A
LIBERAL
CONSCIENCE

Ralph Denton

A
LIBERAL
CONSCIENCE

The Oral History of Ralph Denton, Nevadan

From interviews by Michael S. Green,
edited by Michael S. Green and R. T. King

University of Nevada
Oral History Program
2001

Publication of A *Liberal Conscience* was made possible in part by gifts from:
Robert Faiss,
Michael Ravitch,
and a grant from the John Ben Snow Trust

All photographs courtesy of Ralph Denton.

Publication Staff:
Director: R. T. King
Assistant Director: Mary Larson
Production Manager: Kathleen M. Coles
Senior Production Assistant: Linda Sommer
Production Assistants: Jamie Gradick, Elizabeth Opperman,
and Kathryn Wright-Ross

Contents

Preface

Founded in 1964, the University of Nevada Oral History Program (UNOHP) is building a significant collection of oral histories that illuminate selected dimensions of Nevada's remembered past. These are primary source records—the program's chroniclers are people who have participated in or personally witnessed activities and events important to understanding the history of Nevada in the twentieth and twenty-first centuries. Politics and government are among many subjects so explored by the UNOHP.

In the winter of 1997, at the recommendation of UNOHP advisors, I invited Ralph Denton to participate in an oral history project that would focus on his experiences in state and local politics over a period of almost fifty years. When we learned that Mr. Denton was a valuable source of information on additional subjects of interest to the UNOHP, it was decided to expand the scope of the work and do a full life history. While this book is the result of those efforts, it is merely the last step in a very time-consuming process that required the dedicated work of many talented people, chief among them Dr. Michael S. Green.

Dr. Green, a professor of history at the Community College of Southern Nevada, was eminently qualified to serve as oral historian for this project. Widely published on the history of Nevada, he is also book review editor for the *Nevada Historical Quarterly* and a columnist for two Las Vegas weeklies. When Green and Denton commenced their work in March of 1997, neither suspected that it would lead to fifty-seven hours of tape-recorded interviews spread out over an eighteen month period; but it did, and we are indeed fortunate that they saw the project through to its end.

The tapes yielded a verbatim transcript over 2,000 pages long. Dr. Green edited this down to manageable proportions, subsuming his questions and making of the whole a first-person account in Ralph Denton's voice. Denton then reviewed and corrected the edited transcript before I did what additional editing was necessary to prepare it for publication as a book. In our editing, Dr. Green and I employed only a single device not commonly encountered outside of oral histories: when Mr. Denton laughs, either in amusement or as an accompaniment to ironic comment, it is noted in the text with [laughter].

As with all of our oral histories, while we can vouch for the authenticity of *A Liberal Conscience*, we advise the reader to keep in mind that it is an account of a remembered past, and we do not claim that it is entirely free of error. Intelligent readers will approach it with the same anticipation of discovery, tempered with caution, that they would bring to government reports, diaries, newspaper stories, and other interpretations of historical information.

R. T. King

University of Nevada
Oral History Program

UNIVERSITY OF NEVADA ORAL HISTORY PROGRAM
PUBLICATIONS OF RELATED INTEREST

Jean Ford: A Nevada Woman Leads the Way

Lubertha Johnson: Civil Rights Efforts in Las Vegas, 1940s-1960s

H. Clyde Mathews Jr.: OEO, Nevada Politics and Civic Affairs

James McMillan: Fighting Back, A Life in the Struggle for Civil Rights

Clarence Ray: Black Politics and Gaming in Las Vegas, 1920s-1980s

Charles Russell: Nevada Congressman, Governor, and Legislator

Grant Sawyer: Hang Tough! An Activist in the Governor's Mansion

Art Smith: Let's Get Going! (Las Vegas Banking)

Woodrow Wilson: Race, Community and Politics in Las Vegas, 1940s-1980s

Introduction

Dwight Morrow, a sagacious businessman and diplomat, once observed that there are two kinds of people: those who want to do something, and those who want to be somebody. This is the life story of a man who wanted to do something for his home state, and did.

Ralph Denton is a classic "man behind the scenes." Although he has practiced law for half a century—first in Elko, Nevada, from 1951 to 1955, then in Las Vegas ever since—he has held only two public offices: district attorney of Esmeralda County, to which he was elected, and Clark County commissioner, to which he was appointed. While Denton has had an influential role in state and local politics and government for over forty years, it is a role that has been played, for the most part, off stage.

In 1958, Denton was a key member of the team that overcame an entrenched political machine and helped elect Grant Sawyer governor of Nevada, thereby fundamentally changing how the state would be governed in the future. Over Sawyer's two terms, Denton not only remained a trusted political adviser, but also served as a close confidant—sometimes an emissary, sometimes a hatchet man, sometimes a sounding board. He also served as chairman of John F. Kennedy's campaign in Nevada in 1960, and he later played the same role for Eugene McCarthy in 1968 and Jerry Brown in 1976. He has lived in Boulder City since 1959, playing an influential role as a citizen committed to progress in that community.

Denton's story offers the reader a more nuanced appreciation of some important leaders from Nevada's past than may be found elsewhere. He went through law school on the patronage of Senator Pat McCarran, among others. This forever stamped him as one of "McCarran's boys," as that group of leaders and followers became known, but it also meant that he was close to one of the most important and controversial politicians, nationally and locally, of the twentieth century. Denton's richly textured recollections offer new ways to look at and think about McCarran, those with whom McCarran served in the Senate in the 1940s and 1950s, and other prominent Nevadans and national leaders.

Denton's story encompasses an important era of social and political change for Nevada and the nation. He was born in Caliente in 1925, meaning that he grew up during the Great Depression, and he offers valuable reminiscences of what life was like in an isolated Nevada community during that period. Informative, too, are his memories of the World War II years, when he never left the country during his army service and admits that he is glad of it. Denton went to law school in Washington, D.C., after the war, then came home to Nevada. After serving as deputy district attorney for a few years in the small northeastern Nevada town of Elko, he and his young family moved to the Las Vegas area, where they have stayed as it has grown exponentially. The Dentons retain close ties to Lincoln County, still a sparsely populated area—they have one foot in the older Nevada of mining and ranching, and the other in the modern Nevada of gaming and tourism.

While Denton's story is primarily a political insider's memoir, it is also an important historical account of the evolution of the practice of law in Nevada during the second half of the twentieth century. When he passed the bar, Nevada lawyers usually practiced in small firms and rarely specialized in any single field of law, with the exception of migratory divorce. Today, of course, Nevada has many large law firms and numerous attorneys specializing in criminal defense, personal injury, estate planning, bankruptcy, family law, and any number of fields. Denton still practices in a two-lawyer office, without a Dictaphone and with no typewriter in sight. As might be expected, he has strong opinions about the state of his profession and much to say about its history in Nevada.

History aside, Ralph Denton's narrative reveals his true, multi-faceted nature. Those who know him, know that he is a raconteur par excellence, and this narrative puts on paper stories that have circulated at political and social functions, in living rooms and backrooms, for much of the century. Sadly, the printed word cannot convey changes in tone and expression that are so important to these stories when Denton tells them—the alternating bark and stentorian tone of Pat McCarran; the plaintive sniffling of Walter Baring—but they provide enough to whet the appetite of the reader, who might just be inclined to look for additional information on the people and subjects discussed here.

More than a storyteller, Ralph Denton is a liberal-minded man. He believes in, and has fought for, certain ideals throughout his life: civil rights for all, respect for his profession, activist government, and the value of friendship and loyalty. Naturally, he disagrees with some of what Pat McCarran stood for: the senator was a leader of the communist witch hunt of the 1940s and 1950s. Yet, he has remained friendly with, and an admirer of, many conservatives—he even liked Walter Baring, the man who defeated him in two congressional races.

Ralph Denton's life follows the sense of Tennyson's line, "I am a part of all that I have met." When you meet Denton's parents in the pages that follow, you will understand more about him, and what each of us can be. His mother Hazel was a schoolteacher, an educated idealist. His father Floyd was a miner, a saloon keeper, an undersheriff—a man who held a variety of jobs, as befitted his uneducated, street-smart, pragmatic approach to life. Hazel Denton was a liberal thinker; Floyd Denton was a thoughtful, colorful operator. The title of this oral history, "A Liberal Conscience," reflects Ralph's inheritance from his mother. Reflecting his father's influence is the question Ralph's son Mark asked me: "Did you get in all of the great phrases?" We certainly tried, as you will see.

Conducting the fifty-seven hours of tape recorded interviews that are the basis for this book gave me a great deal of knowledge about Ralph Denton. It offered me insight into him and into myself. Ralph and I had known each other for several years before we sat down to do this oral history. That is different from the usual manner in which oral histories are conducted; usually, the interviewer merely brings training to the table. While I trained with Tom King, and worked with his fine staff at the University of Nevada Oral History Program, whatever merits I brought to this project involved a knowledge of Nevada history derived from teaching the subject for more than a decade and growing up in Southern Nevada, and from my closeness to the subject.

That may have given this a different flavor than most such works. I met Ralph and his wife Sara at an engagement party for Mary Lou Foley, who remains a dear friend of mine and the Dentons, and has encouraged this project and affected my life in many important ways. Her grandfather was a federal judge for whom Ralph had worked as a clerk; her father was a federal judge before whom Ralph appeared in cases; she worked for Sara in Senator Cannon's office; and Mark Denton wore her father's robes for his investiture as a district court judge. If anyone needed a reminder that Las Vegas remains fundamentally a small town, this may serve that purpose. Despite a substantial difference in age, the Dentons and I became close friends: Ralph has been our family attorney, I worked on Mark's campaign for judge, and Mark performed my marriage.

All of which helped lead to Ralph's selection as one of "The First 100," a project completed by the *Las Vegas Review-Journal* and two of its finest, A.D. Hopkins and the late K.J. Evans. You are encouraged to read the book that resulted, and the story on its Web site (http://www.1st100.com). I introduced Ralph to the authors as a source, and was a consultant in choosing who would be included on the list. For one thing, Ralph tells a couple of stories not included here. For another, I stand by something I said for the article: Ralph Denton is a living refutation of every nasty lawyer joke ever told. The title of his article captures a reason for this work: "Good Citizen Ralph." He has been a good citizen, indeed.

By way of explanation, I must immodestly add that Ralph agreed to be interviewed for this oral history only if I would ask the questions. Friends often had suggested that he submit to this kind of questioning. These efforts increased after he helped persuade his friend, Grant Sawyer, to endure questioning; the result was a fascinating oral history narrative. Nor was it a coincidence that Bob Faiss, who succeeded Sawyer as chair of the administrative and gaming law department at Lionel Sawyer and Collins, not only added to Ralph's considerable powers of persuasion with the governor, but also trained his sights on Ralph. Bob and his wife Linda deserve special acknowledgment here for financial and moral support for this project, and for their friendship. Michael Ravitch, another of Ralph's many friends, also made a contribution in support of the work.

Other acknowledgments are important. Gary Elliott conducted the interviews with Sawyer and, later, Dr. James McMillan, a leader of the civil rights movement in Southern Nevada. Gary's work set a magnificent example to be emulated, and the narratives that resulted from his questioning have greatly influenced this one. Gary influenced me in many other, substantial ways. Happily, he saw the interviewing finished for this work. Sadly, he did not live to see this narrative completed. His knowledge and camaraderie meant a lot to me over the years, and would have made this a far better book.

The Community College of Southern Nevada aided this work by providing me with gainful employment, but also through its telemedia department, whose staff copied the taped interviews for me. I am especially grateful to Roger Sieck for his help.

In addition to those already mentioned, friends and family have helped me considerably. My parents endured stories, piles of clippings, papers, and much more. My father, Robert Green, read the manuscript; my mother, Marsha, did not live to see it completed, but aided me greatly while I was doing the interviews. In completing their marvelous book *The First 100*, A.D. Hopkins and the late K.J. Evans generously shared information and materials. John L. Smith, Bob Coffin, and Gene Segerblom offered aid, ideas, and encouragement. Deborah Young arrived in my life as I began composing the narrative from the raw transcripts, and she kept me composed in the process.

I also am indebted to Ralph Denton's friends and family. Joseph A. Lopez, his law partner, offered thoughts and encouragement. Mark, Sally, and Scott Denton, Alice Denton, and Roger Morris often asked how it was going and provided helpful suggestions.

Most of all, we thank Sara Denton. Her memory filled in many a fuzzy or vacant spot. Her hard work, then and now, reduced the need for me to do additional research. And her hospitality, like that of her husband, was wonderful. We occupied parts of her house, and she managed to keep the telephone and grandchildren from bothering us while remaining unfailingly gracious—which, as anyone who knows her could tell you, is typical of her. She and her husband are anything but typical. If you do not know that now, turn the page; you will know that soon enough.

Michael S. Green
Community College of Southern Nevada
September, 2001

1 | Sacrifices and Devotion

As a young man, I had no political ambitions of any kind—how could a poor boy from provincial, Depression-era Caliente ever hope to be elected to public office? Eventually, I came to realize that my background gave me strength, not weakness, and I lost all self-consciousness about who I was.

My heritage is a little Danish, quite a bit English. What else might be slipping around, I don't know . . . and maybe I would rather not! When I was a kid, I just knew that my family were pioneer Nevadans. That was important to me, and it was important to my father and mother. We felt that we were a breed apart from citizens of other states. We were advocates of the great virtue of Nevada: that here a man could do and accomplish whatever he wanted.

When I was a boy, my father would say he didn't know much about his own family, and he didn't want to find out,—if they had money, they didn't want to see him; and if they didn't, he didn't want to see *them*. Later, we learned that the first member of his family to arrive in the U. S. was a Presbyterian minister, the Reverend Richard Denton. Reverend Denton was born in the 1630s in London, migrated to America in the 1660s, and became the minister of a church in Connecticut. Eventually, he established the First Presbyterian Church in the town of Hempstead, on Long Island, New York. In Denton Green, the big park surrounding the church, there is a memorial bust of him.

Richard Denton's descendants spread out across the country. One of them, my great-grandfather, left his home state of Kentucky in 1860 because he opposed slavery. He became a missionary in Nebraska. His son married a relative of John Logan, a Union general in the Civil War. The first time I heard of that connection was when my dad visited me at law school in Washington, D.C., in the 1940s and told me he wanted to go see Uncle John. He took me to Logan Circle, where there is a statue. He said, "Oh, he looks like a Logan. Look how well he sits that horse!"

My grandfather, Lewis Denton, became a cattle buyer in Waterloo, Nebraska. Dad used to tell stories about Grandfather's horse. It was so well trained that when my grandfather'd go someplace to take strong drink with his buddies, the horse could find its way home with him asleep in the saddle.

Lewis's brother James was the first member of the family to arrive in Nevada. He came west building the Union Pacific and stayed in Utah to work in mining. From there, Uncle James went on to Hamilton, now a ghost town; then to Pioche. In the early 1890s, he built a hotel and established a stagecoach line on the site of what would become the town of Caliente. He was elected to the state legislature four times, serving two terms in the assembly (1895 and 1903) and one in the senate (1897-1899).

Apparently, Uncle James quickly became a respected figure in the county. Uncle James served as a colonel in the Nevada militia, which was called to active duty in the Spanish-American War. My Uncle Les was in the militia with him. They made it all the way to Reno before the war ended! [laughter] Uncle James met Pat McCarran, an assemblyman from Washoe County, in the 1903 session of the Nevada legislature. They became lifelong friends.

The house where Uncle James and his family lived was at the bottom of Denton Heights, an area he had subdivided up a canyon before the town of Caliente was established—there was nothing there but the Culverwell Ranch and the Denton Hotel. By the time Uncle Jim died (it was before I was born), the railroad had come through, and Caliente was a town. He willed some water rights and property to the unincorporated town.

James A. Denton, 1898.

My grandmother Denton came to Nevada to visit around 1900 and brought my father Floyd, her youngest. (Dad's nickname was Babe.) All of Grandma Denton's daughters stayed in Nebraska, but, gradually, each of her sons wound up in Caliente in the early 1900s. Uncle Les, her oldest, had been postmaster in Valley, Nebraska. He had gotten a divorce, which just wasn't done back in the 1890s, then bought a railroad ticket to the end of the line. He knew Uncle James was out here someplace, and he would be able to find him. When he got off the train, the first thing he saw was a coach with six horses, and it said "Denton Stagecoach Line."

On my mother's side, my grandmother's family converted to Mormonism in Denmark. They sent their youngest daughter, Nicoline Marie Bertelson, who

Denton Hotel, Caliente (c. 1908), the porch filled with Dentons. *Left to right:* Hazel and Les, Lloyd, Lewis Jr., James and wife Lizzie, Floyd "Babe" and his mother, Sara Rowe Denton.

would become my grandmother, to Utah with missionaries when she was only nine, around 1856. She got as far as St. Louis and couldn't hook on to a wagon train, so for two years she worked as a domestic servant until she saved enough money to get to Utah. Then she walked across the plains to Utah pushing a handcart.

My grandfather lived in Richfield, Utah, and owned a hotel where the Danish girl got a job. She became his second wife in a polygamous marriage. Years later, the federal government came looking for the polygamists to put them in the big house for illegal cohabitation. The men ran into the hills, and I have letters my grandfather wrote, telling my grandmother where she could write him. But after the Woodruff Manifesto, each husband was required to live with the first wife, abandoning any others. This left my grandmother as a single woman with eight children, my mother being the youngest. Grandmother opened a millinery store in Richfield to support her family.

My mother was the only one of the "second" family who kept in touch with her half-brothers and half-sisters. She was close to them. I had great pride, and still do, in the sacrifices and the devotion my mother's parents and their families made to leave Europe and come to Utah to pioneer a harsh environment and maintain their faith.

My grandmother had been trying to save money to send my mother to the University of Utah, but she died a year or so before my mother finished high school. My mother then moved to Ogden to live with one of her older brothers, Ralph Baker. Right out of high school, and maybe with some work at the university, she got a certificate and started teaching school in Utah.

In 1915, Mom got a job teaching school at the Old Prince Mine in Lincoln County, right over the hill from Pioche. Her brother was the master mechanic at the mill, and he helped his sister get a job for almost twice the salary she had been making in Utah. After a couple of years there, she was offered a job in Caliente, where she met my father. At that time, he was in the gambling-saloon business. He was everything she had been taught to abhor in her youth! [laughter] She married my father on December 28, 1916, and that was a blow from which some of her relatives in Utah never recovered.

Other relatives felt differently. My mom's brother, Lewis Baker, had left the Church of Latter Day Saints, but he continued to live in his hometown of Monroe, Utah, to the end of his life. Uncle Lewis was the only non-Mormon in town, yet he was elected justice of the peace every two years and often was a high school commencement speaker. He became radical politically, I think out of bitterness toward polygamy. When my uncle was young, the Mormon bishop had once come to their house to ask my grandmother to tithe. Uncle Lewis threw him out and said, "You ought to be helping her, rather than asking her to help the church."

Uncle Lewis was the oldest boy, my mother the youngest girl in their family, and they adored each other. He was a farmer. When we visited, I'd get to ride with him when he hitched up his one-horse wagon and took his milk to the creamery. He would come to Caliente in the winter when his Utah farmland was frozen. There were no railroads in his part of Utah then, and in Caliente he would just sit at the depot all day long to look at those magnificent big steam engines. A lot of those southern Utah men came here in the winter. Uncle Lewis didn't come just to visit us; he came to work in the mines in Delamar. [laughter]

We would visit my mother's sister and her family. That family was steeped in the church, and I felt uneasy around them. They used to tease me unmercifully about Nevada—Nevada was "terrible;" we had gambling; my dad was in the gambling business . . . It was a little difficult for them to accept that their Aunt Hazel had married a non-Mormon, and in Nevada, to boot!

One night, in Salt Lake City, at my Aunt Etta's house, my Uncle Frank was really putting down Nevada. My dad said, "Frank, let's get in the car. I'll take you uptown and show you more gambling right here in Salt Lake City than we got in all of Lincoln County, Nevada." Some of the hotels there had gambling in the back rooms.

Dad would drive us to Salt Lake for a visit, drop us off at my aunt's house, and he wouldn't go in—he would just drive straight back to Caliente. There were times when he did meet and talk with them, but I always sensed this resentment toward my father—their lack of respect for him.

I don't think my aunt's children felt that way, though; I think they loved their Uncle Floyd. They were wonderful people. One of them was my cousin, Francis Seegmiller. He graduated from college as a chemical engineer and couldn't find a job, so he came to Caliente. My mother, who by then was on the high school board, ignored the nepotism laws and hired him—the best chemistry teacher they ever had, and everybody loved him.

Mr. Seegmiller had an old Model-T Ford you had to crank or push to get started. Once, my brother, eight years older than me, and a couple of his friends were helping him push the car, and I'm helping. They were headed to a little park south of Caliente, Kershaw-Ryan State Park. It was a great place to play, and I figured I'm going to get to go with them. The car starts. They all run and jump on. I'm too little to do that, and they run off and wave at me, just laughing at me. I didn't take too kindly to that.

The next morning, after they left to go to school, I got out my hammer and broke his headlights, windshield, and tail-lights. The only guy who thought it was just was my father. Mr. Seegmiller was absolutely furious. I was too young to be punished as severely as he would have liked. As for my mother, I noticed a gleam in her eye; I knew she resented the constant teasing I got from them about Nevada. But she did make it clear to me that it was improper conduct. My dad said, "Well, it serves them right." A few years back, I spoke at Mr. Seegmiller's eightieth birthday party, and I told what I had done to his car. I was surprised that nobody seemed to be shocked. [laughter]

Quite a few relatives from Utah came to live with us during the Depression. I don't think people nowadays understand how tough that depression was, and how people helped each other. My mother had a sister who lived in Idaho. She had two grown daughters, nieces who were very close to my mother, who had children. They were flat busted, so my mother and I went up to Idaho and brought back one of their children to live with us for the whole year. They were short on food, short on everything, and so you helped.

When we would travel, we never checked into a hotel. We always stayed with relatives. We might sleep on the floor or on the couch, but that's how people helped themselves through those terrible times. In Caliente, until 1935, my dad was doing great, so he was able to offer help. It got so that somebody would come up to him in his saloon, and he would say, "Are you my cousin? Are you my nephew?" [laughter] Often they were. Thank God those days are over.

Whatever was going on in Caliente, my parents were involved—my father in fraternal lodge activities, my mother in school and women's clubs, and both in politics. Dad and his brothers were charter members of the Odd Fellows Lodge in Caliente. (All of the old mining camps had them. The working stiffs belonged to the Odd Fellows; the rich belonged to the Masons. [laughter]) They eventually lowered the age for becoming a member to eighteen, but when I turned eighteen, joining the lodge was the *last* thing I had in my mind. But I came home on leave from the army, and it was made clear I should join the Odd Fellows. I did, and I stayed a member of the lodge in Caliente until it disbanded a few years ago. If I had been gone for a few years and came home, and there was going to be a lodge meeting, Dad or my uncle would want me to go. It was a typical lodge with secret ceremonies, and I'd forget how to get in. [laughter]

Quite a few people were helped considerably by the Odd Fellows. They built a cemetery in Caliente, and my parents were buried there. My father had lost an eye as a child. When he got a detached retina in his other eye, and had to be in a hospital in San Francisco for over six weeks, the Odd Fellows Lodge was a considerable help financially for my family. Yet, I've never been much of a joiner. I did join the Elks in Elko, but the Elks Lodge is a bit different. It's more social. They have one ritual that's very good at 11 o'clock. They're supposed to have a drink in memory of the departed brothers. But I can't think of anything at the present time I belong to, except the Democratic party. Of that, I'm very proud.

My mother got involved in everything. She was on the Lincoln County High School Board while she was a teacher. She was a contributor to newspapers, particularly the *Salt Lake Tribune*, on political issues and matters of that kind. She almost single-handedly started a library. She started getting people donating books, then she got the elementary school to let her put them in a room that she could operate as a library at night. She and other teachers, principally Eula Jacobson, would staff it. I think after my mother's death, they finally moved to the old depot.

I didn't have to go to the library, because Mom made sure our home was full of books. Our living room wall was *all* books. I remember reading Hemingway and Dickens, and we always had the *Saturday Evening Post* and *Colliers* and *Liberty*—they generally ran books in serial form. I became enamored specifically during that period with the Tutt stories in one of those magazines. (Tutt and Mr. Tutt were lawyers in New York City around the criminal courts.) I remember reading Dostoevsky's *Crime and Punishment*, a book Mother gave to me when I was a freshman or sophomore in high school.

Mom started the Delphinian Society. They would meet at least once a month at different members' homes, and books would be assigned to people to make a review. When they would meet at our house, Mom would let me sit on the floor. I'd listen to these women review these books, and then they'd question each other. I didn't always understand the books they were reviewing, but I understood more than they thought I did. [laughter]

My mother got involved in women's organizations. There was a Homemakers' Club in Caliente that she belonged to. She belonged to the Rebekahs, the women's auxiliary of the Odd Fellows. She was an early suffragette worker. I think she and Anne Martin, who ran for the Senate in those days, were friends, and had a correspondence with each other.[1] She became president of the Nevada Federation of Women's Clubs.[2] On my wall is a painting of Mount Rose in Reno given to her as a gift the year she was president.

Keep in mind, in those days, you didn't have television. Mom used the radio to encourage us to have an interest in good music. Every Sunday evening, we'd listen to that Texaco program from New York—opera or symphony music. She played the piano so she could have her kids in school sing songs and put on programs. Mom always encouraged that. I think it was a great disappointment to her when I abandoned all of those pursuits for the sake of playing football and basketball in high school.

Lincoln County High School was in Panaca, about halfway between Caliente and Pioche, and the high school board generally had members from Caliente, Panaca, and Pioche. When the other members of the board would come down to talk to my mother, trying to get something done that she didn't particularly want to do, I'd sit on the floor in the living room and listen to them talk. It was probably because I didn't have anything else to do. I doubt I was particularly interested, but there would be constant discussion around the dinner table about school policies.

One thing my mother was *very* interested in: making certain that vacancies on the faculty were filled, if possible, by University of Nevada students, rather than graduates of out-of-state colleges. She wanted Nevada kids to teach in Nevada schools. (That was always a fight, because other board members liked to bring them in from universities in Utah, I suspect because they were strong Latter Day Saints people.) However, Mom's preference for University of Nevada graduates didn't mean that she couldn't support hiring someone from another school. There's one particular instance of that: Joe Thiriot, who taught in a Las Vegas high school for many years, was a fine man and a fine teacher. Mom was on the board that hired him to Lincoln County. His degree may have been from Brigham Young , but he'd been raised in Pahranagat Valley! [laughter]

I don't remember much about my mother running for the high school board, because I don't think she ever had an opponent. She ran because of her *overwhelming* interest in education. She sincerely believed that education could create a utopian society. If everybody became educated, there wouldn't be this mean-spiritedness. I inherited her point of view, to an extent, but get disappointed all the time, because it seems to me most people are not talking about education today, they're talking about training. You go to college for one reason nowadays: to learn something you can turn into a money-making trade. Why should anybody have to take English, history, philosophy? Why on earth is that going to help you make a nickel? Why should anybody take a course in art? Or music? They think you're a nut.

(I went to law school. That's not what I think of as a classical or liberal arts education. I see an educated man as able to think logically, make good choices in society—who he votes for, what causes he supports, what political and philosophical views he adopts, are based upon his power to think, his ethical standards, his education.)

Mother was *not* one of those persons who was active in the social circles of the community. She wasn't the type who went to a bridge club once a week or was invited to have cocktails or that sort of stuff, but she was greatly respected by those who did. Everybody in Lincoln County, to my knowledge, always treated her with respect; but she certainly had an independent streak.

Uncle Lloyd was a very outgoing man, active in political affairs, and he was closely tied to Clark County, as Lincoln County was in those days. Once, when my mother was in the legislature, and I was practicing law in Elko, Uncle Lloyd wanted me to try and persuade her to support a certain bill some of his friends in Las Vegas wanted. I said, "Well, Uncle Lloyd, why don't you talk to Mom?"

He said, "Oh my God, no! I wouldn't try to persuade Hazel to do something. She wouldn't be influenced by what *I* have to say."

I said, "Well, I'm sure that's true for me too. Mom's as independent as a hog on ice. She'll make up her own mind, do what she thinks is right and proper."

My father deferred to my mother on education. There's an old saying: you never miss what you haven't had. But he knew he had missed getting an education, and it was a serious deficiency. I spent a lot of time with my dad in the mines and the hills—just him and me in a shack or a tent. We'd talk about a lot of things. He would say, even more emphatically than my mother, "Ralph, you *have* to get an education. That's the only thing they can't take away from you."

You could see his Depression thinking—he'd lost everything he had. That's the only thing they can't take away from you, what you have between your horns. He stressed that all the time, and he read all the time. He'd always wanted to be a lawyer, and he'd purchased a complete set of LaSalle Extension University textbooks. We had them in the house, and he would read them.

I like to think of Dad as one of those who understood clearly that the beginning of wisdom is a realization of ignorance. I'm paraphrasing what somebody else said, but he knew that. Consequently, he was slow to reach judgments, recognizing maybe that he didn't have enough knowledge. He placed all his faith politically in the Democratic party, and it never disappointed him. If the Democrats were for it, he didn't have to think anymore. [laughter]

Dad could reduce everything to its lowest common denominator. Here's an example: I never could understand how anybody in Caliente could be anti-Semitic, because there weren't any Jews there. And there was only one Jew in Pioche, Joe Cohen, one of the finest men in the county. Yet, you would hear little anti-Semitic things. I asked my dad about it, and his reply was, "Yeah, I hate every son of a bitch in the country that's smarter than I am." People often are jealous of success. He put it in a nutshell. He had street smarts, but he was also like my mother. They were made for each other, because, like her, he was an idealist. He thought people had the capacity to be decent and good and honorable.

Dad had an absolute legion of friends, but he lacked business sense. Until about 1935, my father was *very* affluent; but, of course, he didn't hang on to any of it. After the bottom falls out of everything in our personal family financial situation, Dad takes to the hills, trying to make a living prospecting. Mother has lost her job, but she supports us by taking in boarders and writing. I've got an older brother in college, and we're having a hell of a time.

On one occasion, Dad came down out of the hills. He'd been gone about two weeks. We get all cleaned up, and Mom gives him a dollar to take me to the show. One silver dollar. It's thirty-five cents for an adult to get in, ten cents for me. So we would have fifty-five cents left over, and after the show, there'd be enough money for me to have an ice cream sundae, and him to have whatever.

We're walking to the show, and as we're walking by the drug store, there's an old guy standing there. I remember him well; his name was Huey. Nobody knew his last name, but he was one of the old hangers-on in town. Huey says, "Babe, I haven't had anything to eat today." Dad gave him the dollar, and we went home. My mother was furious. That dollar! [laughter] He didn't have money sense. If he had any money, he'd give it away if somebody needed it more than he figured he did. So my mother had to control the purse strings. Even after he got back to work, he gave Mom the check. But I was proud of Dad, because old Huey needed something to eat more than I needed to go to a show. And while it created problems for my mother, she would have been equally disturbed if he wasn't a kind and generous loving man. And that's what he was.

After Dad came out of the hills for good, the first job he got was driving a high school bus, and that was ninety dollars a month salary. We thought we'd reached heaven. First cash crop we'd had in the house since 1935.

My father had old values that are probably good values. I remember a Caliente boy, a gambler, a terrible drunk, whose mother and stepfather had a ranch north of Caliente. One of Dad's jobs as undersheriff was to get drunks off the street. When I was home on leave from the army once, I went cruising the town with him. This guy came staggering up the street. They'd thrown him out of all the saloons, so Dad picked him up and took him to the jail, behind the main street. There was nobody in attendance. You took them to the jail, put them in a cell, locked the door, and left. As we were leaving, he started chewing my dad out, calling him filthy names. Dad was just a little old man by then, but he took his gun belt off, set it on the desk, went in the cell, slapped the hell out of this guy, and said, "Now I'm going to take you home to your mother."

The guy kept saying, "Babe, don't do that, don't do that."

"No, you rotten so-and-so, I'm going to take you home to your mother. Maybe she can straighten you out. I can't."

He put him in the car, drove up to the ranch, and knocked at the door. The mother came to the door, and Dad says, "Here's your son. Maybe you can straighten him out. I can't do it. I've done everything I can for him." I don't know how a law enforcement officer could do that nowadays.

In a small community like Caliente, politics was personal. My parents plotted and schemed for whoever their candidates were, and they promoted them among their acquaintances. They would also give advice, if it was sought by their candidates; they'd try and help them as best they could. Politics was always a subject of discussion at our house.

When Mom was taking in boarders, there might be six or seven of us at the dinner table. If Dad was home, and an election was coming up, and Mom and Dad were interested in one of the guys, *that* would become the subject—issues would be debated at the table. Some of our boarders were strangers, but they soon got involved. [laughter] I don't know how to describe it other than just a constant preoccupation with the community's political affairs.

A candidate's need for a job was a big part of these discussions, especially during the Depression. The county commission was *very* big in those days; district attorney, school board . . . they were all important jobs. The question was, who needed the job? That was an important factor to consider if you were going to support somebody: "My God, he's out of work, and he's got three kids! He's as qualified as anybody else. Let's see if we can help him."

It helped if the candidate was a Democrat; as a matter of fact, that was almost essential. [laughter] Most Republicans we knew didn't need jobs. They were the rich folks in the community. [laughter]

My parents couldn't help candidates financially, but in a small town, you talk to people, maybe start rumors. [laughter] Whatever you think you can do to help them: tell them who to go talk to, who's important. There could be rivalry among families, even though they belonged to the same church. You had to know who had married into which families, and that was particularly difficult in Panaca and Pahranagat Valley, where you had large families. Dad was good at that, because he had a magnificent memory. He knew all of the relationships. If a Wadsworth was running, Dad could sit down and count the in-laws—whose kids married whose kids—and figure out that all those related families would be for a given candidate. So, he could predict pretty accurately what was going to happen in a county-wide election.

One that comes to mind is the George Marshall-Roger Foley race for judge in 1940. There was only one judge for Clark and Lincoln counties, and he had to run in both counties. Billy Orr, who was the judge, was appointed to the Nevada Supreme Court, creating a vacancy.[3] The governor [E. P. Carville] appointed Foley to fill it, and he then had to run in the next general election. Marshall from Las Vegas ran against him.

It was allegedly a non-partisan race, but Foley was a well-known Democrat and Marshall a well-known Republican. My family was for Roger Foley for several reasons, not the least of which was that he was a Democrat. But some of the Panaca people were for Marshall—not because he was a Republican, but because he was LDS. Almost everybody in Panaca is LDS. (What the people in Lincoln County *didn't* know was that Marshall was a Jack Mormon. [laughter]) Dad figured out pretty quickly that Foley was going to have trouble, at least in Lincoln County. Even though Dad and Mom and all my uncles really campaigned hard for Foley, he lost in Lincoln County. But not by much.[4]

My parents were not alone in these fights; my uncles were politically active as well. There were times, as I have grown to understand, that the brothers would play good man/bad man so that the family would have a friend in office no matter who won. I didn't understand at the time, and I misinterpreted it as rivalry between the brothers. The gamblers, casino operators, in Las Vegas would do the same thing. I remember when Grant Sawyer was running for governor, the casinos were all for Charlie Russell. But there would be one partner who would come and talk to us, and he would say, "Well, my partners are for Russell, but I really want to help you." So, they always made sure that they had a friend, no matter who won. I didn't realize that my dad and his brothers were as smart as they were. [laughter]

Uncle Les was remarkable. He was first appointed postmaster in Caliente by President Coolidge, and he stayed postmaster until he retired. He was considered 'the man' in Lincoln County if you were running for state office, the political sage of that area, but always behind the scenes. He was a smart politician. He knew the same things my father knew, but he would try and talk people into running. He gave sound advice to candidates. He would make it clear; if he wasn't going to be for you, he would tell you. I've been told by people who ran for office during that period of time, that if you didn't have Les Denton, you didn't have much chance of carrying that county. Yet, the only time he ever ran for office, he got beat. [laughter]

After Les retired as postmaster, he ran for county commissioner. When he got beat, his prestige slipped. There was a bit behind this. Uncle Les was affluent, and there was always a lot of jealousy in the community toward the entire Denton family, anyway. They were pioneers; they had been there forever; they were influential in political affairs, not only of the county, but of the state. (Lincoln County played a much larger role in state politics then than it does now. Lincoln was not the smallest county by any means. Its vote was important and pretty solidly Democratic.) So there were jealousies.

One time, I got in a fist fight with another kid down in the flats, an area below town. I don't know why we got in a fight, but old Stanley and I were going at it. He winds up crying. He says, "My dad says the goddamned Dentons run the town, but they can't run us." [laughter] Yet, the jealousy was selective. I don't know of anybody who disliked my father, and they all respected my mother. She was elected every time she ever ran for anything, but it was close once. She won once by only two votes, I think, or one vote, for the assembly. But I know lots of people who would say things about the whole family, generically.

That doesn't mean the Denton family didn't divide. They were generally together except one time, the 1942 primary election with Jim Scrugham running against Berkeley Bunker for the Democratic nomination for United States Senator . . . and my God, Uncle Lloyd was furious! Uncle Lloyd and Uncle Les had always been strong Scrugham supporters, and so had my father, but in that election, my dad and my mother supported Bunker. They liked him. He was a nice fellow, plus he'd given me a job. You don't repay that sort of thing by not supporting your patron. So dad worked his butt off for Berkeley all over the county, while Uncle Lloyd and Uncle Les worked their tails off for Scrugham.

I'll never forget election night. Scrugham won, but Bunker carried Lincoln County. I came back from Washington in September. I was running the picture machines over at the theater, and about the time the show was over, the results were out in Lincoln County, and Bunker had defeated Scrugham. My Uncle Lloyd took that as a personal insult. "Could not believe how your father could support . . . !"

I said, "Well, Uncle Lloyd, you have to understand, I did every thing I could for Senator Bunker, too. You know, he gave me that job in . . . ." Uncle Lloyd said that didn't make any difference to him. That's about the only time I remember them being on opposite sides of the fence.[5]

Politics was a lot of fun back then; but about the gamesmanship of the time, I don't know how serious it got. I don't know if it ever got out of line, or if it was just spreading little stories. Politics also was serious business and involved deep commitment, loyalty, friendship. They say money is the mother's milk of politics. I suppose it was to a certain extent then, but 'loyalty' was the magic word.

I don't think my parents were ever motivated by expectation of rewards, with one clear exception. When Richard Kirman was elected governor in 1934, his opponent in the general election was Morley Griswold. The Griswold family in Elko County had been friends of the Denton family from the early days, but Mom and Dad didn't feel any particular loyalty to Morley . . . and he was a Republican. So my parents worked like hell for Kirman, who was elected. He was a Democrat, and he got a big vote in Lincoln County.

My father and mother were out of work at the time. Dad was encouraged by Kirman's success in Lincoln County, and he hoped to be appointed warden in the state penitentiary. When he didn't get the job, he was disappointed.

East Side Bar, Caliente, c. 1917. Lloyd Denton behind the "plank."

My parents worked their tails off for Jack Fogliani when he ran for sheriff in 1942.[6] After he was elected, my dad was appointed undersheriff. Whether that was understood when the campaign started, I have no idea. I don't remember it being discussed, except, "We've got to get behind Jack!" [laughter] Other people were after the job too, so we sweated that out. Dad didn't have much faith in getting it. He'd had that experience with the warden's job. He figured he'd be heading for the hills again. [laughter]

I was in Washington during that campaign, but I was home for the general election, and I remember Dad being gone all the time. He was down the canyon to talk to the ranchers and guys who worked on the railroad, the section hands. Or he was up the canyon, or he'd gone up to Panaca to talk to old friends, or he was in Alamo. It was standard campaign practice to do your campaigning in saloons, at least in Pioche and Caliente, but he didn't do that. He didn't spend any time in the saloons. He always said that they don't vote the way they drink, anyway. He would talk to everybody he knew, and just campaign. He used to call it political medicine—"Out making medicine." [laughter]

Notes

1. Anne Martin ran for the Senate in 1918 and 1920, running third both times as an Independent. She also was a noted leader of the women's rights movement.

2. Hazel Denton was president of the Nevada Federation of Women's Clubs, 1944-46, and held several other offices in the organization.

3. William E. Orr served as district court judge from 1919 until March 1939, when he was appointed to the Nevada Supreme Court. Roger T. Foley succeeded him as district court judge. Orr later was appointed to the Ninth Circuit Court of Appeals, serving from 1945 until his death in 1965. Among his law clerks was Caspar Weinberger, later secretary of defense.

4. Marshall defeated Foley, 4,571-4,544. Marshall served until resigning in 1946. He later was returned to the bench and served from 1959 to 1967.

5. Statewide, Scrugham defeated Bunker, 11,461-10,315, and went on to serve in the U.S. Senate until his death in 1945.

6. Fogliani also was a Lincoln County assemblyman for the 1935 session and later superintendent of the prison farm under Governor Charles Russell and warden under Governor Grant Sawyer.

14

Sacrifices and Devotion

2 | Caliente:
One Hell of a Place to Grow Up!

My most vivid early memory is of all of us being together when Dad was home from work, and it just being fun. I also remember trips in the car and being taken to the drug store to have a dish of ice cream and things like that; but my first real memory is of how wonderful and happy I was when everybody was home. Nothing ever happened to change that.

One early thing I remember—this is before we had indoor plumbing—is taking my bath in a washtub in the kitchen, and my mom and dad filling the tub with water heated on the stove. And Sundays, after dinner, Mom would play the piano. We would gather and sing, and Mom's boarders, or any guests we had, would join us. Afterwards, my dad, my brother, and I would go out in the street and play catch.

My brother Lewis was eight years older than me, born on October 5, 1917. While he was growing up, the family was still prospering. I adored him, and I followed him around like a little puppy. On many occasions, when Lewis and his friends were going some place, my mother and father used to insist that they take me too. Lew's friends, who were his age, of course, used to call me Shadow—wherever Lew went, there was a little brother tagging along. He was always so good to me! I looked up to him all of my life. When he went away to college, it broke my heart that he had left home.

I was born September 8, 1925. I was the youngest, Lew the oldest, and we had two sisters in between who died in childhood. In 1921, when she was two, Henrietta Marie died of dysentery, something that would not be serious today. Betty Jeanne was born in 1923 and died in 1926. After one Sunday dinner, Betty reached up on the table, grabbed an olive, and choked to death on it. I can't remember Betty, and Marie died before I was born.

When we were young, I don't think we appreciated the great sadness in my parents' hearts, but it was always present that we had lost two sisters. Mom grieved for her dead daughters. She said the ideal family was two boys and two girls: each girl should have a sister, and each boy should have a brother. She had attained that perfection, but wasn't able to maintain it. At

Ralph and Lew.

the cemetery, there were matching headstones for my sisters; and on Decoration Day, we always went to the cemetery . . . sometimes more frequently than that.

When I think of Lew and our life in Caliente, those thoughts are inseparable from memories of the Great Depression. The Depression changed Lew's life dramatically. It started nationally in 1929, but the bottom didn't really fall out for us until 1935, the year he was to go away to college. Railroad companies were building tunnels up and down Meadow Valley Wash in the early 1930s. There were big crews of workers—it brought a lot of people in there. Business was good, and Caliente didn't really suffer from the Depression that much, even after 1935, because most of the people worked for the railroad. But people who didn't work for the railroad had difficulty: Dad lost his business; my mother lost her job teaching school.

When I got old enough to work, Lew and I were working whenever we could. Lew worked at a very early age for my Uncle Les in the post office, then in Senter's Garage. He later worked for the U.S. Coast and Geodetic Survey, surveying the state of Nevada. Lots of the state had not been surveyed up to that time, so he was off in Elko and Humboldt County with survey crews.

One year, a Caliente family had a son going to Arizona State Teacher's College in Flagstaff.[1] The mother of that boy came to my parents and told them she was happy to pay for Lew to go with her son, and she would provide him with the same financial resources she provided her son. (They were a wealthy ranch family.) Her only condition was anonymity. She didn't want her husband, or anybody in town, to know she was doing that.

Tom Dixon, who lived across the street, also went out of his way to help kids go to college.[2] He was proud that everyone he helped paid him back. One was Della Lee, a Panaca girl—she went to the University of Nevada in Reno. After graduating, she came back to Lincoln County and was one of my English teachers. Uncle Tom Dixon was always so proud of Della—she paid back every penny, and nobody in town ever knew it. Della later became Berkeley Bunker's wife.

George Jeff's sister owned the Blue Front Mercantile, and Lottie Alquist and George managed the big general merchandise store, which sold practically everything, including groceries. The people in that town they fed on credit . . . . Mom and Dad ran a grocery bill there for a long time, but it never bothered George. He stayed a close friend, and in time he got paid. There was a lot of that going on in Caliente, but I didn't know it. It was supposed to be secret. I've gone to members of the family that helped my brother and told them I knew about it and thanked them. The first time I did that to one of the sons, he didn't know about it either! His mother hadn't told him. [laughter]

We were basically a happy family. As far as I was concerned, that was one hell of a place to grow up! It reminds me of a line from *The Bridges of Madison County*, where somebody says, "Really a wonderful place to grow up in; not such a good place to be an adult in." [laughter] It was as near an idyllic childhood as you could ever have.

Life in Caliente seemed wonderful to me—I didn't realize what my mother and father were going through, trying to survive financially and educate their kids at the same time. For instance, the other kids in town would go to the movie show Friday night, but we didn't have enough money for me to go. I solved that problem. Uncle Lloyd started a program at the grammar school: every Friday there would be a spelling bee in each room, and the winner got a free ticket to the show Friday night. I worked like hell on spelling and generally won. That kept me seeing the shows through the fifth grade. Soon I was old enough to get a job at the theater, and eventually I became the projectionist, so I got to see all the shows. I saw "Gone With the Wind" eight times. [laughter]

I experienced no real privations or hardships that I was aware of, but a kid that age, his needs are not that great. My mother and father put up without having a lot of things they would have liked to have had, but it wasn't until Lew went to college that he found there were some financial restraints that made it impossible for him to do some of the things that he wanted to do.

When Lew would come home from the university, he'd bring his yearbooks. I would spend hours going through the *Artemisia*, and I started identifying with the university and taking pride in it. Later in life, when I came back to Nevada from Washington and started practicing law, I'd meet people I thought I knew, because I was familiar with their names from Lew's yearbooks. Of course, they didn't know me from a bale of hay, but their names were familiar, like Louie Peraldo in Winnemucca, Carl Dodge in Fallon.

The schools in Caliente were wonderful. That grammar school under Golden Hollingshead had athletic programs for boys and girls, but mostly boys, in baseball, track, and basketball. The WPA built a nice athletic field, and Tom Dixon donated the land. Caliente even had grammar school basketball tournaments—Las Vegas came, Ely, even Tonopah. They don't have that anymore. There was so much for a kid to do in that town, and I participated. It was a matter of pride. I participated in basketball and baseball in grammar school. Oh, it was tough when we went to Pioche! Pioche and Caliente were great rivals. It was more than you could stand, to lose to Pioche.

I always wanted to compete and succeed, and it was important to me to make the team; but I didn't get much encouragement at home insofar as athletics were concerned. In high school, we had football and basketball, and I played both. I was fortunate to go to such a small school, or I never would have made the team, but at Lincoln County High, I made the first team in football. I had the title of fullback. As a junior, I was first-string fullback and called the signals. (You don't have to be the quarterback to call the signals. It's just become sort of a custom. The double wingback is a fairly complicated system, and the coach trusted me to call the right plays.)

We used to play Las Vegas and Ely and hold our own, but when we went to Reno to play Reno High, they beat the hell out of us. At the end of the first half, it was 12-6, Lincoln County; but during the intermission, the Reno coaches must have taught their team how to defend. The game ended, I think, 34-12.

High school sports weren't all that was going on in Caliente. We had a town band supported by the railroad that even went to the Olympics in Los Angeles in 1932. And each town up and down the railroad had baseball teams, so you would have games in the summertime, where Caliente might play Las Vegas or Milford or Yermo or even San Bernardino. And every Labor Day, Pioche had a fight card. A lot of kids participated and trained, and some became good fighters. Then, you had those hills. You could go any place you wanted.

Left to right: Lindsay Jacobson ("my closest buddy for life"), Ralph, Jerry Arrowsmith, c. 1934.

I took part in boxing when I was twelve or thirteen. Not for long, though. Graham McNamee was the announcer who used to call fights on national radio broadcasts. When I fought Ross Stewart (a big, strong kid from Pioche), Porter Lee, one of the Caliente people, was sitting at ringside, imitating McNamee. He called out, "Oh, Denton's bleeding bad!" I didn't know I'd been hit! That got my attention. I dropped my

Caliente baseball team, c. 1910. *Lower left*, Leo McNamee; *upper right*, Babe Denton.

arms and looked around to see where I was bleeding, and Ross knocked me right on my keister. And I wasn't bleeding—Porter was just making it up. I got up, and we fought to a draw. My fight with Ross made it clear to me that I didn't have a future in prize fighting.

I can't talk about growing up in Caliente without mentioning Lee Liston. At the high school in Panaca, he coached everything—basketball, football, and he ran the physical education program and the intramural sports every boy and girl could play if they wanted to. He also taught history and civics. That school is smaller than it was when I went there, but now they got three or four coaches and assistant coaches. [laughter]

Lee Liston was a Caliente boy, as fine a man as I ever knew—he had a strong ethical influence on everybody who played on one of his teams. It got so you'd heard it before, but he would always say, "If you boys play to the best of your ability, and if you do what we have taught you and what we have practiced, you should win this game. But if you do that, and you don't win this game, it doesn't make any difference, so long as you play to the best of your ability." That sort of attitude certainly is not present in today's athletics, even on the high school level, as near as I can tell.

Although I was second string on the basketball team, I still played a lot. In 1942, we went to the state tournament, and our first game was against White Pine County High School—Ely. For the first and only time, as far as I know, the state tournament was held in Elko. It always used to be at the

University of Nevada in Reno, but in 1942 the war was on, and they had a large army contingent there. The gym had been turned into their dormitory, so it wasn't available. We had beaten Ely twice during the season, but when we played them in the state tournament, they beat the hell out of us. Jack Swedenberg, who became a star at the University of Nevada, was the star on the White Pine team, and he was my man. That day, I don't think he shot from any place on the floor that it didn't go in the basket. [laughter]

One of my best friends on the Lincoln County basketball team was Wendell Mathews. After high school, we all left for the war, and I didn't see Wendell for years. Then, in the 1950s, I'm in Las Vegas practicing law. Earl Monsey and I were law partners. To watch out for conflicts of interest, we put an extra copy of everything we did on the clipboard, so every lawyer in the office could know what the other lawyers were doing. One day, I saw a complaint for divorce by a Mrs. Mathews, and Wendell was the defendant.

Earl was representing Mrs. Mathews. I said, "Earl, we can't represent this woman against Wendell Mathews."

He said, "Why not?"

I said, "Wendell and I grew up together, and we're close friends. We just can't take a case adverse to Wendell."

He got ahold of Mrs. Mathews, told her we couldn't represent her, and explained why. She said, "I don't know why not! He never liked Ralph, anyway." [laughter]

Some of my teammates were better friends than Wendell turned out to be. We'd known each other most of our lives, at least the ones from Caliente. Some of the kids from Pioche and Panaca, we didn't know until we got to high school, but we all became close.

There was something for everybody at Lincoln County High School, yet I didn't get involved in a lot of things. I wished I'd gotten involved in drama, like my friend Lindsay Jacobson, my closest buddy for all my life. He was too small for athletics, but he was in plays and glee club, he was cheerleader, and he made the honor play. Joe Thiriot was a wonderful teacher. They put on readings, and those kids got good training. My brother was active in drama. One summer, Joe took Lew with him back to Northwestern University for a summer session in drama. I don't know where the hell the money came from. That might have been before Dad went busted. [laughter]

Everybody that went out for football could be on the team, but we only had twenty-two game uniforms, and we had thirty-three or thirty-four players on the team. It became a big thing—who would get a nice uniform when we played a game?

We're playing Ely in Panaca. The score is close. Ely's got the ball, there isn't too much time, and they're coming right down that field, right through the middle of our line. There is nothing we can do, as hard as we try to stop them. They're down to about the four or five yard line, and it looks like they're going to score. If they score, they're going to win the game.

Coach Liston didn't know what the heck he was going to do to strengthen that defensive line. He sees Ross Stewart sitting there, a big, strong kid. Ross didn't have a team uniform and had never played in a game, but Coach calls Ross in and puts him in as defensive guard. Ely played the single wing system. Their fullback gets the ball and heads for the scrimmage line. He's going to go through for a touchdown, but BOOM—Ross takes him down right at the line of scrimmage! The same thing happens on three plays thereafter. They don't score. [laughter] Ross hadn't even earned a game suit, but the coach would take a chance on him.

During Christmas vacations, the principal and the coach were out of town, and we felt pretty free in breaking the rules of training. One Saturday night my junior year, five of us on the basketball team went out to a tavern up the road from Caliente called the Cove. Saloons in Caliente at that time didn't pay much attention to the age limits. Fred Lowry ran the Cove Tavern; Christ, if you were too little, too young, he'd come around the bar and lift you up on a stool so he could sell you a drink. [laughter] It was the most popular place in the community. They had a piano player, and you could dance.

The war was on by then, and there were soldiers up and down the canyon in Caliente—they'd sent troops in to guard the tunnels down Rainbow Canyon and Meadow Valley. A bunch of soldiers were at the Cove that night, and, oh, we were having a good time! I don't know how, but we wound up wearing those enlisted men's army overcoats. We thought that was funny as hell. We had a great party, and a lot of the citizens of the community came in.

When Christmas vacation was over, the second day back, we were called to the principal's office, and the coach was there. We were playing Ely, our arch-rivals, Friday night. They asked us what we had done during the holidays—had we broken training? I'm kind of proud of that group of boys, because we all said yes, we had, and told him what we had done. It was exactly what they had heard we had done. They didn't kick us off the team, but said we would not play against Ely. It didn't make much difference if I didn't play; I wasn't a starter. The five boys who hadn't broken training played that entire game and almost won.

We had a hell of a time in Elko when we went to that state tournament. After White Pine beat us the first game, we had to play two other games for the consolation title. Then we were free, so we did about the same thing—they didn't seem too careful in Elko about selling liquor to minors. Coach Liston probably knew what we were doing, but he didn't make any issue out of it. He didn't lock us in our rooms, and we did everything in the world to prevent him from finding out what we were up to. None of us ever wanted Lee Liston to think badly of us for any reason.

In one sense, I regret playing football and basketball. I had been taking piano lessons and doing well, but I quit to devote more time to sports. The high school principal, Frank Wilcox, was equally interested in music. He was not only principal—he taught English IV, English Literature, band, and orchestra. We used to take our band to Ely and Las Vegas for marching contests. Then you'd have the concert at the auditorium and be judged.

I'm inclined to think being in the band and orchestra had a more profound effect on me than playing high school basketball or football. The love of music you acquire will last you all of your life, and there's nothing I enjoy more, even today, than a good military band. When I hear "The Stars and Stripes Forever" with a good piccolo player, my God, it thrills me to death! [laughter] But music and Frank Wilcox, I think, had a more lasting effect on me than football or basketball.

Frank Wilcox also played in an orchestra. He was a fine pianist. The Wilcox Orchestra was famous in Lincoln County, and when I was in high school, I played the drums with them when they couldn't get anybody better. Wilcox was a wonderful teacher and a wonderful man, and likewise a Lincoln County boy.

I played the drums in the orchestra and E-flat alto peckhorn in the school band. The peckhorn is shaped like a French horn, except it has valves. As E-flat alto peckhorn players go, I was pretty good. I love that music. In the dance orchestra, Mr. Wilcox sometimes would play the piano with us, but ordinarily it was one of the students—the Freshman Frolic, Sophomore Hop, Junior Prom, and Senior Ball were big functions that we played for. They were always on a Friday night, generally after a game.

Visits to Pioche were pleasant. They always had a big Labor Day celebration. They had great fight cards. Dances were great. The Wilcox Orchestra would play in Thompson Hall, an old building where they had the dances up on the second floor. If everybody was dancing to the same beat, the whole damn building would sway! [laughter] Pioche was always fun.

I would be remiss if I left the impression my father took to the hills and just hard-rock mined. My brother and I worked with him. We scavenged every mining camp in Nevada and Utah looking for mill parts, and Dad actually got a mill built at Crystal Springs, where he could mill the ore he was mining at Irish Mountain. It would be put in concentrates in big sacks, which would be loaded on a flat-bed truck. My dad, my brother, and I would haul them to Salt Lake City, to smelters at Magna and Garfield, even if we had to ride out on the back of the truck. The smelter would buy the concentrates. We would come back to Caliente, and my dad would pay the grocery bill, gas bill, dynamite bill at the hardware store, and then divide whatever money was left with the men working out there. Most of the time there wasn't anything left over.

Lew always worked. Then, when I got old enough, so did I. I didn't think there was anything unusual about working; other kids were working, too. I ran the projectors at the theater, worked as a dishwasher in the cafe, as a shoeshine boy in the barber shop, as a ranch hand, and I did a little cowboying . . . but not much. I wasn't too good a cowboy. That kind of work history was just thought to be normal for a boy back then. It didn't make you think you were deprived. It was fun being in the hills with my dad, going to Salt Lake City on a truck, shining shoes in the barber shop.

Dad really worked hard, but we just didn't become rich as we thought we would. He believed in that area. He thought it would be productive. Optimism springs eternal in the prospector's heart. Finally. he just had to quit, and that's when he got the job as a school bus driver.

When I was little, in the evening sometimes, we'd drive up the highway towards Panaca. It used to take about thirty minutes, maybe less when my dad drove. We're only talking about fifteen miles from Caliente to Panaca, but in the evening, it would be nice to take a drive and be with my mom and dad and my brother. If Mom and Dad were talking seriously, it was about politics and local things. Dad loved to sing, and loved what they call ragtime music. He was great on "Frankie and Johnny Were Lovers."

We'd ride as far as the Yoacham ranch, maybe even farther, all the way to the old Olson ranch. Other ranch families were around Caliente—Conway, Kiernan, Bradshaw, and Henry. We'd stop at this little place where there was a spring and pick watercress. I got to know that spring location well as I got older, because that's where they built the Cove Tavern. [laughter]

Down the canyon was what we'd call Kershaw, a beautiful place you might know as a Nevada State Park. In those days, it was owned by the Ryan family, who watered cattle there. We could picnic there. I remember going up in the mountains on the summit where Dad would cook in a Dutch oven, and we'd have a Sunday dinner in the hills. We did that a lot. That would be my first memories of going any place, and it was always fun.

Archie Yoacham and his wife were old-timers, close friends of my father and mother, and they had a boy my age. They sort of ran a dairy when I was little, and they sold milk in the days before pasteurization and homogenization. They had a route through town, and they weren't alone. Buck Tennille, down the canyon, also used to peddle milk in town. All of these ranches, in the 1930s, everybody was busted.

Hans Olson was a Swede, an old-timer. Old Hans had a saloon in Caliente. Hans Jr., worked in a grocery store. Otto was a bartender. The daughter married a man that worked for the railroad, and I don't know who was running the ranch in those days. Thomas Clay, who later got the *Lincoln County Record*, bought that ranch, put hundreds of acres under cultivation, and was selling Appaloosa horses.

The Ryans were a pioneer family—became a large cattle operation. Jim Ryan was what we think of as an old cattle baron. He came from Ireland. Probably in the 1880s, he came to Pioche and Bullionville, worked in the mines, took to the desert with a long rope and a few cows, mostly a long rope. The empire Ryan built was hard work. He ran cattle all the way from the Delamar flats down almost into Clark County—real desert. That means he had to chase them and round them up. He ran them north, and I think they ran 5-6,000 head. He was one of the founders of the first bank in Pioche. My dad, who wasn't a cattle man, used to say the only difference between him and Jim was that Jim had a longer rope, implying, of course, that maybe Jim put his rope on somebody else's calf, sometimes. [laughter]

There was a great deal of rivalry between Caliente and Pioche. Pioche was much older; Caliente didn't start until the railroad was being constructed, probably around 1902 or 1903. The railroad was completed in 1905, and the shops were moved to Caliente after the big railroad strike in 1921 and 1922. So, Caliente had a stable population. Pioche, on the other hand, was boom and bust. It was in the mining business. Old pioneers like my family always thought Pioche was up and down, but Caliente will always be a good town, because we'll have the railroad. They didn't anticipate that after steam locomotives were replaced by diesels, trains wouldn't need to stop in Caliente to be serviced anymore.

The first trip I remember is going to the old courthouse for the Mohrlock and Carter murder trial. I couldn't have been over five, six years old. My dad was a witness. Two people were murdered, and he discovered one of the bodies. They later found another down a shaft.

As I recall, two old prospectors had been prospecting at the peak of the Depression. The nephew of one of them came out from Ohio with a friend and went looking for his uncle out in the hills. He found him, murdered his uncle and his partner, and took off.

At the time, Dad was out in the hills prospecting in Logan, Nevada, which hasn't been a town since the 1860s. On Irish Mountain, Dad discovered this body thrown into this manger with a bunch of old cement sacks over it. The sheriff of Lincoln County, Charlie Culverwell, got great credit. The guy was arrested back in Ohio, I think. My dad says, "It's a good thing they did find him, or old Charlie would have put me in jail. They'd have charged me, because I'm the one that found him."

I thought that old courthouse was the biggest place I'd ever seen. Julian Thruston, a new lawyer in Lincoln, was defense counsel. Frank Wadsworth was the prosecutor. As I recall, they were convicted but didn't get the death penalty. It was a sensational case. I remember Dad holding my hand and talking to all the men at the courthouse and on the street during recesses, and wishing the hell I was home. I was bored.

Julian was much older than me, but I got to know Julian a bit as I became a teenager. I even ran into him during the war a couple of times. Julian and my father were close when Julian first came in the early 1930s. He was district attorney of Lincoln County after that. He ran for lieutenant governor once, too. Then he moved to Las Vegas and became a law partner with

George Marshall, and I think he was the lawyer for Guy McAfee, who became an owner in the Golden Nugget. Thruston had a piece of the action.

I don't know what soured my father on Julian, but he really got soured. Julian ultimately shot himself in the head. My dad said, "That's the first time the son-of-a-bitch ever shot straight in his life."

I had a poignant thing happen when I was running for Congress. I stopped at the Minden Inn in Minden. When you're campaigning in small town Nevada, you go into all the bars and buy everybody a drink, if you can. But this was in the morning. There wasn't anybody there. I gave my card to the bartender and introduced myself. There was a young man there, and I introduced myself to him too. He said his name was Julian Thruston.

I said, "There was a Julian Thruston who was a lawyer in Las Vegas. I knew him."

He said, "He was my father. You know, I've never known anybody who knew my father." (This kid was going through a flight school of some kind they had in Minden.)

I said, "Oh, then come to Las Vegas. Plenty of people in Las Vegas know your father."

My first trip to Las Vegas would have been when I was five or six. My parents knew a lot of old-time Clark County people, because in the early days it was all one county. My mother had lots of friends from her women's club activities. Dad would take us to see the Valley of Fire and construction at Hoover Dam, and we'd spend time with Mother's niece, Aileen Baker. She married a Wadsworth from Panaca. My mother taught at the Prince Mine, and her brother was the foreman of the machine shop. Some of those Panaca kids worked at the mine, and one of them married my uncle's daughter Aileen. Joe Wadsworth was a barber in Las Vegas for years.

I used to come down to Las Vegas to see the dentist. (Quannah McCall had been a dentist in Caliente and moved to Las Vegas.) We didn't have a dentist when I was a little older, and that was absolutely wonderful, because I could take the train down by myself and eat on the diner. Then we came down to play basketball and football after high school. It was just a good town. What's interesting about that, though, is that Caliente is right between Las Vegas and Ely. Those towns were about the same size in those days. So, in the summertime, we'd go to Ely, in the wintertime to Las Vegas.

Dad knew most of the Las Vegas old-timers. Ed Clark and my Dad had been close in Caliente. Clark had the Clark Forwarding Company. I have an old Caliente newspaper of 1903 that said Ed Clark, former Caliente businessman, now in The Vegas—not Las Vegas—was in town for a visit. He hoped someday Las Vegas would be as nice a little town as Caliente. He became very successful. Clark Forwarding Company became Clark County Wholesale. He was one of the founders of the power company. He was a banker. He was a Democratic national committeeman for years. What else

Clark owned, I have no idea, but he was prominent, and he and my dad were buddies. My mother was a close friend of Zora Grant. Mom was a close friend of most of the women in those days who belonged to the Mesquite Club.[3]

It was always fun to come to Las Vegas, because it was fun to go any place in Nevada in those days. No matter where you went, you ran into people you knew. When you contemplate only 100,000 people or less in the whole state, spread over 110,000 square miles . . . basically, you were going to run into somebody you knew, no matter where you went! [laughter] There weren't many strangers.

I don't know how these friendships developed, but I suspect the old-timers from the northern part of the county met Caliente people in different civic and political things. In those days, political parties nominated candidates, and county conventions were important—candidates for sheriff, for county commission, for everything were nominated. The people participated in these political conventions. Uncle Jim, who'd been in the state legislature starting in 1893, had to campaign all the way to Searchlight. So, whatever was organized in the area, people from both ends of the county (and often from Clark County) participated.

My mother's friendships, the genesis of them, were more understandable to me, because of her activity in educational circles and women's clubs. When Sara and I moved to Las Vegas in 1955, Sara was immediately invited to join the Service League, because a lot of families still knew the Dentons, just as the Dentons knew the Von Tobels, the McNamees, old families. Mother and Dad generally went together on those friendships—Dad's friends were also my mother's friends. That's not altogether true of Mother's friends, because Dad didn't go to women's club meetings and things like that.

I had a hobby of collecting menus, but about the only restaurants I ever got to go into were in Caliente . . . and maybe in Las Vegas, Ely, and once in a while, Salt Lake. Archie Grant and his wife used to take trips all over the country and the world.[4] Mrs. Grant would see that I got menus from all over, and I had the most magnificent collection of menus you ever saw. While I was away in the army during World War II, my dad threw them all out. I was furious with him. [laughter]

K. O. Knudson was a school teacher in Caliente before he came here. My dad used to mention him once in a while. He had a beautiful daughter, my dad said, who went to Los Angeles and became an actress. I met her sister after I moved here. That's about all I knew, yet when I met this old gentleman, after I moved to Las Vegas, he told me what a buddy he and my father were.

Everybody I knew held Billy Orr in the highest esteem and greatly respected his integrity. He moved up from county judge to Nevada Supreme Court, then to the Ninth Circuit Court of Appeals. We took a *great* deal of pride in his success. The first time after I started practicing that I had an argument at the Ninth Circuit, I was nervous, not because I worried so much about the outcome of the case, as I worried about what kind of an impression

I would make on Judge Orr. I got there and discovered the court sat in panels of three, and he wasn't on the panel I appeared before. But I went to his chambers, and he greeted me as though I were his dearest, closest friend.

My father and mother were fond of Charles Horsey and his wife. They became good friends. When he got out of the University of Virginia, Horsey started to practice law in Caliente. I don't know why he came, although his son Francis told me his dad came west for some health reason. He got involved in mining at the old Prince Mine when my mother was teaching there. There was a newspaper story about this young lawyer from Virginia moving to Caliente. The editor said he was throwing in with Lincoln County folks to make a living.

Leo McNamee enjoyed the respect and love of everybody, at least in my family. My dad and Leo were close as young men. They played on the Caliente baseball team in 1910. I knew the McNamee family, and Dad knew Leo's father.

Leo was born in Eureka, Nevada, and his wife in Eureka, Utah. Leo's father was named Frank. He had a son named Frank who went on to our state Supreme Court. The father had been a barber, studied for the bar, and was admitted. He always wanted to be elected district attorney, but never could win, because he was a Republican. Leo came to practice, ran for district attorney, and they all supported Leo. Leo got elected, even though he was a Republican. He was very young when he took office.

My dad always said we supported young Leo. Everybody wanted young Leo to win, felt bad about voting against his dad. [laughter] His father was still practicing, and I think the firm was McNamee and McNamee—a Pioche firm. Leo moved down after Clark became a county in 1909. Leo and his father were attorneys for the railroad, the father before Leo. Leo and his father practiced until the father died. Another brother, Luke, was an attorney, and Frank, Jr., was an attorney. Luke, I think, went on to California to practice law.

I remember the Wengerts. My mother and Mrs. Wengert had a friendship with Zora Grant through the Nevada Federation of Women's Clubs. Cyril Wengert was a banker, and bankers were not highly regarded in my household at the time. I don't know why. [laughter] Clark and Wengert were in the power company and the bank. Dad used to tell about coming down and seeing Clark at the bank when my dad was in the saloon business, doing pretty good. They'd go to lunch. They'd walk by Second and Fremont, where the Horseshoe now is. Somebody started to build and went busted. Ed said, "Babe, why don't you buy that corner? You can get that for $2,500." Dad looked at Ed and said, "What, you got a bum mortgage on it or something?" [laughter]

What is now Caliente was called Culverwell on the map before the railroad came. The Culverwell family were among the first settlers to arrive in the area, and they picked out that valley. Later homesteaders went down the canyon or up the canyon or up Meadow Valley toward Panaca. The Culverwells must have come in the 1870s or 1880s—that 's about the time you start seeing patents in Lincoln County, with people coming in and taking up homesteads.

Every time a Culverwell died, there was a big lawsuit. When you check titles in Caliente, you start with a Culverwell, then go into the estate of another Culverwell; then this lawsuit, then that lawsuit. Charles and William Culverwell were brothers. They had children, and they sold land for right-of-way to the railroad. There was a lot of litigation over their land.

The Dentons and the second generation of Culverwells were not close in general, but we *were* close to Alice Culverwell. Alice wound up owning most of the land on the north side of the railroad tracks, which is now Caliente. She married Tom Dixon, who was close to us.

We used to laugh. Charlie Culverwell married a Wadsworth from Panaca, Jenny, a nice lady. She was active in politics, as the Wadsworth family was. The only time Jenny ever came to see us was election time. We'd have a lovely time, and then we'd see Jenny two or four years later. [laughter] My dad, for the fun of it, would try and be on the other side in elections. They were not close friends.

Frank Wadsworth was a brother of Jenny's. That's a generation ahead of me. The father was one of the early Mormon settlers in Panaca, and Frank and James were his sons. James became a state senator from Lincoln County in the 1930s and 1940s. James had a lot of kids. Their daughter Martha and I became friends in high school, and she married my best friend in the world from childhood days, Lindsay Jacobson.

Lindsay went into the Army Air Corps in World War II, became an aerial gunner on B-17s for the Eighth Air Force, flew missions out of England, survived, and made it home. As soon as he got home, he married Martha, moved to St. George, and began running a bicycle shop. I was in Washington. I had gone back into the army, and my brother, going to law school, had a patronage job under Walter Baring as an elevator boy. When Lew graduated, Walter asked Lew if he knew somebody who would like to have that job. Lew and I called Lindsay. Lindsay wanted to go to college, but he was married and didn't know how he could afford it. He wound up coming to Washington and taking that job. Marty got a job with Senator George Smathers of Florida.

Lindsay was studying accounting and had a brother in Miami in clothing-manufacturing who had a friend who wanted to open a men's clothing store in Miami. Lindsay went down to manage the store. Later he came back to Las Vegas and got a job as an auditor in the accounting department of the Gaming Control Board. During the Russell administration, Bob Cahill gave Lindsay a job. Lindsay did a good job, then retired and moved to the old family home in Pine Valley, Utah, and later died.

Another part of Lincoln County that was special to us was Pahranagat Valley. The Lambs and the Stewarts of Pahranagat Valley were pioneers, all of whom were close friends of my father and mother, and we had contact with them all of my life. Mame and her husband named their eldest son after my dad: Floyd Lamb. I used to wonder from time to time if I should claim any kinship. [laughter]

Dave Stewart was one of my father's dearest friends in Pahranagat Valley, and he had a passel of sons: C. D., Harold, Gerald, Neil, Alden, and Gilbert. When I came to Las Vegas, C. D. was the Stewart in Wells-Stewart Construction Company. During the Depression, when my dad was trying to work the mine at Irish Mountain, they had to have mules to get the ore down off the side of a hill. They'd rigged a big pulley, and you had the mules on one end who'd come down the hill when they took the sled back up. They'd load the sled with ore, and the mules would go up the hill and let the sled down. Where's my dad going to get mules? From Dave Stewart in Alamo. Dad needs help, so Dave sends up a couple of his boys to help with the mules.

I came to Las Vegas and started practicing law, and Wells-Stewart Construction was a client because of C. D.—funniest man I have known. Practical jokes you can't believe, he would play. One night he calls the house looking for me. I was in Reno. Sara answers the phone.

"Is Ralph there?"

Sara didn't recognize the voice. "No, he's in Reno."

The caller says, "Was Babe Denton his dad?"

Sara says, "Yes."

"Babe Denton went to his grave owing me thirteen dollars rent on my mules at Irish Mountain. Will that kid pay his dad's debts?"

Sara said, "I'm sure if Ralph's father owed you or anybody else any money, Ralph will take care of it. Now, can I have your phone number or address so that Ralph can get a hold of you when he gets back in town?"

He said, "Well, to tell you the truth, I'm kind of down on my luck. As a matter of fact, I'd settle that debt for a bottle of Muscatel wine." Then he started laughing and Sara finally caught on that it was C. D. That was typical.

I don't know when the Amantes came to Caliente. Louie had been a bootlegger, a saloon keeper, and then a gambler, and he spoke with a broken accent. He had a lot of sons—Albert, Carlo, Ernie, and Pete. As far as I know, every one of them went into gambling. Every one of them was very capable, in that they could, if the situation were right, be very "mechanical."

I had better explain. Few people in Nevada today understand old words everybody used to understand. 'Cross-roader' is one, 'mechanic' is another.

Both refer to somebody good with cards to the point they can affect the outcome of a game. I think all of the Amante boys were good mechanics. One time Albert ran for sheriff against Charlie Culverwell. Charlie owned practically that whole street on the south side of the tracks. He was sheriff, and every saloon keeper was a tenant. Louie Amante had been a tenant of Charlie's for years, and they were good friends, or so Charlie thought. Charlie goes to Louie, and Charlie's concerned. According to Charlie, Albert had been telling everybody Charlie was a dirty son-of-a-bitch.

Charlie asked Louie, "How come your boy's telling everybody in the county that I'm a dirty son-of-a-bitch?"

Louie just says, "Charlie, can I help what you are?" [laughter] Charlie won by a huge majority. I wouldn't be surprised if Dad didn't lay a vote on old Albert. He liked Louie.

Old Louie was talking about his kids one day. He said, "Albert's a pretty gooda boy. Ernie's a pretty gooda boy. Pete's a pretty gooda boy. But that God-damma Carlo is a dirty, no-gooda son-of-a-bitcha just like his a god-damn mother." [laughter]

I think the Amantes moved to Las Vegas while I was in the service. Carlo was one of the original owners of the Biltmore Hotel at Main and Bonanza. Carlo was all over. He came to Elko and worked in a gambling joint when I was there. The last I knew of Ernie, he was a floorman at the Riviera, and I think he died. His wife wrote a column about trips out of Las Vegas, to Beatty or Rhyolite. Pete worked at the Showboat for years. I was always glad Pete was at the Showboat, because whenever I went there, Pete saw I got comped. [laughter]

I didn't know Missy Wah until I was an adult, but she ran the boarding house at the Prince Mine at the time my mother was teaching there. Tom Wah brought her, this little Chinese girl, to Nevada as his wife when Missy was only about fourteen. It was reputed that Tom kept Missy locked up at night. As I understood the story, he'd purchased her, and she worked in the boarding house, but her freedom of motion was restricted. My mother raised hell and got that taken care of, then devoted a lot of time to teaching her to speak English, as she

Missy Wah

did with a lot of the miners from Europe. I didn't know this until my mother's death.

At my mom's funeral, at the gym in Caliente, in comes this Chinese lady—turned out to be Missy Wah. After the funeral, she wanted to talk to me. She told me how much my mother meant to her and how much she loved Hazel. My mom didn't do a very good job of teaching her English, but that warmed my heart.

My dad took to the hills, worked very hard. I helped when I could. I've always been proud that he got a mill built, scavenged every old mining town in Nevada and Utah. Sometimes I was with him, picking up spare parts. I didn't realize how tough it was. And his sense of humor! He would come in out of the hills, and the first thing I knew, we were all laughing, having fun. The one thing I never lacked for was love in my family: love and the willingness to sacrifice for each other. The things my mother and father did for me and my brother that we accepted in those days as our due . . . they weren't our due. We worked, but that was thought of as, "Well, who doesn't work? Of course, you work." But a sense of humor makes up for an awful lot. As long as my dad was around, that happened, and he just tickled my mother to death. They would laugh, and we would laugh.

One typical story: We were driving. We'd been to visit my relatives in Utah, Dad had come up to get us, and we're driving back. We drive down through Utah to Cedar City, then across a dirt road to Caliente. It's dark, raining and storming. All of a sudden, on the side of the road, there's a dead animal.

We drive on a little ways, and Mom says to Dad, "Did you see that dead horse back there?"

Dad says, "That was a dead cow, Hazel."

"No, Floyd, it was a horse."

They had the damnedest argument you ever heard over whether that was a horse or a cow. In the rain, in the mud, Dad turns around the car, and they go back and they find out what it is. For the rest of the trip, they were laughing at each other for making an issue over who was right as to whether it was a horse or a cow.

My father's sense of humor was the glue that held our family together in those Depression years. My mother always responded to his humor with a good spirit. One Christmas, he gave her two presents. One was a mirror, and the other was a hatchet. The note was, "Dear Hazel, you have two choices. You can either chop wood or sit and watch yourself freeze to death. Merry Christmas, Floyd." [laughter] Dad had lacked money to buy a nice present as he would have liked, but Mom got a present that raised her spirits.

And I know my mother chopped a lot of wood! [laughter] Dad used to say he couldn't stand to see Hazel chop wood; so every time she started, he'd get up and go into town. But he chopped a lot of wood too, as did my brother and myself and any bums that were around. In those days, practically every freight train that stopped in the yards, bums would get off. Most asked if there was a little work they could do for a meal. My mother never turned anybody down, but they always had to chop wood.

I look back on those years with fondness. I'd see families that had more than we did, but I didn't feel deprived. I worked as a shoeshine boy in the barber shop. That was good, but Lindsay got to work in the Allen Cash Store in the butcher shop for Bob Vowels. Lindsay learned about cutting meat, which left him in good stead. When we'd go to his house for a barbe-cue, he would have known the cut to get.

I didn't learn a thing shining shoes, but I had a good time. You got ten cents a shine, and on a busy day, if railroad men were coming in, you could get three, four shines an hour. (You didn't always get that much, but that was good pay.) I could do three things with a dime. I could save it, which I did quite a bit. I could go next door to Burt's Drug Store, get a Coke for a nickel, and have a nickel left to play the slot machine. Or I could go into the Buckaroo Club, where there were pool tables, and if there were any drunk cowboys, I could take them on in a pool game. They had to be awful drunk for me to beat them, so I wouldn't play unless they were in bad shape. But I had a chance of making a dime or two.

I'd often opt to have a coke and put a nickel in the slot machine, be-cause I had a chance of winning a little. One time I won the jackpot, and Mr. Burt took it from me, saying, "You're too young to play the slot ma-chine." [laughter] I must have been eleven or twelve. I said, "Mr. Burt, you didn't say that when I was losing." [laughter]

I also worked in the old State Cafe as a dishwasher. That was twenty-five cents an hour. That was tough, because you had to be there early in the morning to take care of the breakfast dishes. Then you could go home, but you had to come back after lunch to take care of the lunch dishes. Then you had to come back after the supper crowd and take care of the supper dishes. You'd put in a long day.

From the time I started high school, at night and on weekends, I was a projectionist at Uncle Lloyd's theater. I worked in a service station for a while. I worked as a hand on the Conway ranch. I was a little older and rode on round-ups a couple of times with the cowboys. You'd be surprised how much work there is for a ranch hand. That was two and a quarter a day and board yourself. You dug irrigation ditches, repaired fences. The hay crews in those days didn't have the equipment they have now. You used a buck rake and jayhawk, and you had to stack that hay on top. The irrigating ditches are always washing out. Even if there's nothing to do on the ranch, go into the range area and clean out springs so they'd have water.

When I worked on the ranch, I was fourteen, maybe fifteen. The ranch was three miles south of town. We had to be there at seven in the morning. If Mr. Conway didn't have any work, he'd come out and say, "I don't have any work today, boys." Then you had to go back those three miles. Some-times we'd just been dropped off there, and we'd walk home. Lindsay worked with me. Stiff Bagget was a little older, so he got to drive a buck-rake. Carol Burt worked for a while, and Tom Dula worked on the Conway ranch for a long time.

The job I enjoyed most was shoeshine boy. What was fun about it were the people. Toogey Trower was my first customer. He was a remittance man from St. Louis who had come to Nevada to get a divorce.[5] How he got to Caliente, I don't know, but he stayed and married Stella Grotto, who had the drug store. Toogey was a good baseball player, and he was in the assembly from Lincoln County at one time.

Nobody had told me how to shine shoes. George Ence was the barber—he'd simply given me the stuff and told me I put the polish on and brushed them down. I did that twice. After I did, I took a cloth and polished them. I must have worked a half hour on Toogey's shoes. Toogey got out of the chair and stood. He pulled up his pant legs, looked down, and said, "Ralph, do I have to pay you extra for shining my socks?" [laughter]

Buck Tennille was the sheriff at this time. Buck was all stretched out on Ence's chair getting a shave. He had the big apron draped over him, and his face was wrapped in a hot towel. The damnedest commotion you ever heard took place, and here's Dana Conway on a horse with the horse's head in the barber shop door. Dana throws a rope over Buck's head, backs up with that horse, and pulls Buck out of that chair and right out onto the sidewalk. He's going down the street yelling, "Hey, I got the God-damn sheriff!" Buck and Dana had been friends all their lives, and Dana was just drunker than hell.

Old Bucky Rice, a cowboy, took to strong drink whenever he was in town. He comes into the barber shop. He wants his whole head shaved. He's got cowboy boots on, he wants them shined. Owen Benson was the barber. Owen gives him a complete shave. I shined his cowboy boots. Bucky gets up out of the chair and says, "Thanks," pays neither of us, and out the door he goes!

Here was a kid in a barber shop, and the customers are railroad men. My dad always said of a conductor or a hoghead or a brakeman, "They're the smartest people in the world. They know everything." You'd sit and listen to these men talk, particularly during an election year. They'd all be talking to each other and the barber. I think a barber shop is the best location in any town to know what's going on politically. I used to be fascinated to listen to these guys talk. That was a fun place to work. The barbers were first-class guys. I got free haircuts. They owned the equipment; they owned the chair. I was to sweep the floors and keep the barber shop clean, then they'd give me one haircut a month. And I got to keep what I earned shining shoes; I didn't have to give them anything back.

There was a time when I missed the smallness of Caliente, but I don't any longer. I think we're better off today. We have things in our state now—at least in two, maybe three sections of the state—that we never had before. But I go into the rural counties that still have those small towns, and I'm sure the children in those places feel like I did. I thought Caliente was the most wonderful place in the world, and I felt sorry for every kid who didn't live there. When the state was really small, there were a lot of things we didn't have; and there are some things we don't have now. But with new people and young people and better ideas that aren't tied to the past, it seems to me we have a chance to create a society here in Nevada that will provide more opportunities for young people.

Notes

1. Arizona State Teachers College is now Northern Arizona University.

2. Thomas E. Dixon was a Democrat, an assemblyman from Lincoln County in the 1931 legislative session, and a third-place finisher in the 1938 Democratic primary for lieutenant governor.

3. The Mesquite Club was the first women's club in Las Vegas.

4. Archie C. Grant was a longtime Las Vegas businessman and Democratic politician, and a university regent, 1953-72.

5. E. H. Trower, a Democrat, represented Lincoln County in the 1941 legislative session. He was killed in 1942.

3 | We Thought FDR Was the Savior

I remember Key Pittman coming to our house, talking to my mom and dad, my dad laughing about him. He said, "You know, even a United States Senator, when he has too much to drink, shoots his mouth off more than he should." Any politician or high public office holder should learn that he shouldn't drink in public when he's on a campaign, because whiskey loosens his mouth just like it does everybody else's, and he says some awful stupid things. Dad always had great affection for Pittman. I think it stemmed from the early days when my dad was young and knew him in Tonopah and Goldfield.

I've heard the story that Key Pittman died before election day when he was re-elected in 1940, and I have no reason to believe that it isn't true. I was told this by Bud Lloyd. Bud was county clerk of Lincoln County at the time of that election, and Julian Thruston was district attorney. Pittman was a whiskey head. I've heard that he wet his pants when he was making a speech in Sparks, and he went right on with his speech. Bud said that a few days before the 1940 election, Thruston called him at his office at the courthouse and asked him to go uptown in Pioche, get a bottle of whiskey, and bring it to his house. Pittman was there, and sick, and he needed a drink. Julian was scared. People knew Pittman was visiting him. If he went uptown and got the whiskey, they would know that Pittman was drinking. He asked Bud to get the bottle and bring it, and Bud did. He took it to Julian's house. Pittman, he said, was in bed and obviously sick, and he stayed there. They decided they better get him the heck out of Pioche. Bud wasn't sure whether they took him to Tonopah or to Reno, but he was very sick two or three days before the election.

Apparently, Pittman was an awful boozer. In summer 1942 I went to Washington and got a job as an elevator boy under Berkeley Bunker's patronage. I got to know a lot of the guys that worked around the Capitol, and they would talk about Pittman and how he had whiskey stashed all over the Capitol. He could go any place and put his hand on a bottle, so I was told. I always believed the story about Pittman dying before the election, because it's the sort of story you want to believe, because it's dramatic. A guy's dead, nobody knows, and he gets elected to the Senate. I never asked Senator McCarran about it, but Chet Smith says McCarran said it was not true—he didn't die before the election. Chet was a newspaperman at the time in Winnemucca, and he says that every reporter in Nevada tried to get to the bottom of it and find out. He said, "If that would have happened, you can bet that those guys in Reno would have known it, would have discovered it at the time." I understand, since I've heard the evidence, he might have been alive in the legal sense of the word, but might have been brain dead, as they say. I don't know. I heard people say they were present and he died in Tonopah, and members of their family were present when it happened. I just don't think that's correct.

My parents were strong supporters of Pittman. Part of it was a personal affection for an old-timer, and part of it was his solid support of Franklin D. Roosevelt. That seems contradictory, because they felt equally strong in their affection and support for Pat McCarran, who was not a strong Roosevelt supporter. But I don't believe most people in Nevada, at least in the rural areas, knew of Pittman's erratic conduct. He was president pro tem of the Senate, a great honor for Nevada. He was chairman of the Senate Foreign Relations Committee, a great honor for Nevada. When Roosevelt came to Nevada for the dedication of Hoover Dam, Pittman was with him. Pittman was a strong supporter of free coinage of silver. They liked him, thought of him as an old-time Nevadan, but my mother would have been terribly upset if she'd ever known he went up and down streets in London, shooting out lights with his pistol and that kind of stuff.

The funniest story I heard about any political figure from Nevada, though, was of Congressman Evans back in the 1920s.[1] He went back to Washington with one purpose in mind: to have a gambling game in the House cloak room. He stayed two years, ran games in the House cloak room, and never came back to Nevada, didn't run for re-election. After the war, when I was there, Evans was still in Washington, and he was a Capitol guide. He was a nice old fellow. I asked him about that story. He just smiled with a glint in his eye. [laughter]

My father was fond of Tasker Oddie, and probably supported Oddie until 1932.[2] Why a Republican? I don't know who Oddie's opponents were when he was elected Senator or governor, but there was a lot of the Pittman charm in Oddie. Oddie was an old-time Nevadan. He'd been in Tonopah, in Goldfield, in the mining game. He'd gotten rich, and he'd gotten busted. They thought he was a real gentleman, and they really liked Oddie. It was painful to them in 1932 when they supported McCarran over Oddie. I remember Oddie as a pleasant man, coming to our house.

In those days, we stood in awe of people in high public office. It was hard for us to believe that a senator put his pants on like everybody else. We ascribed more honor, integrity, and devotion to people in high public office then, and it's a shame that such things have since happened in our country that people no longer have that respect. When I ran for Congress in 1964, I called on old Joe McDonald, the editor of the *Nevada State Journal*. When I came into his living room, he stood up and welcomed me as though I were somebody. People had more respect in those days for people in high public office than they do now.

The only times I ever saw George Wingfield were after I was practicing law in Elko and I'd be in Reno. I was in the Riverside Hotel a couple of times, and he walked through. In my family, he was not highly regarded. He was thought of as a tinhorn huckster who robbed the people of Nevada, and who engineered false convictions of murder cases, trying to fight the unions in Tonopah and Goldfield.[3] I'm sure opinion was divided, depending upon your views. A lot of people didn't see anything the matter with having false testimony convict a radical! [laughter]

In addition to the trouble in Tonopah and Goldfield, with the banks going busted, with Wingfield having so much power, he could get the legislature to forgive part of a debt for an embezzlement of state funds.[4] He was the patron saint in Reno of Jim McKay and Bill Graham, who ran the bootleg joints, whorehouses, that stuff. What kind of a man are we talking about who was so powerful, he turned down a seat in the United States Senate so he could be king of Nevada? I forget that quote, but it was a quote where he would rather be, in effect, the king.

I have a friend, Virgil Wedge, who went with the Woodburn firm, did Wingfield's work, and is a great admirer of Wingfield's. I have a great deal of respect for Virgil, but I never could have any respect for Wingfield. I don't care how much money he made, how much power he gained, or how much charity he did, if any—he destroyed people. It appeared to me he was willing to do anything for a dollar.

The first candidate to visit our home whom I really remember with clarity is Morley Griswold, who had been Fred Balzar's lieutenant governor, and who had become acting governor when Balzar died in office. Griswold was from Elko. (When I lived in Elko after the war, I discovered that he and Jack Robbins had been close friends, and the two of them had owned a little saloon there, the Palm Saloon, a "gentleman's resort." [laughter] Wouldn't let any women in, and the bartender wouldn't serve you if he didn't know you.) In 1934, Griswold ran for governor. Richard Kirman was the Democratic nominee, and my parents supported Kirman. I could always understand them opposing a Republican, even if he was a friend—there was no doubt about what we were!

Only a couple of times do I remember my parents giving aid and comfort to a Republican candidate. One would have been George Malone in 1952. Franklin Roosevelt was God in our house. He was the culmination, in my mother's view, of everything Progressives had stood for since the 1890s. For the first time, the government seemed to feel a responsibility to see that people were fairly treated; before that, it had always been laissez-faire.

"Government has nothing to do with economics." Mother saw it in those terms. My father saw it in the same terms, but Dad was a little less ideological and a little more pragmatic. His take was that when the Democrats won, he always seemed to do better. He used to say, "A Republican's nothing more than a Democrat that's got the wrinkles out of his belly." (When Sara and I got married, I learned her family felt exactly the same way. They lived in the South.) Years later, I thought, "How could the Dentons be such strong supporters of Roosevelt, and at the same time strong supporters of Pat McCarran?" But they were. Knowing people in our part of Nevada were such strong supporters of Roosevelt, how did McCarran have the courage to take some of the steps he took? How did he have enough magnetism and charm to retain the support of those people?

I remember sitting in the living room, listening to Roosevelt's "Fireside Chats," and agreeing with everything he said in that magnificent voice. We had a belief in those days that They (the Democrats) would not permit bad things to happen to the country. They would see things were put right. They would see that the right thing was always done. As I grew up, I was shocked to learn that the Democrats ain't no They!

When I was young, though, we thought Franklin Roosevelt was the savior; and, by God, I still do! [laughter] I remember how happy we were when he was elected. Oh, my Lord, everybody was happy! (At least, as near as I could tell. There must have been some people that weren't.) The great thing I remember was when he ended Prohibition, and beer came back! [laughter] The town went wild. All the saloons over town brought the beer out into the open, and there was celebration. In the bootleg days, when I was a very little kid, I'd go to the bootleggers to sell them empty bottles. Lindsay and I and everybody, we'd go up the alleys looking for empty whiskey bottles and beer bottles, and then you could take them to the bootleggers, and they'd buy the bottles from you.

Notes

1. Charles R. Evans, a Democrat, was elected to the House in 1918 and defeated in 1920.

2. Tasker Oddie was governor (1911-14) and U.S. Senator (1921-33). He was defeated for reelection in each case.

3. Sally Zanjani and Guy Louis Rocha, *The Ignoble Conspiracy* (Reno: University of Nevada Press, 1986), details the radical unions and violence in Goldfield in 1907, and the miscarriages of justice involved.

4. State Controller George Cole and State Treasurer Ed Malley embezzled state funds for private purposes in the 1920s. Although they were Wingfield men, and illegally deposited the money in Wingfield banks, they went to jail, and, as Wingfield wished it, the legislature raised taxes to make up the loss.

4 | The Summer That Changed My Life

Lewis was older than I was; he was eligible for the draft even before the war started. In 1940 or 1941, he went to Washington and got a job in the General Accounting Office, knowing it would be just a question of time until he had to go into the service. I missed my brother desperately. I thought I would never see him again, because he would probably get drafted and get killed. But there was nothing I could do about that until, fortuitously, my dad came down out of the hills. He couldn't make it mining. It got to the point where he had to close the mill, shut the mine, and find a job. He found one tending bar at George Shuman's Nevada Club, next door to the theater in Caliente.

I would go to work early and stop in to talk to my dad before I'd go into the theater and get the machines ready. It was probably late May or June 1942. The restaurant and casino were up front, the bar in the back. A nice-looking young man with dark, wavy hair was talking to my father. My father introduced me. It was Berkeley Bunker, the senator from Nevada, appointed when Pittman died. He was out campaigning to be elected. I mentioned, "My brother Lewis lives in Washington; I hope you have a chance to see him." We got to talking about that, and he offered me a summer job as elevator boy under his patronage. It was a great salary of $100 a month, and you only had to work four hours a day. That was magnificent to me, and I accepted on the spot. He said when he got back to Washington, he'd write and let me know when it was available and when I should be in Washington.

I was thrilled to death. I was going to get to see my brother and spend the summer with him. Then I would come home, he would go in the army, and maybe this summer would be the last time I would have a chance to spend any time with him; either he or I or both of us would, in all probability, not survive World War II. Thank God, it didn't turn out that way, but that's what I thought. As things turned out, that summer spent in Washington changed my life—Bunker giving me a job opened the world up to me.

I left Caliente on train 14 at 10:00 at night, in late May or early June of 1942. I remember being a bit scared, my mother and father both crying. I kind of remember me crying a bit, too. It was my first big trip alone, across the country. Oh, God, it was wonderful! When I left Caliente, I knew most of the crew, the brakemen and conductors, until I got past Milford. Some of the crew went all the way to Salt Lake in those days. Most of the people in the car were going all the way across country, too. I fell in love with train travel—eating in the diner for three, four days. After a couple of days, you knew the people in the coach, at least people sitting with you.

Doc Demman was later a doctor in Las Vegas, but in those days, he was in Caliente. His wife Mary, from Omaha, had a passel of sisters. Mary had written them to meet the train in Omaha. That was a big thrill. I got off the train, and here were three or four beautiful girls to meet me and wish me well. I was kind of happy to see Omaha, because that's where my father's family had come from a lot of years before.

When I arrived in Washington, my brother and Hugh Norton, an Ely boy, were at the train to meet me—came into Union Station, got my luggage, walked out, looked right up the hill, and there's the Capitol! We went to the boarding house, dropped my luggage, and walked up to the rotunda. I couldn't believe what I was seeing. Just magnificent! The beautiful paintings, the frieze about halfway up, the art in the top of the dome—absolutely beautiful!

Then we went to the boarding house. There were three beds in the room: my brother had one, and Lorenzo Chavez, who was going to law school, had one. (Lorenzo became a lifelong friend. His son Martin became mayor of Albuquerque. Lorenzo had a job under Senator Dennis Chavez's patronage in the Library of Congress.[1] He didn't object to people thinking Chavez was his uncle, but I don't think they were related.) One bed had been vacated by a Nevada boy, Dyer Jensen, who had left to go in the service. (Dyer has been a lawyer in Reno for many years.) That bed was mine. I had to make financial arrangements with the landlady, Loma Gordon, and the board was $40 a month. My two war bonds came in handy. With my first paycheck, I paid the rent and redeemed my bonds.

Our house was at 128 B Street, Northeast, half a block from the Senate Office Building. In those days, there was one Senate office building; that one is now the Russell Building. B Street Northeast is no longer there, because they built two additional Senate office buildings on what was B Street. But it was filled with Nevada people, and we called it "the Nevada Embassy." There was Jon Collins and Fritz Arlang. Cal Cory had just left and gone to Las Vegas. Jimmy Johnson from Fallon had just gotten married and lived in an apartment around the corner. Grant Sawyer had just left to go into the service; he'd boarded at the Nevada Embassy.

The next day, I went to Bunker's office. He was not there. He was in Nevada, campaigning. His administrative assistant was Florine Maher, whom I later got to know in Nevada. She married Ted McCuistion and moved to

Elko, but I didn't meet her in Washington, because she was out campaigning. The lady in charge, Billie Heckey, wasn't from Nevada, but had a lot of experience on the Hill. (I call it the Hill now! See how sophisticated I am? I didn't know it was the Hill then.)

After I went there, my brother took me to Senator McCarran's office to meet him. I was nervous. I sure wanted to make a good impression. (I'd seen him at our home in Caliente, but he was talking to my mom and dad, and I'm sitting on the floor.) I had purchased a white wool coat. It is 90 degrees and 90 percent humidity, and everybody's sweating like a stuck hog. I get dressed up and wear this coat and a red bow tie—clip-on, because that's what I wore in the orchestra in Caliente, and what I thought was the most appropriate. My brother smiled, but I didn't have anything else, to tell you the truth.

I went over there and met Eva Adams, McCarran's assistant, and that was the start of a friendship that lasted throughout her life and mine. (I've never known anybody like Eva. I was honored to be asked to speak at her funeral. She returned to Nevada after she was no longer McCarran's or Bible's administrative assistant, was no longer director of the United States Mint, was no longer on the board of Mutual of Omaha. Dean Robert Daugherty, of the University of Nevada medical school, told me he was once talking to Eva and my name came up. She told him she remembered the first day she ever met me, with my white coat and bow tie, and how I'd really tried to get dressed up as best I could.) [laughter]

I went in to see the senator. I felt like such a fool! He's very charming, glad to see me; he shakes hands.

"How are you?"

I say, "Fine."

I just sit there, looking at him. Can't think of anything appropriate to say. There's silence for a few minutes. Then the senator stands up, sticks his hand out and says, "Now, come back and see me again." [laughter]

The next day, my brother takes me to see Congressman Scrugham. (I'd seen him in our home too.) I hadn't learned a thing from my visit with McCarran. Shook hands. "How are you?" he says.

I say, "Fine," and sit; cannot think of a thing to say to the great man.

Finally, Scrugham says, "Well, sure glad you came in. You come

"That's what I wore in the orchestra."

back and see me, now." [laughter] I never felt that I could, in those days, say the right thing. If I did say something, it was stupid.

I never saw Scrugham again, but I did see McCarran. Not in his office, but while I was at work—I ran a "senators only" elevator. I'd see quite a bit of McCarran, and he always took the time to be pleasant, ask about Caliente, my mom and dad. Always, "Is there anything I can do for you? Do you need a few dollars?" He'd reach in his pocket.

I wasn't under his patronage. I'd say, "No, I don't need a thing."

On a couple of occasions, he said, "Well, here, take five dollars anyway. Go out and have dinner or something."

I'd go to McCarran's office. By then, Cal Cory had come back. I think Cal was married—he didn't stay in the boarding house. At that time, Cal was general counsel for the Senate District of Columbia Committee, and McCarran was chairman. Cal was back, he was fun, and he was around the office all the time. Jimmy and Millie Johnson lived in an apartment around the corner. They would invite me over for dinner, tried to teach me how to play bridge. They weren't very successful.

The women in Berkeley Bunker's office were wonderful to me. They knocked themselves out to make certain everything was OK. They told me I should stop in at least once or twice a week so they'd know how I was doing. A lot of patronage people were obligated to go to their senator's office and work. They never asked me to do anything, but imagine this: on a Sunday, Billie took me to the Congressional Country Club for brunch.[2] I had never seen a place like that—the landscaping, everything so magnificent. And this lady, who I hardly knew, had taken her Sunday afternoon to take me there. Driving back, she took us into the district. We went by the Pentagon, which was in construction, way the hell out in beautiful, open northern Virginia country, Arlington County. Now it's part of the metropolitan area.

I had no sense of the political rivalry between the members of Nevada's delegation. Everything was just happy and wonderful. Bunker was in Nevada, as was Scrugham most of the time, because that's who Bunker was running against in the primary. McCarran's position was "a pox on both their houses." [laughter] I never noticed any great friendship between the three offices—you would hear little digs from people about the other members of the delegation, and when I went back after the war, there was *outright* rivalry.

I had gone to Washington to be with my brother. Oh, I was happy to see him! But I was there only a week before he got drafted, and he was gone. Then I was the most homesick kid you ever saw in your life. But it wasn't far from the boarding house to the Congressional Library periodical room, and I'd read the *Caliente Herald* and *Pioche Record*.[3] And Lorenzo and Fritz took me all over that town to see monuments, museums, baseball games at Griffith Stadium.[4] After my brother was gone for about two weeks, I got over the homesickness and enjoyed every minute.

I had one experience involving Eleanor Roosevelt. Queen Wilhelmina of the Netherlands came to Washington. She was going to speak to the Senate—not a joint session of the Congress, just the Senate, which is unusual. I was told the day before by the nice gentleman in charge of all the elevators in the Senate that I should have my elevator on the street floor of the capitol at twelve o'clock, and, no matter how many senators rang, I was not to move. Mrs. Roosevelt would arrive at noon, and I was to take her up from the street floor, which in those days was called the 'basement'. Below it was the 'subway'.

Ralph and Lew with Mom and Dad, 1942.

I'd been told that when anybody rang the bell three times straight, that's a senator. Consequently, no matter where your elevator was going, if somebody rang three times, you immediately went to pick up that senator. If another senator was on the elevator, you were to say, "Do you mind if I pick up your colleague?" If he said no, or he wanted to go wherever he was going before I went to get his colleague, you had to do that. You were scared, if you got three buzzes, that you did not answer them.

It's twelve. I don't see anything. I get "bzz, bzz, bzz," three buzzes in the subway. I think, "I can go down and take care of that. It's not quite twelve."

I go down to the subway, and here's Senator Gerry of Rhode Island.[5] Gerry wants to go all the way up to the gallery, the fourth floor. Just as I'm passing the street (basement) floor, I get another three buzzes from the Senate floor. In accordance with what I had been taught, I said, "Senator, do you mind if I pick up your colleague on the floor?"

He says, "I'm in a hurry, don't stop." I went past the senator on the floor, went to the gallery, let Gerry off, then came down to the Senate floor and opened the door. Senator Gerald P. Nye of North Dakota got on and started cussing me out for passing him up and wanted to know whose patronage I was under.[6] He'd see I'd lose my job. He wants to go down to the subway. He gets on the car. As he's chewing me out, there comes a steady "bzz, bzz, bzz, bzz, bzz" on the street floor, where I should have been to get Mrs. Roosevelt.

I passed Mrs. Roosevelt and took Senator Nye down to the subway, where he wanted to go. Then I came back up to the street floor to get Mrs. Roosevelt. I was a nervous wreck, as you might imagine. I suspect the whole thing didn't take over forty-five seconds or a minute. Mrs. Roosevelt, with a large smile, got on the elevator, followed by a Secret Service guy, who started chewing me out. He also wanted to know whose patronage I was under, because they would get my job. She told him to be quiet and mind his own business. She put her arm on my shoulder and patted it and said, "Don't you worry, young man."

I took her where she was to go . . . to the gallery. I was supposed to wait at the gallery until Queen Wilhelmina's speech was over, then take her to the street floor. I stepped out of the elevator, and by the elevator was a big window where you could look down and see the parking lot in front of the east portico of the Capitol. Seated down there in an open car was Franklin D. Roosevelt. He had brought Queen Wilhelmina and Mrs. Roosevelt to the Senate.

I could see down the street to Union Station. Soldiers with full battle regalia, all standing at parade rest, with their rifle and bayonets fixed, lined both sides of the street up to the Capitol, then down Pennsylvania Avenue to the White House. They really put on a show for Queen Wilhelmina, and it was the most impressive thing I'd ever seen.

I looked down at President Roosevelt. I had seen him once before, when he came through Caliente to dedicate Hoover Dam and made a little speech in the back of the train. There was a gloss to him that, all my life, I saw in presidents of the United States . . . except I never saw it in Richard Nixon or anybody since. I saw it in Harry Truman. I saw it in Jack Kennedy—a glow, to me, that I'm sure nobody else has seen.

After the speech, Mrs. Roosevelt came out and got on the elevator. I took her down to the street floor, the level where the Senate dining room is. I opened the door of the elevator. I couldn't believe it: All of the black waiters in the dining room had come out, and they had lined both sides of the hall. As Mrs. Roosevelt left the elevator, they bowed to her, and she stopped and shook hands with every one of them.

My experiences in Washington that summer were wonderful. It was a wonderful town if you were white, but I could not believe the way blacks were treated! Behind our street, within a stone's throw of the Capitol, were the worst slums. Behind big houses, black people lived in a completely seg-regated town. I could not accept this, but aside from that, my summer in Washington was a wonderful experience.

Oh, it was a grand thing, indeed, to get on the street car that came right by the Senate office building, and, for a ten cent fare, go to F Street to the Capitol Theater, where you could see a double feature and four acts of vaude-ville for fifty cents. And, if you could get one of the Capitol cops, who were also patronage guys going to school, to loan you their badge, you could get in for nothing. The ushers at the Capitol Theater got onto it, though. They would look at that badge. If it said "Capitol Police," you didn't get in for free. [laughter]

We would scam. Often, we would scam the taxi or streetcar outfit. You could buy a weekly pass, so you'd have one guy get on with the pass, and he'd quickly go to the back and hand it out the window to you. Then you'd wait for the next street car and use it, so you didn't even have to pay the dime.

We would save our money, particularly Hugh and I, to have a nice dinner on Sunday at Cannon's Steak House in the market area of Washington. We thought that was the grandest place in the world. There was also a fancy French restaurant on Vermont Avenue called Michel's. They had a dish I'd never heard of. We thought this was fancy: coq au vin. So, we would have coq au vin, Michel would stroll around the room playing a violin, and we just thought we had gone to the top. And I learned of a chain restaurant called the Little Tavern, all over town. You could buy a hamburger for a nickel. They were small, but you'd go in and order five for a quarter. [laughter]

So many things were free. You could go to the National Gallery of Art on a Sunday afternoon. There might be a string quartet—didn't cost anything. You could spend hours in the Smithsonian—didn't cost anything. Every Monday, Wednesday, and Friday night, there was a band concert on the east portico—the Army, Navy, and Marine Corps would alternate. You could sit on the lawn in front of the Capitol and hear these magnificent bands.

After I knew the town, I could go by myself, because I worked in the morning and got off at noon. I could spend all afternoon and get home in time for supper at the boarding house. By then, the guys working all day would be there, and maybe we'd go to a movie or something like that. I couldn't believe things could be any better any place than they were right there.

I used to sit in the House and Senate galleries. However, I soon learned there wasn't much going on on the floor. It was summer. There were a lot of recesses, and might be a great big debate going on, and wouldn't be anybody on the floor listening to it. But I got so I knew a lot of the newspaper guys in the press gallery. They were always sitting back there playing cards. I'd go back and talk to them a little and mostly listen to them talk. It was fun. I think I was too young to really realize these were important people. They were just nice guys working around there like I was, as far as I knew.

There might be a debate going on, and eight guys on the floor. I was surprised at that, but I learned most of the work was going on in committee. You learned the bell system. If a vote was coming, the bells rang all over, and the congressmen would show up. A lot of them might have just been in the cloak room, sitting there, working. They weren't interested in listening to the debate. They knew how they were going to vote. They'd read the committee reports or their staff had. It could be kind of boring, I imagine, just sitting there listening to a bunch of speeches you weren't particularly interested in. There's so much legislation passed, and so much of it any given senator doesn't have much interest in, one way or another.

In my job, you had to learn the names of the senators. You had to be able to recognize them. That came naturally after a while, particularly if you were working on a "senators only" elevator. Many of them would be pleasant; some would not be. Theodore Bilbo of Mississippi and Kenneth McKellar of Tennessee, Robert Taft of Ohio, were charming men, nice to the working stiffs around the capitol, even though you might abhor their views on some things. Burton K. Wheeler of Montana was a passionate man, always in the middle of whatever fight was going on, if there was a fight going on, but noncommunicative insofar as we peasants were concerned.[7]

There was one woman member of the Senate, Hattie Caraway. She always wore black. She was still mourning her husband. He had been a senator, and she'd been appointed to take his place. I don't remember her ever saying a word. She'd get on the elevator, and I'd say, "Good morning, Senator," or "Good afternoon, Senator." Never say a word, but a nice little old lady.[8]

I have memories of Senator David Walsh of Massachusetts.[9] Every time he would get in my elevator, if he was the only one there, he'd pat me on the keister. I didn't know about things like that. I didn't know what to make of it. I didn't know what the hell he was doing! I thought, "Well, maybe he's just trying to be friendly." Not knowing what to do, if anything, I didn't do anything; and that was probably wise. [laughter]

Some of the kitchen personnel in the Senate dining room would bootleg sandwiches to us. If it cost you fifteen cents for a cheese sandwich in the dining room, you could put your order with one of the busboys or people back in the kitchen for five cents, things like that. [laughter] I remember guys selling numbers and booking horses, but I didn't know what the hell they were doing. I learned more about that when I went back in 1947. But it was just a wonderful experience, and it showed me a world that I never would have seen.

I saw these Nevada boys, all of them older than I was. My brother had known most of them at the university in Reno. That's not true of Hugh Norton, who had gone into Salt Lake at Westminister College, then come back to Washington and was going to George Washington University. At that time, I think he had a patronage job under McCarran, but I don't recall what. We became lifelong friends. He's a retired professor of economics at the University of South Carolina, and we're in touch all the time.

Most of the guys from Nevada I met in Washington, I met there again after the war. I decided if these other kids from Nevada could go to college and law school, I could do it. There was no doubt in my mind from that summer on what I was going to do. Depending on what happened during the war, I was going to go to college in Washington; I was going to become a lawyer; and I was going to go back to Nevada to practice law. That was my ambition then, and my ambition now, and nothing else: to be a lawyer in Nevada. I was a long way from Caliente, and I was sensitive about my background, but, after the war, when I went back to Washington and worked in the sergeant-at-arms office, I began to realize most people were just like me. This was a new world for them too.

The truth of the matter, though, is that I did not want that summer to go on forever. They had in those days, and I guess they still do, a special school for pages. I looked into finishing up at the page school, yet I wasn't that serious. I missed Caliente. I missed Mom and Dad. School was starting in early September, and I was looking forward to my senior year in high school, to football and basketball. I had really mixed emotions, but I was glad to go home.

Notes

1. Dennis Chavez, Democrat, represented New Mexico in the House, 1931-35, and the Senate, 1935-62.

2. The Congressional Country Club has been the site of many PGA tournaments and United States Open championships.

3. The *Pioche Record* was published by Edgar L. Nores, alone or with partners, from 1920 to 1958; he was a Democratic state senator from Lincoln County, 1949-53. Philip Dolan worked briefly for Nores, and edited or published the *Caliente Herald* from 1931 to 1946.

4. Griffith Stadium was the home of the Washington Senators of the American League until they moved in 1961 and became the Minnesota Twins.

5. Senator Peter G. Gerry, a great-grandson of Declaration of Independence signer Elbridge Gerry, served from Rhode Island, 1917-29, 1935-47.

6. Nye, an isolationist, served in the Senate from 1925 to 1945 and was best known for chairing a committee that investigated munitions makers in the 1930s and concluded that they helped cause World War I.

7. Bilbo, known for his blatant racism, was governor, 1916-20 and 1928-32, and senator, 1935-47. McKellar was in the House, 1911-17, and Senate, 1917-53. Taft, the president's son and a Republican presidential candidate, was in the Senate, 1939-53. A noted progressive, Burton Wheeler represented Montana in the Senate, 1923-47.

8. Thaddeus Caraway represented Arkansas in the House, 1913-21, and Senate, 1921-31. His widow was appointed to succeed him, and remained in the Senate until 1945.

9. David Walsh served in the Senate from 1919 to 1925 and 1926 to 1947.

5 | Most Miserable I Ever Was . . .

Things had happened while I was gone that affected my life at school that year. Our coach had quit his job and taken a job as coach at the college in Cedar City, Utah. I respected and admired Lee Liston so much that I couldn't conceive of him not being there. We had a new coach, who I didn't know, and most of my teammates the year before had left. Quite a number of them went to Cedar City to play college football for our coach.

The new coach introduced a new system. We had played the Warner double-wingback system, and I had called signals the year before, although I wasn't a quarterback. This coach insisted on me becoming the quarterback. Well, I couldn't pass. Our season was a disaster, and the coach and I did not get along. It created problems.

The coach was scared of me because my uncle was president of the school board. He thought I would complain and maybe get him fired. I never did, yet the coach called on Uncle Les one night to state his case about what a jackass I was, assuming I had complained. That came as a surprise to Uncle Les. He protested that, "Ralph hasn't said anything to me about it at all." A couple of days later, Uncle Les sent for me and asked me what was going on. I said, "Oh, everything is fine, Uncle Les. I don't know."

Now, we start basketball. I make the team, but Coach doesn't play me. We went to Cedar City. I didn't play in the first half at all. During the half, Coach Liston came in the dressing room to say hello to the Lincoln County boys. Everybody, of course, was glad to see him. On his way out, he put his hand on my shoulder and whispered in my ear, "Ralph, don't worry about it. It doesn't mean that much." He could see what was happening. That made me happy that a man would take that interest in a kid.

Aside from that, I was glad to be back in Caliente, to see my friends, to be home. I think I regaled them too much with stories about how wonderful Washington was. I think kids began to think I thought I was a big shot. Everybody's attitude was that you get a job like that because you got politi-cal pull, that the Denton family thought they ran the county. There was resentment. On the other hand, teachers would ask me in class to tell things about Washington. Some of the kids and parents resented it.

The Spanish Civil War was followed and discussed by Mom and Dad. Our household was sympathetic to the Republicans, as, I believe, were many Caliente families. In grammar school, I remember maps up in the classroom and Mrs. Jacobson explaining the war in Spain. Then, when the 1938 Munich conference occurred, and Neville Chamberlain, the prime minister of Great Britain, came back to announce he had secured "peace in our time," I remember the joy in our family. My father always said, "If a war starts in Europe, we can't stay out of it. You can't be the biggest frog on the bank and not jump into the puddle."

As war approached, my mother and father worried about their sons winding up as soldiers. I remember them telling me that Key Pittman had come to town and given a speech at a large gathering at the depot, in which he raised the specter of Japan and was seeking legislation to prevent the United States from selling steel and shipping scrap iron to Japan. My father was certain Pittman was right. My mother wasn't certain. She had a higher belief in the good in man than my father did.

We got in the war December 7, 1941. I was a junior in high school, and all of us knew that as soon as we were eighteen, we'd be in the service. You kept hoping beyond hope that the war would end before that. You tried to plan what you should do. Should you wait for the draft? What were the advantages of enlisting now? I don't remember many of us being gung-ho to get in. [laughter]

Some enlisted right away. You could join the marines, army reserve, or navy at seventeen, but you had to have the consent of your parents. You weren't drafted and couldn't go on active duty in the army until you were eighteen. You could join the reserves, then be called to active duty. The advantage of *that*, as far as the army was concerned, was you could pick your branch. You could avoid the infantry—most kids saw a lot of glamour in flying, and they thought aviation cadets would be a grand program to join. Even when you were young, the war was constantly on your mind.

One thing I've always been deeply grateful to my parents for: they always gave me the right to make decisions that affected my life. They might state a view and advise me differently, but my mother used to laugh. She'd say, "Since you were a little kid, I can hear you saying, 'Let me take care of my own affairs.'" And they let me.

Because of the war and all of the kids having to go in the service, the University of Utah had started a program that would admit, as probationary students, kids who had completed fourteen credits with a certain average. They were working out agreements with the high schools that wanted to participate, where the high school would, if the kid was successful and passed, give them credit. I knew I was going in the service in September 1943 or soon thereafter, when I reached eighteen. I wanted to get as much college or education as I could so that I could take advantage of it in the army. I thought I would have a better chance of succeeding. If possible, I wanted to be an officer, and I wanted to be an aviation cadet to start with. It was that simple. I saw no reason to sit around Lincoln County if I did have an opportunity to go to college.

I applied to the University of Utah. I was accepted, and discussed it with Principal Wilcox. He wrote a great letter of recommendation. My mother and father thought it was a wonderful idea, although it was putting another financial burden on them, because I didn't have a job in Salt Lake, although I tried to get a job as a motion picture projectionist and couldn't make it into the union. When I told the coach I was leaving, he said I was letting down the school and should stay because of basketball season coming up. I thought that was unusual, in as much as, in games we played before the season started, I hadn't had any game-time. I wasn't that good a basketball player, anyway. As a matter of fact, I wasn't that good a football player, either.

So, late in 1942, I went up to Utah and started school; but then I decided I'd join the Marine Corps. I went to the recruiting station in Salt Lake City, got the papers, and filled them out to enlist. Then, since I was not yet eighteen, I had to get my parents' consent. I got on the train in Salt Lake and went back to Caliente on a weekend to discuss it with my parents. My mother was strongly opposed; so was my father. Both made arguments as to why it was not a wise decision, but eventually they signed the consent form.

I got on the train and went back to Salt Lake. It was an eight- or nine-hour trip, maybe more, and I sat and thought. When I got to Salt Lake, I decided they were correct. I tore up the application and didn't join the Marine Corps. But the point is, they had signed my application. They let me take care of my own affairs. That was true in many decisions I made that affected my life, some of which were correct, and some of which were not.

I came away with great respect for the university, but I wanted to be in Nevada. I found out there was quite a social strata at the university, and what high school you went to made quite a bit of difference. If you'd gone to East High School in Salt Lake, you were pretty much in the "in" group. If you came from a little town in Nevada, you weren't entitled to much consideration. That doesn't mean that they wouldn't recognize ability and give it to you if you earned it. They would, of course.

I had great respect for every professor I had. One professor of sociology who was attacking segregation and stereotyping of races, creeds, and colors. That's 1942 at the University of Utah in Salt Lake City, Utah! A professor I had in history went on to the University of Chicago, and I understand he became president. He was a Utah man. A professor I took a course from had married a woman from Alamo, Nevada. He was an outstanding political scientist and active in Democratic party politics in Utah—great teacher. ROTC was even a great program—field artillery ROTC.

When I came back to Caliente in May of 1943 to graduate with my high school class, some parents objected to me being on the platform and getting my diploma, notwithstanding that Lincoln County had agreed that my first two quarters at the university would credit toward my high school graduation. My Uncle Les, who had been chairman of the school board, had died while I was at the University of Utah, and they'd appointed Uncle Lloyd to take his place. Uncle Lloyd handed out the diplomas, and as soon as I got mine, I took off for Reno. I wanted to go to the University of Nevada, where I belonged. I didn't have any place to stay; I didn't have any money; but I was bound and determined, so my parents said OK.

Dad raised a little money to get me to Reno and to eat until I could find a job. They'd help any way they conceivably could, never tried to dominate my decisions. I regret is that I was a grown man before I began to realize the sacrifices they made for me and the freedom they had given me.

Money was a serious problem. I was looking for work and got a job at the Ross-Burke Mortuary. Si Ross, a regent of the university for years, always gave university students a chance to get at least free room.[1] My pay was a free room. My job meant sleeping in the mortuary overnight, answering calls, and going out to pick up bodies and bring bodies back.

The room was in this old Victorian home in Reno. I lived in the attic by myself, scared to death, because down in what they call "slumber rooms" were dead bodies. To go to the bathroom, I had to go downstairs through what was called the prep room, where they embalm the bodies. The first night, I was just terrified, and put it off. In going up to my room, I had gone through the prep room, and there were no bodies. I'd heard some activity, and I hadn't been called. That was my first night, but I got to the point where I really had to go to the bathroom. I did and, God, there was a body on the table! I made it to the bathroom, and made it back upstairs to my bedroom. I've never admitted to a soul . . . but that caused me to catch a bus, go back to Salt Lake, and register for the summer session there at the University of Utah. [laughter]

In those days you could enlist in the army at seventeen, but they wouldn't call you to active duty until you were eighteen. You became a member of the army reserve. That's what I did. I enlisted on July 9, 1943, in the Army Air Corps, another thing significant in my future army career: that meant they couldn't transfer you to another branch of the army without your consent. I went on active duty and went to enter the army through Fort Douglas, Salt Lake City, and was sent to Buckley Field, Colorado, for basic training and classification. In the Army Air Corps, classification means you hope you're going to become an airplane driver, a navigator, or a bombardier. I went through and did not qualify for pilot or navigator or bombardier, and I'm not sure for what reason. They told me I flunked the psychomotor, a test that tested your blood pressure, your pulse rate and stress under different situations, and your reaction.

At that time, probably early 1944, you had other possibilities: armament mechanics, armor and aircraft mechanics, aerial gunner. I had been trying to get an appointment to the academy, and Senator McCarran gave me a third alternate's appointment to West Point. If you were appointed to one of the academies, if you were on active duty, you were immediately transferred to one of three prep schools: Lafayette College in Easton, Pennsylvania; Amherst in Massachusetts; Cornell in New York. The minute I got that appointment, I was transferred to Lafayette, and I became a member of what's called the United States Military Academy Prep Unit and started college there. That was great, because I was able to get a full semester of college.

But I learned a couple of things there that dampened my enthusiasm for the military academy. The minute you got there, they started telling you that you were the cream of the crop. "You are superior." I knew better than that. I knew kids there had their appointments the same way I had: through political connections and influence. A couple of kids were the sons of Army officers. They got the appointment every year and came up and spent the winter at one of the prep schools, never wanted to go to the academy. Go back to the troops in the summer, and come back when they'd get another appointment for the next year. I'd love that.

There were some really bright kids. A kid from Palo Alto—a Stanford graduate—was superior, no question about it. But most were kids like me: seventeen, eighteen year old high school graduates. I was fortunate that I had one year of college. Most of them were smarter than I was. A lot of them were just regular kids. No matter what, it wasn't true that they were superior. And I thought, "Is this what they teach you . . . ?" I've been kind of an egalitarian through my life, and I couldn't accept that the United States Army was telling these kids, before they know anything about them, that they're superior. Maybe there was a reason for doing that.

In June they picked the class. Those of us who didn't go to the academy were sent back to the troops. I was sent to Camp Gruber, Oklahoma, to join the Forty-Second Infantry division as a rifleman in an infantry company. On my way, I had a day in Washington, and I was surprised. I wanted to stop by, see McCarran, thank him for the appointment, and tell him I hadn't gotten in. I discovered he wasn't at the office or the Senate wasn't in session. I looked in the phone book, and lo and behold, there's his name. I called him at his home and thanked him. He said, "Well, I'm sorry you didn't make it."

I still had time, so I went to the House office building. A new congressman, Maurice Sullivan, had been elected when Scrugham left in 1942.[2] He'd been lieutenant governor. He was a Reno lawyer, and I had met him when he was campaigning through Caliente. I didn't know him well. I went to his office. He was in committee. His secretary said, "Oh, he'd love to see you. Go over to the committee." Things were so much less formal then than they are now. I felt uncomfortable doing that, but I went to the meeting of the House Interior committee. I sent a note in. The congressman came out to see me, and we had a nice visit. I explained what was happening. He said, "I'll appoint you next year if you want me to." I said, "No, Congressman. I appreciate it, but I've lost my enthusiasm for going to West Point." He told me, frankly, he didn't like very much being a congressman.

Then I went on to Oklahoma and joined the Forty-Second Infantry division. I started training. I hadn't known when you enlisted in the Air Corps, they couldn't transfer you to another branch without your consent. All of the troops at Lafayette, and I assume in Amherst and Cornell, were sent to fill up infantry divisions, because the Normandy invasion had taken place on June 6, and they needed infantry. I'm in a rifle company, and this division is getting organized, getting ready to go overseas. Most miserable I ever was in my life, crawling around on my belly out there in the middle of the summer in Oklahoma with chiggers, little ticks I'd never seen or heard of before all over you, overnight bivouacs, marching and that sort of stuff all the time, and I'm really a miserable son-of-a-bitch then. [laughter] And lo and behold, in the barracks early in the morning, we were getting ready to go on a forced march, got our rifles and packs and all ready to go, and the guy comes in from the orderly room looking for a Private Denton. "You're wanted in the company headquarters." They told me I was being transferred to Keesler Field, Mississippi, back to the Air Corps. I had to leave that afternoon.

Keesler was a replacement center. All you do is pull KP and that kind of stuff in the big mess halls. After three weeks to a month, from Keesler, I was sent to B-17 aerial gunnery school at Kingman, Arizona, where I spent almost a year as a gunnery instructor. It's funny. It was like working at the mortuary. I never got in a lower-ball turret that I wasn't scared to death. I flew almost every day, except not in the lower-ball turret, but in the waist, because I was the instructor. A wonderful airplane, but I never got on it that I wasn't scared. [laughter] So, I was no hero.

But I met one of my best friends, Hank Hoover, who started gunnery school with me and died a few years ago. We stayed together the rest of his army career, because we finished gunnery school together. I don't know how this happened, but both of us were held there as instructors. He had already graduated from Indiana University. He was older than I was, and he was affluent, much to my pleasure. His family owned a business back in Rensselaer, Indiana, and he was married.

Hank and I became almost inseparable. We'd come to Las Vegas. We bought a 1928 Graham-Paige automobile for $75, got leave, and drove to Los Angeles one time, because he was a friend of the great football player Tom Harmon. Hank always had plenty of money, and he was generous.

By now, the war is winding down. They were phasing out B-17's. The B-29 was going to become the new plane. Rumors go through the army—just unbelievable. Everybody thought B-29's were dangerous from a gunner's standpoint, because they had a new system of gunnery. I guess you could even call it a computer with automatic sights. They had blisters on the side of the aircraft, and the gunner sat in these blisters. The rumors were these blisters were always popping out, and the gunner was going with them.

Hank and I decided, by God, we don't want to go to B-29's. Rumors were that they were closing the B-17 school, which they did, and instructors were going to be either shipped to B-29's to go into combat in the Pacific or they would be replacements on B-17's in Europe. Neither one of us being anxious to get into combat, we looked for some easy way out. (I hate to admit it, but that's true.) We applied for officer candidate school.

While we're waiting to go in the spring of 1945, a friend of ours, a buck sergeant in squadron headquarters, came in the barracks one night. He said, "You won't believe it. A request came in today. They want to send three men to Camp Pinedale, California, to go through clerk typist school."

I piped up, "God, put me down!"

He said, "I already have, and I put myself down and Hank."

So, the three of us went off to Camp Pinedale in Fresno, California to be part of what was called the MTP project. (We never knew what that meant.) I think they were trying to get occupation troops ready for Japan. They had other staff, training people for the book-keeping stuff that was going to have to be done with units. I got so I could type over a hundred words a minute on an old Underwood or Royal typewriter.

It was like heaven after Kingman. Among other things, Hank could have been a professional golfer. Before long he's playing golf on all the country clubs in Fresno, even the private ones. They'd let a soldier play. Then they'd see him play, and he was invited back. The first thing you know, he's getting invitations to these people's houses, and always taking me along. It was just wonderful. We're loving life.

I found a girl I liked, and we got engaged. Hank and I took two girls to dinner. It must have been arranged by somebody Hank knew at one of the country clubs. I don't know who paired us up, but the girl Hank was with and I hit it off immediately. We had a nice evening. Her mother was on the faculty at Fresno State College, a widow or divorced. The father had been a congregationalist minister. The girl had, just that spring, graduated from Stanford. An absolutely charming girl, so we became quite serious, and then I went to Fort Sill.

I got a leave when I graduated and got commissioned. She had gotten a job in Carmel, and when I graduated from OCS, I had a ten-day leave before reporting to Fort Bragg, North Carolina, a field artillery replacement training center. I made it to San Francisco. She met me in the lobby of the St. Francis Hotel. We caught the train to Monterey. I spent that leave with her in Carmel, we became engaged, then I went to Fort Bragg.

We communicated with each other and wrote very dear letters. She went to Caliente and met my parents . . . but ultimately we just drifted apart. "Let's wait until the war's over and life gets back to normal." We never saw each other again. She was two or three years older than I was. There just wasn't enough in common.

Hank and I have to leave paradise. Here we are in clerk typist school in a wonderful community, meeting wonderful people, just having a grand time, when all of a sudden, whoom, it all ended when the orders come down that both of us had been accepted to officer candidate school, field artillery. We take off for Fort Sill, in Blocker, Oklahoma, in the summer of 1945.

That school was the best, most efficient school I have ever attended. I learned more in a short time than I thought believable. I had struggled in college algebra and hadn't learned geometry in high school. I never could see any purpose in it. But in field artillery, I learned to survey. They taught you that you could solve any triangle, at least for our purposes in artillery, if you knew the sine, cosine, and tangent functions. I learned why it was important to solve a triangle. It's hard to learn how to survey in on a firing chart, a gun, a target, and measure the deflection and range. They taught you that, they taught you why, and you could see its purpose.

The tactical officers, on the other hand—that wasn't too bad unless somebody got on your tail. A tactical officer can ruin you, because if you get so many gigs—a gig would be a demerit—they can kick you out. They could give you gigs for almost anything. We lived in five-man, tar-paper huts. Your textbooks have to be on a shelf above your bunk. If a tactical officer runs his hand down the top of the books, if one is sticking up a little, and it stops him, that can be a gig. The steel helmet has to be on a certain place on that shelf right back against the wall. If the tactical officer pushes your helmet, and it moves, that can be a gig. If you're an officer candidate, you're lined up to march into the mess hall. The tactical officers swarm all over you, get their face about an inch away from yours and yell at you, call you dumb and all sorts of things, check to see how close you've shaven. If they don't think you've shaven close enough, it's a gig.

This guy got on my tail. No matter what I did, at the end of the day, there would be posted on the bulletin board certain gigs for me. They could do two things if you got too many gigs: kick you out or wash you back to a class behind you. That's what they did to me on the gigs. So, I'm back to this class behind me, re-doing the same thing. I'm enjoying it very much, but this same tactical officer is still on my keister.

I decide I'm not going to go down without a fight. Keep in mind I was an Army Air Corps boy, I had a patch on my left sleeve, an air corps patch; and on my right, the OCS patch. There was always a great deal of rivalry between the ground forces and the Air Corps. I think I was the only one in either of these classes from the Air Corps, but they would refer to you as "fly-boy." This guy in particular, whenever he's chewing me out, "Hey Fly-boy, how about this?" So I write a letter to the commander, resigning from the school.

I told this officer I wanted the form to submit a resignation. Oh, God, he gleamed. He threw me this form, and didn't realize they had a place for reasons. In all of the subjects I was at the top, or at least successful—I ran a good survey, I knew how to lay a field artillery battery—all of the things you had to know to be a field artillery officer, I was doing well in. I said I wanted to resign and gave as my reasons that I saw no possibility of completing this course because of the absolute prejudice that Lieutenant so-and-so had toward Air Corps personnel.

I didn't know, but I learned later that that complaint had been made to the point where General Hap Arnold, commanding general of the Army Air Corps, requested an investigation a year or two before.[3] I'm getting ready to go when I'm ordered to report to the brigadier general, who wanted to discuss my letter of resignation with me. I can't remember his name. I was in a daze. I had really worked hard and done well in the school. I remember the conversation. When it was over, he said, "Well, you go back to your class, Mr. Denton." They called you Mister when you were a cadet. He said, "I don't think you'll have any trouble with Lieutenant so-and-so."

I didn't, and I graduated. If I had not resigned and used the reason I did, he would have gotten me. I was doing too well for him to wash me out. That's why they washed me back. But if the same thing happened to me twice, I would have been gone.

I went, then, to Fort Bragg, North Carolina, a field artillery replacement training center, in early 1946. Recruits were coming into the army still. They'd had their basic training, and we were giving them basic instruction in artillery, training them on 105 mm howitzers and the weapons you use and the equipment you use, prior to their assignment out to division.

From there, I was sent to Camp Campbell, Kentucky, now Fort Campbell, where I joined the field artillery battery. The Third Infantry Division had come back from overseas. They were filling it up with new people, and I was Able battery, Thirty-Ninth Field Artillery Battalion. After I became a field artillery officer, I loved the work, the guns, everything about it. I loved teaching it. In a ground force unit like a field artillery battery, the troops come to you, and they've been through basic training. They're assigned to your battery, and they're taught this in the unit. It's *your* job. The officers and

Lt. Ralph Denton, U.S. Army

the senior sergeants teach them. So, the battery executive officer, like I was, and the battery commander know everything about what everybody has to do, because they're the ones who taught them.

Take the gun crew on a 105 millimeter Howitzer: You've got the gunner, the people who cut the fuses, the people who put the powder in the canister, based upon the commands from the battery executive officer, the type of fuse on the shell, then the people who put it in. I'm the one who taught them. I knew everything every man on a gun crew had to do, and could do it better, because I have taught them. I won a lot of accolades in the division when we'd have firing demonstrations in the field, when senior officers would come out to the observation post and witness it.

One time I was so proud of my battery—battery has four guns in it. The division artillery commander or brigadier general was on the observation point with most of his staff, as well as the battalion officers. My battery's firing air bursts, when you have shells explode above the ground; they don't explode on impact. For a battery to fire all four guns, and for the rounds to explode at the same height above the ground and separated the same distance, it means everybody in that battery did their job just right. Each gunner measured the angle correctly when he turned the tube in response to the battery executive officer's commands and sighted on the aiming stakes. Each one did it just right—the gunners, the guys who cut the fuse, the guy who set the elevation of the tube.

At this one program, they call for air fire. I give the commands to the battery: deflection, range, fuse setting, powder charge. Then the battery all fires at one time, and you look out, you see these bursts way out there, all hanging exactly where they should be. It gives you a great feeling of pride. The phone rang from the observation post. It was the general, and he told the operator he wanted to speak to the battery executive officer. I got on the phone. "This is General so-and-so. I'd like to compliment you, Lieutenant, on your battery and invite you to join me at the observation post." That was a thrill. I just loved it.

That's why the day I got discharged in November 1946, I applied for a regular army commission. I wanted to stay in. I loved the field artillery battery in the infantry division. But I didn't want to stay unless I was a regular army officer, because they could kick you out any time they wanted.

I got out of the army a few days before the general election of November 1946, filed an application for regular army commission, and tried to get to Caliente before election day so I could vote for Berkeley Bunker against George Malone in the Senate race. I blew about all of my severance pay on transportation trying to make it in time. I made it to Las Vegas, but didn't make it to Caliente, so I didn't vote; but I spent the election day mostly with Bunker in his headquarters, in the Cashman Garage on Main Street. And Bunker lost.

I was sad. Bunker had given me that job as an elevator boy in Washington. At that time, it was hero-worship. I thought Berkeley Bunker was just about the greatest thing that ever came down the pike. In subsequent years, maybe I've become a little more realistic about human frailty and human character, but I thought it was a great tragedy that Bunker lost.

Notes

1. Reno businessman Silas Ross served as a university regent, 1933-57.

2. Maurice Sullivan, a Democrat, was lieutenant governor, 1915-27. Defeated for the House in 1926 and 1930, he was again elected lieutenant governor in 1938, and won the state's lone House seat in 1942 before losing to Berkeley Bunker in the 1944 primary.

3. General Henry H. "Hap" Arnold (1886-1950), a longtime advocate of air power, became commander of the Army Air Forces in 1941.

6 | Doing the Postwar Shuffle

Back home in Caliente, I did some cowboying for the Conway ranch; then, after Christmas, I left for Washington and got there before New Year's. My brother was back from the war, and when I got off the train at Union Station, Lew and Hugh Norton, who had also been there in 1942, met me. They took me to Grant and Bette Sawyer's basement apartment on Ninth Street in the ghetto, and that's when I first met them. That friendship started then and continued the rest of Grant's life and will the rest of my life. That's when I started meeting all of these Nevada kids.

My plan was to find a job and start college. The Republicans were in, so I didn't see much chance for old Ralph to luck out with a patronage job, but I went to the House to meet Charlie Russell, the new congressman from Nevada. He only had one patronage job, elevator boy, and he gave it to me, notwithstanding I was a Democrat. Among the Nevada delegation, your politics didn't make any difference. If you were a kid from Nevada trying to get an education, and needed a job, all of them would do anything they could to help you.

So Russell gave me a job. With that and the G.I. Bill of Rights, hell, I was in hog heaven and started classes at George Washington University. Those jobs were designed for kids going to college. You worked four hours a day, so you could go to college full-time. If you had the morning shift, you might have to take evening classes. I started George Washington and was thoroughly happy.

Everything was wonderful. All of a sudden, I get orders to report to the Pentagon to take the examinations for a regular army commission. At that point, I'm liking civilian life, so I was ambivalent. It took three days. It was like a bar examination. I didn't feel pressure, because I wasn't sure I wanted to go back in the army. After the third day, I went on with my life. Then I get another order to go before the selection board.

Although I had a reserve commission, I'm a civilian and wearing civilian clothes. Had I thought about it, I'd have worn my uniform. Every board

I'd ever been before in the army, the candidate sat at attention in the chair in front. All the officers sat behind a long table and asked you questions. I went in, and they were sitting in overstuffed chairs, like it was a living room. They were general officers—there were three or four—except the secretary, a colonel. This colonel says, "Sit down, Lieutenant. Make yourself comfortable." I sat down, crossed my legs, and started talking. They started asking questions like we're not an army board. I'm not sitting at attention.

They asked a lot about Caliente. "Where's Caliente?" and questions like, "I see you played football in high school."

One general said, "Has Nevada produced any great men?"

I said, "Yes," before I thought.

They followed with, "Who?"

I'm at a loss. No matter how much I admired some of our political leaders, I hadn't found it possible, at that stage in my life, to call any of them I knew 'great'. I answered, "My father." That was the last question. I shook hands with everybody and left. (I've since been persuaded this may be the reason I got that appointment.)

Grant and Bette had moved into a magnificent apartment on Massachusetts Avenue to house-sit for a couple that had gone to Europe. My brother and I had taken over their basement apartment. I remained happy. I loved being on the Hill again, even though only in the capacity of an elevator operator. Everybody on the Hill thinks they're a big shot, no matter their job. I thought I was a big shot, and I'm meeting these great Nevada kids back from the war.

Everything is going fine until one Saturday morning, about September. My brother and I are sitting in this apartment, reading *The Washington Post*. He says, "Oh, the list of regular army appointments is in the paper."

One kid I met at George Washington had also applied. I said, "Well, did Bob Hart make it?"

He says, "No, but you did."

I thought, "Oh, God." About forty-five minutes after that, I get a telegram from the War Department, from J. A. Ulio, the adjutant general, advising me of the offer of an appointment as a regular army field artillery second lieutenant. If I accepted, I would be stationed at Fort Bragg. I had forty-eight hours. Now I am absolutely confused. Do I want to go back in the army? My life was good in Washington. All these Nevada boys hung out together and spent a lot of time with each other. I was thoroughly happy, particularly with the university.

One of the reasons I had wanted to stay in the army was I was frightened of going back to college. When I was sixteen, the University of Utah had been a struggle for me. I worked like hell to pass, but my grades were mostly B's and C's. But when I started George Washington, I found it a breeze. I loved the classes, did well in all of them. We had a Veteran's Club, and for practically every class, if a veteran was having trouble, the club would arrange a tutor. I became a tutor in philosophy. I was going to night school.

Now I get this opportunity. I had really wanted it, but now I wasn't sure. My brother and I talked. I thought, "Well, let's see . . . a lot of military installations around Washington. If I could get stationed here, I could continue to go to night school."

Monday morning, first thing, I go to see Eva Adams in McCarran's office. I wasn't under their patronage, but the Nevada people hung together—they really did. I told her I'd gotten this appointment. Immediately, she took me in to see the senator, and he was furious with me. Why? Because my residence was on all my papers: 939 Massachusetts Avenue, Washington, D.C. I hadn't listed my home as Caliente. He calmed down and wanted to know if I was going to accept it. I said, "I really haven't made up my mind, Senator. I just don't know if I could get stationed here in Washington, so I could continue to go to school at night. Then I think I would accept it. I don't particularly want to accept it if I'm going to have to give up college and just go back to a field artillery battery again." Of course, for a regular army officer, they have your whole career planned. He indicated to Eva to do what she could. Eva assigned Grant, who worked in McCarran's office, the chore of trying to talk the army into stationing me in Washington, D.C.

Some people feel McCarran assisted in getting me the appointment, but he did not. I hadn't told him or anybody else. I'd forgotten about it, to tell you the truth. But Eva put Grant on the job of seeing if he couldn't talk the army into stationing me in Washington, the rationale being I couldn't compete with guys in the regular army if I didn't have a college degree. (I went past that by saying a graduate degree.) The army would not hear of it. They had their career plan, so, as usual in McCarran's office, when one of the people in the staff couldn't get the job done, they would tell the senator. Then the senator would take over.

The next thing I knew, I had a call to report to Lt. General Wilton B. Persons, later Eisenhower's chief of staff. I wore my uniform and went to the Pentagon. Here I am, a second lieutenant, going in to see a general. He advises me the army decided I would be stationed at Arlington Hall Station in Arlington, Virginia. He said, "Lieutenant, you don't know what the Army Security Agency is doing. You will learn. It has nothing to do with artillery. And in your career plan, if you accept this appointment, the army will send you to college. The army wants to be certain you're well qualified for advancement, but we have agreed, at the request of Senator McCarran, that you be stationed at Arlington Hall Station."

I saluted. I was going out the door. He said, "Oh, lieutenant, just a moment."

I turned around and said, "Yes, sir."

He said, "Would you do a favor for me?"

I said, "Certainly, sir."

He said, "Now, would you keep that gray-haired old son-of-a-bitch off my back?" [laughter]

I went to Arlington Hall Station—the greatest decision I ever made. Had I not, I never would have met Sara, because she was a civilian employee in the headquarters. Sara and I became close friends. We would have lunch on the post. Sometimes we'd ride the bus home together at night. We didn't live far apart. We just had fun. And she never would go out with me.

The next greatest decision was when I resigned my commission. A couple of weeks after I got out of the army, I went to the post to see some of my friends, ran into Sara, and asked her out for dinner that night. She accepted. For over a year, I'd been asking her to go out, and she wouldn't. Over dinner I asked her why, finally, she had accepted an invitation to go out with me. She said, "Well, to tell you the truth, I didn't want to get seriously involved with anybody who was stupid enough to make the army their career." Had I not resigned, she would not have married me. I would have missed a lifetime with the most magnificent and remarkable person I've ever known. I can't conceive of what life would have been like without her. That's why my experience with the regular army was very, very good.

I was assigned to headquarters, because I didn't know any of the technical stuff. That's the agency whose cryptographers broke the Japanese code. It's now called the National Security Agency, but at the time, the army and navy had security agencies. This one was administered by the army, and Sara was a secretary in army administrative headquarters, where I was in the chief-of-staff's office, because I didn't know what the hell the agency was doing and couldn't be of assistance to anybody. What do I know about breaking codes? All these people were signal corps officers, PhDs. God, what an operation that was! There were only four regular army officers on that post. The general was a regular army officer. Captain Vernon Robbins was my immediate superior, a West Point officer. I had great respect for Captain Robbins, who retired as a colonel and lives in Massachusetts. We still correspond.

You have a tendency to remember the good and forget the bad, but the army was a wonderful experience—memories I treasure, friends I made. Something was looking over me that I was never sent to combat, never fired a shot in anger, although flying B-17s in training was not the safest occupation in the world. For that reason I didn't have what you would call a distinguished military career. I had been in the army five years, only about three and a half on active duty, when I resigned. Consequently, I don't feel entitled to special privileges. The government put me through college, through law school, and the people of the United States certainly provided me with everything they ever owed me. I never felt the government owed me anything for doing nothing more than I was supposed to do. I went in the army, responded to commands, did the best I could, and was not injured. Although people say you lost that many years of your life, they weren't lost to me.

Nor did the military shake my faith in the essential goodness of the government. You'd make fun of the military, say there's three ways to do anything: the right way, the wrong way, and the army way. [laughter] I had difficulty accepting the separation of the ranks. When I became an officer, I understood, because it's based upon the doctrine of "familiarity breeds contempt." After I became an officer and got to know other officers, I knew damn well it wouldn't work if the men were that familiar.

Of course, I didn't know what I was doing at that headquarters. But everybody lived off the post. A certain number of enlisted men, maybe a hundred, worked in the army offices and some of the scientific areas. Because I couldn't do anything else, I was assigned the job of trying to make soldiers out of these guys. [laughter] The other officers were signal corps officers. We played soldier—short-order drill and that kind of stuff. Whenever they had a little ceremony, I would march them half-way decently up to the flagpole. But I became disillusioned. The army had gone to pot. They just demobilized so fast after World War II! I knew people there at Arlington Hall Station just fighting to try and stay in. I became disillusioned. It wasn't the kind of army I wanted to be in.

I started thinking about resigning. An adjutant major was lining me up with his daughter. She was nice, but I wasn't interested. I was really interested in Sara, and she wouldn't go out with me. [laughter] He was going to transfer to an Army Security Agency unit in Germany. He called me in and told me he was going to cut orders, and I would go, too. He was a career officer, and he wanted his daughter to be, I think, the wife of a career officer. He was adamant. That was the straw that broke the camel's back, so in September 1948, I wrote a letter of resignation.

When you resign from the regular army, you send a letter to the president. You get a letter back accepting your resignation from the president. Mine was signed by Harry Truman. One of the things that attracted me to Sara, and Sara to me, was that we were Democrats, and as near as I could tell, we were the only two people in Washington supporting Truman. [laughter]

I had heard about Truman; when I was an elevator boy in 1942, he was a senator. I didn't remember anything that distinguished him until he became vice president, other than stories about his work in that Senate committee to investigate waste within industry. He got quite a reputation for doing a good job on that. The contrast between Roosevelt on the one hand and Truman on the other to the American people, myself included, was tremendous. Here is this plain, simple man. In those days, we didn't know his qualities. If we knew anything, we knew of his ties with Pendergast in Kansas City—a corrupt political machine.[1] Yet he soon started to demonstrate a strength of character. Those of us who were Democrats to the degree I'm a Democrat really wanted him to succeed. We were defensive of him, and a little disappointed in some of the scandals that took place in his administration.

I remember the dropping of the atomic bomb, and how I felt about it. I think everybody in the army expected the next move was to invade Japan.

Why were they still training artillery officers, forming divisions? The feeling was one of "Thank God we beat the Germans. Thank God Harry Truman dropped that bomb and saved all of the American lives." Whether that's correct, history questions. Based upon what I knew then and even what I know now, I've never questioned it. It took a lot of courage, I think.

After the 1946 Republican landslide, and during the 1948 campaign, nobody thought Truman had a chance. But by 1948, quite a few things happened that had shown real strength of character. He fought that Eightieth Congress tooth and toenail. [laughter] Sara had belonged to the Women's Democratic Club of the District of Columbia before I dated her. She'd met Mrs. Truman, gone to receptions at the White House for the members of the club, and she was charmed by Mrs. Truman.

One of the guys from Nevada, Bud Bradley, now an attorney in Reno, just knew Thomas E. Dewey was going to be elected president. Election night, he forsook the Democrats and was at the Dewey party at one of the hotels. Sara was where she lived, I was where I lived, and she and I were on the phone all night long. The next day, Truman had won, and oh God, Sara and I were happy! Bud was one of my roommates. Oh God, he was sick! He'd gone to the Dewey party and tried to make points, and he had a menial job McCarran got him down at the justice department. He was in the enemy's territory that night.

When Truman came back from Independence, Sara and I were on the sidewalk in front of Lafayette Park when this limousine came up. Truman and Alben Barkley were waving at everybody. They drove under the north portico of the White House, and somebody set up a microphone. The president made a speech, and everybody cheered. Then Barkley, from Sara's hometown of Paducah, Kentucky, got up and said, "I feel like Minnie Pearl of the Grand Ole Opry. I'm just so proud to be here."[2] God, it was really a happy occasion.

By the inaugural, I'm out of the army. We met and went out Pennsylvania Avenue to Seventeenth or Eighteenth to watch the inaugural parade. They had garbage trucks lined up that would come in as soon as the parade was over and pick up all of the stuff. Sara and I had the best view of anybody, standing up in this garbage truck to watch. [laughter] The parade went right by us.

Of course, it was a great day for me, because Democrats took control of the Congress, which meant McCarran got back his committees and patronage. When I resigned from the army, I had needed a job on the Hill, and George Malone, a Republican senator, had given me a patronage job as an elevator boy. In January, 1949, Senator McCarran gave me the best job he had—one in the Senate sergeant-at-arms office. So, that election meant a lot to us personally.

In 1960, I was chairman of the Kennedy-Johnson campaign in Nevada, and Truman came to Reno to make a speech for Kennedy at Mackay Stadium at the university. To contrast ex-presidents then and now, Truman flew into Reno in a two-engine airplane that belonged to his friend John Snyder in St. Louis.[3] I was one of the people to meet him at the airport. There had been a platform set up for the president to make the speech to the crowd at the airport.

On the platform were President Truman, Governor Sawyer, and me. My job was to introduce Sawyer, who would introduce Truman. I introduced Grant, Grant got up and introduced the president, and the president makes this speech. A lady in the audience wearing a pair of western pants and a western shirt had a cigarette in one hand and a drink in the other. She kept yelling, "Give 'em hell, Harry!"

When we came down off the platform, I was on one side of Truman, Grant on the other, and we walked by this lady. She shouts, "*Give 'em hell, Harry!*" He looks at her with the coldest eyes I've ever seen and says, "You don't know me well enough to call me Harry." That surprised me. He took a few more steps, turned to me, and said, "I can't stand a drunken woman."

My brother had an experience with him: Lew quit his job at the general accounting office. Walter Baring, our congressman, had one elevator job and gave it to my brother. Lew operated the elevator that took Truman from the street floor up to the House floor to make his State of the Union speech to a joint session of Congress. When he got on, Lew didn't say anything. He took him up, then waited. When the president came back out, Lew said he stuck his hand out to shake hands and said, "Congratulations, Mr. President." Truman said, "I'd rather plow forty acres than talk to that group of men." [laughter]

Truman had an unusual relationship with Nevada's delegation. The other senator was Malone, and the other member was Baring, a freshman congressman. So it was Truman and McCarran, and they *hated* each other. McCarran never said anything to me about it, though. He wouldn't. Very seldom did I sit in their circles.

Jimmy Johnson's is a tragic story insofar as what it did to Jimmy, but it's funny insofar as politics is concerned. There's a vacancy in the United States attorney's office in Nevada. Truman played by the rules, and McCarran was the senior Democratic senator. That appointment belonged to him, and he submitted Johnson. Truman appointed him. At the time, Jim was district attorney of Churchill County. He resigns and moves his wife and kids into Reno, getting ready. McCarran is Senate Judiciary chairman. There's not going to be any problem with confirmation. The tradition and the rule were that that appointment was McCarran's. The president would appoint whoever the senior senator recommended in that situation, and he did that.

The Senate confirms Jimmy, but Truman will *not* sign the commission. Nothing in the rules said he had to sign or when he had to sign. Jimmy's busted. He doesn't have a paycheck. Truman waits until just before he goes out of office and signs the commission in time for Jimmy to get the job and get fired by Eisenhower. All the pressure, all the power McCarran could command could not budge Truman to sign that commission. [laughter] It had a terrible effect on Jimmy. The poor guy had a hell of a time. I don't know how long he actually served, but it wasn't long. I can see Truman chuckling, "Fixed that Irish son-of-a-bitch." [laughter]

I had never known Charlie Russell before he gave me the patronage job. I later learned he ran a newspaper in Ely. Vail Pittman had the daily, and Russell the weekly. He knew my parents. One of the nicest men I ever met. He had brought with him as his administrative assistant, Dutch Carlson, who'd worked in Reno for Standard Oil for many years. Hugh Norton was from Ely. Charlie and Marge, his wife, used to invite Hugh and me to their house for dinner. I learned so much about Russell and the kind of man he was.

Riepetown is up in White Pine County, on the side of a hill, with shacks where a lot of the miners—as we called them, unfortunately, "bohunks"— from Eastern Europe lived.[4] One girl whose parents lived in Riepetown was Helen Delich. Her brother Sam was one of the bosses at a casino on Fremont St. for a time. Charlie and Marge saw something in Helen, took Helen to live with them in Ely, and sent her to Stevens College or the University of Missouri School of Journalism. I had known Helen when I was in high school when we'd play White Pine in football and basketball. Helen was one of the student body from Ely that would always yell at us and throw things. When I got back to Washington after the war, Helen was labor editor of the *Baltimore Sun*. Tough gal. Richard Nixon appointed her to the Maritime Commission, and she was a congresswoman from Maryland, and a couple of elections ago, ran for governor. Her married name was Bentley. Charlie and Marge were very proud.

Kind of a sad story, my relationship with Helen. She had an apartment, not in the best part of town. Oh God, we'd have some big Nevada parties with Grant and my brother and Nevada people sleeping on the floor and everything, taking to strong drink to excess. We became good friends. When Grant ran against Charlie for governor, it became difficult for me, because of my respect, admiration and love, if you will, for Russell. I had to choose. I talked to Charlie about it, and he was a gentleman as always. He said, "I understand, Ralph. No hard feelings with me." What a nice man. But Helen never forgave me, and I don't think she ever forgave Grant for running. I shouldn't limit it to men—but of all of the men I've known in high office, without question, Russell is the most decent, never the least bit of arrogance or desire to exercise power. A fine man. Republican, no question about it. Republican, but some kind of good guy. [laughter]

I felt bad when he lost, but McCarran was going to be chairman again of the E.C.A. joint committee, which supervised the Marshall Plan, and as soon as he found out about Charlie's defeat, he sent him a telegram offering him a good job on the committee staff. So, Charlie didn't leave Washington. He just moved from the House down to that committee. McCarran liked him very much. What's not to like in Charlie Russell?

Before Russell was defeated, I'd left that job running the elevator. He filled that job with my brother. I'd been going to law school at night while I was stationed in Washington. I resigned my commission, and I'm looking for work. I get all dressed up in an army white dress uniform and go up on the Hill to call on Malone to see if I could get some kind of a patronage job from him. He had an administrative assistant, Ed Beaupert, a fellow from Reno I had met after I'd come back to Washington this time. Ed set up this appointment with Malone.

I'm dressed fit to kill in a beautiful uniform. I must have spent forty-five minutes with Malone, wherein he's telling me all about his flexible import-export tariff, Malone's chief interest at that time. He finished and ushered me out. Ed met me at the door and wanted to know if I'd gotten a job. I said, "I don't know, I didn't have a chance to ask him for one." [laughter] But he did give me a patronage job as an elevator boy. When I got out of the army I went right to work in the Senate office building on the night shift, which was wonderful, and stayed there under his patronage until the Democrats took over in January 1949, at which time McCarran gave me a job in the sergeant at arms office—best job I ever had.

Malone was helpful to me, because after Sara and I got married, getting an apartment was almost impossible. Some were under rent control, but those that weren't, were expensive. We moved into an apartment where the rent was killing us. A company called Kafritz owned nice apartment buildings all over Washington. Most were under rent control. They were social arbiters in Washington. There was always a story in the paper about that Morris and Gwen Kafritz party and who attended. I read one time George and Ruth Malone were at a party. I thought, "Wow! Maybe we got some tie to the Kafritzes here . . . ." God, it was difficult. You'd go to any of those Kafritz apartments and go on a list four miles long, because they were still under rent control.

You know how politicians are. On the floor, I went up to Malone. He's glad to see me, hello and everything. And, "Anything I can do for you?"

I knew I had him. I said, "Yes, Senator, as a matter of fact, I understand that you and Mrs. Malone and the Kafritzes are good friends."

"Oh yes," he says, "we're very close friends."

"Do you suppose you can help me get an apartment in one of the Kafritz buildings?"

"Well, I'll see what I can do."

I thought, "That's nice. I'll wait and see what happens."

About two hours later, I'm back in the office. I get a call from a lady in the Kafritz office asking me what building I want to be in and what kind of apartment. "Just efficiency apartment?" she said. "Is that all right?"

I said, "Oh, that's just fine."

"What building would you like to be in?"

I said, "Well, if possible, I'd like to be in the Empire," because that was just a block away from the law school.

She said, "We have a fine vacancy there. You can move in tomorrow."

So Malone was of great help to me. We never would have gotten in that building or any other. Old George Malone helped me there.

I remember another occasion, though, when Senator Malone was speaking on his flexible import tariff bill. He'd been speaking for an hour or two. There was nobody on the floor except him and some senator in the majority leader's chair, and one in the minority leader's chair to make sure nobody slipped anything through. Old Tom Connally of Texas came waddling in.[5] I was standing on the side of the room, just listening to Malone. I didn't have any place else to go at the time. Connally wound up standing right next to me. He poked me with his elbow, and said, "Is he still speaking?"

I said, "Yes, Senator, he is."

Connally says, "I thought there was no such thing as perpetual motion." He turned around and waddled out. [laughter]

Notes

1. Kansas City Democratic political boss Thomas Pendergast, who was largely responsible for Truman's election to the Senate in 1934, went to prison for tax evasion in 1939.

2. Minnie Pearl (Sarah Ophelia Cannon), a member of the Grand Ole Opry for more than 50 years, began all of her monologues, "How-DEE! I'm just so proud to be here."

3. John Snyder had been an aide in the Truman White House and treasury secretary.

4. "Bohunks" refers to Eastern European—Bohemians and Hungarians.

5. Democrat Tom Connally was a representative from Texas, 1917-29, and senator, 1929-53.

7 | McCarran Expected Loyalty, and He Gave It

Frankly, I didn't get a decent education when all was said and done. I missed something, not having a normal college experience. By the time I got out of the service and started college again, guys my age didn't have a heck of a lot in common with nineteen and twenty-year-old kids. Some of us had been in the service four or five years. George Washington isn't a campus type of university, anyway. But a lot of social things at George Washington, guys my age felt were silly. I missed the fun my brother had had in Reno. God, he *loved* it up there. Those guys had something going all the time.

When I started at George Washington, most law schools only required two years of college. Because I'd been in ROTC at the University of Utah, when I became a commissioned officer, they gave me credit for four years of ROTC, which gave me more credit hours than I'd earned as a student. I had sixty hours after a year or less at G.W. I'd gotten interested in philosophy. I was questioning whether I should go to law school now. In most schools, even George Washington, you could get in with three years. Then they give you a combined degree, and I couldn't make up my mind whether to stay in college and pursue philosophy a little farther.

I was trying to make up my mind and ran into McCarran in the Capitol and had a little visit. I said, "I can get in George Washington's Law School now. I've got sixty credit hours. Or should I stay and get my degree?"

He said, "You came back here to go to law school, didn't you?"

I said, "Yes, sir."

He said, "Well, then, go to law school."

I thought, yes. That's what I did. I've regretted I didn't get a bachelor's degree before I went to law school.

Patrick McCarran greatly affected my life. Anybody who wants to know about McCarran should read *The Last Hurrah*. There's an awful lot of Pat McCarran in that book, based on Mayor Curley of Boston.

When McCarran got me the patronage job in the sergeant at arms' office, I reported to the Senate Sergeant at Arms, Joseph Duke, who became a dear friend. Most people are not aware the sergeant at arms is important. In effect, he's business manager of the Senate. He is in charge of patronage jobs and is on the board of the capitol police. He has the same pay and privileges as a senator. He has a limousine, which he made available to senators. It was a big job then, and I'm sure it is now. Joe was just taking over—a very important promotion. It's really the choice of the majority leader, who was Ernest McFarland of Arizona.[1] Joe was an Arizonan and had come to work in the Senate in the 1930s.

Joe told me he didn't know where to put me or what to do, but as soon as he got organized, he'd let me know. In the meantime, he asked if I would mind working in the Senate post office on the afternoon shift. I didn't object. I'd be to work at one in the afternoon and get off about five. One thing the Senate postmaster did that I wasn't aware of: whenever a member of the cabinet or a high sub-cabinet official was going to testify before a Senate committee, formal invitations were sent from the Senate, a respect for the separation of powers. The Senate post office would have those invitations delivered downtown to the executive departments. On occasion, the postmaster would ask me to take an invitation to the secretary of labor or the attorney general's office or some place, generally in the afternoon.

I was envious of some young men in Washington—some young men who were from Reno, from affluent families, had graduated from the university, had gone into the service as college graduates, and who immediately became officers. They were older than I, and they had no trouble financially. Most of them had graduated from college before the war. I hadn't.

Joseph C. Duke

I started getting over that when I was in the sergeant-at-arms office, and I was sent to New York to serve a subpoena. The sergeant-at-arms is responsible for serving subpoenas on people to testify before committees. During the McCarthy era, Irene Bentley was a well-known communist who was going to "spill her guts." Mr. Duke, the sergeant-at-arms, saw a chance to give me a trip to New York, so he sent me. I got on the train at Union Station, had dinner in the dining car, had a drink in the club car, and spent the night in the Pullman. When I got off at Grand Central Station, my instructions were to go to the U.S. marshal's office in Foley Square, the federal building. They would be expecting me and assign a deputy U.S. marshal to go with me to serve the subpoena.

We went into the bowels of the earth and got on the subway and went uptown. We got off uptown, and we're walking. We look down a side street toward the Hudson River. It looked like a canyon to me, big tenements on each side. Across the river, you could see New Jersey. The deputy marshal said, "I was born down that street." He let me know he'd never been off the island of Manhattan. I said, "Oh, partner, you've just done me a great favor. I always thought I was a hick for where I was born and grew up. But I've been all over this country. You're the hick. You've never been off this island." And that did give me, for the first time, a little feeling of self-confidence. As far as he was concerned, the rest of the United States was like New Jersey across the river. But he just knew everybody else were the hicks. We found the apartment and served the subpoena. I got to ride back on the train, had a nice trip to New York, and thought I was a big shot marching around with credentials showing I was an officer of the United States Senate. [laughter]

I had a couple of night classes in law school with Eva Adams. A couple of times, I was late. That worried Eva, and she asked me why. I said I was working as a riding page this afternoon and had to deliver a couple of invitations. She said, "Oh, aren't you in the sergeant at arms office? Are you still down in the post office?" I said yes. I didn't mind.

The next day, I went up to the Hill. I didn't have to be to work until 1:00, and stopped in McCarran's office to say hello. As I'm getting ready to leave, in the door to 409 come McCarran and Eva. He said hello and I said hello. I'm trying to get the hell out of there.

Eva said, "Senator, do you know that Ralph is *still* down in the Senate post office, he's having to handle those riding pages, and it's making him late for class?"

I fumbled around and said, "That's all right. It doesn't happen often," and I left. I only had to go down to the post office, on the street floor of the Senate office building.

I came in at 1:00 and started sorting mail. The postmaster got me. He said, "Take that apron off and report to the sergeant at arms office immediately."

Mr. Duke's secretary said, "Mr. Duke wants to see you right now."

Duke said, "Whatever you do, don't go near that Senate post office again."

I said, "What should I do?"

He says, "I don't know. Just stay out of my sight and keep that gray-haired old son-of-a-bitch off my back! As soon as I've got a place for you, I'll let you know." [laughter]

I didn't have anything to do in the sergeant at arms office. I was to read the telegrams sent out by senators to make sure they were official business. I soon discovered that was useless; even if I picked out a telegram that didn't appear to be official, it's a cinch the sergeant at arms wasn't going to call the senator about it. I'd look for big stacks where some senator sent a telegram to every registered voter in his state. Wayne Morse used to do that all the time—stacks of telegrams.[2] I'd take them to Joe, and they'd sit in Joe's office for a while. Joe would throw them all away, then we'd wait until they all came in the next month. Another deputy was supposed to take care of the same thing on telephone bills. [laughter]

I did basically what I was asked or told to do by the senator. I wanted them to know I was available, but I wasn't around him that much. Eva knew: anything I could do, let me know. Most of the time, when people from Nevada came, Eva would call me. She'd introduce me, and I'd take them on tours of the Capitol or to lunch. I took Nevada people to dinner at night, on the senator's tab; to Mount Vernon; on a tour of Washington, that sort of thing.

How best to describe it? I had been a career officer, and, from the time I was seventeen, subject to discipline and to respect authority. So, I was just as uncomfortable around the senator, in many ways, as I was when I had to report to a general officer.

After I moved into the sergeant at arms office and had floor privileges, I'd spend a lot of time on the floor. I would see the senator on the floor and in the hall. (Lawyers will appreciate this.) One day, he asked how school was going. I said, "I think I'm doing fine."

He says, "You understand the rule in Shelley's case?"

"Yes, sir. I think I do."

He smiled, says, "You're the only son-of-a-bitch in the world who does," and laughed.

There were times when he'd reach in his pocket and ask, "Do you need any money or anything?" Yet I still felt self-conscious around him, couldn't really be myself, always acted, as I look back on it, like a God-damn fool.

After I got to know him in Nevada, I became more comfortable around him. I had a few contacts with him. I learned he was a good man, an emotional man. His heart was on his sleeve. I don't think a lot of people realized he was as sensitive as he was. He suffered wounds, but I don't believe the average person was aware of that. He didn't show it—a few conversations where he indicated how sad he was about a couple of people who'd been close to him, how their excessive use of liquor injured their careers.

The boys who came back from Nevada and went to school—McCarran took an interest in them. It wasn't just giving them a job and then forgetting them. He was always interested in how they were doing. In some cases, he would ask them at the end of the semester to bring their grades in, so he could discuss with them how they were doing. Consequently, he would be hurt and react if any of them didn't give him the affection and loyalty back that he was entitled to.

He was very sensitive. He expected loyalty, but he gave it. He told me one time, "You only need a friend when you're in trouble." Everybody's your friend when everything's going well. But when you're in trouble, maybe in

To My Friend Young Friend Ralph D'Enton
Sincerely Pat McCarran

the wrong a little, that's when you need a friend, somebody who's going to stay with you through thick or thin, and he did that.

One example is Jack Sexton, a Nevada boy who went back to Washington with McCarran before World War II.[3] I didn't meet Sexton until after I came back to Nevada. Sexton was one of the first, and close to McCarran. Old-time Nevada family—Jack's father and uncle owned the old Eureka Palisades Railroad. When Jack went back in McCarran's first term, I think he even lived with the McCarrans for a while until he found a place to live.

Jack was in the navy during World War II, came back, and went to law school. He had it all lined up. He was going to be district attorney of Eureka County. He took the Nevada bar, and flunked it. Jack's idea was, "If Nevada doesn't want me, they can go to hell." When he made his application to take the bar, he swore under oath he was a resident of Nevada. He goes to California, because he'd gone through high school there, to take the bar, with an affidavit that he's a resident of California.

You can't be both. He gets a call from the Supreme Court clerk. According to Jack, he said, "Jack, do you really want to be a member of the bar in Nevada, or are you going to go to California?"

Jack said, "Sure, I want to be a member of the bar of the state of Nevada, but those so-and-sos didn't pass me. The hell with them!"

"Well, the Supreme Court's been reviewing the exam papers. There are three that we think should have passed, and you're one of the three."

Jack told me they wanted to get in two others below him. They couldn't let them in without letting Jack in. The two below him later practiced law for a long time and came from judicial and political families in the state.

Jack was admitted to the bar and got his job. He and his wife Louise moved to Eureka, where he came from. Later he got a call from McCarran, and the senator says, "I can't talk to you on the phone, but I'm going to be in Las Vegas next week. I want you to come and meet me at the Thunderbird Hotel. I need to talk to you." Jack wondered what the hell he wants. He drove down, went to the Thunderbird, and saw McCarran.

The senator said, "Jack, I get through the grapevine that the bar is gonna try and revoke your license upon the grounds that you perjured yourself in your application. I'm going to be touring the state. I want you to stand right beside me every place I go. Those sons-of-bitches are gonna learn that they're not just fighting you, they're fighting me, too."

The state bar did move to revoke Jack's license. McCarran got an old friend of his in Reno, Gordon Rice, who'd been his law partner, to represent Jack. The senator personally filed an amicus curiae brief on Jack's behalf, and the Supreme Court ruled in Jack's favor. Now, how far does a United States senator go in helping a friend or a young man who happened to have been under his patronage? Can you think of anybody else who'd do that?

McCarran expected loyalty, but he gave full measure in return. I can tell you this: never, even after we were in Nevada, did he ever discuss with me any political philosophical questions. I recognized his right, because I think he was a true believer, although I disagreed with him. He never asked me or, as far as I know, any of the other guys to embrace fully his views.

I met one boy from Eureka, Bob Tognoni, after I got back to Washington. The Tognoni family was well-known. Bob and his brothers had been the garbage collectors in Eureka, and in the wintertime, they did it with a dog-sled. It wasn't much income. Most people would take their garbage to the dump. One of his brothers, Nye, became a lawyer in Nevada and now is a lawyer in Arizona, and worked for a while under McCarran's patronage on the Senate Interior Committee. Another brother, Hale, was in the state legislature.[4]

Bob worked on the Capitol police force under McCarran's patronage and was a classmate of mine in law school. In 1950, when the senator was running for re-election, we all had to come out to Nevada to do whatever we could in the campaign. (I say "had to." God, I wanted to.) Bob worked his tail off all over Eureka, Lander, Humboldt, Elko, White Pine, counties in which he knew people, then went back to Washington after the election and told Eva he was quitting, because he was completely out of sympathy with what McCarran was doing: the immigration-naturalization bill, internal security sub-committee, the search for communists. He couldn't, in good conscience, continue to work under McCarran's patronage. He felt indebted to the senator for the job he had, so he had done everything he could to help re-elect the senator, and he felt he had paid his debt to him.

Eva called and said the senator wanted to see me. I went, and again felt tense in McCarran's presence. He always tried to put me at ease; I just never could feel it. He told me about Bob. He felt terrible. "Eva tells me you and Bob are good friends. I wish you'd talk to that boy. I don't want him to quit. He doesn't have to agree with me on things. He should stay here and finish school. There are no hard feelings with me. Would you talk to Bob?"

I did. He's one of the guys I admire most. I talked to Bob like a Dutch uncle, and he just didn't feel it was correct. He could not accept money as a result of McCarran's actions. He never came back to Nevada, either. The last I heard, Bob was a justice of the peace in Colorado.

Eva Adams played a large role in my life—and everyone else's. Eva was bright, devoted to the Senator, knew how to use power, and used it. Insofar as patronage jobs are concerned, I think Eva decided who got which. I'm sure the Senator concurred. I think he left that to her unless he had somebody in mind. Eva held us together. She was the one we dealt with all the time, at least patronage people. In those days, in the bullpen, you had Grant Sawyer, Jon Collins, and Chet Smith. I'd mentioned the people I met when I was there in 1942, but when I got back in 1946, there was a whole host of guys from Nevada. Most of them had jobs with the senator or in agencies that he'd gotten for them. Most of them came back to Nevada.

Everybody else was older. I'd been fortunate to get in some college and law school, so I was almost where these guys were in academic levels, but younger—and quite a bit younger than Eva. I was always treated like the kid. That's a difficult position to be in.

A lot of the guys had trouble with Eva, or thought they did. She was ambitious. She was thrifty. Even though she was administrative assistant to one of the most powerful senators on the Hill, she went to law school and didn't stop at just getting her degree. She got a graduate degree in law. All I can say about Eva was I was fond of her, grateful to her for everything she did for me.

And not just for me, but Sara, too. The senator—we were told—didn't want any of his boys to get married. He thought they were too young. At bottom, he thought if they marry somebody back here, they won't go back to Nevada, and Nevada needs its young people to stay there, at least the ones who have gotten an education. So, we all knew that we hadn't better get married, and if we were thinking about it, we better keep it secret.

Eva Adams

Sara and I were going to get married anyway, and we sent an invitation to Senator and Mrs. McCarran. Eva, I think, interceded with the senator. One morning about 7:00, McCarran called Sara at her boarding house and wanted to see her right away, if she could come to his office. He always got there early. She called me and said she was scared to go up there by herself. I said, "I'll meet you there, then." We met up there. Eva took Sara in to talk to the senator, and I wasn't invited in.

You went through Eva's office to get to the senator's office. Eva told me to sit in her office, and she and I visited. She was afraid the senator was going to try and talk Sara out of it. I think Sara impressed him. He asked her a lot of questions, just like it was his son getting married—where she was from, how she felt about moving to Nevada—she'd never been there. I don't know what Sara said, but when she came out, she had a smile.

I said, "What did he say?"

She said, "Well, all he said after he asked me these questions, was, 'Mrs. McCarran and I will be pleased to attend your wedding.'"

When we were walking down the aisle after we were married, I look down on my left. There's the Senator and Mrs. McCarran, and he has a big smile as I go by. [laughter] But some of the guys, I think, were scared to get married.

Even as a classmate in law school, Eva wouldn't mind giving me her notes. She was a magnificent secretary. She took notes in shorthand, and she'd type them up. And she always invited me to cocktail parties she was giving for people, but she did that with most everybody on patronage.

Eva was shrewd. One time, she had a party at the judiciary committee room, and the conference table was covered with costume jewelry, all for sale. She was selling it! [laughter]

Joe McDonald used to joke about how tight Eva was. She must have had a ton of money when she died. After the war it was hard to get new automobiles, but she'd always find a way to get one. She bought a new Studebaker. She wanted to get it out to Reno for her mom and dad, and she knew I wanted to go home that summer, and it was tough coming up with the money. She said, "Why don't you drive my Studebaker out to Reno," which I did, and delivered it.

I don't know why some of the other boys had trouble with her. I think they resented her dominance. Say, she had a cocktail party at her apartment. Trying to teach us, she might say, "Don't just sit there. Circulate." Some resented that. Some resented that she'd ask you to do personal things for her that didn't involve your actual work. She might send them out to get a sandwich, or tickets to New York.

Almost every one of the guys, to various degrees, was ambitious, and some were arrogant: "After all, I work for Senator McCarran." I don't know how to describe it, but it's typical of young men resenting the boss. When you can't say anything about the boss, you take it out on the underling. When Grant was governor, if I did something on his instructions, and it was wrong, nobody blamed him. They blamed me. I picked up a few enemies for things everybody in office, like governor or senator, need to distance themselves from.

Eva was always as democratic and down-to-earth as anybody I've known. Some have said she was "Senator Adams," but I don't think anybody ever thought that. McCarran left Eva to run the office, and it was obvious he relied upon her heavily. He was fond of her, would protect her, but he was, without question, *the Senator*. (He even looked more like a senator than any of the rest. You'd be in the Capitol with him, and people would point, "Is that a senator?" The lionesque head, the flowing silver mane—he looked the part and played on that. He would stand straight up.)

This is typical McCarran, defensive of his boys. My desk was in the assistant sergeant at arms office. The assistant was Bill Reed. Bill's father was a Republican congressman, had been chairman of Ways and Means in the Eightieth Congress.[5] There had been a tradition I don't think is followed anymore. If the Democrats were the majority, the sergeant at arms would be a Democrat, but they would make the assistant a Republican. That was a good job. He did a lot of the actual work. If the Republicans came in, he would become sergeant at arms, and the Democrat would become assistant. It never worked that way afterward, because it didn't change that much.

A fight came up between Duke and Reed. Joe wanted to be rid of Bill, and thought he had the muscle to do it. The majority leader was McFarland of Arizona. Joe was from Arizona, and had gone there with Henry Ashurst, the first senator from Arizona.[6] Carl Hayden was the other senator, and they were close.[7] Joe tried to fire Reed, and did. But Bill wouldn't leave. It became one of these behind-the-scenes battles of the Senate. Of course, I sided with my friend Joe. I figured, "He's my boss. He's a Democrat, I'm a Democrat. I'm here by virtue of Democratic patronage, so I'm with Joe Duke."

Joe had the locks changed on the door to the office, so Bill couldn't get in. Well, Joe lost the fight. McFarland and Hayden didn't stay with him. Hayden was chairman of the Rules Committee, where jurisdiction was, and Bill stayed. Then Bill figured he'd get rid of me. He goes to McCarran on the floor and complains I'm not doing any work. I learned this from Joe. McCarran said, "He didn't come back here to go to work, he came back here to go to law school. Now leave him alone." Apparently, McCarran went into Duke's office and had a good laugh about it, told Joe what Reed had tried. [laughter] Reed and I later became friends.

Another story that shows a little about McCarran: There had been a terrible Democratic convention in Tonopah in 1950 with a knock-down, drag-out fight over who was going to be elected state chairman. McCarran's candidate was Jim Johnson, an attorney, one of McCarran's boys from Fallon. The Las Vegas bunch—the Vail Pittman wing—wanted Archie Grant. McCarran had to win that fight, in his view. He went to Tonopah. It was bloody. My Uncle Lloyd was a delegate from Lincoln County, and Lincoln always aligned itself with Clark. The Clark bunch—Big Jim Cashman and those guys—were for Grant, so Uncle Lloyd was for Grant.[8] Jimmy ultimately won, I understand.

I didn't know anything until I get a call from Eva. The senator wants to see me. I go to the office, and he starts telling me about this convention. "Lloyd was on the other side. I sent for him and asked him to come to my hotel room in the Mizpah to talk to him about it. I told him how important it was that Jimmy Johnson be elected state chairman," he said. "Your uncle would not go with me. I said, 'After all, Lloyd, I've got your nephew on my payroll back in Washington.'"

Lloyd said, "If the son-of-a-bitch can't earn his own living, he ought to starve."

Very dramatically, McCarran doubles up his fist, puts it to his forehead, and says, "Having a member of the Denton family, after the years we've been friends, say that to me was like a blow to the forehead."

I thought, "Oh, my God." [laughter]

A couple of months after that, I got a letter from Uncle Lloyd telling me he had been working on Cashman, and Cashman agreed he would support McCarran in 1950 for reelection. Uncle Lloyd says, "I want you to go tell the senator that." I call Eva and tell her I need to talk to McCarran. She told me when to come over. I go in, and he's sitting there, not much expression on his face. I read him this letter from Uncle Lloyd. He thought he'd be making up with him pretty good; if he could get Cashman to commit to support him, that would be helpful. I finished the letter, and McCarran said, "That son-of-a-bitch has never been for me, and he won't be for me now." [laughter]

It comes the time of the election. We all come out from Washington. Eva drives from Reno all the way to Caliente, spends the night with Uncle Lloyd and Aunt Mabel just to discuss that and patch up that friendship. Eva didn't have to do that. No detail was too small or too large that they didn't try to take care of it. She intended to just visit with Uncle Lloyd and talk to him, but wound up spending the night, and that took care of that one. [laughter]

I took care of a lot of Nevadans coming to Washington, serving as a tour guide. I got pretty expert on the Capitol building, its history and art. Sara and I would show Nevada folks around Washington on McCarran's dime, and we met people from all over the state. I enjoyed that, and it wasn't a burden. That and working with Mr. Duke up in his office, and pouring whiskey for senators—that was enjoyable. That kept me out of sight. If I was on the floor, I wasn't where Bill Reed could really see that I wasn't doing anything. [laughter] I'd be on the floor, and I was available.

McCarran never, in my presence, discussed another senator, and I never saw any evidence of close friendship with other senators. I think he was close to Richard Russell. He might have been close to Harry Byrd of Virginia. He had a friendly relationship with Styles Bridges of New Hampshire.[9] I'm not proud of him for this, but I think he developed a friendship with Senators Welker of Idaho and Jenner of Indiana, who were Republicans with the McCarthy group.[10] I know Chet Smith drove him from Reno up to Boise one time to make a speech for Welker. Whether it was a friendship or just a political friendship, I don't know. He was a loner, pretty much. He rarely came in the sergeant at arms' office and joked with other senators. Once in a while he would have a drink with Mr. Duke, and if there happened to be another senator there, maybe, maybe not.

From time to time, I would act as receptionist in Mr. Duke's office. One of his big jobs was to have plenty of whiskey for senators who wanted a drink. I got to know quite a few senators when I was fulfilling that responsibility. Any number of them would have a drink, just visit—get off the floor away from everybody.

Senators were in there all the time, like Dennis Chavez. I had to be there for one night session. I was handling the phones, and senators are coming in off the floor getting a refill. Chavez was drunk. Mr. Duke asked me to get him off the floor, or the news people would discover it, maybe get pictures and a story. I got him into the Senate car with a driver. We're taking him home. He's madder than hell at me, wants to know whose patronage I was under. I said, "Senator McCarran."

He said, "That son-of-a-bitch. I can't stand that God-damn McCarran. I liked Key Pittman. He was a hell of a guy. As a matter of fact, I was on the committee to go to Pittman's funeral in Reno. I set out from Albuquerque driving, got to Tonopah, checked into the Mizpah Hotel, got drunk, and never made it to Reno." [laughter]

A great surprise to me was that some people whose political views I agreed with, I didn't find personally attractive. In other words, they were rude to the help. Some whose political philosophy I disagreed with, I found to be the nicest. Senator Taft of Ohio was one of the nicest men I ever worked around. I didn't know him. Even when I was an elevator boy, if he got on the elevator, it was always pleasant. Another was Senator James Eastland of Mississippi.[11] I couldn't have sympathy for his views, yet as nice a man as you'd ever meet when you just were dealing with him. The same was true of Senator Theodore Bilbo—a vile man.

I think the greatest shock to me as a boy—this happened more when I was in Washington in 1942 than in 1946, 1947—was to realize that senators are like everybody else. What you have to do to avoid becoming cynical is to develop a healthy respect for the institution and the office. The average guy's head would get turned if all you hear everyday is what a great guy you are, the privileges, the way they're treated, they're fawned over. Some of them get to believing it. Some of them keep their feet on the ground, but a lot of them don't.

Just a little thing, like ringing the elevator button three times. That elevator, no matter where it's going or who it's got on board, is going to answer that call. I think the hardest thing for a young person to do is to not become cynical in working there. That's why I have a lot of sympathy for my friend, Bobby Baker, who I got to know well there.[12] He came there too young and stayed too long. Lots of problems and troubles, but Bobby's basically a good, down-home country boy, a good guy . . . not racist and never was.

Some Republicans I admired as men and disagreed with their political philosophy. I admired McCarran so greatly as a man, but disagreed with his political philosophy. Yet I was proud of him that he was not reading the polls, deciding what to vote. He was a believer. The immigration and naturalization bill that was defeated the first time in the night session—he stood on that floor and introduced, I think it was, ninety amendments, each one of which was defeated. He knew after the first vote they were all going to be defeated. This man stood on the floor that night, exhausted, introduced each one of them, and explained each one of them. Soon as he sat down, they'd have the vote: "No." Move on to the next one. I was proud of him for that.

When I first had those privileges, I was amazed that debate could be going on, a member would be making a very impassioned speech, and few senators would be present. That puzzled me for a while, but I came to the realization the senator might have been building a record. He was making a speech that would be in the *Congressional Record.* If it wasn't crowded with other senators, he still took the time and work to do it, rather than just submit a written statement to a committee. I admired a man who could stand up for an hour and make a speech with the knowledge that few are listening to it.

Then I enjoyed spirited debates. I'm surprised when I see on television all the people standing in the well, and each senator has an aide next to him. I remember senators in a free-for-all, the senator making a speech, another asking him to yield, yielding only for a question, not wanting to give up the floor, and questions and answers. I found that fantastically interesting. It could have been something I had no interest in or didn't know anything about, but these men standing in the open and asking questions and showing each other great respect, sometimes hostility, often not.

I was so impressed with Senator Elbert Thomas of Utah. It must have been after the election of 1950, when Thomas was defeated. Thomas had been a senator for a long time. He was a Democrat, a nice, bright man. The last day of that session, some of the senators were paying tribute to senators who wouldn't be back in January. Thomas got up and paid tribute to the Senate in response. He said it was the greatest deliberative body in the world and should be that last place of gentlemanliness where men of conscience debated issues as gentlemen and maintained friendship. That, to him, was what the institution was. Thomas did it so eloquently, and was such a basically decent man, that there were tears on the floor of the Senate that day.[13]

I don't know whether McCarran felt the same way I did about the Senate as an institution. The people I knew respected him a great deal and were afraid of him; they knew he was a very strong, powerful senator; but the newspapers in Washington, particularly *The Washington Post*, were very critical of him. The people who work around the Hill treat all senators with a great deal of respect and make sure they don't say much, and I never saw any open hostility toward McCarran. But neither did I ever see him behaving collegially with another senator or group of senators.

One time, they were in the main chamber. McCarran's seat was right on the front row—he had that much seniority. There had been a vote on something, and Connally came waddling by him and says, "Hey Pat, I thought when you were bought, you stayed bought." He waddled on out into the cloakroom. I don't know what the issue was. McCarran just laughed.

He had a great sense of humor. He was a practical joker. He liked to tell jokes and laugh at his own jokes. I never had any social contact with the senator, was never in his home, but I remember him telling stories at a picnic in Nevada. He was sitting on the grass with his back up against a tree. All of us were sitting in front of him, and he was joking about the old days in Tonopah and Goldfield, the labor strife and the union. He'd tell a story, and he'd laugh.

Joe McDonald told a story about the 1950 campaign. They were staying at the Thunderbird, and McCarran would go to bed earlier than the others. The rest of these guys were out carousing. They came back, and McCarran had short-sheeted all their beds, done it himself.

Notes

1. Ernest McFarland, a Democrat, was a senator from Arizona, 1941-53. Later he was governor of Arizona, 1955-59, and defeated for the Senate in 1958. Both times, he lost to Republican Barry Goldwater.

2. Wayne Morse of Oregon served as a senator from 1945 to 1969. He was elected twice as a Republican, then became independent and switched to the Democrats. He was one of only two members of Congress to oppose the Tonkin Gulf Resolution, which effectively allowed a blank check to President Lyndon Johnson, to send troops to Vietnam.

3. John F. Sexton later served as district court judge for Eureka and Lander Counties from his appointment in 1953 until his death in 1975.

4. Democrat Nye Tognoni represented Eureka County in the Assembly, 1941-43, and the State Senate, 1943-46. Republican Baptista Tognoni represented Eureka in the Assembly, 1953-55.

5. Daniel A. Reed served in the House from 1919 until he died in 1959.

6. Henry Ashurst, a Democrat, represented Arizona in the Senate from its statehood in 1912 until he was defeated in 1940. He was born in Winnemucca, Nevada.

7. Carl Hayden was a Democratic representative from Arizona, 1912-27, and senator, 1927-69. No one has served in Congress longer.

8. "Big Jim" Cashman was a longtime businessman, first in Searchlight and then in Las Vegas, and helped found the annual Elks Helldorado celebration. Cashman Field complex in Las Vegas is named for him.

9. Richard Russell, a Democrat, represented Georgia in the Senate from 1933 until he died in 1971. As chairman of the Armed Services and then Appropriations Committees, he wielded great influence. He also was a leading opponent of 1960s civil rights legislation, despite his close relationship with President Lyndon Johnson. Democrat Harry Byrd was governor of Virginia, 1926-30, and senator, 1933-65. Styles Bridges, a Republican, was governor of New Hampshire, 1935-37, and senator from 1937 until his death in 1961.

10. Senator Joseph McCarthy of Wisconsin was known for his irresponsible anti-communist tactics. Two of his fellow Republicans were Idaho's Herman Welker, who served from 1951 until he was defeated for re-election in 1956, and Indiana's William Jenner, who served from 1944 to 1945 and 1947 to 1959.

11. James Eastland was a Democratic senator from Mississippi, 1941, 1943-79. A longtime Judiciary Committee chairman, he continued and perpetuated McCarran's anti-communist tactics while also fighting much civil rights legislation.

12. Robert "Bobby" Baker was a protégé of Senators Lyndon Johnson of Texas and Robert Kerr of Oklahoma. He was secretary to the majority leader until financial scandals eventually led to his resignation and subsequent conviction and imprisonment.

13. Elbert Thomas served in the Senate from 1933 to 1951. He was defeated by Wallace Bennett.

8 | McCarran's Boys

McCarran was a great public speaker, and he thought very well on his feet. But in his older age, his voice was not as impressive as it could be. It was not a voice like Grant Sawyer's.

Sawyer was just one of the guys in the office back then. Elizabeth Heckman, Marge Pence, and then Grant, Chet Smith, and Jon Collins back in the bullpen, and later, Joe McDonald and Joe McDonnell. We were all doing the same thing: going to school. We'd have Nevada parties at somebody's house, a bring-your-own-liquor party. We got to know each other well.

McCarran had a hide-away office in the Capitol. Jay Sourwine was there and became counsel to the Judiciary Committee. They had the committee staff. It wasn't as big as it is now. It grew when he became chairman, when the internal security sub-committee was created. The Immigration and Naturalization Sub-Committee wound up with a big staff. But in the office, it was basically the ones I named. Eva and the women, and three or four men who were part-time. Sourwine was very important to McCarran. He did a lot of legislative work, helped with speeches. He was a formidable character who looked like Teddy Roosevelt; in fact, the rest of us used to call him Teddy Roosevelt. Wasn't very civil to anybody. All business. To the Nevada society parties, formal ones, he would go, but never to my apartment or Tom Foley's.

Elizabeth Heckman, I think, was on the Interior Department payroll. They'd loaned her to him, and he had her for years. They didn't have an administrative assistant and legislative assistant. Hal Lackey from North Carolina wasn't on the office staff, but was involved with legislative matters. I think he was actually on the Judiciary Committee payroll, did not have an office up in the senator's office. In those days, each senator only had three rooms. If you'd been there a long time, you got a fourth one. The fourth is what we call the bullpen.

A senator was allowed so much money to run his office, and could split that any way he wanted. Instead of hiring one person, McCarran would hire two part-time to give jobs to kids back there to go to school. Instead of one working all day, two worked half-time. Everything went through Eva. The rules were strict. Every letter had to be answered no later than the next day, and followed up. If the first answer was simply, "I've received your letter. I'm taking the matter up with the so-and-so at the Department of Justice. I'll be back to you," it was followed up *very* closely, to make certain none slipped through the cracks. Had to be very careful with it if they were friends of the senator, that they were addressed properly.

One part of my job is that Sara and I would clip the Nevada newspapers. They'd all come to the office. McCarran would read every Nevada newspaper, then I'd take them home. At night and over the weekend, we would underline and clip any article in which his name appeared or any other member of the delegation, or prominent political figure—the governor, Malone, Russell, or Baring. Sara and I became familiar with parts of Nevada I didn't know. We would read the Yerington paper, the Reno, Elko, Ely, Caliente, Pioche, Eureka, Austin, and Tonopah papers, and clip all of those. That gave Sara a good understanding of Nevada, because she'd never been here until 1950. I'd turn them in, and somebody else had the responsibility of putting them in big scrapbooks.

Joe T. McDonnell was from Reno. Joe had been graduate manager at the university before the war, and he came back to Washington to go to law school. He was older than the rest of us. He went to work in McCarran's office, later moved over to the Appropriations Committee, made a career, and stayed there with Alan Bible. Joe T. was his trusted lieutenant. There was a Joe T. McDonnell and a Joseph F. McDonald who worked back in the bullpen at the same time. No confusion there: everybody just said Joe T. or Joe F.

But they were so different. Joe T. was staid, prim and proper. Joe F. was the opposite, and it was fun to go in the bullpen and listen to them jab at each other. I was on the Hill and didn't have to be over at the office until I wanted to be there. I got out of school at noon and went up to the Capitol. I had great privileges in the sergeant at arms' office. We assigned the parking spaces, so I had a parking space in front of the Capitol on the east portico—can't even drive through there anymore. But I'd have time to go up to the office and visit with Grant and those guys. I'm sure I bothered them. They had work to do, and I'm in there yapping at them.

McDonald had the distinction of being, as far as I know, one of the few kicked out of the Naval Academy twice. Before the war, McCarran appointed Joe, and he got kicked out, I think, for academic reasons. Lord, they wanted to get him back in! McCarran appointed him again the next year, and that's not supposed to be done. Frank Knox was secretary of the navy, and McCarran put the pressure on.[1] Chet laughs when he tells the story; he read a letter McCarran sent to Knox, urging him to give this young man a chance, called him another John Paul Jones. Joe F. got back in, and got kicked out the second time for disciplinary reasons. Joe was so scared about what his parents were going to do to him, he didn't go home for a year. He bummed around the country on freight trains for a year before he went home. [laughter] Then he went to work for Morrison-Knudson Construction and was taken prisoner by the Japanese at the beginning of the war. After he came back, he came back to Washington, where I got to know Joe. His father was editor and publisher of the *Nevada State Journal* in Reno. Bob, his brother, is a lawyer in Reno.

Chet Smith, one of my dearest friends, was from Winnemucca. Chet had been a newspaperman in high school or just out of high school. He worked for the *Humboldt Star* and was a stringer, I think, for one of the wire services. During the war, he was a correspondent in the Marine Corps. He saw an awful lot of front-line combat carrying his typewriter, which, as far as I know, he still has. He worked in the bullpen and became a trusted lieutenant of McCarran's. As a matter of fact, Chet drove McCarran from Reno to Hawthorne the day he died. Chet would always accompany the senator around the state.

Anybody who's doing any history of Nevada would be well-advised to talk to Chet, because Chet was a note-taker. Chet has notes on everything he thought significant, from the time he was a boy in Winnemucca. He really knew Nevada. He had a deep knowledge of Nevada political history from the time he was a boy and remembered all of the political stories he covered. He told me about being in the depot in Winnemucca when the train came through taking President Warren Harding's body back to Washington when he died in 1923. Chet remembered all of the political stories he covered.

Later we practiced law together, but he went back to Washington and worked for Senator Bible. I think he ran all of Bible's campaigns. After Bible retired, he worked for Senator Cannon. Chet worked for Carville when he was senator. He worked for McCarran. When Russell was governor, Chet came back and was budget director. Chet had been best man when Charlie and Marge married. When Lyndon Johnson was running for election in 1964, Chet was loaned to the White House and did advancing for Johnson's political tours.

What made him the classic "man behind the scenes" was that everybody who knew Chet had confidence in his intelligence and political sense. Chet was efficient, a natural staff man. It was all business when Chet was doing his job. Chet was just as reliable, as decent, as any man I've known. Chet was a good writer, good newspaperman, good Democrat, a sober, trustworthy man. He didn't engage in a lot of the festivities some of us did from time to time. Chet got married in Washington. John Snyder was secretary of the treasury under Truman, and Chet married his secretary. Her sister worked in McCarran's office—Marge Pence. Chet married Betty Pence, now deceased.

I met Chet the day I enrolled in George Washington and took my first class. Hugh Norton and I were standing on the steps in front of the government building. Chet came out of a class and down the steps, and Hugh introduced me to him. Immediately, he knew all about Caliente and remembered the music festival in 1938, when Lincoln County High School had come to Winnemucca and participated. He just knew all about Nevada, all about everybody in Nevada. I don't know how anybody could not like Chester Smith . . . just a nice man, smart, efficient, interesting.

Bud Bradley wasn't above letting people think he might have been Omar Bradley's nephew.[2] [laughter] He wasn't. Bud grew up in Ely, where his father was a doctor, and moved to Reno. Bud graduated from the University of Nevada. He had started flying at an early age in Ely, before the war, when they were trying to encourage civil aviation.

Bud came to Washington to go to law school, and he was going to G.W. He got a patronage job at the Justice Department running the elevator. It ran up to the assistant attorney general's office at the top. (His name was Payton Ford.) Bud ran Ford's private elevator on the night shift, and he didn't have much business. He went to work at five, and maybe would have somebody there until six. It was a good job, and he could go to law school full-time, which he did.

The Justice Department decided they didn't need an elevator operator on the night shift. If the assistant attorney general wanted to use the elevator, he could push the button that said "floor one" or "floor two." They removed it from the budget, and Bud was going to be out of a job next fiscal year. But they didn't count on Senator Patrick Antonio McCarran. [laughter] McCarran had the appropriations bill in his subcommittee. For some reason, it wasn't coming through committee, and they're getting to the end of the fiscal year. Then, I understand, the senator had a discussion with Ford. The elevator operator's position was put back in the budget, it was approved, and everything was all right. Bud continued in his work. That's an example of the ends the senator would go to, to protect the Nevada boys.

Bud had come back to Washington in 1949. Joanne Shaef, a McCarran girl, married Bud—Joanne was from Reno. Then Bud came to Reno to practice law, and he has done well. Bud and I were roommates for a while after my brother left Washington.

We had great Nevada parties in Washington. [laughter] When somebody had a place, everybody would bring your own liquor. I had a couple of G.I. foot lockers, which I would stack on top of each other back of the living part of our basement apartment and put a G.I. blanket over them, and that would be the bar. Everybody would bring their own liquor, and we'd chip in to go get the mix. They would play records, and folks would dance and drink and just have one hell of a time. [laughter] We really got to know each other that way. A couple of the kids were married, so we had a couple of great parties at Tom Foley's house. His wife Lucy . . . oh boy, she'd fix up grape leaves and things like that. Lucy is an Armenian and a wonderful cook.

I remember the first party. I hadn't been in Washington long. Grant and Bette lived in that basement apartment at 939 Massachusetts Avenue. I looked like an albino in that neighborhood in those days. [laughter] Some rich friend of Eva's had a beautiful house on Massachusetts Avenue in the Embassy Row area. They were going to Europe and asked Grant and Bette to house-sit for the summer. Shoom! Grant and Bette went up there.

Lew and I had been living in the rooming house, so we took over the Sawyers' basement apartment. The first party we had, everybody was there. Grant and I, maybe Don and Hugh, were heading toward Seventh where we could buy cokes and mix. I saw this animal on the sidewalk in front of me. I'd never seen anything like it. I said, "What the hell is that?" Sawyer says, "It's a rat, and it's yours!" [laughter] I discovered that neighborhood was full of those big ugly rats. Whoa! It was a bad area.

Lew graduated from law school and, I think, went home in the summer of 1948. Don Leighton got out ahead of him, and they were going to be partners in Winnemucca. Lew was full of optimism, came home, and failed the bar examination. It broke his heart. He took it again. I won't mention the names, but three other guys who failed at the same time petitioned the Nevada Supreme Court to review the papers. My brother wouldn't do that. He didn't think that was right. If he hadn't passed, he hadn't passed. These other three guys were admitted. He took it again and failed it, and then left the state. That broke his heart; broke my parents' heart, too.

Without question, Grant Sawyer was the leader of that group. If there was going to be a party, Grant would sort of decide when and where, and everybody went along.

"Why don't we have a party?"

"OK, Grant."

"Why don't we all go ice skating?"

"OK."

Grant was kind of the natural, and I think everybody recognized his abilities. It wasn't talked about, but it was obvious. Years later, back in Nevada, some of the guys might have had a little bit of jealousy. There was just something about Grant. I don't mean to be misunderstood—Grant was a human being, not without warts like the rest of us, but it was obvious that he possessed an indefinable spark. You had confidence in him. If you had problems, you felt at liberty to talk to Grant about them.

A lot of people were in Washington on patronage from senators' offices. A South Carolina guy was postmaster in the Senate Post Office. Olin Johnston, the senator from South Carolina and chairman of the Post Office and Post Roads Committee,[3] generally named the postmaster. Those jobs were arranged for patronage people, slinging mail. You had half-shifts. I remember one guy, when I was slinging mail there for that short time, related to Senator Byrd of Virginia. I don't know where the hell he lived, but when he took his apron off, hung it up, and stopped slinging mail, he'd go out and get in his limousine, and be chauffeur-driven home to Virginia. [laughter]

A couple of old guys worked full-time. I don't know whose patronage they were on. They delivered registered mail. One of them was selling numbers in the Senate office building. Taking bets on horses. Who was buying? [laughter] Patronage changed when the politics changed. Boy, when Republicans were elected in 1946, the morning they took office, every elevator boy, door-man, post office employee—every one of them got their pink slip. They knew they were going to be replaced by the Republican majority. Well, to the victor belongs the spoils. Nobody objected. That's the way it worked. In 1949, the Democrats came back. The fellows came back to work. [laughter] It was a grand thing to be home.

This is when I met Bobby Baker. As I recall, Bobby was from Pickens, South Carolina. The senator was Burnet Maybank.[4] I left Washington in late August or September 1942 to come back to Caliente. Bobby came in January 1943. When I came back after the war, I didn't meet Bobby. When I got back on the Senate side in 1949, Bobby was still a page boy, but he was chief Democratic page in the Democratic cloakroom. He was probably nineteen, maybe twenty, but he was well known. He'd been there since he was just a kid. He knew all of the Democratic senators well, because he was on the Democratic side. That didn't mean he didn't know the Republican senators, because both Democratic and Republican pages responded to calls from any of the senators, of course.

In January 1949, Lyndon Johnson of Texas and Robert Kerr of Oklahoma came to the Senate. Bobby became close to those two men. He was still chief Democratic page. Kerr and Johnson thought Bobby was the greatest thing in the world. They really took him under wing. When Johnson became Senate majority leader (he didn't become leader immediately), Bobby became secretary of the majority, a big job. He had a great deal of influence. He was well liked. Other guys who had worked there longer were jealous of him.

I'm not sure when Bobby and Dottie got married, but she worked for Scott Lucas of Illinois, who had been Senate majority leader and was defeated by Everett Dirksen.[5] She was so well qualified, she went to work in the Judiciary Committee. That put her in the Nevada group. Dottie and Bobby married, so when we had a Nevada party, or Eva would have parties in the senator's office in Judiciary, Bobby would be at some of those. I would see him, because I had floor privileges in the sergeant at arms office. So, I'm on the floor a lot, and Bobby and I are laughing and joking. We weren't close friends, but I called him Bobby and he called me Ralph. We'd have a cup of coffee together.

A classmate at law school, Ernest Tucker, from West Virginia, was under Senator Matthew Neely's patronage—a doorman.[6] That's a great job, because they only work when the Senate is in session. Ernie's wife became secretary to Hale Boggs, the House majority leader, of Louisiana. She and Dottie were friends. That got the Bakers and Tuckers together. Tucker and I belonged to the same legal fraternity. We'd go to the same parties. Bobby hadn't started law school when I was there, but he went to night school and through law school. He and Ernie became law partners and opened an office in Washington, and that's what led to all of their trouble.

I communicated with Bobby. After I came back Nevada to practice, I'd been to Washington a couple of times. When we went back to present the statue of McCarran to Statuary Hall in the rotunda of the Capitol, I saw Bobby. When Senator Cannon went back, he and Bobby became friends. Bobby was riding high and wide in those days. I did see him at the Democratic Convention in Los Angeles in 1960, and we had a yelling match. He's giving me the devil for not supporting Johnson, and I'm telling him it's none of his business.

But we were friends. A few years ago, Bobby and Dottie spent the night with us in Boulder City. Bobby's living in Florida. He's charming, bright, decent at heart. Bobby was convicted of tax evasion, regarded as a juice peddler—all of the worst connotations. In my view, Bobby never did anything he wasn't taught by his parents—namely, the Senate, where he grew up. He learned from Johnson and Kerr and other people in that August institution. I've always been apologetic for Bobby. I don't believe he deserved the rap he took. It ruined Tucker's life, too, although Ernie was never charged.

I met another South Carolina boy, David Jennings. Senator Johnston was his uncle. David wound up Senate postmaster, and he was jealous of Bobby. Here are these two South Carolina kids, Bobby obviously moving up in influence, and David in the sergeant at arms office with me. We're not doing anything but sitting around, but I'm going to school, and David isn't. After Bobby had his trouble, and David was set at postmaster, Johnson was president. I was in Washington and went into the post office to see David. I said, "David, I'm glad you got this job, because I don't think you can handle sorting that mail. I'm not sure you could read all of those letters." He laughed and I laughed. It was a joke.

He was telling me a delegation from the South Carolina farm bureau had been in Washington. They were going to have some meeting in the White House rose garden with Johnson. Uncle Olin, being senior senator, planned to introduce them to the president, but he couldn't do it, so he asked David if he would escort this group. He was standing in the rose garden, next to Johnson.

When Johnson had a chance, he whispered in David's ear, "David, how's Bobby?"

I said, "What did you say, David?"

"I said, 'Bobby? Bobby who, Mr. President?'" [laughter]

People said Johnson abandoned Bobby when he got in trouble. I don't think that's correct. Bobby spent a lot of time with Johnson not long before he died. If they had any grievances toward each other, they fully resolved them and made up. Bobby still is an admirer of Johnson's.

Bobby's circumspect about the whole thing. He believes he was not fairly treated. I think he believes there might have been a Kennedy vendetta to undermine him, and discredit Johnson by discrediting his chief aide. Bobby did indicate that some new things are developing in connection with his case, and he's optimistic he can still get that conviction set aside.

I got out of the army in 1948. Sara and I started to date. In 1949, when I went into the sergeant at arms office, we continued dating. By then, Grant had graduated and left Washington, so Sara didn't meet Grant and Bette. When there was a Nevada party, Sara went with me, started meeting the Nevada people, and liked them all. She met three girls back there from Nevada. They became, and are to this day, close friends. Sara just fit grandly into the group. She liked them, or most of them, and I think they liked her.

There was plenty to do for young folks courting in Washington. One grand thing was the Capitol Theater, on that circuit of theaters up and down the East Coast where vaudeville acts played. You could see a double-feature and four acts of vaudeville at the Capitol for 50 cents. When we had enough money, we'd try to go to the National Theater to see a Broadway show. You could do great things for free. Concerts down at the National Gallery of Art didn't cost you anything. Down at the Potomac, just north of the Memorial Bridge, they would have concerts. There were seats up the bank of the river.

Sara had friends in Washington not connected with Nevada. You'd go to people's houses, maybe to dinner. I met wonderful friends of Sara's—her roommate when she worked at Arlington. Her roommate was from Massachusetts. Two of her sisters lived there. They were all graduates of Smith College. One was cellist for the National Symphony, the other a magnificent pianist. We'd go to concerts. We'd entertain each other, because we didn't have much money. Don Leighton and I were baseball nuts, so we'd go to the Senators' baseball games.

My father had come back to my brother's graduation from law school and met Sara. He told me, "You ought to marry that girl, son. She stands out like a diamond among a bunch of horse turds." [laughter] That was his attitude. My mother was thrilled, particularly after she met her in 1950, when we took her to Nevada for the first time; Mom just adored her, as I can't see how anybody who knew her would not.

We married, but neither my parents nor hers could come to the wedding. It was not financially possible. No members of my family were there. One of Sara's brothers came from Paducah to give her away. It was a grand wedding. Who to choose as best man was tough, because here were all my good buddies. I got Vernon Robbins, my superior officer in Arlington Hall Station and a good friend. He was best man, and the Nevada boys were groomsmen. (I had more political ability than you thought.) [laughter] Lindsay

Founders Day banquet, Delta Theta Phi fraternity, April 1949. *Left to right:* Tom and Lucy Foley, Lew Denton and date, Bob and Betty Joy, Bob Ely, Ralph and Sara Denton.

Jacobson was in the wedding, and his mother Eula Jacobson was there. She was the closest I had to family there. She taught third grade and my mother fourth grade alongside each other for years. She was there to see her son.

The Western Presbyterian Church was near the G.W. law school. That became a problem. I had little religious training, and what I had was LDS. I discovered I couldn't marry in the LDS church; you had to go to the temple. Sara was raised Baptist. We attended this church a couple of times and liked the minister and the church. We made an appointment to see the minister, and he spent a lot of time with us before he would agree. He questioned us both. He was a fine man. For years we stayed friends.

Sara put on the wedding. I had no more idea than the man in the moon what I was supposed to do. Was I to arrange some kind of a dinner or something? I didn't have the money to do it, whatever it was. So, Sara just arranged the whole wedding. Her best friend, her roommate, who was going to be matron of honor, was Catholic. In those days, Catholics had the rule that none of their people could participate in any Protestant service. Martha looked around, went to priest after priest until she found one that said it was OK. It was a nice wedding.

We got married on a Friday evening. I had taken the evidence examination that morning; and the following Monday morning, I started the second summer session, so we didn't have much of a honeymoon. It didn't make any difference. Washington was—and I think still is—a great town. You don't have to have a lot of money to do a lot of things. Sara had bought a car just

Left to right: Lindsay Jacobson, Jack Wedge, Hugh Norton, Ralph and Sara, Martha Treml, Capt. Vernon Robbins, William "Omar" Bradley.

before we got married, and, of course, we had to make monthly payments on it, but Saturday mornings would be fun. You could drive to Rock Creek Park, drive into the creek, and wash your car. You'd see other young people doing the same thing.

Notes

1. Frank Knox was Alfred Landon's running mate on the Republican ticket in 1936. A longtime newspaper executive, he supported Roosevelt's foreign policy and joined Henry Stimson in a wartime coalition cabinet, serving as secretary of the navy from 1940 until his death in 1944.

2. Omar Bradley was one of the outstanding battlefield commanders of World War II and later general of the army and first chairman of the Joint Chiefs of Staff.

3. Olin Johnston, Democrat, was governor of South Carolina, 1935-39 and 1943-45, then a senator, 1945-65.

4. Burnet Maybank was a Democratic governor of South Carolina, 1939-41, and senator from 1941 until his death in 1954.

5. Democrat Scott Lucas of Illinois was a representative, 1935-39, and senator, 1939-51.

6. Democrat Matthew Neely represented West Virginia in the House, 1913-21 and 1945-47, and Senate, 1923-29, 1931-41, 1949-58. He also was governor, 1941-45.

9 | McCarran: He Was Just "Pat" to Them

I graduated from law school in January, 1951. Sara was pregnant. In March, I drove from Washington to Reno to take the Nevada bar exam, and I stopped in Elko to see Grant and Bette Sawyer and spend the night with them. Grant had been elected Elko County district attorney in 1950. He offered me a job as his deputy district attorney if I passed the bar. I was certainly interested.

When I got back to Washington, Eva called and said the senator wanted to see me. I went to see him, scared to death as usual. He said, "How was the bar?"

I said, "Well, I thought it was pretty tough."

"How do you think you did?"

"I think I passed."

"Well, it's time for you to go home, then."

I wanted to keep my patronage job until after we had the baby. I tried to explain that my wife was pregnant, which he apparently knew, and I would appreciate it if I could stay until the baby was born in September. He said, "No. Ralph, you came here to go to law school. You finished. Now you've got to make room for another Nevada boy who wants to go to law school." He told me he had arranged for Jack Barry from Battle Mountain to come back and take my job. Then he said, "But don't worry, I've got a job for you in Carson City. You'll be deputy clerk in the federal court until the bar results come out."

Not only had he done that, he had gotten in touch with friends of his to make sure they could find a place for Sara and me to stay when we got to Reno. I started that meeting being told I'd been fired, and walked out grateful for what he had done. It was funny. When I got to Carson City, I reported to the clerk, an old racehorse tout, Amos Dickey, a good friend of McCarran's. The bailiff was Mickey Kloskey. He couldn't have kept order in a courtroom—he was an old decrepit guy from Beatty. McCarran always called him the admiral of the Amargosa River fleet.

I started work in the clerk's office. I didn't know anything about the law on the subject of the hiring of clerks, and I assumed everything was fine. I'd been there about a week, and the chief deputy clerk told me Judge Roger T. Foley wanted to see me.

Judge Foley was cordial. He said, "Ralph, the statute provides that the clerk may hire deputy clerks with the approval of the judge. Mr. Dickey hired you, apparently, because Senator McCarran told him to hire you, but I wasn't even consulted."

I thought, "Oh, oh. Here I am again, mixed up in that fight."

Then Judge Foley said, "But don't worry. It's perfectly all right with me." He was so nice to me. He and Mrs. Foley went to Las Vegas for a month to hold court and invited Sara and me to live in his house while he was gone, which we did. We lived there even after he came back. He said, "You might as well stay until bar results come out."

When I was staying at Judge Foley's house, McCarran would call me. There's a three-hour time difference. It'd be about 6:00 a. m. in Reno, and he knew Judge Foley had to answer the phone. Then he'd just say, "Is Ralph there? I need to speak to Ralph."

Poor old Judge Foley would have to come down, wake me, and tell me, "Senator McCarran wants to talk to you."

I'd get on the phone, and, "Yes, Senator, what can I do . . . ?"

"Oh, how's everything going?" He had nothing to talk to me about. He just wanted to annoy Judge Foley. [laughter] Tells you a little bit about Senator McCarran.

My relationship with McCarran changed when I came back to Nevada. (I hate to just call him McCarran. I think "the senator" better reflects the attitude of old-time Nevadans toward him.) I was self-conscious around him in Washington—held him in awe. That didn't change, but I saw a different side to him in Nevada. I'd gotten glimpses before . . . . In Washington one time, the Nevada people all went to a picnic. McCarran was sitting on the grass with his back against a tree, telling stories about Tonopah, his days herding sheep. I sat and listened. He seemed happy to be surrounded with Nevada kids he knew from home. His love for Nevada was not just a front. He really did love and miss Nevada, but I didn't see much of that side of the senator in Washington.

The first contact I had with McCarran after coming back was the Democratic convention of 1952 in Wells. I had never been to a convention, had no idea how a convention worked or that planning had been going on that I was not privy to. I was selected to make the welcoming speech to the delegates on behalf of Elko County. (By then I was Grant sawyer's deputy district attorney.)

Grant was elected convention chairman. Once that fight was over, he appointed committees, and I was appointed chairman of the resolutions committee. I had no idea what the chairman of that committee did. The convention was held in the Wells Theater, and I repaired to where the resolutions committee was supposed to be and met Tom McLaughlin, a committee member from Las Vegas who became a friend. We sat down, and Tom said, "Ralph, did the senator give you the platform yet?"

I said, "No." As a matter of fact, I didn't know the senator was going to give me a platform. The senator wasn't at that convention.

I was pondering that when Joe Cleary, from Reno, came to that part of the theater. He said, "Is Ralph Denton here?"

I said, "I'm Ralph Denton."

He said, "The senator said to give you the platform," which we immediately enacted.

That was the end of the committee's work. None of us had any idea what was in the platform, but it was adopted unanimously. Apparently, the senator arranged all of this. I did not rise in righteous indignation—if that's the way they do it, that's the way they do it. That seemed to be the attitude of the other people, too, and they'd been doing it for years. I just wanted things to go smoothly.

The speaker at the convention was Senator George Smathers of Florida.[1] He was flying in on a private plane, and I was sent to meet him. The Wells airport was out in the desert. This airplane landed on this dirt strip, and I picked up Smathers. I knew him a little, because he had come to Washington in January, 1951. I had seen him on the floor a time or two, and we had mutual friends. At least I could visit with him a little when I drove him to the convention. We got him there, so it appeared to me the convention was a great success.

McCarran faced a situation new to him: the rapid growth in Nevada, particularly Clark County. The senator had a paternalistic view toward Clark. He had done everything he could to help its growth by securing federal projects. It was almost like he had created a monster, and the monster was about to turn on him. I don't think Jimmy Ryan of the Clark County delegation was on his side, even though the senator was a great supporter of organized labor. I think he had been responsible, in the Nevada legislature, for the eight-hour day and a few things like that, and he had voted against the Taft-Hartley bill. But I don't believe Ryan was in his tent.

I decided it would be nice if all of us who had gone to school under McCarran's patronage had a dinner for him, where we could meet and express our thanks to him for everything he'd done for us. I think that was the first social meeting I had with McCarran after I came back to Nevada. There were no political implications. I was surprised nobody had thought of that before, because a lot of guys under his patronage had been practicing law for years. I decided I would check with Eva. She thought it was a good idea and said she would talk to the senator. He thought it was great. We decided we would have it at the Riverside Hotel in Reno. Then he suggested we wait until after the primary. He said, "Ralph, if you have it before the primary, it's going to be misinterpreted in the press as me calling all of you boys together to give . . ." and he would laugh, "my machine orders as to what to do."

He was happy we did that. I learned he felt deeply about how some of the boys had behaved after they came back to Nevada. He'd call and tell me, "Don't invite this son-of-a-bitch," or "Don't invite that one." [laughter] He wanted to be sure Jon Collins was not invited. Jon had worked right in his office, so I'd invited Collins, but I had to withdraw the invitation.

(In the 1952 Democratic convention in Chicago, Adlai Stevenson had been nominated. McCarran had wanted Nevada to support Senator Richard Russell of Georgia on the first ballot. He knew it wouldn't go past there, but McCarran could rely on Russell for help where he might have needed it—gambling and things of that kind—and he didn't want the Nevada banner in the demonstration for Stevenson.

McCarran's holding the state banner on a standard. He looks up. Going by him is a Nevada banner for Stevenson carried by Collins, George Rudiak, and two or three Clark County delegates![2] McCarran says, "Where in the hell did *that* come from?" He goes after it. He winds up in a beef with Collins and takes a poke at him. It hurt McCarran that they wouldn't give him the courtesy of that first ballot vote for Russell.)

In September, 1952, we had the dinner. It was a wonderful evening. The senator was warm and jovial, and there was no political discussion. He had a good time laughing about the old days, telling stories about Irish and Swedish miners in Tonopah, and how they had an even number in the union, and, consequently, had a hard time electing a president. I had a short discussion with him. He thanked me for putting on the dinner and told me what a nice time he had.

Testimonial dinner for Sen. Pat McCarran at the Riverside Hotel in Reno, September 20, 1952. *Front row, left to right:* Ralph Denton, Virgil Wedge, Alan Bible, Sen. McCarran, C. E. "Dutch" Horton, Jim Johnson, Grant Sawyer. *Back row, left to right:* William Hammersmith, Chester Smith, George Hadley Hynes, Donald Leighton, Jack Sexton, John Matthews, Clark Guild Jr., Leslie Leggett, Fran Breen, Julian Sourwine, Calvin Cory.

In the party primary that year, Alan Bible was running for the Senate against Tom Mechling, but Mechling didn't really run against Bible; he ran against McCarran. He accused McCarran of everything under the sun. He voiced a lot of the objections Democrats had to McCarran's policies, legislation that McCarran had enacted or supported, and he accused McCarran of all sorts of things, among which was that all of us were in his machine, and his machine controlled the state. He beat Bible, but even though we had this dinner *after* that election, the paper still said it was McCarran's way of getting us together and giving us our orders.

I remember McCarran saying that night, "My God, here I am, and they call you guys a machine!" [laughter]

McCarran *was* the power structure, but if he had a machine, and we were part of it, we weren't an integral part. We were just a bunch of kids practicing law. (Of course, some of our group were older and more influential in their communities.) Mechling, whom nobody knew, came into Nevada, and by doing a door-to-door campaign all over the state, which you could do in those days—television was not a factor—took on the power structure and won. Those who had political aspirations—and I was not among them, frankly—had to start taking a look. What is the situation in Nevada? Maybe we don't have to wait to be hand-picked to run, even if we're not in good favor with certain people. I think that idea went through the minds of several of the boys.

Among the boys, everybody had been stunned by the results of the primary. The general election really got hot. Mechling, whom I had known in Washington and considered a friend, continued his attacks, not on Malone, who he was running against, but on McCarran. I guess he figured that had worked in the primary, and he'd continue with it in the general. Of course, I had supported Bible in the primary, and I had thought I was prepared to support the Democratic candidate in the general election, but I changed my mind. Nonetheless, it was difficult for me to openly support a Republican for the Senate, and I felt I had an obligation to tell Mechling why I was going to support Malone. I wrote a long letter to Mechling and went through chapter and verse explaining why I could not support him for the Senate, and I mailed it to him. [See the Appendix for the complete text of the letter.]

Then I got worried. I should not have done anything without checking with the senator. I called Eva and told her what I had done. She said, "Read me the letter." I read it. She didn't make much comment, as I recall, but said, "Air-mail me a copy." I thought, "Oh God." A day or two after that, the senator calls to thank me for writing that letter. He said, "You didn't have to get my OK, Ralph. I'm glad you feel that way," very warmly.

I understand Malone's people had thousands of copies of the letter printed and dropped out of airplanes over the Admission Day parade in Carson City on October 31, a few days before the election. I didn't find out until I came to Las Vegas the weekend before the election. In those days, all the locals sort of hung out at the El Cortez.[3] Malone's campaign manager, Pete Kelly, came up and thanked me for everything I'd done for Malone. I didn't know I'd done anything except write that letter. I tried to explain it wasn't for Malone; it was that I just could not have Mechling in the Senate. I don't know why I did that, because I liked Malone. He was a nice man, and I'm glad he won . . . but McCarran was so nice when he called me about that.

I was still in the DA's office, and my support for Malone had a personal effect on me in Elko County that I didn't anticipate and, frankly, didn't care about. One of the active Democrats was Johnny DiGrazia, a saloonkeeper in Wells, and his daughter was married to Mechling. She worked under McCarran's patronage—the Judiciary Committee. DiGrazia became a life-long political enemy, because I'd gone against his son-in-law.

Other Democrats were teed off at old Ralph. Taylor Wines, the judge, had been a friend.[4] His office was on the same floor in the courthouse as mine. I would drop in and visit if he wasn't on the bench. He was interested in politics and a strong Mechling supporter. I got back from Las Vegas and went in to say hello. He said, "I'm busy. Get out." It changed my relationship with the judge.

The consequences of my foray into politics should have taught me a lesson: a lawyer shouldn't get involved in politics, particularly if the judge—if he's in a town where you only have one judge—is on the other side. [laughter] But I never gave much thought to consequences when I did something of that kind if I thought I was correct, and I certainly thought I was—I couldn't stand by and see McCarran pilloried. McCarran didn't deserve it from the nominee of his party. While the incident did have some negative effects on my life, that didn't bother me at the time and still doesn't. In Elko, Harvey Sewell and I became close, and one of the things that made us close was our admiration for McCarran. Harvey was president of Nevada Bank of Commerce, a Northern Nevada chain. He and his brothers owned a chain of stores—Sewell's. He used to have a store on Third and Fremont in Las Vegas. He used to laugh: everybody assumed he was a Republican because he was a banker. The Republicans used to have precinct meetings at his house. He wasn't at any of their meetings, but they could use his house. [laughter]

He told me of things McCarran had done to help him during the war. Harvey had a slaughterhouse and packing plant. He was having a terrible time getting an allocation of material from the War Production Board. He said the senator came to Reno, stopped in to see him, and asked how things were going. He said, "I told him about the problems I was having, and your office has been doing everything they can."

The senator said, "Let's go now. You come with me to Reno, and we'll catch a train and go to San Francisco." With his constituent Harvey in tow, the senator walked right in to the head office for the West Coast in San

Francisco and demanded, by God, they approve his application, and they granted it. I can't think of too many United States senators who would get on the train and go to San Francisco to help an old Nevada constituent, but McCarran did. They'd been friends for many years.

At one time, when McCarran was practicing law, there was a big arson case in Elko County to do with a store the Sewells owned in Tuscarora. Somebody burned it down, and there was a big lawsuit over it with another Elko County family. McCarran represented the Sewells to a successful conclusion. Doby Doc (Robert) Caudill apparently was their star witness. Doby Doc's name is well-known in Elko County and Clark County, and McCarran told me one time in Elko, "The best witness I ever had on the witness stand was Doby Doc."

McCarran knew all those old guys and was friends with all of them. He was down to earth, decent, good. Hard to see it if you stood in awe of him, but these old-timers were his friends for years, so they didn't stand in awe of him. He was just Pat to them. If Pat's your friend, Pat's your friend. They all knew that. Pat was your friend when you needed a friend, if you were maybe in a little bit of grease or something. He didn't judge you.

McCarran came through Elko on several occasions while I was there. He just dropped in. I couldn't believe that. I was flustered and fumbled around. He wanted to see how things were going, told me jokes about practicing law, and asked, did I represent any Basque sheep men. He knew about the practice of law in Nevada and was good-humored.

The FBI agent, Dick Lubben, came to my office one afternoon and said McCarran was coming that night on the streamliner and wanted me to meet him. He was bringing his son Sam back to Nevada to practice medicine. He was going to stay at the Stockmen's Hotel.

The train tracks went through the middle of town. We stepped across the street to meet the senator. I never saw a man so happy and proud. He was happy to be home, to be in Elko; the next day he was going to take Sammy to his mother's family's ranch in Clover Valley and show Sammy the ranch where Mrs. McCarran had grown up. Sam was going to start practicing in Reno, and I never saw such a demonstration of parental pride. I think they stayed in Elko a couple of days, and he showed Sammy around. It wasn't political. He was so proud his son was coming home! And, of course, the senator had a hand in setting him with another doctor.

I was pleased that the senator had asked me to meet him. Politics was not a subject of discussion. Again, it illustrates a point I've made: his great love for Nevada and his love and devotion to his family. That love and devotion went beyond his family to other people he'd been close to, some of the boys who'd worked for him. I think he felt closer to some than others. Cal Cory, for example, in Las Vegas, was almost like a son to him . . . was a son to him.

One time he came to the Elko County Fair. It's a great fair: horse races, cattle cutting, exhibitions of quilting and produce, kids showing lambs and calves and horses. They have a big parade. I was assigned the job of driving him. We had a convertible, and McCarran's going to sit on back of it. We line up before the parade at the front of Hesson's Store. The tracks bisect the town. Hesson's is on the south side of the tracks on the east end. The parade would come down the tracks heading west, cross the tracks just below the Stockmen's, then go up Idaho Street to the Ranch Inn.

I look down the sidewalk, and here comes C. D. Baker, mayor of Las Vegas.[5] I don't know how C. D. felt about it, because he was a nice guy, but in the senator's mind, Baker was an enemy, because he'd beaten Ernie Cragin for mayor. Cragin was McCarran's friend, and McCarran had done all he could to help Cragin. At that point, Baker was thinking of running for governor. Charlie Russell was governor, and he was in the car with his driver, a young lady, Billie Glock.

I got to know C. D. after I moved to Las Vegas, but I wasn't sure who he was; McCarran knew exactly who it was. Baker spotted McCarran and came over. He stuck out his hand to shake hands. I saw the senator's arm go up to shake hands with him. I see Baker's face turn red as a beet. He didn't say a word. He turned and walked off. McCarran turned to me laughing. "I sure fixed that son-of-a-bitch," he said. "When he stuck out his hand, I just gave him one finger, and he clamped down on it before he knew." [laughter] McCarran thought that was funny. I thought it was kind of funny, too.

The parade's ready to go. The marshal was an Elko businessman, Zeke Daly. Zeke's in the middle of the street. I don't know where we're supposed to line up, so I go up to talk to Zeke. He said, "Governor Russell will be in the lead, then Senator McCarran will be second.

I said, "No, Zeke. Senator McCarran will be first."

Zeke said, "No. Protocol says the governor has precedence over a United States senator."

I said, "Zeke, I'm not going to drive that old son of a bitch second. If he's going second, you're going to have to get somebody else to drive him."

Zeke was adamant. "You go second."

I thought, "I'm not going to drive him second. I got to do something." I went over and talked to Russell. I said, "We've got kind of a problem here. Zeke says you're to go first and Senator McCarran's going second. I can't drive him second."

Charlie smiled. He says, "I know. When the parade starts, you pull out in front of us and get in the front."

I said, "OK."

So, the parade starts, and Charlie's car is leading it. I pull up on the left. Charlie hadn't told his driver. Billie speeds up. We're going about half a block side-by-side. I finally get up enough speed to get in front, and I look back at McCarran. He knew what was going on, and he was laughing. He thought that was the funniest . . . . [laughter] But we led that parade. That's how the senator operated.

Back then, DA's and their deputies commonly had private law practices along with their public responsibilities. It was perfectly acceptable, and it was the only way you could make ends meet. I hadn't been practicing long in Elko when I'm looking out the window of the courthouse, and this limousine pulls up. I wondered, what's a limousine doing in Elko? A chauffeur gets out, goes to the back, and opens the door. A distinguished, gray-haired man gets out. The next thing I know, my secretary tells me, "A Mr. Dave Kessel would like to see you."

Kessel came in and told me he and Bill Pechart had purchased or taken a lease—I don't recall which—on the Palace Club in Reno. The tax commission had turned down their license application because of Pechart. He said, "I have bought out Mr. Pechart; Mr. Pechart no longer has anything to do with it. My application for a gaming license is coming before the Nevada Tax Commission"—a 'gambling' license, we called it then—"at its next meeting. You've been highly recommended to me. If you will represent me, I'll pay you $10,000, and I'll give you $5,000 now. After the hearing, I'll give you the remaining $5,000." More money than I'd ever made in a year. He gave me $5,000.

I didn't know Pechart from a bale of hay, but Kessel said, "He no longer has any interest in the Palace Club. It's just me. I'm the only applicant, and I assure you Mr. Pechart is no longer involved." So, I believe that to be true.[6]

The time came when we went before the tax commission. In those days, they met in the governor's office. The tax commission consisted of the governor, the chairman of the public service commission, and three other citizens appointed by the governor. You didn't have a gaming control board. You'd go into the governor's office and put on your case, then you'd leave, and the next applicants would come in. After all the applicants had come in, they would vote on each one. Then, you would find out.

I got there early and thought I'd say hello to the governor. The secretary says, "Oh, yes. The governor would be glad to see you, Ralph." I went in, we exchanged greetings, he wanted to know how Sara was, and then, "What brings you here?" I told him. He didn't say a word. We made our presentation, and I staked my reputation that Pechart had nothing to do with this application, that Kessel was sole owner of the Palace Club. I made personal representations on his behalf that I'm ashamed I ever made.

We went in the hall, and I told Kessel, "It looked good, but it'll be late this afternoon before we know, so why don't you go back to the hotel." He was staying at the Mapes. "I'll stay here and wait and get the results, and I'll call you or come to the hotel." About four o'clock, they voted. By God, much to my shock, Kessel's application was denied unanimously. I couldn't believe it. I hadn't smelled any wolf manure or anything when Kessel had come to see me. I had just believed, "This practice of law is a wonderful thing. I have only been practicing a few months, and already, my abilities are recognized, and people are coming to me from Reno. Isn't that wonderful?" I didn't even consider that I was a deputy district attorney representing a gambling applicant before a state agency.

I tried to call Kessel from Carson, but the line was always busy in his room, so I got to the Mapes Hotel and called his room on the house phone. He told me to come up. I went up and started to tell him they had turned him down. He interrupted me. He already knew. He did not seem mad at me, but a tall, skinny guy was in the room. Kessel turned and said, "Pay the kid off." The guy came over and gave me the second $5000 of the $10,000, which I put in my pocket, and I never took my hand out until I got to Elko.

A few months later, I get a call that McCarran's coming on the streamliner and going to Reno. Would I meet him? I met him at the depot. We walked across to the Stockmen's and got him checked into a room. Then we went down to the bar, and we're having a drink. The senator asked me: Did some people come to me and want me to represent them in connection with a license at the Palace Club in Reno?

I said, "Yes."

He said, "What happened?"

I start telling him the story. A big grin on his face, and he starts laughing. When it's over, he said, "I'll teach those tin-horn sons-of-bitches to try and buy me." Then he told me the story:

They had come to Washington to see him. They thought they could get the fix in through him. He didn't promise them anything. "Tell you what you do," he said. "I think if you went out to Elko, Nevada, there's a young lawyer out there by the name of Ralph Denton. If you go out and see him— he's very good—and pay him $10,000, I think everything might be okay."

They thought they had the fix in. They misjudged their man. McCarran did not take a penny from them. He didn't raise a hand, but he got a friend $10,000 the friend could well use. [laughter] I think he did that for a lot of people. When they asked his help, he would do it.

From this experience, I learned never to make a personal representation. As for why they were turned down, it's obvious: the tall, skinny guy in the room turned out to be Pechart. The state didn't believe Pechart wasn't still part of the deal. I got to know Pechart later, and there was no way he could get a license, but he ran the gambling in the Mapes Hotel for years.

After Grant became governor, the control board entered an order that Pechart could not be on the premises of the Mapes. But the attorney general, Roger Foley, said that was unconstitutional and modified it: he could be in the hotel, but couldn't be in the casino.[7] The result was, Pechart ran that casino from the cocktail lounge for years. He'd been in Las Vegas, left in the 1930s, and never come back to Las Vegas. I heard rumors as to why he couldn't get a license. I think he's dead now. He was the one that paid me off.

After that, Mechling wrote columns in *Las Vegas Sun* and Hank Greenspun ran them—I didn't know Hank at the time—referring to me as a mouthpiece for mobsters. Might have been true. I don't know. But I'll tell you, that $10,000 was gratefully received. [laughter]

Senator McCarran came to Elko several times and was so friendly and nice. Then, one time, I was in Reno, and he invited me to have breakfast with him at the Riverside. This shows how naive I was. I pick up the check. He kept saying, "No, Ralph, let me have it." I thought, "No, you've taken care of me all my life. It's my turn to start." I paid, never dreaming in those days those joints comped everybody, particularly senators. But McCarran tried to tell me. [laughter] I learned about comps. Geez, did I learn about comps.

The Democratic convention in Boulder City was coming up in 1954, and McCarran or Eva told me I was to be state chairman. I accepted that in my naiveté as a fait accompli. I decided I'd better learn the rules of county and state conventions—and learn them *well*, because you needed to know what you were doing in one of those places.

We had our county convention. Lo and behold, somebody offered a resolution that the county Democratic convention go on record memorializing the state convention to elect Ralph Denton state chairman. That sure pleased me. Nobody voted against it. I thought, "That's just grand!" With McCarran behind me, this ought to be a lead-pipe cinch. The only problem was, what the hell do I do if I get elected? What does a state chairman do? I discovered when I got to Boulder City that most of the small counties had adopted a similar resolution. McCarran had caused these resolutions to be prepared and gotten the people in the small counties to get them passed.

A couple of days before the state convention, the senator called and wanted to know how I was going to Boulder City. I said, "I'm going to drive down."

He said, "Would you do me a favor?"

I said, "Certainly, Senator."

He said, "Would you go to Winnemucca and get my old friend Roy Persons. He doesn't have a way to get there."

I said, "Oh, I'd be glad to do that."

I didn't know Roy Persons. He might have been county assessor in Humboldt County. I think he'd been a barber by trade. Sara and I drove to Winnemucca to get Roy, whereupon Sara and I had the opportunity of meeting one of the most delightful men I've ever known. The first thing that endeared him to me was when he said, "I can hardly wait to get to Boulder City and find out who I'm mad at." [laughter] His presence was important, because he had the proxies of all the Humboldt votes. I think Humboldt had eleven votes at the convention, and old Roy had all eleven. I'll never forget, it was dark when we were coming in. We're coming down past Indian Springs, and we get where we can see Las Vegas and all those lights. Roy was amazed, couldn't get over the size of Las Vegas. He probably hadn't been there for twenty years.

We got to Boulder City, and I discovered Joe Foley was the Clark County candidate for chairman. That created a problem for me, because I considered Joe and Betty our close friends. All things being equal, if Joe wanted to be chairman, that would have been fine with me. I didn't have any desire to be chairman. I would have withdrawn, but I was not a free agent. It always puzzled me that Joe was bitter toward me for running against him, because I thought he should understand that I considered this to be an obligation to McCarran. If McCarran wanted me to run for chairman, that's what I would do. I would have expected anybody to understand. But it did create some hard feelings. I learned later on my name was never offered as a candidate. Keith Lee, who became state treasurer at the same time Grant became governor, was elected.

The senator explained it later. He knew the minute it was in the papers I was going to run for state chairman, the anti-McCarran part of the Clark County group would oppose it. They had a large number of votes. They would make a knock-down, drag-out fight over it. He'd gone through that in 1950 with Jim Johnson. He'd won, but it created problems in the party. So, his real candidate was Keith Lee. When my name didn't go up, Lee's did, nobody tied him to McCarran, and he was elected.

The senator later apologized. He said, "Sometimes, Ralph, we have to be a little bit smarter than they are. And I knew I could count on you, and you wouldn't be too offended by it." I wasn't! I thought, "Gee, it's great! The old man won again." [laughter] But I decided I would learn as much as I could about procedures, so that in the future, I'd have some idea of what was going on.

McCarran wasn't at the convention, but a lot of his old work-horses were there. I think they were kind of running it, and a funny thing happened. I don't know how many votes Burt Hanks had from White Pine, but he and Roy were buddies. The first night we were here, the Foley forces recognized the power of Roy with the Humboldt vote and Burt with the White Pine vote. They decided they'd take them into Las Vegas, get them drunk, and leave them there. Then they wouldn't be at the convention the next day to vote. [laughter] They took them to the Sands. They miscalculated. Roy and Burt could hold three times more whiskey than John Mendoza and whoever was with him.

Sara and I went into town that night and ran into Persons and Hanks at the Sands. They were sitting there wondering where Mendoza had gone. They were stone-cold sober, it appeared to me. We said, "We'll take you back." They were present at the convention, but I don't think Mendoza showed up. [laughter]

The senator was facing a reelection campaign in 1956. Although he hadn't had trouble in 1950 beating George Franklin, in 1944 he had barely won the primary. Vail Pittman had come close to beating him.[8] I don't think McCarran figured he'd run against him. But Pittman was a participant in the Clark County group that opposed McCarran. It was not only the newcomers; a lot of the old-timers had lost their affection for Senator McCarran.

The senator did not fear defeat in the general election. If he was vulnerable, it would be in the primary. He always believed it was important to control the party organization, which had a little more significance in those days—it didn't have much power then and has even less now. When the state was smaller, it gave you a few people in every county. Those active in party politics were involved. If you had control, it meant people in those counties were with you. Not that you could do so much with the organization if you had control, but nobody else would have control—my theory on why McCarran believed it was important. As history shows, Grant Sawyer believed in party organization and political parties; that healthy political parties were in the best interest of good government—the two-party system.

In 1954, McCarran was thinking about 1956. Where was his vulnerability? The Democratic primary. Where was he vulnerable in the party? Clark County. He recognized that. He was emotional about it. He felt betrayed when all of these newcomers didn't seem to appreciate him, because if ever a senator had gone the extra mile to help southern Nevada, it was McCarran. No one can doubt his effectiveness in the things he produced for Clark County. You look at Nellis, the airport, all that McCarran did for this part of Nevada.

That's the year he died, and when he died, he was touring the state with the entire Democratic ticket and speaking for the ticket with some candidates who, I know, he did not feel should be in the high offices they were seeking. Nevertheless, he was doing it. That included Pittman running for governor. McCarran told me at one of our discussions in Elko that he was going to make this last attempt to be with the party. But if the party still was going to oppose him, he would consider doing what Senator George Norris of Nebraska did and run as an independent.[9] Of course, he dropped dead while he was making his speech from the party platform in Hawthorne [September 28, 1954].

I was still in Elko, and cannot leave my account of those days without expressing my appreciation to Eva Adams. She saw that I was given the opportunity to be part of any group that did anything to remember McCarran. I was an honorary pallbearer, but so was everybody else in Nevada. She knew I didn't have money to make a substantial contribution to the collection of monies to pay for a statue of McCarran in Statuary Hall in Congress, and the money was raised quickly by some of his rich friends in Reno, but she wanted my name on the list. She said, "Send me $75. I want your name on that list of people who remembered the senator." I always appreciated that.

Jack Sexton had been under McCarran's patronage before I went to Washington. In Lander County, he was district attorney, D. W. Priest was judge, and Francis Escobar was deputy sheriff.[10] Jack prosecuted some guy, and he was sentenced to thirty days in jail or something, but Jack would see him on the street in the daytime. It turned out Escobar would let him out and make him come in at night. Jack didn't think that was right, so there was a meeting in Priest's chambers. Jack wanted the judge to order Escobar to keep that guy in jail. He got into a discussion, and Jack invites Escobar outside to settle it. Escobar says, "I'm not a fighting man." Sexton says, "You ought to be, because you're an insulting son-of-a-bitch." With that, Jack cold-cocks the deputy sheriff—right in the judge's chambers.

We didn't have television, and we got our late news at night on the radio. We used to get KFI.[11] I'm listening, and it says, "High noon at Austin!" It describes the district attorney cold-cocking the sheriff in the judge's chamber. I thought that was funny as hell. I sent Jack a telegram offering to promote a fight on the Fourth of July with him and Taylor Wines in Elko. Jack called and told me what happened. We laughed about it, but Jack was arrested for assault and battery. The district judge in Humboldt County, Merwyn Brown, was assigned to hear the case. (The J.P. in Austin didn't want to hear it, so a district judge could be a magistrate.)

Jack's case was dismissed. In the meantime, Priest resigned, and Jack wanted to be appointed judge! Of course, he asked McCarran to help him. McCarran was willing to help. Although the Lander County courthouse was in Austin, Jack lived in Battle Mountain. Sara and I happened to be at Jack's house when he got a call from McCarran from Dayton, Nevada. He'd been in to talk to Russell about appointing Jack. He was scared to call him in Carson City—he thought all the phones were bugged—so, he'd gone out to Dayton to a pay-phone. He told Jack, "It's OK. Charlie's going to appoint you. There's only one thing. He's got to get the OK of the Woodburn firm." Again, even under those circumstances, McCarran went to bat for Sexton, and the governor appointed him district judge. That's another example of McCarran helping his boys.

It also was another example of the power of the Nevada old-boy network. It was near the end of the power of that group in Reno, which included the Woodburn law firm, then Woodburn and Foreman. (Originally, it was Thatcher and Woodburn. They represented George Wingfield.) Noble Getchell, who claimed residence in Lander because he owned the big mines, was a political power there. They had approval rights on almost anything. The only one who fought them was McCarran, and they wound up as friends toward the end, but he always ran against them. Most political officeholders, before they did anything of an essentially political nature, would check and get the OK.

Obviously, gambling was vital. It had been legalized in 1931, and if it had not been, God knows what would have happened to the state in the years following. If we lost gambling, people said, Virginia Street in Reno and

Fremont Street and the Strip would be a ghost town. Consequently, the industry had to be protected. McCarran recognized that. I think everybody agrees that without his service, in the time of the Kefauver hearings and the attempt to tax gambling, there might have been federal legislation.

That doesn't mean he liked gambling. He regarded it as a necessity, but it should not control the state. He recognized it, as most old-timers did, as a vice, and a regulated and controlled vice was better than an uncontrolled vice. He resented it, because he believed that because gambling was legal here, no political figure from Nevada could ever hold high national office—the rest of the country would not permit it, considering their attitude toward Nevada and gambling in those days. I think he resented that, because I think he realized, as many of his colleagues did, that he was a superior intellect and senator. Many of his colleagues would have been willing to support him for higher office. But it was never a possibility, because he came from Nevada. Whether he was correct, I don't know; but that *was* his view. At bottom, he believed in legal gambling in Nevada, that we had to keep it clean, we had to convince the rest of the country it was well-regulated and controlled, and we were a pioneer state—a frontier state—where gambling had always been present.

Also, if you examine his legislative career, he wasn't a right-winger or an ideological ogre on social legislation. He supported much of Roosevelt's social legislation. But he fought with Roosevelt. He was in his first term when a vacancy for U.S. attorney came up in Nevada. Under protocol, the senior senator of the president's party could make that appointment. Key Pittman was senior senator. Pittman made the recommendation. The president appointed. McCarran opposed confirmation on the Senate floor, and finally, as I understand it, he had to adopt the extreme statement that is part of the Senate's unquoted rules. The one circumstance in which the Senate would not confirm was if another senator in that state said the appointee was personally obnoxious to him. McCarran went to that length, the Senate didn't confirm, and McCarran won his fight against his bitter enemy, Pittman. Somebody else got appointed not personally objectionable to McCarran.[12]

So, among other things, he had a lot of courage. A junior senator is supposed to kind of listen and learn before he starts. In his first term, he became active in opposing the President's court-packing legislation.[13] He's back there locking horns with the best of them and *winning*. He was strong; he was smart, and he had the courage of his convictions. He suffered a lot of defeats when I was there on the floor of the Senate, but he carried on. He was a strong-willed man, an emotional man. I will always be grateful to him for everything he did for me, even when I had little contact with him after I came back to Nevada. All he required was that I be a Nevada boy.

The senator introduced two pieces of legislation with which he is most often associated, the Internal Security Act and the Immigration Act. I don't believe I formed any real opinion about either act. I did form an opinion about his committee and his friend Joe McCarthy. It was incredible to me that McCarthy could get away with destroying people's careers. I'd graduated from law school and had some idea of what due process meant. I could not believe the Senate would permit McCarthy to do the things he was doing.

The greatest social thing in Elko was a bridge party. Everybody played bridge. (The two worst bridge players in the history of Elko were Ralph and Sara Denton, and the worst was Ralph Denton.) You'd have these parties, and I would be incensed when support would be voiced for McCarthy: "Where there's smoke, there's fire."

Where's the evidence? Sara and I were disappointed. It seemed so clear that McCarthy's conduct was outrageous, and people didn't pay attention to what we had to say. [laughter] But people don't need evidence to form conclusions. I don't think the first ten amendments to the Constitution would pass if they were on the ballot today. Certainly, they didn't pay any attention to them in the McCarthy era. That was my first really deep feeling, and I made no friends as a result of that. I was shocked at how people in whom I did have great respect stood silent. Not only the papers in Elko . . . but few of them ever took him on. I was proud of Hank Greenspun when Hank took him on. Good friends decided I was a left-wing fanatic because I would complain about McCarthy. And few who supported him, after he was brought down, ever said they were sorry, that they were wrong.

I couldn't understand McCarran's position on this, because he was a fine lawyer. He had the group with him, like Jay Sourwine, Hal Lackey, the committee staffs, the Internal Security subcommittee, and the Immigration-Naturalization subcommittee. That's who he talked to. He never discussed anything with me. I was just a peasant. But I couldn't understand how a judge could ignore basic fundamentals of fairness.

McCarran opposed Adlai Stevenson. He never mentioned it when I was actively supporting Stevenson, making speeches. They had speeches in Elko, where Orville Wilson would speak for the Republicans, and I'd speak for the Democrats. Never did McCarran ever suggest that I adopt any kind of a political view or suggest that I should agree with his views.

When McCarran died, I was in Elko. I'm trying to remember how I heard, because the first thing I did was call Harvey Sewell. Although he lived in Reno, there was a branch of the bank and a Sewell's store in Elko, so he was in and out. We talked about it—we were shocked, because we'd just seen him. He'd been in Elko not long before. I don't remember what he was doing, but he seemed in good enough health, although I knew he had had a heart attack. I felt a personal loss. Harvey felt the loss of a dear friend. I wasn't at that point in my thinking about the senator that we were close friends. I regarded myself pretty much as what I was, I guess—a soldier.

I remember thinking, "What happens now?" On a weekend, I went to my office and got the statutes. I concluded the central committees of each party were going to have to nominate a candidate, whereas the papers up to that time said, because the primary had been held, Ernie Brown, whom Governor Russell had named to succeed the senator, would serve until 1956, rather than till this next general election in 1954. They went to the Nevada Supreme Court over that quickly. The court ruled they had to go on the ballot.

Meanwhile, Harvey and I took off on what the papers called the abortive mission to get Eva nominated. [laughter] The central committee had to have nominations thirty or forty days prior to the election in November. It had to be done in a hurry, and it was. I don't know whether Eva wanted to be a senator, but she never gave me hell for doing it. [laughter] I don't know if Harvey talked to her. I doubt he had. Harvey was old enough to be my father, but he was as naive as I was. Sure, we'll get the central committee guys signed up before anybody else knows about it, then call Eva and say, "By God, Eva, you're going to be senator if you want to be." [laughter]

We discovered by the time we got through Winnemucca that Bible's people had been to them long before we ever got to them. They were all committed to Bible. Then we went to Norman Biltz's house in Reno. Those guys, the power structure, were sitting around figuring they were going to get Bill Cashill the nomination. Cashill was a lawyer in Reno—old politically active family. I think he'd been assistant U.S. attorney, a successful lawyer in Reno and was part of that group.[14] He had a brother, Tom, who kicked a field goal in the 1930s for the University of Nevada, and they beat St. Mary's or Cal; I'm not sure, but Tom lived that kick until he died. He was a hero.

Harvey took great pleasure in telling Norman it was too late. "Norman, you guys don't have any idea what's going on. Bible's already got it, and you guys sitting here talking about it. He went out and got it." [laughter]

Biltz made some funny remark to Harvey. Harvey's hair was kind of red. He said, "Well, Red, what have you been doing?" There was a little banter, but that was all. They thought they could get the job done.

Cashill was sitting there, and Biltz, and Johnny Mueller, and I forget who else in that great power structure that thought they controlled everything. We have people like that in Nevada now, who sit around, pat each other on the back, and convince each other they know how to handle what's going on. They forget a couple million people out there aren't privy to their conversations. [laughter]

The Democrats nominated Bible, the Republicans nominated Brown. I knew Brown a little. He was a well-regarded attorney in Reno, out of Eureka or that area. Jack Sexton hated him and told me what a rotten, no-good son-of-a-bitch Brown was, because Brown was with a group trying to move the county seat from Austin to Battle Mountain. Jack was a district attorney, and they were in this litigation.

Years later, when Frank McNamee was appointed to the Supreme Court and ran for a term in his own right, Brown filed. After Sexton became judge and got down here, he and McNamee didn't get along. He called one time and asked me to support Brown against McNamee. [laughter] I said, "Jesus, Jack, I'd like to help you if I can, but I've never heard anything good about Ernie Brown. The only son-of-a-bitch that's ever told me anything about Brown is you, and you've told me what a dirty, no-good, untrustworthy so-and-so he is. And now you're asking me to support him for the supreme court? My goodness, Jack, I can't do that." [laughter] As far as I know, Brown was a fine man. And he lost to McNamee.[15]

Brown went back, was sworn in, and moved into the office. Eva told me he was awfully nice. Brown kept McCarran's staff, when Eva and the people were trying to wind up everything. I don't know if other senators have done it, but Eva went through the files and sent back every letter constituents had sent and every reply from the senator's office. I know my mother got back every letter they'd written McCarran over the years with copies of the replies. That took some doing. That was a nice gesture.

McCarran's death had the effect of snapping the connection between his boys. While the senator was alive, we were all unified in whatever political activities any of us went into or did. That unity didn't survive his death, because he was what tied us together politically. Once he was gone, the knot that tied us was gone. Many of us didn't share the same political philosophies, but most of us remained friends through the years.

Notes

1. George Smathers, a conservative Democrat, represented Florida in the Senate in the 1950s and 1960s.

2. George Rudiak was a Las Vegas attorney who, as an assemblyman, introduced civil rights legislation.

3. The El Cortez, opened in 1941 at 6th and Fremont in downtown Las Vegas, was run by longtime casino executive J. Kell Houssels. McCarran, among other Nevada politicians, often received a suite there for visits and campaigns. At one time, one of its owners was Bugsy Siegel.

4. Taylor Wines was a Democratic assemblyman from Elko County, 1945-47, and was appointed district judge for Elko County in 1947 and served until 1966, when he was defeated. He was appointed to district court in Clark County in 1969 and resigned the next year. He later was a member of Lionel Sawyer and Collins.

5. C. D. Baker served as a Democratic state senator from Clark County (1947-51) and mayor of Las Vegas (1951-59).

6. The Gaming Control Board was created in 1955. The Tax Commission continued to rule on license applications until a separate gaming commission was created in 1959.

7. Roger D. Foley was the oldest son of U.S. District Judge Roger T. Foley and succeeded his father on the bench, serving from 1962 to 1993. He was elected attorney general in 1958, the same year in which Grant Sawyer was elected governor.

8. In 1944, McCarran defeated Pittman, 11,152-9,911, amid rumors that McCarran supporters engaged in voter fraud.

9. George Norris, a renowned progressive reformer, represented Nebraska in the House, 1903-13, and the Senate, 1913-43. He was a Republican until 1936, when he was re-elected as an Independent Republican. He was defeated for re-election in 1942 by Republican Kenneth Wherry.

10. D. W. Priest was elected district judge for Eureka and Lander Counties in 1950 and served until he resigned in 1953.

11. KFI-AM-640 was one of the first radio stations in Los Angeles. As a 50,000-watt clear-channel station, it carried through much of the West.

12. William McKnight, state Democratic chairman, was Pittman's choice. When McCarran objected, he eventually forced the selection of E. P. Carville, later to serve as governor and U.S. senator, then to have a falling-out with McCarran.

13. In 1937, angry at a highly conservative Supreme Court's rulings against the New Deal and his inability to appoint a justice, President Franklin Roosevelt proposed a law to allow him to name a new justice for each of the six justices over the age of seventy. The plan was defeated, thanks in part to McCarran, whose re-election Roosevelt unsuccessfully tried to derail in 1938.

14. William J. Cashill also served one term as a Democratic assemblyman from Washoe County, 1941-42.

15. Frank McNamee, appointed to the Nevada Supreme Court on December 15, 1958, won a term in his own right in 1960, defeating Ernest Brown, 48,523-47,177.

10 | There Wasn't Much Crime in Elko

When the bar results were announced in May, 1951, Sara and I left Carson City and went to Caliente to see my mom and dad and tell them I passed. My dad was prospecting. I drove to the mine, way up the side of Irish Mountain, to tell him. He was so happy. We stayed one day, went to Elko, arrived on June 7, ready to go to work doing whatever I was supposed to do. I assumed I would be prosecuting criminal cases, but I had little knowledge of county government. I had to start familiarizing myself with Nevada statutes and procedures.

We had an awful time finding a place to live. We stayed with Grant and Bette before we found a little apartment over Wally White's Furniture Store on Idaho. It was more like a loft, and a neon sign for the store right out our front window flickered on and off all night long. The city hall was across Idaho Street and over a block. They had this big siren that went off whenever there was a fire or something. In the middle of the night, we heard that thing go off, and it was just like it was right in our bedroom. Scared us both to death. But it was close to the courthouse. [laughter]

We didn't know anybody in Elko other than Grant and Bette, and Sara was pregnant with Mark. But Elko's a great town, and we got meeting people right away, found a house on Juniper to rent, and got in before Mark was born. We were happy in Elko all the time we lived there.

My work wasn't difficult. There wasn't much serious crime. [laughter] Grant was there if I had questions. Justice court was in the basement of the courthouse. The justice of the peace, George Boucher, also the coroner, was all stooped over with rheumatoid arthritis. I tried misdemeanor cases and preliminary hearings before him. To this day, I would say Boucher was as fine a judge as I've seen, and he was a lay person, as fair and decent a man as I ever knew. Then I got to know the sheriff, Jess Harris. I worked with Jess a lot. Jess was an old-timer, and indeed a legend.

I had less to do with the Elko police than with the sheriff's office. Jess only had one deputy. You had police departments in each city: Elko, Wells,

118

*There
Wasn't
Much
Crime
in
Elko*

and Carlin. Jess was responsible for the rest of the county. In most of those areas, there would be a constable. Jess, I thought, felt fortunate he didn't have a bunch of deputy sheriffs to worry about. As a result, Jess was like horse manure: he was all over the county all the time. Many times, I was with him. If a felony came up, for example, in Wells, Jess would go, and I would go with him if there was a death or something of that kind.

That winter, we got a call that one of the old-timers in Midas, in northwest Elko County, had died. Ordinarily, Jess would have taken George and had an inquest, then brought the body to wherever it was to go. This time, it was cold, and George wasn't physically able to take a trip over dirt roads through snow to Midas. So, he made me a deputy coroner. Jess and I took off down the highway to Reno, turned north at Golconda, and spent hours getting to Midas. I had an inquest and ruled his cause of death was natural causes. Then we put the body in the back seat, and Jess and I drove to Winnemucca, where there was the closest mortuary, the Halley Eddy Mortuary, and delivered the body. It was snow in that country, and dirt roads. We didn't get to Winnemucca till after midnight, and we had left Elko at six-thirty or seven in the morning. It's not far, but we were fighting snow and getting stuck all that time. That was part of being a sheriff in a big county. Jess never bitched about it, and I kept asking him what I was doing there. [laughter]

But I didn't bitch either; that was part of the job. Truthfully, I enjoyed my work every minute I was in that district attorney's office. I enjoyed the people I was working with. I enjoyed working with Grant, who helped me a great deal and overlooked my impulsiveness. One time, when he and the sheriff were out of town, the deputy sheriff and I yanked the license on a bar outside of town for serving liquor to minors. We didn't realize until the district attorney and sheriff got back that maybe we shouldn't have done that. That was a very responsible person in Elko who had that license. We had a hearing before the commission. They restored his license. [laughter]

Jess was remarkable. Jess was an Elko County boy. I think Jess's father had been sheriff before him. Jess had gone to California in the 1930s, maybe before, and I think was a city motorcycle policeman in Burbank. Jess learned to fly in the late 1930s, and, I think, even became a test pilot for Lockheed. After the war, he came back to Elko. He flew a lot. Once, he was flying a prisoner to the state penitentiary, there was a weather problem, and he had to land. The plane turned over, and he was injured. Had it not been for that prisoner, Jess probably would have died. That prisoner stayed with Jess until help got there. I think Jess died soon after that. But here's this man—in his seventies at that time—flying an airplane, himself, with a prisoner he's taking to the state penitentiary sitting next to him.

Jess used to scare the hell out of me driving a car. He was fearless. In the wintertime, with the highway a sheet of ice, we had to go to Wells. Jess is driving; we'd be going down that sheet of ice at seventy-five miles an hour. There's a story—I don't know if it's true—in a small airplane, he flew through one of the railroad tunnels. The railroad comes down to Carlin Canyon, and Jess in this plane just swoosh, flew right through that tunnel. [laughter]

He was a dead square honest, kind man. The thought that Jess would ever abuse or take advantage of a prisoner or anybody would never enter your mind. He would walk into situations—drunks, guys with guns—and just take them. "Come on, give me your gun . . ." wouldn't even pull his. He was an old-time lawman. I enjoyed that, because my dad had been undersheriff of Lincoln County. My dad knew Jess, and they were the same type; they liked each other.

I got to meet Bob Stenovich, the Western Pacific Railroad policeman. They called those guys railroad bulls. I might have prosecuted people where Bob initiated the arrest, but Bob was a law officer and cooperated. They worked together—Jess, Bob, Dick Lubben, the FBI agent, Pinky Smithers was a highway patrolman, and game wardens.

One game warden, Dudley, arrested his brother, for God's sake! You're supposed to put a tag on a deer when you kill it. The brother said, "I just got here. I haven't had time to put the tag on." He arrested him anyway, and I had to prosecute him. That became a cause célèbre. It was one I lost that I wasn't so sad about. He was acquitted. You had fish and game violations all over the county. Very seldom did they get involved in court, but if Dudley was around, they did. [laughter]

We got a call from the justice of the peace up in Jarbidge. A guy had been arrested for fishing without a license. The warden hauled him into court and got a complaint against him. The Jarbidge river comes right down that canyon; it's close to the Idaho line; the guy had an Idaho fishing license; he thought he was in Idaho. The game warden said he was in Nevada. He put up a $75 cash bond, and the judge released him and set a trial date.

There was a bar in Jarbidge where the court was—the judge was the owner and bartender. I get a call telling me I have this case. Jarbidge is in the northern part of the county—it's beautiful. I'd never been there, so I was glad to have a chance to go. So few people, particularly in the southern part of the state, have been in that part of Nevada—Mountain City, near the Idaho border, the Owyhee Indian reservation, an old mining and ranch town. When you go to Mountain City even today, you think you're stepping back to the Wild West.

Grant said he'd like to go. He hadn't been there since he ran. Grant and I leave the county seat and go to this bar. The judge is there, we're early, and we're waiting for the defendant, so we buy a drink, as you're supposed to do in a Nevada bar. You buy one for the judge, too; it's his bar. The first thing you know, several people are around. Grant, a big district attorney, having recently gotten their votes, buys everybody a drink. The defendant doesn't show up. We continue until a sum equal to the amount of his bail—$75— was spent on drinks. Then Grant and I went back to Elko. That's the last we ever heard of the case. [laughter]

120

*There
Wasn't
Much
Crime
in
Elko*

I met an awful lot of nice Indian people in Elko. An Indian hung around the streets, kind of the town character. They called him Skeezix. It was against the law to sell liquor to Indians. Skeezix used to hang around the bar at the Commercial Hotel. He knew a couple of the bartenders, and they were friends. He'd just sit and talk to them. During the Korean War, in comes this soldier dressed in a United States Army uniform. He comes up to the bar, he orders a drink, and the bartender says, "I can't serve you."

The soldier says, "Why not?"

The bartender says, "Because you're an Indian."

The soldier says, "I'm not an Indian, I'm a Hawaiian."

Skeezix says, "If he's a Hawaiian, I'm a Mormon cricket. Give me a drink, too!"

I was upset about the treatment of Indians at the Owyhee reservation, but I didn't have any idea what to do about it. I made a speech to the Rotary Club up there, without knowledge and nothing more than a desire to right a wrong I had no clear idea how to right. I suggested complete emancipation. Get rid of the Bureau of Indian Affairs, let them take title to the land allotted by the tribal council, give them a chance to sink or swim on their own, because it was a heartbreaking situation. I'm ashamed to say I thought I knew all the answers. Of course, I didn't. But how many people think?

When we moved to Las Vegas, we brought a young Indian girl with us. I thought it would be helpful to her and us. When we moved, Mark was four and Sally was two. I thought if she lived with us, she could go to school and help Sara take care of the house and the kids. But she was so lonesome. She missed her friends, her family. I don't think, growing up in Nevada, I had any concept that Indian families had a heritage, a structure, like everybody else. It didn't work. I brought her to an alien society where she didn't know anybody and would stand out like a sore thumb if she went to school. She stayed a couple of months and said she would like to go back. I arranged to take her back. I just jumped to conclusions about how to solve what obviously was, I thought, a great human problem, and that therefore, there was a way for us to solve it. I, of course, would lead the way. [laughter] Which I didn't do.

There wasn't much crime in Elko. The court was busy on petty misdemeanors, and we had a few felonies. One of the first felony cases I had to prosecute was a case in which a guy came into town, hung around, and forged a man's name for a check, Bernadotte. He misspelled Bernadotte by leaving out one of the "t"s. The bank cashed the check. When Bernadotte saw it come through, it was an obvious forgery. He came to the district attorney's office, and we pursued a complaint. It was large enough to be a felony.

It's my first jury criminal trial. I'm handling it fine. We got the jury selected. I have Bernadotte on the stand identifying the check. The attorney objected to the introduction of the check into evidence; the information alleged the check had been drawn on Bernadotte, as listed. We looked at the check. It was only one "t." Therefore, it was not the same—ridiculous! The attorney called forth the great legal doctrine of *idem sonans*, one I'd never heard of and haven't heard of since. We made a little bit of argument.

Judge Wines—that was after the 1952 election, when I had backed Malone—said he wants both attorneys in chambers. The first thing his honor said, before any argument, "Ralph, it looks like he's got you." [laughter] It was regarded as getting *me* rather than doing what should have been done, no matter what I said about getting the information amended. Obviously, the pronunciation's the same. I felt like an absolute fool and worried about the effect it would have on Grant, because here's one of the first felony cases we'd had since I'd been there, and I blew it completely. With his usual class, Grant just told me not to worry about it; it didn't make any difference. [laughter] That made me a little gun-shy.

I'd been trying cases before Judge Wines before November, 1952 and hadn't had any problems; but after that, I had considerable problems. It was not *the* reason, but one of the reasons I left Elko and came to Las Vegas: if you practice law in a community where there's only one judge, that judge can have a great effect upon your life, your success, your reputation. Judge Wines took his job seriously. I heard him pronounce many wise, compassionate things from the bench—particularly as juvenile judge. In many respects, Taylor Wines was a fine man and judge, but . . . .

You've heard Nevada referred to as the Mississippi of the West—that was true of Elko. When buses came through and black people got off, they wouldn't be permitted in the hotels and restaurants. They could go in, order something, take it outside, and eat on the curb.

Only two black people lived in Elko. Sam Herron had a bar and restaurant across the tracks, a couple of doors from the Star Hotel, around the corner from the whorehouses. It was kind of a skid-row place. Another black, Earl Dunlap, worked for the Railway Express Agency. Even though he lived there, he couldn't go in the Commercial or the Stockmen's, but he could go to Herron's place. He's there having lunch, and a couple of guys get in a beef. One of them pulls a gun and shoots the other guy. (Believe it or not, he shot him in the head, and the guy lived! I learned a lesson there.)

Grant and I prosecuted the guy who did the shooting. I'm having Earl describe how he was sitting at the counter and could see the whole thing. I said, "And now, at the time the shot was fired, Mr. Dunlap, what were you doing?"

Earl said, "Man, I was sitting there wishing I was elsewhere." [laughter] The guy was convicted.

I don't regret one minute I was in the district attorney's office with Grant. I got to meet the county officers, all interesting and bright, or they couldn't

122

*There
Wasn't
Much
Crime
in
Elko*

have gotten elected in a small community where you know everybody. The judge, for example: if he left the office early, and some citizen saw him on the street during working hours, they'd complain. In those small towns, they know what their officeholders are doing, and they're not afraid of them.

Grant and I stayed close, but to a certain extent, we went down different paths. I don't want this misinterpreted—we developed a different group of friends than Grant and Bette's, although they were our friends too. We just had some different interests. My interests didn't include bridge. [laughter] Neither did Sara's. As a matter of fact, we were terrified of the game.

You would have parties at somebody's house, and it was always a bridge party. Sara and I couldn't play, and I lacked the capacity to learn! Grant and Bette were excellent players, as were their friends: the McMullens, Stenoviches, Wunderlichs, Gartezes. They would invite us, and we'd play. I'd go home thinking I was an absolute dunce. Sara sometimes would go home with tears in her eyes. That bridge group didn't take the game very seriously, but there were groups that would scare you to death! The judge's was one.

Judge Wines and his wife Barbara were excellent players. They would have a bridge party, and I'd screw up everybody's game. I didn't know how to bid and had no interest. I suppose I'm one of those guys who doesn't have good card sense. Later, I got so I enjoyed bridge if the pressure was off.

Some of the other group were not bridge players. My friend Tom Gallagher, as far as I know, never played bridge in his life, but he was a great hunter and fisherman. I didn't particularly enjoy that, but I enjoyed going in the hills, and we camped a lot. Sara and Dorothy became good friends and belonged to this women's club in Elko, like the service league here.[1] It started out as one of these sororities, then they decided, "Why are we sending in dues?" They dropped out and formed their own club.

There was never any diminution of my friendship with Grant, although we did, to a certain extent, run in separate circles. Ran together a lot, too. Grant and I and Sara and Bette used to have a lot of fun together—the four of us. Grant and I might leave the office at five or six and pick up our mail at the post office box. Just coincidentally, the Stockmen's was right across from the post office. Sometimes Grant and I would stop in there to visit with the boys and have a drink. Time just flew. The next thing we knew . . . . [laughter] Sara and Bette would be there to let us know they didn't appreciate our doing that. Didn't happen often, particularly after Mark was born. (Little Gail was older than Mark. What a little doll she was—and is!)

During your life you have a close friend, and maybe you don't see him for a long time. Then you get together—it's just like you were never apart. That's the way it was. This would be particularly true after I went into Jack Robbins's office. I wasn't seeing Grant every day. It didn't make any difference. Grant and I could have been apart ten years, then run into each other, and it would be like we'd never been apart.

Under Grant's tutelage, I became active in darn near everything. I became a member of the Lion's Club, the Junior Chamber of Commerce, the Elks Club, the Toastmasters. I remember I was chairman of the Right-on Red Cross Fund drive, the Cancer Fund drive, the Heart Fund drive. In writing letters to all of the people in the county seeking contributions, I got to know the names of people and where they lived, and the names of little towns, valleys, little settlements like Starr Valley that I'd never heard of before I went to Elko.

I was invited to give the graduation speech at the school at Montello, on the Southern Pacific

Grant and Bette Sawyer, Sara and Ralph: "We'd have a lot of fun together."

right-of-way going across northern Elko county. It is desert country, and it took me a long time to get there. Sara went with me, and we got there in time for the ceremony. I was on stage, Sara was in the audience, and I made a speech. After it was over, Sara said two ladies sitting behind her wanted to know, "Who's that kid?" They didn't know who the heck I was, just some kid they didn't know. But you could take part in almost anything as far as your interests and your energy would take you. You were welcomed.

That does not mean you were welcomed into the old structured Elko society automatically. It took a while before old timers started including us in social affairs like weddings. Once they opened their heart to you, though, you felt like you'd been there forever. I suppose we had the same thing in Caliente with old-time families there since the turn of the century.

When I started as deputy district attorney, I didn't have a salary. Grant was throwing cases to me if he could, and paying me, but I was having a hard time. Roger Foley was district attorney in Clark County and was going to hire another deputy. He only had two, John Mowbray and George Dickerson.[2] Roger offered me a job. I took off for Las Vegas. I met with Roger, accepted the job, moved into a little office all in one day, and started on a case.

And I got to thinking, "What I'm doing is running. I haven't given either me or Elko a chance. I'm not going to leave until I have been a success, if then. But I'm not going to just put my tail between my legs and run." I was looking for the easy out, where there was a bigger salary, and coming up with reasons to justify why I was doing it and ignoring the real reason: it didn't look to me like I was making it. I called Sara and discussed it with her, and I said, "I'll be home tonight." I went in and told Roger. I left. That's when Johnny Mendoza took that third deputy spot.[3]

124

*There
Wasn't
Much
Crime
in
Elko*

I went back to Elko. Not that the people in Elko knew what I had done, but soon after I got back, people seemed to open up. My practice got better. I got to know Harvey Sewell and some of the businessmen, and Harvey loaned me some money. There were old-time families since the 1800s—ranch families, all so nice—in Ruby Valley and Clover Valley up in the Independence Mountain area.

The Palm Saloon played a significant role in Elko. (But I don't want you to think I was hanging around saloons all the time.) The Palm Saloon was run by a Basque, Pete Brust. Underneath the sign, "A Gentleman's Resort," it was a typical old Nevada bar in a storefront building, with a bar on one side and a card room in the back. They wouldn't let women in. They didn't want to serve anybody if they didn't know them well. All the old-timers and ranchers, when they were in town, about five o'clock, they'd all be at the Palm. I went, oh, once a week just to see the old-timers. It was a riot every time you would go there.

You couldn't go in the Palm and come out sober, because if there were fourteen people at that bar, you were going to have fourteen drinks. Everybody bought a drink for the house. You knew your turn would come. I would try and buy my round early, so I could get out. [laughter] I really felt good when they accepted me there. Strangers come in and sit at the bar, and Pete wouldn't serve them. He was too busy serving the old-timers. It's no longer there.

Allegiances to friends, associates, and relatives over all those years mean something. You don't cut into that right away. The elite of Elko were ranch families—nice people like the Glaser family; Norm Glaser was a state senator from Elko.[4] The Weeks and Bradish families in Clover Valley, the Gardners, the Vaughan, Smith, and Wines families in Ruby Valley; Gene Segerblom was a Wines, and her aunt Lorinda Wines still runs that ranch. What a woman! She's run that ranch with her sons since her husband died, she's been president of the national cowboy organization, and she still raises a lot of beef cows.

Some of the big ranches—like the Seventy-One; I think it was the Seventy-One—were owned by out-of-state companies. The Horseshoe ranch at Beowawe was owned by Dean Witter. Bing Crosby owned the ranch on the North Fork. Joel McCrea owned a ranch in Clover Valley. Another old western star owned this ranch, I think, got in trouble with it, and his friend McCrea bailed him out. That was after I left, but everybody told me what a wonderful man he was.

The business community, all old families: Warren, Ogilvie, Pearce, the old Hesson Hardware Company, Reinhart. Milton Reinhart was a lawyer, but his family had been merchants in Nevada at the turn of the century. There's a big Reinhart store in Elko, had been one in Winnemucca. Milton

Reinhart was as fine a man as I ever knew—a gentleman in every sense. George and Eva Ogilvie were old-time, George from an Elko ranch family. She and George met at the University of Nevada, or she came to Elko to teach school. George was county commissioner—active in politics, served on state boards, had run for Congress in the 1940s.[5] They became dear friends. They were an absolute blast. They were *just fun*. Eva was the cutest little lady I ever knew. She could tell the cutest jokes, and she laughed—great senses of humor, both of them.

Dorothy Gallagher's mother was a Short. They were pioneer ranchers in Ruby, I think. Tom Gallagher's mother was a Gedeny, and they were ranchers. The early Gedeny family had known the early Short family. These ties go back. Morris Gallagher, Tom's brother, was one of our dear friends. Chris Sheerin, one of the owners and editor of the *Elko Daily Free Press*—an old-time family. I think Chris was born in Virginia City and graduated from the University of Nevada in Reno. Snowy Monroe—not an oldtime Elko family—had been in Nevada for many years, and his wife was a Winnemucca woman, an old family.

It was just solid permanence. Most lawyers who came to practice law came from one of those families. Grant and I were about the only two who didn't have family in Elko before we came to practice. It was a stable community economically, and progressive. These old families sent their kids away, many to the University of Nevada in Reno, many to Stanford and eastern schools. They came back and brought with them a degree of sophistication you wouldn't expect in cow country. Tom and Morris Gallagher's mother went to finishing school in Chevy Chase, Maryland, I think because her family were friends of Senator Newlands, a developer of Chevy Chase. I think her father was sent to the University of Michigan to law school and became a judge. The kids came home because of the depth of their heritage. With most small towns—and Elko was a lot smaller when I lived there than it is now—if the kids go away, they never come back. The brain drain, so to speak. Elko kids came back in many instances and became ranchers, carrying on the family operation.

My dad told me when I went to Elko, "You call on every lawyer in town and introduce yourself," or I probably wouldn't have thought of doing that, but I did. When I was there, counting the judge, there were sixteen lawyers. Orville Wilson was one of the leaders of the bar, also the Republican Party, highly regarded, well deserved his reputation. There was Milton Reinhart. Another attorney, George Wright, later became a judge.[6] He ultimately defeated Wines. Joe McNamara could have been considered—when he was alive—the leading criminal lawyer, not only in Elko County but maybe around the state.

It was a wonderful place to practice law. As you might suspect, there were probably a few petty jealousies, but it was never mean-spirited in the courtroom or negotiations. All of them helped me when I first came there to get started by giving me powers of attorney, loaning me files. All the lawyers

126

*There
Wasn't
Much
Crime
in
Elko*

tried to help each other then, but that's not the case any more . . . certainly not around here.

Every lawyer I went to encouraged me, told me what a fine community Elko was, "Yes, you'll be able to make a living here; there's plenty of room, and we'll help you any way we can," except one—George Wright: "Oh, we got too many lawyers now. You shouldn't come here." George is the only lawyer I ever saw that used to charge his clients an extra fifty cents for notarizing their signature on a divorce complaint. [laughter] George and I later became friends.

The local priest at the time, Monsignor William J. Devlin, one of the old Irish priests, was a grand man. I got to know him through the Gallaghers and started going to his rectory at St. Joseph's one night a week for him to educate me on Christianity. I thought, "I've got a family coming along. I'd better learn something." Sara would go with me; she did have a fairly good religious education. After I moved to Las Vegas, Monsignor Devlin was transferred, became pastor of St. Joan of Arc's, and we renewed our friendship. Through him, I got to meet that group of delightful priests who pioneered this diocese: Monsignor Peter Moran, Father Hugh Smith, Monsignor John Ryan, Father Vanning. Those men enriched my life just sitting around having lunch together—not a religious education, just listening to them. I consider my association with those men among the most interesting I've had.

There was as much to do in Elko as in Las Vegas—many civic groups, lodges, and charitable organizations. You could be busy every night of your life if you wanted to. And it was hard not to, because you couldn't be anonymous. It would be fun, taking a trip—maybe the road company of a Broadway show at the Capital Theater in Salt Lake City. Tom and Dorothy Gallagher and Sara and I went there to see "The King and I," the original cast, including Yul Brynner. Sometimes you'd go to Reno. There might be something at the university.

Reno is the economic center of that whole eastern slope of the Sierras and the Humboldt River. Elko, Winnemucca, Lovelock—that whole area funnels into Reno. A lot of people in Elko had come from Reno. Maybe young women married Elko men they met at the university, or came to teach school. There was a lot of social and professional relationship between Elko and Reno. The tradition in Reno had been—and I suppose still is—that people go to San Francisco for a long weekend. That was true in Elko. In the old days, they would take the train. Later on, they'd fly and drive. Sara and I would go to San Francisco once in a while, and Lake Tahoe. Oh, how beautiful it is!

Boy, you can be as busy in a small town as you want to be. In the hotels, you had shows. Big-name entertainment didn't start in Las Vegas; it started in Elko. When we lived there, Rowan and Martin used to play Elko regularly before they became big stars with *Laugh-In*. Tennessee Ernie Ford, Sophie Tucker, and Joe E. Lewis used to appear regularly. Tommy and Jimmy Dorsey appeared when we were there. You can just go on and on. You didn't have shows every night, but always during the holidays and fair time. I remember seeing Burl Ives and a musical group called the Weavers. Pete Seeger was one of the Weavers. I'm not sure whether Newt Crumley or Red Ellis canceled their engagement because Seeger was a communist.[7] I think everybody in town except Grant, Bette, Sara, and I believed that they did exactly right. [laughter]

Notes

1. Dorothy Gallagher was elected to the Board of Regents in 1980 and was still on the board at this writing.

2. John Mowbray later served as a Clark County district judge (1959-67) and as a Nevada Supreme Court justice (1967-93). The son of Acting Governor Denver Dickerson and brother of three-term Attorney General Harvey Dickerson, George Dickerson later served as Clark County district attorney and Gaming Commission chairman, and is a distinguished longtime Las Vegas attorney.

3. John Mendoza served as Clark County district attorney, a district court judge (1967-91), and chairman of the Nevada Public Service (now Utilities) Commission.

4. Democrat Norm Glaser represented Elko in the Assembly (1961-72) and State Senate (1977-84).

5. George F. Ogilvie was defeated in the 1946 Democratic congressional primary, 11,254-8,892, by Malcolm McEachin, who went on to lose in the general election to Charles Russell.

6. George F. Wright served one term as judge, 1967-70.

7. Newt Crumley was a Republican state senator (1955-58). He served as a university regent from 1950 to 1955, and was a supporter of President Minard Stout's repressive policies toward academic freedom, which included dismissing professors whom he considered critical of the administration. In 1958, Crumley was returned to the Board of Regents, and served one term.

11 | We Were Liberal Democrats

There was no rub that we were liberal Democrats in a conservative area, but Grant was always smarter than I am. Grant was smart enough to keep his mouth shut. I don't mean he lacked the courage of his convictions; he was just smart enough to know you couldn't change others'. I wasn't. I would take them on in parties where McCarthy would come up. I couldn't believe it. I got the reputation of being . . . well, in those days a liberal wasn't that bad.

The two words, 'conservative' and 'liberal,' have taken on new meaning, if anybody knows what either means. Many people think they do. Extreme reactionaries believe liberal is a terrible word, an obscene word to them. And the word conservative is a very complimentary term. I suspect most of them don't know the meaning of either one. They were allowed to become catch words in our political process, just like communist was a catch word. You accuse somebody of being a communist, that's the end of his career. Just accusing! Accuse somebody of being a liberal, it's almost that bad now.

Grant was district attorney, elected by the people in the county. If I was embarrassing him, he never said so. When we would have discussions about issues, Grant never tried to influence what I did. Like that letter I wrote to Tom Mechling. God Almighty! I signed it Ralph Denton, Deputy District Attorney, Elko County, Nevada. That's the way all my letters were going out. That could have been embarrassing to Grant. Under today's standards, I guess, if anybody in public office wrote a political letter on official stationery, oh my God, all sorts of terrible things would happen!

A good example: Right to Work was a hot issue. The people of Elko County were certainly for it. As far as most of them were concerned, labor leaders were communists. Walter Reuther, my God, what a communist! The longshoreman in San Francisco, Harry Bridges, was the best example.[1] The sentiment was obvious. Some in Elko—mostly people who worked on the railroad—opposed the bill. I made speeches against the bill—not only in

Elko, but in Winnemucca, other places. That didn't endear me. That added to the belief I was some radical liberal. It didn't affect personal relations in Elko when I lived there, but it had an effect in 1964 when I ran for Congress. A lot of those people I considered my best friends didn't vote for me when they had a chance. They wouldn't admit it, but all you have to do is look at Elko County returns. [laughter] It hurt my feelings, because I always believed reasonable people can differ. Just because you and I might differ on an issue doesn't mean that I wouldn't vote for you, my friend, if you were running for something.

The first time I was invited to speak before the Elko Rotary Club, I spoke on controlling the gambling industry. I said gambling was important to the state. We had to protect it. The best way was to have strict control, or we ran the risk of the government taxing gambling out of existence, or the people voting it out. I'd probably been in Elko only a year and was young. I don't think I knew much about anything, particularly gaming control, except that had been the real thrust of the 1952 senatorial election and, before that, the era of the Kefauver committee, when everybody thought, "Boy, we're going to have to do something here, or we're going to lose gambling." That became a major issue, so I was probably just parroting what I'd heard.

Benny Binion had a couple of murders on his record in Texas, and his gambling license was controversial. State Senator Edgar Nores from Lincoln County owned the *Pioche Record*. Edgar had run for various offices and was a strong supporter of McCarran's. They had a meeting of the tax commission—the first time they met in Las Vegas. (They ordinarily met at the capitol.) Binion's license was on the agenda. Nores drove to Las Vegas and testified as a character witness for him; then he drove back in a new Hudson Eight automobile. Everybody in Pioche called it the Binion Eight. [laughter]

That license shocked a lot of people, although there were people in Elko supportive of the Binion license—namely, Doby Doc and Delpha Jewell. Doby Doc had moved to Las Vegas and brought all that stuff from Elko and installed it next to the old Last Frontier. Doby had a lot of friends back in Elko. Delpha Jewell, an insurance agent in Elko, was a close friend of Doc's, and Doc was a close friend of Binion's.

The Elko Free Press wrote about me a few times. The Steninger family and Chris Sheerin owned it. My recollection is that Chris ran the paper, and Steninger ran the mechanical aspect—the printing. I don't recall knowing him or him taking an active part in editorial policy. One of the reporters when I was there was Gene Evans. Gene played football at UNR and graduated in journalism, then worked for the *Free Press* as a reporter and covered the town well. He represented Elko County in the legislature, and later moved to Reno and does work in P.R.[2] Chris would hate, I think, to write anything bad about somebody. I don't remember Chris being that active in politics. I feel certain he must have been a McCarran supporter. Wasn't everybody? [laughter]

Warren "Snowy" Monroe, on the other hand, was very active in party things.[3] Snowy ran the *Elko Independent*, a weekly. He wrote a column, "Hot Copy." Where Chris sort of stayed out of controversy at the *Free Press*, Snowy was in the middle of it all the time. Snowy represented Elko in the state senate after Newt Crumley's death. Snowy had a great sense of humor. His one crusade—I'm sure there were several—Snowy just could not understand why they felt it necessary to put a speed limit on Nevada highways. He'd hunker down that road about as fast as that car would go. Snowy once bragged he drove a car so fast between Elko and Carson City, he beat an airplane making the same trip. I can believe that. [laughter] He was a strong and effective supporter and adviser to Grant.

Snowy also was on the first Nevada fish and game commission. Snowy was a very avid sportsman. He used to hunt ducks and geese, did a lot of fishing, and took a proprietary interest in the hatchery in Ruby Valley— tried to make sure it was properly funded and maintained, although a story going around Elko one time was that even while he was on the fish and game commission, he got caught fishing in one of the breeding ponds, illegally. [laughter]

During fair time or the Silver State Stampede, Snowy put out a paper called the *Bull Sheet*, filled with the funniest stories about local people. I wished I'd saved them. Howard Eppling owned the pharmacy at Dupont Drug. The *Bull Sheet* had a headline, "Howard Eppling Has Popcorn Balls." [laughter] I think Howard thought it was funny. It got his name in the paper.

Paul Leonard was manager of the Stockmen's when Red Ellis had it. Before that, Paul worked on the Ely papers. Later, he moved back to Reno and went to work for the *Nevada State Journal*, had a distinguished career, and was its editor before he retired. If you were in Elko a while and active, you met everybody in different clubs and organizations. If you went to the Stockmen's, you were going to see Paul. If you belonged to a service club, you're going to see him. I don't remember Paul being active in politics, but I'm sure he was, like everybody in a small town. He was public-spirited, which meant he was involved in almost everything.

M. E. "Ted" McCuistion was a Democrat. I can't remember the names of all the brothers. Ted, Burt, and one other brother had the Texaco station. Ted had the garbage franchise in the city. I think the family was from Montello. His wife Florine had been Bunker's administrative assistant in the Senate. Florine's first husband, Billy Mayer, was a deputy mine inspector back in the thirties and was killed in a cave-in or disaster, leaving Florine a young widow. (Mayer's sister Alice was right-hand person to Governor Carville and perhaps Governor Pittman. She's still alive, in Reno.) Ted and

Florine and Sara and I became friends, and that friendship ripened after we moved to Las Vegas, because they moved to Las Vegas. Ted was a real estate broker here until his death.

I didn't fully comprehend how deep the animosity was between Carville people and McCarran people. In 1953, Democrats had a majority in the assembly. My mother was in that session. The caucus designated Jimmy Ryan to be speaker. Some Democrats wanted McCuistion, joined with the Republicans, and Ted was elected speaker, rather than the one who'd received the majority vote of the caucus.[4] My mother stayed with the party and voted for Ryan. I think Ted understood. It didn't affect our friendship. If it didn't make it clear to everybody who knew the situation, it sure as hell made clear to Ted that there was no way my mother was going to let *me* tell her what to do, so, I never tried. [laughter]

If I had to go to Carson or Reno on business, I'd go see Mom and try to get her home to Elko with us on weekends. Mom pretty much marched to her own drummer. Her interests were in education, libraries, and things of that kind. I remember discussing with Mom what is now UNLV and Mom's commitment to try to get a university in southern Nevada, and talking to her about forming consolidated school districts; she believed in and worked for that. She wanted to see financing for schools changed from just school district property taxes. I remember the phrase I heard her use many times: a kid in Eureka is just as entitled to a good education as a kid living in Reno or Las Vegas. She was interested in state parks and got three designated in Lincoln County: Beaver Dam, Kershaw-Ryan, and Eagle Valley.

When Jack Robbins died, Ted McCuistion ran for the state senate. His opponent, Newt Crumley, was a nice man, well-known in the community. Newt had been a general in the Army Air Corps, an airplane driver. He owned the Commercial Hotel. He built the Ranch Inn. The family owned ranches. Newt was raised in Elko County, and had gone through the University of Nevada. Everybody knew Newt was a class act. The worst you could say was: he was a Republican. He ran for the senate. Newt won big, but I always thought it was a close election in everybody's mind. I think people struggled as to which one of these nice men to vote for. The returns indicate everybody decided at the last minute to vote for Newt. As I recall, you couldn't get people to say who they were going to vote for. It was a vigorous campaign, and Newt won. I made a few talks for Democratic rallies, for Ted, but I always regarded Newt as a friend.

A lot of Elko people got involved in politics. Harold Anderson represented Elko in the Assembly for two terms (1949-53). He owned an equipment company or worked for one. Harold was active in the Mormon church and the community—later moved to Las Vegas and was in business for a long time. I don't remember Harold being active in party organization. J. F. McElroy was a loyal Democrat.[5] Fred worked for the railroad company, was attuned to the labor movement and well-liked—he and his wife Pearl. Pete Walters was first-class in every respect, an insurance man, had worked in Reno and been a desk clerk at the old Golden Hotel, an old-time Nevada guy.[6] Pete and his wife Connie were popular. When Bible was in the Senate, I think Pete was made head of the FHA in Nevada. Then Grant appointed him to the gaming commission. Pete was a Republican. I think, when he retired, he moved out to Fallon until he died.

Johnny Oldham, who was in the Assembly, was a cattleman, had a ranch in Elko County up on the North Fork. I didn't know Johnny well. About the only time I saw Johnny was in the Palm Saloon. He was a devout Carville man, and one of the Democrats in 1962 that joined to help defeat Bunker for lieutenant governor and supported Paul Laxalt.[7]

Doug Castle was another Republican assemblyman from Elko (1953-55) and an attorney. His father had been an attorney before him, H. U. Castle. When I first went to Elko, it was Castle and Puccinelli—Leo Puccinelli.

Jack Hunter came from an old business family. They had the Hunter Theater and the Rainbow Theater. I think his father had had other businesses in town. Jack grew up there. He and his wife Jean were active in the Democratic party.[8] Jean became national committeewoman, if my memory serves me. Jack's father, maybe even his grandfather, had been in the retail business in Elko.

I didn't know Hugh McMullen well. The McMullens were an old time northern Nevada family. Sam McMullen was a CPA in Elko. Hugh, I think, was also a CPA, maybe in Reno. He recently died. Bob Vaughan, a Republican, came to practice law after I did. He was raised in Ruby Valley, I think—a pioneer ranch family. Bob's still practicing in Elko. If memory serves me, after Crumley died, Bob ran against Snowy for the state senate, and Snowy beat him. Roy Young was a Republican. Roy's ranch was between Elko and Carlin. Used to see Roy in the Palm Saloon.

Notes

1. Walter Reuther was the longtime head of the United Auto Workers Union. Harry Bridges was the longtime head of the International Longshoremen's Union.

2. Democrat Gene Evans represented Elko County in the Assembly, 1957-60.

3. Warren "Snowy" Monroe owned the *Elko Independent* from 1937 to 1974, and continued writing for it until his death in 1987. He was a Democratic assemblyman from Elko County, 1941-45 and 1947-49, and state senator, 1959-76.

4. M. E. "Ted" McCuistion was a Democratic assemblyman from Elko, 1939-43 and 1947-55.

5. J. F. McElroy was a Democratic assemblyman from Elko, 1939-47, 1951-53, 1955-57.

6. F. E. "Pete" Walters was a Republican assemblyman from Elko County, 1951-55.

7. John Oldham was a Democratic assemblyman from Elko County, 1935-41 and 1953-55. "Carville Democrat" refers to those who supported E. P. Carville, a U.S. attorney for Nevada (1934-38) and governor (1939-45). Carville appointed Berkeley Bunker to the Senate in 1940 to succeed Key Pittman; as mentioned above, Representative James Scrugham defeated Bunker in his quest to win a term in his own right. In 1945, Scrugham died, and Carville resigned as governor; his successor, Vail Pittman, appointed him to the Senate. In 1946, Bunker, apparently with Pat McCarran's encouragement, ran against Carville in the Democratic primary for the Senate and defeated him. Carville supporters then backed Republican George Malone, who defeated Bunker in the general election. When Bunker attempted a statewide political comeback in 1962—a subject to be discussed in this book—many old Carville supporters worked in behalf of Bunker's Republican opponent for lieutenant governor, Paul Laxalt, who was elected.

8. Jack Hunter represented Elko County in the Assembly, 1955-57 and 1959-61.

12 | "This Office Never Sends a Bill"

Jack Robbins went to the legislature from Elko County as an assemblyman in 1925, and later served twenty years as a senator. I wish I knew more
about Jack's background. I think he came from the Bay area. He came to
Reno or Carson City and worked for the Nevada land office when patents
were granted to a lot of ranches. How or when he got to Elko, I don't know.
He had never gone to law school.

Old Doc Gallagher used to tell a story about Jack: In those days, the bar
exam was an oral exam before the Supreme Court in Carson City, or so I was
told. Jack was scared to do it. Some of his friends got him drunk and put him
on the train. He appeared before the Supreme Court, was admitted to the
bar, and came back to Elko.

Jack and Joe McNamara were law partners for years. McNamara was one
of McCarran's closest friends. There was almost a paternal relationship between the senator and Joe. When I knew Jack when I first came to Elko,
McNamara was no longer alive, and Jack was practicing law by himself. I
saw him in the courthouse a few times. Of course, I called on him when I
first went to Elko, introduced myself. He was nice to me. He lived on Idaho
Street. Doc and Ruth Gallagher lived across the street from Jack and Millie.
That's where Tom and Morris Gallagher were raised. The two families were
close. Jack and Doc were hunting and fishing partners, good guys with magnificent senses of humor.

Jack was national committeeman from Nevada and a loyal McCarran
supporter. I think all the time Jack was national committeeman, he gave
McCarran his proxy. [laughter] He was chairman of the local party all the
time I was there. I don't think anybody would consider running—at least a
Democrat—without talking to Jack about it. Classy dresser, down-to-earth,
smart—I assume he was Irish, because he had all the qualities of a good Irish
politician. [laughter] I think he was as honest as the day is long.

This would be typical Jack Robbins: After Jack and I became law partners, people would tell me how Joe had taken to strong drink and wouldn't

136

*This
Office
Never
Sends
a Bill*

show up for work. Both of them had been through the Depression. They didn't trust the banks. Put their money in the bank? Hell, the bank might go broke and they'd lose it, so they kept their money in the office safe! Joe hadn't shown up at the office during the day for three or four weeks, but he'd come into the office in the middle of the night and empty the safe. Jack's friends told him he ought to put a stop to Joe taking all the money. Jack says, "Hell, he took care of me for twenty years when I was drunk. I'll take care of him his twenty years."

Jack told me this story about Joe, which is typical Nevada. He defended a guy in Mountain City for assault and battery—misdemeanor. He got him off, and the guy asked Joe his fee. Joe said, "$50." Well, $50 is tough for the guy to come up with, so he offered him $50 worth of Rio Tinto mine stock, a defunct copper mine near Mountain City, at five cents a share. Joe said no, he'd prefer to have the $50.

The miner scraped up $50. World War II comes along, and that stock went to $17 a share! Poor old Joe. Jack never turned down mining stock after that, but he never did hit one. Most old-time Nevada lawyers, myself included, got a lot of mining stock in the files. It's worthless. Still waiting. [laughter]

Jack told me that in all the time he'd been in the legislature, he never introduced a bill. That was the trouble. There were too God damn many laws, except the Elko County salary bill. Back then, the legislature set the salaries of county office holders. Whatever that county's delegation wanted the salaries to be, the legislature would go along. You had varying salaries all over the state. The clerk in Lincoln County might not get as much as the Eureka clerk. That was true of judges too.

The fourth judicial district was Elko County. Regrettably, Judge Wines's salary was the lowest of any judge in the state, or very low, but I never heard Jack say anything bad about Wines. I think Jack just figured he was young and hadn't had enough experience when he was appointed, and he ought to work his way up. [laughter]

Jack was always chairman of the fish and game committee. If Democrats had control of the state senate, he was majority leader. All he had to do if he didn't like a bill was move that it be referred to the fish and game committee. Then it went in his desk, and that's the last anybody saw of it.

Johnny Mueller, Norman Biltz's partner and lobbyist for many big commercial interests in Nevada, was a close friend of Jack's. I was shocked—one time I went to the legislature and was told I could go right on the floor. I'd worked the U.S. Senate, where nobody gets on the floor. Next to Jack was a chair. Mueller was sitting in it, giving him the benefit of his views and advice. [laughter]

When the legislature was over, Jack always took off for Santa Anita. The racing season started about when the legislature was over. Jack and Millie would have a couple of weeks vacation before they came back to Elko. Jack liked to play the races, hunt, fish. I saw pictures of him and Doc

Gallagher when they were young, in hunting garb with their rifles and so many ducks on the ground in front of them you couldn't believe it.

I am not certain how I came to be Jack Robbins's law partner. It was late 1952 or early 1953. I was deputy district attorney. I made my living in private practice. Jack represented many ranchers, many Basque ranchers. Jack was sick. He had a younger lawyer with him for a while—Pat Mann. Something happened. Pat had to leave that office. Jack had emphysema and stayed home. He was on oxygen most of the time. His secretary, Verla McFarland, had been with him for years. She'd go to the house, but he needed a lawyer in the office. Tom and Dorothy Gallagher and Sara and I had become friends, and Doc Gallagher was close to Jack. Maybe Doc suggested to Jack that he should consider me. I went to talk to him, and it was that simple. I became a partner and moved to his office in the Henderson Bank Building. Almost every night, I'd go see him.

Through Jack, my life was really enriched, in that I got to know so many Basque ranchers. Basques would become successful, starting as sheepherders and becoming ranch owners. Basques were found where the sheep industry was. Had it not been for Jack, I don't think I would have had an opportunity to get to know that interesting group—Xavier Goyeneche, Fernando Goicoechea, Pete Itcaina, Pete Elia. By naming those, I'm forgetting some. I met *wonderful* Basque people.

As attorneys, we were always concerned about the language barrier. If one of the Basques perceived we had not done an adequate job, true or not, you ran a risk of losing all of them. When Jack died, I thought, "That ranch business is going to split up, particularly the Basque ranchers." Three days after the funeral, I think they sensed my feeling. Pete Elia, a big sheep operator in Idaho and Nevada, came by—I wasn't there—and gave Verla a check written to me for $1,000. He says, "Tell Ralph this is my retainer for next year. We all stay." It was so nice. God, when Verla told me that, I was just thrilled.

Xavier Goyeneche was going to the old country, and I had to get his passport from our State Department—also a right to reenter the country. Xavier hadn't been back to the Pyrenees for a long time. He was retired and lived in town. He came to the office to see how things were, and I told him I hadn't received it yet. My desk was covered with books and papers, and Xavier said, "Oh, Jeez Christ, Ralph, I wish I smart like you, so I could read all of these books and papers."

I said, "Xavier, who's smart? Who can afford to go to the old country? I can't even afford to go to Carlin."

I learned a lot from Xavier about the life of young Basques who came to the country as sheepherders, and the exploitation of them. He told me he got off the train in Elko—right after World War I, I think—with just a tag around his neck, "The Johnson Ranch." He was picked up at the depot and taken to the Johnson ranch, out between Wells and Wendover, around the

138

*This
Office
Never
Sends
a Bill*

Pequop Mountains. He said he was out in the hills thirteen years before he got to town. He says he couldn't speak English, no Basque, just "baaaaa."

In those days—I think a lot of this has been forgotten—before the Taylor Grazing Act, the herder would take care of the bummers; they would become his. After he got enough bummers to have his own band of sheep, he could take off across the country, and he was in the sheep business himself—maybe with one band. Gradually, his herd would increase. That's what Xavier and a lot of early Basque ranchers did: taking care of the bummers and then going out on the public domain and grazing, and later on being able to buy a ranch and increase their holdings. I couldn't conceive of that sort of thing.

Maybe people should remember how they imported the Basques. There was an organization in Sacramento called the California Range Association. If a ranch needed herders, they would contract with the association. Our office—Robbins—had a legal relationship with that association and would help arrange this. Their agents would go to the Pyrenees and recruit young Basque men to come to this country to herd sheep. The rancher would advance the money for the ship fare or plane fare or whatever got them here. Over the years, the Basques would pay them back out of their salaries.

Old Pete Itcaina—Christ, he ran sheep and cattle all the way from White Pine into Idaho, owned that whole Mary's River country. He was convinced there was a conspiracy between the Mormon church and the government to steal his land. Each year, the grazing service would cut down his grazing license, and Mormons would move into the country. So he just lumped the two together.

Many of the herders were out in the hills for a long time. All of them sent money back. Pete was one of them. We kept his payroll in the office. Sometimes three or four years would go by that an employee had not received his salary. When he came to town, he could come to the office, and Verla could look it up. We had paid the NIC premiums, the withholding, if there was any, and had a clear record of how much this herder had coming. We'd give him a check in the office. I signed some awful big checks on account for guys who had been out in the hills for years and came in and asked for the money.

One time, a guy had to hitchhike in from Curry, the southern headquarters of Pete's holdings, and wants his money. Pete wouldn't bring him. I have Verla looking it up, how much he's got coming. I think he'd gotten money before, but he'd worked for Pete for eight, nine, or ten years.

Pete comes running in. "Don't pay him! Don't give him anything! He's no good!"

I said, "What do you mean, Mr. Itcaina, he's no good?"

He said, "He quit! No good! Don't pay him anything!" [laughter]

I went to the house to see Jack. He says, "You go back and pay him what he's got coming."

In those days, there were about 5,000,000 head of sheep in the state. Today, there's less than 100,000—give you an idea of what's happened to the sheep industry since the 1950s. I think it's a combination of things: everybody blames the importation of Australian wool and sheep, and that may be part of it. Part of it is all of the new clothing materials that aren't wool. The demand for wool isn't as great as it used to be.

A large part of it is the protection of predatory animals. One of the last sheep outfits in Elko went out of business not long ago because of depredation of their herds by coyotes. The government used to have a program to kill coyotes. Now they got a program to save them. Never could understand why anybody would want to save a coyote. [laughter] It's a sad day, because it used to be a great time in Elko, when the shearing and lambing were going on, big trucks were bringing these big bundles of wool to be shipped on the railroad out of Elko, and the sheep were being transported to feed lots and markets.

I remember, just up the Mount Rose Highway in Reno was a restaurant on top of the hill. Sara and I were there having dinner. We looked toward Reno. Here's a big band of sheep coming down that valley, with the herders and dogs. It was a dramatic thing to see. You don't see them anymore. It's too bad.

My friend and client Pete Elia and Celso Madrietta, a big Elko County cattle, sheep, and wool buyer, put on a big barbecue in the Ruby Mountains each Fourth of July. The Basque herders came out of the hills and mountains from all over. Few non-Basques were invited. Some old-timers they did business with in town, like the Gallaghers (they were dentists) were there. Sara and I got invited. I can't tell you what that scene was like! All of these young sheepherders out of the hills, still wearing their berets, with their bota bags. As far as you could see, lambs on spits being roasted, open fires, boys dancing the old country dances, accordions. You'd have thought you were back in the Pyrenees. What a wonderful party it was. After that, Sara and I were invited each year we lived there. You don't stereotype any group, but all of the Basque people I met in Elko were wonderful. That is my greatest gift from Jack Robbins. Had I not gone in that office, I would not have had that association.

Jack taught me another lesson. Maybe it was never valid in most places. With our clients, it was valid. "This office never sends a bill," he said. "If you send a bill to one of these ranches, and they don't have the money to pay it at that time, they're going to be terribly embarrassed about it. When they sell the wool or the lambs, they'll come to the office and ask, 'What do we owe you?' They'll probably leave more than you tell them they owe you, and they'll probably tip your secretary." He was right. Maybe you'd done a big piece of legal work, and it would be several months, but all of a sudden in one would come and talk to Verla. "How much I owe?" She'd look in the books. Pay it and give her maybe a $25 or $100 tip.

140

*This
Office
Never
Sends
a Bill*

Danny Bilbao, who was Basque, bought the Stockmen's. In the 1950s, Idaho shut down, and a bunch of gamblers came to Nevada. Danny and two other guys from Boise bought the Sonoma Inn in Winnemucca, then the Stockmen's in Elko. One of them was a banker—Joe Dollard. Dollard and Virgil McGee were his partners originally. Then Danny had another partner who wanted us to send bills to him, so we did. The partner always complained about them. That embarrassed Danny, though he never said anything.

Every time I'd go into the Stockmen's after work, which I did on occasion, and sat at the bar, Danny would sit next to me and buy me a drink, and we'd have a nice visit. I'd go home. When I got home, I'd reach in my pocket. Danny would have stuck a $100 bill in my pocket. He was embarrassed his partner was objecting, so he would just give me a little extra, which was very nice. [laughter] Danny later retired and moved to Palm Springs, and his son ran the hotel and sold it.

When I joined him, Jack and I had a general practice. We did a lot of ranch work. We did a lot of probate work. Like every lawyer in Elko, we did our share of migratory divorce and personal injury, commercial work. It's a busier town now, but it was a busy town then. From a revenue standpoint, it was the ranchers and probate—estate work. And we represented the Stockmen's.

Red Ellis, who sold the Stockmen's to Bilbao and that group and was out of business, later bought the Commercial from Newt Crumley. I handled that, one of the most interesting legal transactions I was ever involved in, because Red and Newt did not get along, wouldn't sit in the same room. I'm representing Red, Bill Woodburn from Reno is representing Newt, but most of the negotiations are taking place with me as intermediary. I'd go to the Commercial and talk to Newt, then I'd talk to Red. We got a deal, but trying to negotiate a deal when neither of the principals would negotiate with each other was interesting. I'd never done anything like that, and never negotiated the sale of a casino. Woodburn had, so the contract was well-drafted. Red came back in business, so we were representing both the Commercial and the Stockmen's.

I have no idea why Newt and Red didn't get along. They were different men; their backgrounds were different. Red had come up from Salinas, California. He had a partner who was a saloonkeeper there. Red had been one of his bartenders or maybe one of his partners. They had come up and bought the old Mayer Hotel and changed its name to the Stockmen's. Red ran it and later acquired his partner's interest. Newt was a patrician, an appropriate word to use, if you could apply that—and I think you can—to an old-time Elko family. Newt's roots were so deep in Elko County, and Red was sort of a newcomer. I don't know what the difference was, but they didn't get along.

Jack was a Democrat; I was a Democrat. He was a McCarran man; I was a McCarran man. Ted McCuistion and some of those guys would talk to Jack and plot and scheme. I think Jack had a lot of Republican friends. I don't think he regarded the legislature as partisan. Partisanship was for elections. He always spoke at rallies. When I was first there, I remember him speaking at a Democratic rally. When we had the Democratic convention in Wells in 1952, in the theater, Jack came and parked his car in front. He didn't go in, but stayed in the front seat outside, so everybody could come up and shake hands. Everybody running for state office called on Jack, and many times, Jack would call and ask me to come down to the house and meet so-and-so. I met a lot of people that way. Republican candidates always called on Jack too. But we never discussed political strategy or that kind of stuff.

One time people were trying to get me to run for the legislature. I didn't want to. I asked Jack. He says, "Wait until you've been here a little longer if you want to run. I don't think it's a good idea for you to get in any political fights right now." But he said, "If you want to, I'll do anything I can to help you." In 1954, when McCarran put my name out as a candidate for state chairman, I discussed that with him. He said, "Well, if that's what the senator wants you to do, you better do it. But they tie horses to state chairmen in Carson City."

Soon after I got to Elko, I drew up a deed for somebody and got $5. I remember saying to Sara, "At least, I know now, being a lawyer and admitted to the bar, I can make a living." I took comfort from that. I might be the lousiest lawyer in the world, but I'd be able to make a living. That gave me a security I'd never had, because before, I was always working for somebody else.

I was a child of the Depression, and I'd lost the best job I ever had in my life in Washington. McCarran had sent me back to Nevada, and I thought, "Oh God!" All Sara and I had when we went there is $500 I borrowed from the Bank of Pioche with my father co-signing. That's what we had to start out with, and I started as deputy district attorney without a salary. I've got rent to pay, so it was a great comfort to me when I realized I could go any place in Nevada, might not be the best one, might not get rich, which wasn't important to me anyway, but I could make a living.

It wasn't very different to work in the D.A.'s office with Grant and then in private practice. When I was with Grant, my private practice was conducted in the district attorney's office. When I went to Jack's office, I left the district attorney's office, but I'm still dealing with the same people. I did miss the law enforcement aspect of it: working with Jess Harris and being in on what was going on in the community. And I missed working with Grant. Several cases after I went over to Jack's office, I would associate Grant in, if I felt two heads were better than one. Grant had a good relationship with every lawyer in town . . . . There might have been exceptions—I don't know

142

*This
Office
Never
Sends
a Bill*

what his relationship was with Alex or Leo Puccinelli, but I know that most of the lawyers had a high regard for Grant. You couldn't help it. Everybody liked Grant. As a matter of fact, not only was Grant well liked, but Grant was respected by the other lawyers

Leo Puccinelli was the one Grant beat for district attorney. I've found through the years that political opponents develop a personal feeling. Leo was born and raised in Elko County. Grant comes in in 1948, and in 1950 gets elected—only there two years, and he beats Leo. Leo wouldn't be normal if he didn't have some resentment.

There had been difficulty between Grant and Alex Puccinelli, Leo's cousin. Alex had been district attorney before Grant. Alex might have felt the carpetbaggers were taking over. Grant and I used to laugh about that. He was a newcomer, but he'd been there longer than I had, and I was a newcomer. We'd leave the courthouse to go to lunch and speak to everybody we saw. If somebody's sitting in a car, stop and say hello, try to get acquainted.

We were going to the courthouse one time, and two ladies are sitting in a car. Grant says hello, I say hello, and God, we had a hell of a visit. I looked back, and the license plates are from Illinois. I said, "Christ, Grant! We're even trying to get acquainted with the folks from Illinois!" [laughter]

But I think we were about the first two for several years that came to practice law that didn't have a previous tie to the county. They married an Elko girl, or they were from Elko. Every lawyer in town when we were there had a deep tie to Elko, with the possible exception of Pat Mann. But Pat had a tie to the rest of the state, to Mineral County, and was a fine lawyer too.

All of these people, Democrats and Republicans, many belonged to the Toastmasters Club, where we did discuss political issues. Orville was a member—Pete Walters, McCuistion, Taylor Wines, Grant and I, some railroad people, two or three doctors. That club didn't operate according to the general rules of Toastmasters. Each night, in addition to maybe three short speeches by members, you could choose your own table topic. Then everybody would discuss it. Table topics generally dealt with political questions. Boy, you'd be surprised at things you would hear—McCarthy, sales tax, economic policies, Right to Work. It was really a debating society. Here are all these guys of different parties, all friends, and it never got out of hand.

I really enjoyed that club. I don't think in those days Republicans had yet been as successful as they have been in turning liberal into a bad word. I don't think we painted each other with words like that: liberal or conservative. It was mostly Republican and Democrat. Republican was a bad word to Democrats, and Democrats was a bad word to Republicans. [laughter]

There were three reasons for my decision to leave Elko—not equally weighted. One, Jack Robbins died, I think in October 1954. I had gone to Ely on a legal matter that day and seen Jack before I left. I drove back, and when I came into town, I stopped at Jack's house to tell him the outcome, and I was told he was dead. I found myself in partnership with his widow—a wonderful woman, but it was difficult, at my age, to be partners, and I liquidated the partnership with her.

The second reason was that I was not getting along with Judge Wines. I found it unpleasant to be in court. It may be my difficulties were as much my fault as his.

Third, I had done well in Elko. I was young and ambitious and perhaps a little arrogant. I thought I had reached as far as I would go in the practice of the law in Elko, which, of course, wasn't true. You can always do better wherever you are. But Las Vegas was growing. I had family in the southern part of the state. I had an offer from a close friend for a partnership—Joe McDonald. It was a combination of those things.

When we left Elko, Tom and Dorothy Gallagher had a big party for us, and that was it. Sara moved down before I moved, because we sold our house and had to get out. We rented a house in Las Vegas. She was pregnant with Scott. That was about the first of August. She and the kids are in this heat. God, I felt sorry for her, because it was so hot. But we got used to that.

With Sara and the kids gone, I moved in with George and Eva Ogilvie. To just open their house and let me live with them . . . ! I must have lived with them a month-and-a-half. I had to wind up whatever work I was doing or get other lawyers to take it over. I had one case the day before I left—I argued a divorce case before Judge Wines. Of course, he ruled against me! We appealed it, and it was reversed. The arguments to the court were on Friday, and I left Saturday morning for Las Vegas.

13 | Lawyers Up One Flight

While I was still practicing in Elko, I went down to Las Vegas to see Lindsay Jacobson, who had moved there from Miami. Joe McDonald had also moved to Las Vegas and set up a practice. His firm was called Bible and McDonald, because Alan Bible and Joe's brother Bob were partners in Reno; but actually, the office in Las Vegas was independent. It was at 425 Fremont, on the second floor of the Carl Ray Professional Building, with a drugstore on the first floor. There was a sign on the side of the building, a finger pointing upstairs: LAWYERS. UP ONE FLIGHT.

Joe said, "Why don't you come down and practice law with me? This town is really going." I said I'd let him know. I had so much fun with him and Lindsay, and saw so many old friends and family members, that I thought, "This would really be great. Las Vegas is booming, and there's more than one judge." [laughter]

It was going to be Joe, me, and David Goldwater. Dave was in his own office in the Friedman building at Third and Fremont. When I got here, there wasn't any office space for rent. Joe's office was not big enough, and Dave's wasn't, so we thought, "We'll do it this way until there's an office building we can get into." By then, Joe and I were happy and David was happy, so we never pursued that. And it would be the most exciting time of my life, the time that Joe and I were law partners.

I didn't learn for a long time that Sara was sad about leaving Elko. She had a lot of dear friends, things she did and belonged to. But she never said a word when I discussed the move. It was fine with her. Very soon after we got here, she began liking Las Vegas, and has liked it ever since.

I hated to leave Elko too. Every time we got a chance, I'd visit. Glendale is between Las Vegas and Mesquite. It was on old US 91, about 48 miles from Las Vegas. Going to Elko, you would go there and turn north on US 93. Joe used to ream me: "God, every time we get close to Glendale Junction, Ralph wants to go on up to Elko," another 400 miles or more.

[laughter] I was called up there a few times as a witness in a will case, and tried two or three cases and had a client from Wells for years until he died.

I didn't sense this was going to be a major change in my life. One of my friends said, "I'd rather see you commit suicide than move to that God-damn town." [laughter] That man was from Reno. The feeling toward Clark County in that part of the state was that everybody here was nuts or a hood-lum, and I suppose, to a certain extent, they still feel that way. [laughter] To be honest, I had a jaundiced idea of Las Vegas, because I wanted to move to Reno, but I figured Reno was too hard to crack . . . to just go and open an office. You've got the old established order, and I didn't have much money. But from everything I'd heard, I could make enough money in Las Vegas in two or three years to move to Reno. Never admitted that to too many folks, but that was the plan.

I loved Reno . . . just *loved* it; but Las Vegas is a young man's town. You're accepted at face value. You're not going to confront an established hierarchy. Opportunity is here for everybody. Not to say that isn't true in Elko or Reno, but both of those towns have a core of old time salt-of-the-earth people who have fairly tight control. Las Vegas still is open. I tell young lawyers, "Don't think you have to go to work for a law firm. Open an office. You'll make it. Might be tough, but other lawyers will help if you'll ask. Let them know you'd like to have any referrals they could give you." The wonderful thing about Las Vegas is that, by and large, people will judge you on your relationship with them, and not on where you came from or your past or what church you belong to,.

When we moved to Las Vegas, we lived on the 1000 block of Bonita. It was a small house with a swamp cooler. We had quite a few friends by the time we left. We bought a house under construction at 715 East Oakey. When it was finished, we moved in. That was a leading neighborhood. Around the corner to the north was Sixth Street, and Sixth between Charleston and Oakey was a prime residential area. As we looked south, we looked across desert, believe it or not, all the way to St. Louis, the next major street. The kids had lots of places to play, but it started to fill in, and quite a few houses had gone up before we moved to Boulder City in 1959.

Next to us was Jim Archer, one of the owners of Vegas Village.[1] He and his wife remained our friends until both passed away. Up a block, the Wakely family became close friends. They had a little girl Mark's age. Oh, they were good buddies, but they decided to move back to Missoula, Montana. The morning they were leaving, Mark was so excited and sad about little Wynn Wakely, he got up, put on his jeans, got on his two-wheel bike with training wheels, went pedaling up the sidewalk to say goodbye again. When he made it home, we discovered he had his pants on backwards. [laughter] Behind us lived George and Ida Fox, who built each house, all custom houses. Around the corner, Cal and Beth Cory's house was under construction on Sixth next to the Wengert house on Sixth and Charleston. Art Ham lived on Sixth. Across Oakey, both sides of Sixth to St. Louis were developed. A lot of people on that street became friends: Dave Zenoff and his wife; Kell Houssels, Jr., and his wife; Dave Goldwater and his wife; Vince Sanner, a dentist; Ollie and Marilyn Gardner.[2] Parry and Peggy Thomas moved into a street that bisected Sixth or Seventh. Peggy and Parry had a passel of kids. All those kids played together.

We felt immediately accepted, thanks to Mary Gene McDonald and our old friends. Most of the women were in Service League, now Junior League; Sara became a member and got to know them. We had so much in common with our neighbors. Everybody was busy, and all were social—people used to have dinner parties, or cocktail parties.

Joseph F. McDonald, Jr., was a remarkable guy. He was game for anything. Hard-working, but seeking out opportunities. Funny, too. Knowledgeable and interested in political affairs. The sign on the door downstairs said "Bible and McDonald," because that was the name in Reno. But we had no connection with that firm! It said Bible and McDonald, and on the door below, Alan Bible, Robert McDonald, Joe McDonald, and Ralph Denton. That was helpful.

Joe knew all of the old political figures in Las Vegas. He and Mary Gene were close to Julian Moore and his wife, Fran, a McNamee, and used to do a lot together socially. Joe and Mary Gene had a big reception for us at one of the hotels. They must have invited half the old-timers in town to introduce us to Las Vegas society. It was fun. Las Vegas was a happy town, a happy group of people. It was exciting to me.

I had known of the McNamee family all my life, but I'd never met any except Leo's daughter Patricia when she worked on the Senate Judiciary Committee under McCarran's patronage. They're a remarkable family. It's like Will Rogers said: he never saw a man he didn't like; I've never met a McNamee I didn't like. They were involved in the community and a lot of social functions. Their house was on Third or Fourth and Bridger, in that area. Every evening after Leo got home, it was kind of an open house. Anybody in town was welcome to have a drink. You didn't have to have an appointment to drop by and see Leo and Fran McNamee.

Leo McNamee wouldn't handle divorce cases. To show how isolated he was . . . . Jerry Geisler, a prominent lawyer in Los Angeles, represented a lot of movie people, and referred clients to Leo. Ava Gardner came up to get a divorce, and Leo wouldn't handle it. The name meant nothing to Leo. She got ahold of Geisler. Jerry insisted that Leo handle this case to get Ava's divorce from Mickey Rooney. Leo said, "Mickey Rooney? That name is familiar. Did he go to school with one of my kids?" [laughter] But Leo wouldn't handle the divorce.

Joe was smart. Our office was on the south side of Fremont. The bread and butter legal business was migratory divorce, and most of the lawyers were on Fremont. Joe figured if people came to Fremont looking for a lawyer, they came down Fifth, which today would be Las Vegas Boulevard South, where the bus stop was. They would walk up the north side to the depot, looking at offices and trying to make up their mind. Then they'd cross and come down the south side. All of a sudden, they hadn't selected anybody, and here they are back at the bus stop. "Well, we better take somebody." That's where we were! So, he figured we got a lot of walk-in business for divorces.

Joe was on top of his work. He would come to the office at 6:30 or 7:00 in the morning. He'd get everything done, then he might go home at 4:00 or 5:00 and go to bed. He'd get up at ten at night, go to the Strip, and circulate until 12:30 or 1:00 in the morning. He'd stop and say hello to every dealer, every cocktail waitress he knew, and his theory proved to be true: we got more uncontested divorce business out of the working people in the hotels. Somebody would ask for a lawyer, and one of them would say, "Joe McDonald or Ralph Denton." Through uncontested divorce, we were able to meet the overhead and make a little profit before we got well enough established to be representing some of the people in the community.

Joe believed lawyers screw up a lot of deals simply by delay and being too careful to make contracts exact. The thing to do: two businessmen want a contract, draw that contract! Even if it doesn't appear to be a pearl of great price, and a lawyer said, "God, this is a terrible contract," Joe's position was the parties understand it and want this deal put together. He'd draft contracts off the top of his head. Sometimes I'd take my scissors out and cut our name off the bottom of the paper. But there never was a lawsuit over any of them. If you came to him and were buying "business A" and wanted this done by day after tomorrow, Joe would have it done. The clients didn't complain about lawyers screwing up their deals. [laughter]

He was smart, yet he didn't feel that comfortable trying a case if the legal points involved required scholarly attainment. I don't know why; he was a fine lawyer, and he understood the law. He just wasn't interested in spending a heck of a lot of time doing legal research and that kind of stuff.

One time Joe, Lindsay, and I decided we'd go up to Lincoln County and prospect. Joe liked to get out in the hills. He knew this state like few people I know. We drove up to Irish Mountain, kicked around for a few hours, looked over my dad's old claims, walked in the tunnels, and went into Caliente. We took a bath at the hot springs and decided we'd go up to Pioche and have dinner. I think it was the Alamo Club. I'd gone to high school with the guy tending bar. We were having a drink. Jim Bilbray was shooting craps, and boy, he'd taken to strong drink.[3] Bilbray was throwing money around like you can't believe. You don't see that kind of money in Pioche often—big money on the pass line and other people getting it. Joe figured we could get Bilbray in a poker game and take him off. [laughter]

There was a poker table in the back of the room with a green lamp over it. I asked my friend tending bar, "Do you ever open that poker game?"

"Oh, not often," he says. But another guy I had grown up with dealt when they had a game. He called him to come open up the game.

We figured we'd get Bilbray, no matter what we had to do. But we get him in the poker game, three of us trying to figure out some way to steal his money, and we couldn't win a bet! He was the luckiest man I ever saw. He could draw two to an inside straight. [laughter] It was a lark with Joe to do something like that.

The almost two years I practiced with Joe were the most exciting years in all of my practice of the law. He was a complete pleasure to be around. You never knew *what* was going to happen, who was going to be in your office, who you were representing. They could be the biggest con men in the world, and it would be a circus with Joe. That was the impression Joe left, that he was not serious. He was putting himself down; but that was not Joe at all. He was a serious and good man, and smart. Life was a ball to Joe. And Joe knew everybody—in Reno, of course, but everybody in Nevada that had gone to the university over the period he was a student there. I've never heard anybody say anything bad about Joe, and I've never known anybody, when you mention his name, you don't get a smile in return. He was one of those guys.

We had a client, Lou Davidson, a Jewish businessman from New York who still spoke with a thick accent, and he loved Joe. Joe loved him. Lou was active in business—he built the Carver House Hotel on the Westside— and Joe did all of his work. Lou was a builder, a visionary. We might be out for lunch on Fremont, and Lou would say, "You boys will live to see this valley full all the way to Sunrise Mountain that way and to Red Rock that way." What is he, some kind of nut?

Sometimes, Lou would get a little far out. He and Joe would yell, then Joe would get mad and tell him to get out of the office and never come back. One day, I looked up, and Joe had Louie by the collar his shirt and the seat of his pants, and he rushed by my door and threw Lou out of the office.

Soon, Lou comes back up and knocks on Joe's door. "Can I come in now, Joe?"

Joe said, "Aw, come on in, Lou."

Joe absolutely loved con men. This was the day of penny uranium stock. We represented many promoters putting together corporations and peddling penny stock. They were interesting, and that's why Joe liked them, because they were so much fun.

You'd get that phony stock in Salt Lake City—where most of these con-men came from—and it would get on that stock market. The first thing you know, stock they sold to the public all over the country for a penny a share was up to ten and fifteen cents a share . . . but the mining claims the corporation owned were worthless, and everybody knew it.

I asked this one guy . . . . (I'd read these letters they were putting out. Their chief stock in trade was the sucker list they'd built up over years of being in the stock fraud business.) This one guy was putting out this letter to send to his sucker list, offering to sell them this chance in uranium mines. I said, "Who buys this stuff?"

He said, "Well, I'm just getting this letter out. In about two weeks, you come and ask me, and I'll tell you."

In two weeks I did. God, the money was coming in! He was getting checks, stacks of mail every day for about a week after he sent his solicitations. He said, "I'll tell you. School teachers, lawyers, doctors, dentists and everybody that wants something for nothing. You've got a chance to make a big killing. They're the ones who buy it, and they repeat. The same people I sold stock to last year are buying the stock this year." [laughter]

The first divorce of any prominent person I ever got was Hazel Stone, Lewis Stone's widow. Lewis Stone was an actor for years, started on Broadway, came to Hollywood almost at the start, was in many great movies, best known for being Judge Hardy in the Andy Hardy series—Mickey Rooney being his son. After he died, Hazel married Gilbert von Klatt, thinking he was some sort of a titled man from Europe. They took a trip to Europe. By the time she got back, she knew she'd made a mistake. She came to Las Vegas to get a divorce. They had just been married a few weeks, and there was no community property, but the husband wanted money. Hazel didn't feel inclined to give him any. For some reason, the case was being delayed. I don't know how she got to us, but she fired the attorney she had and brought the file to us. We got it set for trial, almost immediately.

While Hazel was here, she became acquainted with JoJo Mannarino. He wasn't in the gambling business, but he was reputed to have connections with what we referred to as "the organization," or the mob. He'd been a client of our office, and he brought Hazel here. He had his eye on her. Every time she came to the office, he'd come, too.

Once we started to try the case, then the case was over, because the husband and his attorney were, frankly, just trying to make it tough enough on Hazel that she'd give him some money and he'd go away. So, we try it, and JoJo came to the office to walk to the courthouse with us. On the way over, he looked at me with a very cold look in his eye and said, "Ralph, you better win this case." I thought to myself, "I sure as hell better win this case." I don't know what he had in mind. But we won the case. Judge Ryland Taylor was incensed this man was trying to get some money out of this nice lady when there wasn't any community property. They'd only been married for about three months.

One of my first clients was Z Louie, a Chinese man who played quite a role in Nevada life thereafter. Z Louie was referred to as a mystery man of Nevada politics. People couldn't understand how he knew practically every politician in the United States, not just in Nevada. They all knew Mr. Louie, and he knew them all well.

Z Louie became a client because Bible referred him to us. These were the days when Las Vegas was completely segregated, and the Westside was, for all intents and purposes, a separate area—its own commercial district, bars, stores. One of the popular bars was the Town Tavern, run by Earl Turman. Louie took a lease on part of the bar to put in a Keno game. (We used to call it "Race-horse" Keno, the pretense being that the numbered balls represented race horses. I think this was because Nevada has a constitutional prohibition against the lottery; and certainly, a pure Keno game is nothing more than a lottery.)

Ralph Denton with Z Louie, "mystery man of Nevada politics."

Louie came here from San Francisco, and we negotiated the agreement and handled Louie's gambling license to operate the game. He did well to the point he decided he wanted his own place. He acquired a building catty-corner to the Town Tavern, and leased and opened his own club, the Louisiana Club. I think it was at Jackson and D, a block west of the Carver House. We negotiated the lease. The lady who lived on the Westside, who owned it, had a secret partner in it, former sheriff Glen Jones. He owned the building.

We applied for Louie to have a full gambling license. We didn't have a fight with the state, but had an awful fight with the city of Las Vegas. We had a gaming control board, and there was a thorough investigation, but we're getting held up by the city because the head of the licensing department contended Louie didn't own the place; that his tong owned the place, and Louie was just a front. The tongs, ipso facto, were evil—of course, there was no proof anybody owned the Louisiana Club but Louie.

Louie showed the source of his money. (Like most successful Chinese businessmen, Louie did belong to a tong. He would tell me: "It's not like they used to be. It's like a social club.") We appeared before the council, and it almost developed into a shouting match between me and Joe and the licensing director. The poor council is wondering what's going on, disgusted with our presentation. It was continued to a date certain.

Before the continued hearing, I was contacted by the licensing director. He didn't want to talk about Louie's application. Rather, he told me he had a son trying to get an appointment to West Point. I inferred, I think for appropriate reason, that he wanted to make a deal: if I could arrange for Bible to get his son an appointment, Louie wouldn't have any problems. I'd never been confronted with anything like that. I made it clear there was nothing I could or would do. The next hearing, the talk about Louie's involvement with the tong was not that serious anymore, and the council gave him his license.

Louie knew everybody in political life, not only in Nevada, but all over. Now, his was a typical Westside joint. He had this dining room, and he would have big parties. It would not be unusual to have the governor, senators, sheriff, county commissioners, city councilmen, business leaders for a dinner at Louie's. But he never did invite black people, and he was located in a black community.

People didn't refuse Louie's invitations. I know Bible got concerned about who his friend Z Louie was. He was able to find out . . . and was pleased to learn that Louie was prominent in the anti-communist Chinese community, had been editor of a Chinese newspaper in San Francisco. Then everybody felt better. We're not scared about him being a member of an evil tong. [laughter]

Louie and I became friends. I thought the world of Louie. On several occasions, we'd gone to San Francisco and been entertained with him. One time he went to New York with Sara and me. I was going on business, and he just went along. There was a reception arranged for Louie in Chinatown in New York, and J. Wellington Koo, the nationalist Chinese ambassador to the United Nations, paid great respect to Mr. Louie.

One time I went to Washington, D.C., on business. Louie came just to go along. We were taking the subway from the Senate office building to the Senate side of the Capitol. As we were getting on this subway car, a man got off the subway car that was coming to the Senate office building, and he saw Louie. He said, "Oh, Mr. Louie!" Louie said, "Oh, Senator Lausche!" How he knew Senator Lausche of Ohio, I have no more idea than the man in the moon.[4]

Louie sold the Louisiana Club after maybe ten years. He went to San Francisco, and I never heard from him. Then, one day, he came in the office and wanted me to draw a will. He looked terrible. I learned he'd been very sick—he'd had a heart attack. He'd been in Sunrise Hospital, and in Las Vegas about a year. I didn't know it, he hadn't called me, and I gave him the devil. He said, "I was sick, and I didn't want to bother you." I drew his will. Soon thereafter, he died. I handled the probate of his estate.

Wherever you went with Louie, you'd wind up in a Chinese restaurant, and Louie would be in the kitchen. You didn't order off the menu; Louie would tell the chef what he wanted for his party. That even happened in Amsterdam. Louie went on that trip in 1964 billed as the "Sell Nevada" tour. A lot of Nevada business and political people had meetings in European capitals and preached the virtues of Nevada. Every place we went, Louie knew somebody. He'd always invite everybody to a Chinese dinner, and be back in that kitchen telling the cooks what to serve. And they did! Just remarkable!

There was a lot of resentment on the Westside toward Louie.[5] He had no black employees. No blacks were invited to his parties. His dealers were Chinese. That became a big issue. I represented Louie trying to negotiate something with Jim McMillan and Charlie West.[6] They were incensed. Here's this man in our midst, and none of our people getting work. We worked out a deal, and Louie started hiring black dealers. They were a little resentful even after they got hired, because their bosses were all Chinese. After that, the games weren't doing as well as they were before. [laughter] So, what do you do about that?

I asked my friend Jimmy Garrett to watch one night and tell me what was happening. Jimmy was hysterical. He was describing the action on the crap table. He said, "There's a Chinese sitting on the box. Then you got a stick man across from him, a dealer to his right, and a dealer to his left. The Chinese fellow looks down to the right side of the table to check the bets and what's going on in the field. While he's looking down at the right, the dealer on the left is taking money out of the rack and placing bets. Then, the box man looks down the left side of the table, and while he's looking, the dealer on the right is taking money out of the racks and making bets." I never told Louie. I did talk to Jim and Charlie and told them the dealers had to quit stealing from Louie. They did.

Over the years, many of my clients became some of my closest friends. Jimmy Garrett, Lou DiGregorio, Verne Phipps, and Snap Staley were all dealers, and they all had the same problem. They contracted to buy a house from Bert Tait. So did George Deverell. They had gotten loans from Silver State Savings and Loan or First Western Savings and Loan. They purchased the land, so they owned the lot. They signed a note for construction money and left the money to disperse to the contractor during the course of construction. When they came to me, the homes were not finished, some barely started, all the money gone, the savings and loans foreclosing on their mortgages. Not only had the contractors not completed the houses, they hadn't paid the suppliers for the material. It became a long and complicated piece of litigation, during the course of which I got to know these guys.

We pursued the cases for a long time, to a successful finish. Not only did I sue the savings and loan and get that straightened out, I defended the lien cases of over forty 'mechanics'. We were successful in all except one—a lumber company appealed, and the Nevada Supreme Court reversed.

I mention these guys because they all stayed friends of mine. Some of them are dead. I learned so much from them. They were all dealers. With the exception of George Deverell, a local boy, who, I think, had graduated from Las Vegas High School and gone to the University of Nevada, all of the others had worked in gambling outside Nevada, where it was illegal. They were very knowledgeable.

When we had time to just talk, they piqued my interest in gambling—the vocabulary of the trade, how gambling houses really worked. I learned what 'mechanic' meant to them, which was someone able to cheat from the outside or inside. I learned that 'cross-roader' meant a guy that goes around to different gambling houses to cheat them. When they referred to cheating, their term was 'flat'. They would call a gambling house a 'store'. "That's a flat store," meant a gambling house that regularly cheats.

They would laugh about some of the ways people on that side of the table, sometimes inside the house, operated. Through them, I got to know some well-known cross-roaders. [laughter] And bust out people . . . "bust out" meaning a game that's going to cheat the player. That's just from the inside. The ones I got to know were motivated by a desire to make money, but mostly, it was the excitement of the thing. The risk was funny to them. I owe Jimmy and these people a debt, because I learned so much from them, how it was important to a gambling house to protect itself from outsiders, from cross-roaders, and the pressures on dealers when they worked for a flat store. It was a great education for me.

I used to know dealers as a kid in Caliente. When my dad was in the business, a lot of those guys who worked for him were cross-roaders who worked the state. They'd work in Caliente for a while, then Ely; sometimes for the house, sometimes against. In those days, dealers were paid in cash out of the cage. I think it was ten silver dollars a day. You didn't have to keep records in the sense of workmen's comp or withholding, so you didn't have to know their names. My dad told me, often he never knew their name—just their nickname.

Jimmy Garrett told me a friend of his had said, "The whole world's a flat store." [laughter] When I repeated this to my friends, nobody laughed. They didn't know what I meant by a "flat store." I don't know how you could grow up in Las Vegas, and not know what a flat store was. [laughter] Jimmy coined another phrase that brings a smile to my lips and a glow to my eyes: "The only thing on the square in Clark County, Nevada, is the crap tables." Recent news events will lead you to the conclusion he may be right.

Jimmy, in particular, remained one of my closest friends. He was a dealer at the Thunderbird when I met him. He's retired, but he wound up his career as casino manager of the Flamingo. Anything Jimmy would tell me, I would accept as the absolute truth, and that is the case of most old-time gamblers. Their word was good—particularly Jimmy. Jimmy played a very important role in Sawyer's campaigns for governor. Most old-time gamblers were generous and decent, but each of them had a great sense of humor.

These people became dear friends. George Deverell wound up as a high executive. He was at one time at Caesars, also at the Desert Inn—closely associated with Burton Cohen.[7] Louie DiGregorio wound up, I think, as casino manager at the Union Plaza. He'd been in Atlantic City and was high at the Flamingo here. Verne Phipps was a craps dealer at the Golden Nugget. Snap Staley sat on the box at the Dunes. I don't know where Snap learned the trade, but he'd come here from Kansas City or some place like that. He's dead. Verne is dead. That leaves, out of that group, just Jimmy. They could tell me a lot—and did—about people they worked for in Kentucky, Chicago, Florida. Some of the people they told me about working for were also in Las Vegas.

The one guy that pops to mind that Jimmy knew was Tommy Callahan. I never represented Tommy, who became a friend of mine, but Tommy was a gambling executive here and in Kentucky. He and Jimmy were friends. Tommy and Benny Goffstein had the Pioneer Club on Fremont. Jimmy worked for the two of them; Jimmy was sort of their casino manager. The two of them put together the deal for the Four Queens. Jimmy went with them, and was casino manager until he went to the Flamingo not long after Hilton bought it.

The story was that Hilton bought the Flamingo to start assembling his organization for the Hilton on Paradise, which had been the International. The Flamingo, from the time Hilton bought it up until the time Jimmy went to work there, had been in the red constantly. It was never in the red one day after Jimmy became casino manager. There's been all that renovation since, and it became, I think, the biggest cash cow of the Hilton gambling empire. Jimmy got it into the black when it was still the old hotel and may have been dying. Jimmy's very proud of that, and well he should be.

Oh God, did McDonald attract an interesting group of clients. When I came down, Joe represented the Hotel New Frontier, the Silver Slipper, and the Royal Nevada, which had opened about the same time right next door and been taken over by the Stardust later. I'll never forget the Royal Nevada opened with "Guys and Dolls," the original Broadway cast. Those guys in the cast would be in the casino playing and joking. It was a different town. B. S. Pully and Stubby Kaye were in that cast. They did the movie. Robert Alda was in the cast at the Royal Nevada.[8] I had read some Runyon, and it was funny to hear all these guys sounding like some of the characters I met in Las Vegas!

The Royal Nevada went busted and closed at midnight, December 31, 1955. I got a call from Joe. I was in bed asleep. It was about eleven at night. He says, "Get to the back door of the Royal Nevada with your station wagon." He didn't tell me why. They were closing because they couldn't pay their license fee. They had to have it paid before December 31 to open in the next quarter. They prepared all of these New Year's dinners, all on trays, ready to heat the next day. They were all going to go to waste. Joe had a station wagon, and we loaded our wagons. We took turkey dinners to every friend we had in Las Vegas and some of the charitable organizations. We hauled away as much as we could. We left a bunch at the hospital. I don't remember every place we went, but boy, you never saw so many beautiful turkey dinners in your life. Old Joe was on top of it. [laughter] Joe didn't miss a bet. And we had plenty of turkey dinners for ourselves New Year's Day.

The majordomo at the New Frontier in those days was Maury Friedman, a very interesting man I got to know well. Very early, I got to know the Las Vegas-type gambler. On the one hand, I was dealing legally with owners, principally Friedman, and on the other, I was dealing with dealers, really opening my eyes. I'd been around gambling all my life, but I had no idea what real gambling was. In Elko those were small operations, and mostly local guys were working in the joints.

Maury was one of the most interesting men I ever knew in my life—absolutely brilliant. He had a great sense of humor, and he was fun. When the New Frontier opened, Joe was given, as counsel, the power of the pencil, meaning he could sign comps. That was available to Joe's wife, Mary Gene, another character. She would take her friends for lunch, maybe have a bridge party, and comp the whole thing. One day Maury called Joe. He said he didn't mind Mary Gene signing for all of this, but he did object to her comping the tip. Maury was laughing, and so was Joe. Joe said, "Jesus, Mary Gene, you can't comp the tip!" [laughter]

After Joe left, I continued to represent Maury. Maury was the president; he had put that New Frontier deal together. There were about forty minority stockholders. (There used to be a limit under Nevada law, and everybody who was a stockholder in a corporation had to be licensed if they shared in the profits.) Maury brought all of them in with a certain amount of their money invested in capital in the corporation and a certain amount in notes. A lot of them were square Johns. A "square John" is a guy who isn't in gaming; a square John is in some kind of other business.

The joint wasn't doing well. One minority stockholder, a car dealer in southern California, had become disgruntled. He'd spent a lot of money, and he was going to try to take over the corporation. He had to persuade a lot of other stockholders to go along with him. I'm the corporate attorney. I have to rule on all sorts of questions. They'd have meetings at night. It was the darndest thing I ever saw. I learned a lot of corporate law representing Maury. You'd start a meeting at four in the afternoon, and they'd recess about six. Everybody would go to their room or wherever they were, get all cleaned up, and see the show that night. After the show, they'd start again. After about a week, the man from California was able to get enough votes to elect a new board and throw Maury out as president. It wasn't ten minutes after the meeting that they'd reached that decision, they went to Maury's office, threw everything in the hall, and locked his door so he couldn't get back in. [laughter] Maury was one of the owners of the Silver Slipper, the Western Village, so he moved over there. (That company was the landlord for the New Frontier. The one going busted was the New Frontier operating company.)

The fight with this stockholder from California had been bitter. This guy had even hired FBI agents to try and find something. About three weeks after Maury was kicked out and moved to the Slipper, Maury wants me to come out. The Royal Nevada had gone busted, and Maury's going to meet with the guy who had taken over the New Frontier. They were going to buy the Royal Nevada as partners. [laughter] And did! I couldn't believe it! These guys had been at each other's throats!

I represented them. We went to Carson City, and, for some reason, they wouldn't give Maury a license, but would license this other guy and T. W. Richardson. For a time, they took over the Royal Nevada, but Maury was not supposed to have anything to do with it. T. W. was Maury's partner. I don't know how they got together. T. W. came out of Mississippi. He and Benny Binion were close. There were quite a few in the business from Mississippi and Texas. Joe W. Brown came from Gulfport or Biloxi, and ran the Horseshoe while Benny was away at "college," as they say. (He was in jail.) T. W. had been involved in gambling there for a long time. He and Maury became friends and partners. T. W. was well-liked, a typical southern gentleman.

I represented Maury in matters other than at the New Frontier. When he put together the deal for the Lake Mead Marina, I represented him and some other people. The game was exciting to him—putting deals together and getting the edge. Maury was later convicted in federal court of cheating in a gin game at the Friar's Club in Los Angeles. Hank Greenspun was one of the guys he allegedly cheated out of a substantial amount of money. Hank's one of the guys who wrote the judge asking him to give Maury probation, although Hank was one of the victims. After Maury was sentenced and did time at Lompoc, Hank wrote to the parole people trying to get Maury out. By that time, I was not representing Maury any more. Our relationship came to the point where I said, "I want to be your friend, but I don't want to be your lawyer." And I suspect he thought he needed somebody different than me.

Maury later built what is now the Frontier. The New Frontier went busted. Doc Bayley had it for a while. It didn't do well, but he kept it open for a long time without gaming; just the hotel was open. Ultimately, it was torn down, and the present Frontier built. I understand, from what I read in the papers—I had no personal knowledge—Maury was licensed there, and was the boss. There was trouble with the control board concerning people brought into the deal from Detroit, I think.

Maury died too young; T. W. is dead . . . a lot of the color of the community, as it was then, has died. I think those characters are missed. They kept the town exciting and interesting. And they participated in community affairs. Everybody knew Maury. Everybody knew Rich. Everybody knew everybody. They supported and participated in charitable events, things of that kind. You'd see them around, at functions.

They participated in politics, generally on both sides. They spread their money around evenly. [laughter] They didn't really try to control anybody, they just wanted to be left alone. Those who had been gamblers out-of-state, I believe, honestly appreciated that for the first time in their business lives, what they were doing was legal. Therefore, I think they wanted to be part of the community. Many of them made this their home and stayed here even when they were no longer in the business. When they retired or sold out, many of them returned to where they came from, but most of them stayed, particularly the working guys, and made Nevada their home.

Joe and I were new insofar as practicing law in the community, although both of us were known around other parts of the state. We were in general practice, and we were busy. All those stock promoters, penny uranium stocks, they were promoters. We did our share of migratory divorce. I had some good mining cases. It's just a shame we didn't stay together longer, really, in the sense of the fun. Joe was the type of guy that attracted those people, because Joe was one of them! Joe was dead square honest, but he enjoyed that type of activity, associating with the smart guys.

One time Joe represented Sammy Mannarino, out of New Kensington, Pennsylvania. He couldn't get a gambling license—he never even applied for one in Nevada—but he had a bridge club out on the Strip. Joe represented the guy that owned the building and leased it to Sammy. Joe was going to Washington on business, and he decided he'd stop in New Kensington and see Sammy. Joe came back and was really laughing. Sammy had showed him around New Kensington, and he wanted to give Joe a present. He gave him a pistol. [laughter] And he happened to be at that Appalachian meeting. That's how we found out what were alleged to be his connections. He was at the big meeting that finally may have convinced J. Edgar Hoover maybe there was a mob organization in this country. [laughter]

JoJo Mannarino was Sammy's brother. JoJo stuttered. JoJo told me one time, "I was the o-o-only m-m-man in Am-merica Al Capone was s-s-scared of." [laughter]

One time, when the old airport was on the Strip, Sara and I were going some place. JoJo was there. I said, "Where are you going?"

"D-Detroit."

I said, "When are you coming back?"

He said, "Tonight." It made you wonder why he was going to Detroit on such a short mission. [laughter]

When Joe was there, the office was full of characters out of Damon Runyon, without question. Not all of them, but many of the people we represented: there were cross-roaders, good old fashioned madames . . . not objectionable as clients, but we drew the line at pimps.

We had this one guy . . . Bill O'Reilly, who was high up in the sheriff's office, was always rousting him. He wanted him out of town. Joe represented him. O'Reilly would just pick him up and throw him in the can. He wouldn't charge him. (They have more rules now than they used to.) We'd have to file for writ of habeas corpus and serve it on the sheriff, and they'd let him out. He'd be out a couple of weeks, and they'd do it again. Joe finally had a petition commercially printed. The minute he got arrested, all he had to do was sign that petition and file it, and they'd let him out. [laughter]

1. Vegas Village was a Southern Nevada grocery store with several outlets.

2. David Zenoff later was district court judge (1958-65) and a supreme court justice (1965-77). J. Kell Houssels, Jr., son of a longtime casino operator, became an attorney and hotel-casino owner and executive. His then-wife, Jeanene, was his law partner.

3. James Bilbray was Clark County assessor and a longtime politician and businessman. His son was a university regent (1969-73), an unsuccessful congressional candidate (1972), a state senator (1981-86), and a representative in the first congressional district (1987-95).

4. Frank Lausche, a Democrat, was governor of Ohio, 1945-47 and 1949-57, and senator, 1957-63.

5. Westside refers to West Las Vegas, specifically A to H Streets and from Washington to Bonanza. First developed by surveyor J. T. McWilliams to compete with the railroad townsite in 1904 and 1905, it became predominantly a black residential area, thanks to the segregationist policies of the railroad and the city.

6. James McMillan, Las Vegas's first black dentist, and Charles West, the town's first black doctor, were leaders in the NAACP, active in Democratic politics, and involved in the beginnings of the black community newspaper, now called the *Sentinel-Voice*.

7. Burton Cohen is a longtime casino executive, associated with several resorts, most notably president of the Desert Inn, and is now a consultant.

8. Robert Alda appeared in the Broadway version. In the 1955 film, Marlon Brando played the role of Sky Masterson. B.S. Pully played Big Julie and Stubby Kaye played Nicely-Nicely both on Broadway and in the film.

14 | A Law Firm, or a Political Firm?

In Alan Bible's campaign in 1956, Joe McDonald was the manager. (My role was insignificant.) If Bible hadn't been so straight-laced, I can't even imagine the things Joe might have dreamed up, because Joe was good at dreaming up things. [laughter]

Early in 1956, Cliff Young, our congressman, announced he was going to run for the Senate.[1] There were stories that Bible was not going to run for reelection. Mahlon Brown filed for the Senate, thinking Bible was not going to run.[2] I didn't even plan to go to the state Democratic convention in Lovelock, but Joe went. Then Joe called and asked me to come up, and I'm not certain why. But I got in the car, drove up, and was in several informal meetings with Senator Bible and Joe and Bob. I don't recall who else might have been there. Fred Anderson might have—some of Bible's friends.[3]

Bible told us he was not going to run. That was a disappointment. I was and am a great admirer. I supported him in 1952 as best I could when I was in Elko and in 1954. I remember using the phrase that to my knowledge, Bible was the first real senator we had—more than just an ambassador from Nevada. He didn't want to introduce legislation unless it had merit. [laughter]

We were all used to having private bills introduced to keep Basque sheepherders in the country. I think that was done regularly by attorneys in counties that had a large sheep industry. The government wanted to deport a sheepherder, and the rancher wanted to keep that sheepherder. Senator McCarran would introduce a private bill that would suspend deportation immediately. The first time I had to write Bible to see if he'd introduce a special bill for this, I thought it was routine. He wrote back and wanted to know the merits. I remember talking to Bob McDonald about it—he had the same experience. I admired him greatly for that. Nothing ever happened—I should make this clear—to lessen my admiration for the man. Some things happened to him and me politically through the years, but nothing that caused me to lose my admiration for Bible.

162

*A Law
Firm,
or a
Political
Firm?*

It looked like he was not going to run, and Young and Brown were. I'll never forget Joe McDonald—all of a sudden everybody's going to run for the Senate. Jay Sourwine decided *he* was going to run. He'd been around northern Nevada and came to our office in Las Vegas to talk to Joe. Joe was a very open and frank man. He told us all the support he had, like he had talked to Dan Shovelin in Battle Mountain. Dan was national committeeman. He said, "Dan Shovelin's for me," as though that made a hell of a lot of difference. Jay thought that was big. He's telling us all these people are supporting him, and asked what we think. I didn't know what to say, so I kept my mouth shut. Joe says, "I got it figured this way, Jay. If there are four people running, you're bound to be fourth. Dead last." [laughter] Joe told him the truth, and of course, Jay got mad. Jay didn't believe him, but Jay finished *dead last.*

Not only was the Senate wide open—at least in the primary—but the House was open. Lo and behold, who's going to be the Democratic candidate? Walter Baring is going to try again. He'd been defeated in 1952 and 1954. There were stories Grant Sawyer might run. Grant didn't confirm or deny those. Joe decided *he* might run. The fire in his belly got burning. But he didn't want to if Grant was going to run. Joe decided I should get ahold of Grant, and we should meet. I talked to Grant, and sure, he'd like to meet. We decided to meet in Salt Lake City. Grant went over from Elko, Joe and I went up from Las Vegas, we stayed in the Hotel Utah, and we had a meeting.

I *knew* this was going to be the funniest meeting I'd ever been in, and I *knew* the main thing I should do is keep my mouth shut, because I knew exactly how Grant would handle it. [laughter] We get there, and Joe keeps explaining to Grant why he would like to run and thought he would have a good chance. He would appreciate it if Grant could tell him whether he was going to run, then Joe wouldn't run, but if Grant wasn't going to run . . . . Grant looked Joe right in the eye very calmly and said, "Well, Joe, I haven't made up my mind yet."

Joe says, "In case I do, would you run against me?"

Grant looked him in the eye: "If I decide I'm going to run, it won't make any difference who else is running." [laughter] That's exactly what I expected. I didn't break out laughing, but I was snickering to myself.

Grant kept his own counsel in many instances. He would make a decision as to what he was going to do and would not be influenced, except on rare occasions, by what somebody else was going to do. So, that ended the meeting. We went downtown, went out on the town a little bit, had dinner and had a nice time, and Joe decided he wasn't going to run for Congress.

Then Bible changed his mind. I thought that was good news. There's been a lot of speculation; a lot of people said Lyndon Johnson put pressure on him. I suspect that may be part of it. Joe decided we had to give him an excuse, some basis. So, Joe drew up a bunch of petitions. [laughter] He had me going up one side of Fremont Street and him the other side in all the bars and having everybody at the bar signing these petitions. He had that going on all over the state, so God, we had a big stack of petitions respectfully asking Senator Bible to reconsider, which he did. Some of them, I guess, were even registered voters!

Then Bible ran, and I think he was sensitive about having changed his mind. I remember him saying he would stay in the Senate as long as the people of Nevada wanted him to stay. I think he felt that quite strongly and stayed in the Senate a long time. But in our discussions in Lovelock, I gathered that he didn't really like it. He missed Nevada. He didn't really like Washington, but I'm sure he came to like it.

Now the campaign's on. Joe is working hard, but we're trying to build a practice. I'm starting to get work. Joe represented a couple of hotels, and I was meeting some of those guys. We were doing well, working hard, and getting started, and my participation in the campaign was limited. I sat in on meetings when the senator was in Las Vegas, and sometimes I drove him.

There was a convention that summer in Ely, which must have been the state labor convention, and all of the candidates went. I drove Bible from Las Vegas. The big money in campaigns today . . . it wasn't there then. Bible and I shared one room at the Hotel Nevada in Ely rather than buy two rooms. He was comfortable talking to people. We left Las Vegas and got to Alamo at sunset and spent the night at the old Dave Stewart home. The Stewart home took in roomers. Bible always stayed with them when he was campaigning that area. He was welcomed like an old friend. We went through the valley to Hiko and to Caliente. I took him around and realized he knew practically everybody in Caliente. He'd campaigned before and was highly regarded. Then in Pioche, we'd stop. I'd go with him up and down the street to all the business houses, and he had people in each of those communities he knew. We'd go to their house and visit with them. It was an old-time Nevada campaign.

We got to Ely and the labor convention. All the politicians would show up at the labor convention. They'd be scheduled to make a speech. Grant Sawyer was running for the board of regents, and he was to speak. Right to work was still an issue in Nevada in 1956, and how on earth is Grant going to address the question of right to work? He didn't want to take a position. By the same token, he wasn't going to make a false statement to them—say he opposed it, when he wasn't really opposed.

I was Grant's deputy district attorney the first time the Right to Work bill was an issue, and I had opposed the bill, done it publicly in speeches, and not hesitated to express my view. Now, at this convention, Grant addressed the issue like this: "I didn't think it was appropriate for me, as district attorney, to take a position one way or another on that bill. And the people are going to decide it. I don't think it's appropriate to take a position now. However, you may recall that my deputy, Ralph Denton, opposed the right to work bill all over the state, and I did nothing to stop him from doing so." [laughter] That satisfied them. He handled it very well.

While the Bible campaign was going on, Grant's campaign for board of regents was going on, and there was no money for it. In Las Vegas, Grant

164

*A Law
Firm,
or a
Political
Firm?*

knew me, Cal Cory, some of the Washington guys, and a few lawyers. He came down here. How do you campaign in a town like Las Vegas, even back then, when you don't have a lot of money? There was no television. You could take newspaper ads. We sat in our kitchen, Sara and Grant and I, and would take turns calling everybody in the phone book. That was mostly the campaign. But it was good experience for Grant. In those days, you campaigned the whole state. He was able to personally get around the whole state, and he met some people here.

Although he didn't win, in the next session, the legislature increased the size of the board and gave Russell the power to appoint new regents, and he appointed Grant.[4] Grant served at a crucial time. He and Bruce Thompson went on when the regents needed a common sense approach to problems, particularly with the administration of the university trying to restrict the academic freedom of some of the professors.[5] This is about the time they discharged professors for expressing their views on certain subjects that Minard Stout, the then-president of the university, opposed. Grant's level head helped leaven some of the extreme positions on the board.

I flew with Bible once. Joe got ahold of a helicopter some place. He'd have a little schedule in the paper, like he was going to land at the park in Maryland Parkway at a certain hour and then another place. Skipped all over town. One afternoon, I flew with him just for fun, more than anything. He had to have somebody with him, so I went. We'd come swooping down out of the air and land in the park. The senator would get out, he'd greet people, shake hands, and say a few words. The main thing was the press coverage. Most of the people around were kids that wanted to see the helicopter.

I went with him to the nuclear test site. We flew up in a military helicopter. By this time, I was developing friends on the Westside of Las Vegas. There were some active political organizations. I took Bible there. I'd accompany him on things like that. I certainly was not what you'd call an integral part of the campaign, plotting strategy. The significant thing, compared to now, is everybody who worked at headquarters pretty much was a volunteer. In those days, the Senate staff could just move out here and work. Whether they were on leave of absence, I don't know, but I don't think anybody saw anything the matter with a man's staff working for the man. They seem to forget that part of the job of being a senator is political. It has to be.

Other things were going on politically. You had this congressional race: Baring, Howard Cannon, Nada Novakovich, Cyril Bastian, Eugenia Claire Smith. Oh God, I was strong for Walter. I have to admit that. Like everybody else, I felt sorry for Walter. He was going around the state, "All these people are ganging up on me, and I don't have anybody. [sniffs] God, it's just awful." I didn't know Howard Cannon. I knew who he was and had a couple of legal matters with him, but I had no reason to support him; and I had no reason *not* to support Baring, a man I'd met in Washington when he was first in the Congress and I had supported in 1952, 1954, and 1956. Finally, he's a winner.

The general election was tight. That was a tough election for Bible. I think the world of Cliff Young, but he exhibited a quality in that campaign that isn't generally recognized. He could get snide and critical. It was not until late the morning after election that we found out Bible had won. Bible had lost that election until Clark County came in at about 11:30 at night, midnight. We got pretty low. We kept saying, "Well, when Las Vegas, when Clark County comes in, we're going to be all right."[6]

To me, that was a lesson that people up north, in the Democratic party, should stop this anti-Clark County feeling. If it wasn't for Clark, there wouldn't be a Democrat in office. Bible realized that was where his success or failure would be determined in an election. Bible was born in Pershing County, and I believe Young beat him there; Cliff was from Pershing, too. Before he went to the Senate, Bible lived most of his life in Washoe, and I believe Young beat him there. That was another reason I was always proud of Bible: there was not the least bit of regionalism in him.

During that campaign, Grant and I had gone to some sort of a Democratic function at the Desert Inn, and were standing in front talking to Nada Novakovich, a lawyer in Reno whom we had known in Washington. She had been a secretary in Senator Malone's office. We made some comment about how beautiful the hotel was. She said, "Well, it's really beautiful, but this isn't really Nevada." I thought, "What do you mean it's not Nevada? You're down here getting some votes. If you're going to get elected to Congress, you're going to get elected in Clark County. You're not going to get elected in Nye County where you came from or Washoe." That early on, as a transplant to Clark County, I began resenting the northern Nevada attitude toward Clark.

The main reason Clark came through for Bible is that it is overwhelmingly Democratic. History has proven, I think, a lot of Clark County Democrats in those days were Republicans, but registered Democrat. They couldn't vote for Young in the primary. If they were going to vote, they had to vote for a Democrat. Bible was well-known. He'd been not only attorney general, he'd been on the ballot a lot of times. Name recognition, even then, was big. He knew a lot of people in Las Vegas. He played the lead role in acquiring the Basic Plant in Henderson for the state while he was attorney general. After he went out as attorney general, he was still retained by the state as special counsel to the Colorado River Commission.

When I got to Las Vegas in August 1955, it had already been determined that Joe McDonald was going to be Bible's campaign manager in 1956. Joe really wanted to go back to Washington to become a big lobbyist.

166

*A Law
Firm,
or a
Political
Firm?*

Lobbyists are like the people we're talking about, most of them. They're smart. They're operators. Joe had met quite a few of them when he was working for McCarran. [laughter]

It didn't work out. I don't know how long Joe stayed in Washington—two or three years. Then he came back to Reno and promoted all sorts of different ventures. I missed Joe. Eva called one time. I had some old McDonald fees still due, and when they'd come in, I'd immediately write a check to Joe for half of it and send him the check in Washington. Eva told me Joe had come prancing in and says, "Look what I got. That Ralph Denton, he's on the square. Look at this. Don't worry about me, Eva, I've got plenty." [laughter]

Back in Las Vegas, Joe did fine. He had a saloon, the Roaring Twenties. He had a swing from the ceiling and a girl in the swing. He went into construction, opened an office here, and had some success. He opened some sort of store in Reno. Joe and I stayed close. I thought the world of him. He called me the night before he left to go to Sacramento to have a bypass operation. It came as a complete surprise to him. He had a routine physical, and they decided he needed a bypass. He came out of surgery, everything was fine, and he went into a coma and spent the last two or three years after that in a coma in a convalescent home in Reno and died in the early 1980s.

One story about Joe should indicate his nature. In Reno, he had a Mexican fellow working for him, Jose. I don't know if the guy was legal. Joe liked him. (Joe was always good to people. He could scream at you, but you wouldn't get mad at Joe.) Joe opened a savings account at a Reno bank and put it in joint tenancy with his wife and Jose. Every time Joe was around that bank, if he had a few dollars in his pocket, he'd throw it into that account. It built up to $10,000. Then Joe was in this coma. The account sat there. Joe had the foresight, with help from Loy Martinet, that he bought a large insurance policy. I'm sure it had been a burden on Joe to keep that policy, but when he died, Mary Gene was well taken care of. She discovered this account. Jose had long since returned to Mexico, to his home in a little village north of Guadalajara, where he had died.

Mary Gene took the money out of that savings account. We happened to be in Puerto Vallarta at the time, and we saw Mary Gene. She had flown to Guadalajara by herself, rented a car, and driven to this little Mexican town and found Jose's family—his wife, kids—and gave them more money than they had ever seen or hoped to see. I'm told they had a party in that town that lasted for a long time. [laughter] Mary Gene did exactly what Joe would have wanted her to do. I thought it typical of Joe. I don't know many guys that open a savings account for somebody who works for them in a very menial capacity. Joe put it away hoping he wouldn't have to use it some time, that there would come a time when he would feel at liberty to give it to Jose. He would have if he'd lived. He'd have probably given it to him when Jose went back to Mexico.

When Joe had left our partnership in Las Vegas to go to Washington, I had thought, "Well, for Christ's sake, here I am left alone in Las Vegas to try and make a living practicing law on my own." But that didn't scare me. I figured I'd make a living some way. The overhead wasn't too high in the old professional building, and in those days, migratory divorces would at least keep food on your table. [laughter]

About that time, Cal Cory had a heart attack. He had good accounts, but he was not going to be able to devote full-time to the practice anymore. His wife Beth

167

A Law
Firm,
or a
Political
Firm?

"We happened to be in Puerto Vallarta . . . ."

came to see if I would consider becoming a partner with Cal. She had talked to Cal, and Cal said I was one of the few young lawyers in town he would feel comfortable being associated with. I had an office going and wanted to move to another office for three lawyers and get out of the old Carl Ray building. Then Chet Smith, who had been working for Bible, finished law school, passed the bar, and wanted to come to Nevada to practice law. He came out, and we formed a partnership in the United Mortgage Building at 212 Las Vegas Boulevard South, now part of the old Nevada State Bank.

We were all busted. None of us had any money, or at least Chet and I didn't—I don't know Cal's condition; he'd been practicing law a long time. But we had to put in leasehold improvements. One of the old McDonald and Denton clients was a builder, Mel Schroeder. He said, "Oh, hell, I'll come and put in your partitions and everything." He put in all of our partitions and walls and electrical work. Mel just did everything and said, "We'll write it off against fees in the future." So, we were able to get that lease hold and stuff done. It was a big rent in those days for three of us.

God almighty, I took too much space! We had a reception room and an area for secretaries and three offices. I thought they were awful big. And we had a conference room. Oh, boy, did I think we had a rent—$600-$700 a month. I was nervous as a proverbial whore in church about taking on those expenses. But we did.

That practice was different. There wasn't the hustle, if you will, that there had been with Joe. [laughter] I missed the con men, the characters. I continued to represent a couple of the guys at the Frontier. I met Jimmy Garrett and a lot of dealers, and was representing them. I continued to meet

168

*A Law
Firm,
or a
Political
Firm?*

a lot of the working guys in the gambling business for whom I took on great affection.

That partnership must have started in the spring of 1957. It continued through 1958. Cal would come in half a day there for quite a while. I know we were still partners when Grant ran for governor in 1958 and after he took office in 1959. The firm broke up toward the end of 1959 or early 1960. Law firms are funny. There are two times when law partners have trouble. One is when you're not making any money, and two is when you're making quite a bit. If you're not making any, then everybody's complaining. Partners start complaining, "Well, I'm bringing in more than him." If you're making a lot of money, then a partner will say, "Well, I ought to get more, because I'm doing more." Ours started to break up because we weren't making any money. [laughter]

I think Cal became city attorney. He represented the Union Pacific, so if he became city attorney, he could still handle that account. Chet decided he wanted to go back to Washington for Bible, and I think Bible approached him, needed him. I don't know for sure, but Chet went back to Washington and said it was going to be temporary. The firm stayed Denton and Smith, but Chet never came back to practice law. So, there I was, stuck with that big rent, that overhead. [laughter]

There were a couple of interesting political things at the beginning of the Sawyer campaign for governor. Cal and Grant had been close in Washington. They had been there before 1942. Cal was close to Charlie Russell. They'd worked on the ECA committee under McCarran, when he was chairman. Chet had gone back and forth from Las Vegas to Washington, but he was on that committee payroll in those days, and they had become close. Chet was a Democrat, Chet and Grant were good friends, but Chet was likewise a close friend of Russell's.

When Grant comes to Las Vegas and he's going to run for governor, he comes to see us. I'm the only one completely free to help him, although I worked under Russell's patronage. It did give me a bit of concern to the point where I talked to Charlie and told him I was going to support Grant and work in his campaign. Charlie was a perfect gentleman, said he understood. Cal and Chet were more sensitive to that, although both of them remained good friends of Grant's, and I think did what they could to help him. That didn't cause any problems. They understood why I would support Grant.

So, as a brand-new partnership, we were already involved in politics. The two do not mix. You're going to be a law firm or a political firm, because the minute you get as active in politics as I was, your reputation changes from that of lawyer to politician. A lot of potential clients didn't come to us because of our involvement. If you think about it, big business clients want to be able to operate no matter who is in office. If their lawyer is active in the Democratic party and you've got a Republican governor, they're going to feel a little nervous before a state agency. To a certain extent, that was one of the reasons we were not making it. Cory, Denton, and Smith weren't making more than just a bare living. So, Cal became city attorney; Chet went back to the Senate, and I stayed in the three-man office with a three-man rent by myself. [laughter] It was fine. I made a living.

Notes

1. Clifton Young defeated Walter Baring for reelection to the House in 1952. He subsequently served as a state senator from Washoe County (1967-83) and a Nevada Supreme Court justice (1984-).

2. B. Mahlon Brown was a Las Vegas attorney who served as a state senator from Clark County (1951-75). His son was a U.S. attorney and his grandson is now a municipal judge.

3. Dr. Fred Anderson lost to Howard Cannon in the Democratic primary race for U.S. Senate in 1958, then was a member of the Board of Regents from 1957 to 1979. He also has completed an oral history for the University of Nevada Oral History Program.

4. In a four-man race for two seats, Sawyer ran third, behind Dr. Fred Anderson and Archie C. Grant.

5. Bruce Thompson, later a longtime federal judge, was elected to the board of regents in 1954. Thompson was defeated for re-election in 1958. He was appointed federal judge in 1963.

6. Bible defeated Young, 50,677-45,712.

15 | A Lot of Color in the Bar

I had wanted to come home to Nevada and practice law. I felt confident in any field of the law. We weren't specialists. If it was a divorce, I'd take a divorce. If it was a contract, I'd draw a contract.

When you think about it, the law is a culmination of human experience, what the best minds have created as basic rules to govern our conduct. How well the system works is remarkable. I came away from law school with great respect for the law and tolerance for those lawyers who don't feel the same way I do. [laughter] I don't know how you could complete law school without great respect for the law and a realization—to me, this is important—that the practice of the law is tinged with the public interest. We're part of the judicial branch. We have an obligation to serve the public. I lose patience with those who regard it solely as a vehicle for amassing money.

I know I'm out of touch with today's standards. The minute the client can't pay so many dollars per hour, you let the door hit them in the hind end. That's not the way the profession should be practiced. Enough people with money will pay you for your work, you ought to be able to work for those who can't. The attorney-client relationship is based on mutual trust: trust by the client in the attorney, and in the client by the attorney. I have brought a couple of suits against clients. I filed one against an Air Force colonel, who appeared at court with his wings and ribbons. He was charged with shop-lifting in a pornographic shop in Las Vegas. [laughter] I got him off, and he wouldn't pay. To me, that was a matter of principle.

When I got here, Las Vegas had a fascinating legal community. One of the most important firms was Jones, Wiener, and Jones. The other big firm was Morse, Morse, Graves, and Compton: Harold and Bill Morse, father and son, Maddy Graves, and Bill Compton. They were about the only big firms.

I met Cliff Jones when he ran for lieutenant governor.[1] I had never met Herb, nor Louis Wiener. I'd read all the stories about that firm's connection with peddling juice to applicants for gambling licenses. Cliff and Louis boasted they could guarantee a hoodlum a gambling license, plus they had the *Re-*

view-Journal in their pocket.[2] There had been a lot of publicity. The Democratic central committee had a meeting and were going to remove Cliff. (He was given the appellation of "Big Juice." His brother Herb was referred to as "Little Juice.") I came to Las Vegas with a very unfavorable impression of them, but I met them as soon as I got there and became, I think, a good friend of Louis, Herb, and Cliff.

McCarran said one time, "Cliff wants to be the Thatcher Woodburn of southern Nevada," the political boss. I never had many dealings with Cliff, but, for a while, Herb and I were both on the board of directors of the Bank of Las Vegas (later Valley Bank). Herb and I became friends, our wives became friends, and our children, for that matter.

My first dealing with another attorney in Las Vegas was with Louis Wiener. I was new in town and didn't know Louis. My client, a man, had been sued for divorce. Louis was the attorney for the plaintiff. In asking the client when he was served with the complaint, he told me it was more than twenty days before, and he hadn't answered. I called to see if Louis would give me an extension. I said, "Hello, Mr. Wiener. My name is Ralph Denton. I just moved here from Elko. I represent Mr. So-and-so. I'd appreciate it if you could give me an extension of time to answer."

He said, "Gosh, I've already taken a default."

I said, "Could you stipulate to set the default aside?"

He told me his client would just kill him if he did that, but to file my motion, and we should go over to the court about fifteen or twenty minutes before the hearing. He said, "We'll go in and talk to Frank." He was referring to Judge McNamee.

We went into chambers. Louis told the judge he felt bad he couldn't stipulate to set aside the default, and his client would read the riot act to him if he did. But he didn't mind if the judge granted my motion. We then went into court. I argued as best I could; Louis put on a great argument against, and of course, McNamee granted my motion. I can't think of a better example of collegial courtesy. Attorneys like to cooperate on procedural things, particularly a default. It should go to trial on the merits. His client wasn't injured, and Frank might have granted the motion anyway.

Through the years, I had many dealings with Louis, all of which left me with a good taste in my mouth. He wanted to do the best he could for his client. Louis didn't want to book any losers, as a gambler would say. He was a gentleman, courteous, and respected the profession. I thought no matter what Louis did, no matter how involved he got in business, no matter how successful those businesses were, to himself, Louis was just a lawyer.

Louis was indeed a character. That's what I miss. There was a lot of color in the bar. There isn't anymore. Everybody wears three-piece suits. They all look alike, sound alike, and talk alike. What happened to Louis and George Franklin and Harry Claiborne and people like that? [laughter]

George Franklin wasn't D.A. when I came here. He was practicing law. He'd run against McCarran in 1950. I knew Franklin and his family. One of his wives was a Caliente woman whose family was well known to me, and she was known to me. Her name was Laura Gentry, a sister, I think, of Lillian Barnum, a Gentry from Caliente married to Bruce Barnum. George was colorful.

George was also effective. I had one case with him. I represented the wife. The husband had taken $40,000 out of their savings account. We're trying to get the community property divided in divorce, and I'm trying to get him held responsible for the $40,000, at least get her her half back. George believed it's not community property. He'd already spent it. He lost it gambling. I couldn't believe a judge would swallow that, but the judge did! [laughter] When clients ask me if they should take the money and hide it, it's generally my view it was community property, and they might want to protect the money, but not hide or spend it. Now when that question's asked me, I wonder whether I ought to tell them to swing with anything in sight. [laughter]

Before I was Hank Greenspun's attorney, George sued the *Sun* for libel. The jury gave him a judgment. Hank had insurance. The insurance company wanted to pay it off. Hank wanted to appeal. The company gave Hank $75,000, and he released them from liability. Hank appealed, and the Supreme Court reversed. Hank made $75,000 out of Franklin's suit against him. [laughter] George never forgot that. Oh God, they battled. George took a little ad in the *Review-Journal* almost every day, George says. [laughter] He would be tearing after Hank. I'm not sure what Hank said about him.

George had taken on a practice common in those days. Adoptions were handled privately. The ob-gyn may have a pregnant girl. The ob-gyn would call a lawyer, and the lawyer might know somebody who wanted to adopt. We didn't have agencies where people could get babies. The statute provided an adoption could not be granted without the welfare department having filed a report. These private adoptions would be arranged between an ob-gyn, a lawyer, and the adoptive parents. The consent to adoption was to be sent to the welfare department. Then they were to make a report. But the statute gave the judge the right to dispense with the report. Of course, the natural mother had to give consent. There was no provision if it was illegitimate that the father had to. In my judgment, it meant the name of the adoptive parents had to be in it.

In those days, people didn't want the natural mother to know the identity of the adoptive parents. I was familiar with that. I arranged adoptions for close friends and clients, but I always made sure the name of the adoptive parents was there, and the natural parent read it; always referred it to the welfare department for an investigation, and never charged for adoptions. But large sums of money were changing hands involving attorneys.

Clarence Breeze was Dean Breeze's father, an old-timer, kind of an old man when I got here. He'd been justice of the peace, and he was entitled to and wore with pride the appellation of Judge. Dean was a young man with a great conscience, one of the early leaders of the ACLU in Nevada. He devoted his life to trying to help people who really needed help and couldn't afford it. I think he started a Unitarian church in North Las Vegas. He was the type of man that makes you proud of your profession.

Oscar Bryan was the funniest man I ever knew. He and Cal Cory had been partners. I remember Cal telling me the senator was mad at him because he didn't put his name first in the firm; it should have been Cory and Bryan. [laughter] Oscar should have been a professional entertainer. Jones, Wiener, & Jones used to have a big Christmas party at their office. Every lawyer in town and their staffs were invited. The first I got to know Oscar was at those parties. He was the preeminent center of attention. Oh, God, he was funny—he would have everybody in hysterics all of the time.

Oscar did an awful lot of divorce work. Soon after I got here, I ran into him in the courthouse and said, "How are things going, Mr. Bryan?"

He said, "Oh God, it's already ten o'clock, and I've only made $3,000 so far." Just joking. He'd probably been over on a couple of uncontested divorce cases.

Later, Oscar became justice of the peace. He told me the way he decided cases: "I take a yellow notebook and write 'plaintiff' on one side of the paper and 'defendant' on the other. If the plaintiff makes a good point, boomp, a point for the plaintiff. If the defendant makes a good point, oop, a point for the defendant. When the case is over, I add up the points. The one that has the most points wins." [laughter] I had a great feeling of warmth toward Oscar. I got to know his wife, Lillian, and was fond of Lil.

Harry Claiborne was colorful, as fine a trial lawyer as I have seen. At one time, Harry was an evangelical preacher in Arkansas or Tennessee. He carried that persuasive ability to harangue a crowd and was very effective. He thought fast on his feet. Harry and I tangled many times, mostly in the courtroom. In those days, criminal law was not remunerative. Most accused of crimes are busted. Harry was in general practice, handled private cases. He'd get high-profile murder cases, and he was good. The big federal crimes, where the defendants had lots of money—it wasn't until then that Harry became exclusively a criminal lawyer.

Bill Compton was from the firm of Morse, Graves, and Compton. They did most of what insurance defense work there was in town. Vegas hadn't developed a big bar and big firms that had great reputations, so a lot of big cases were handled by Reno lawyers or Salt Lake or Los Angeles law firms. Bill did a lot of insurance work and did it well. He was judge for a long time (1960-75). Everybody thought he was a fine judge, but you'd wait for a decision a long time. Then you'd get it, and it would be well-written. Attorneys generally prepare findings of fact or conclusions of law after the trial; in complicated cases, Bill would prepare his own. When Bill was defeated for re-election, he went back into practicing law. I gave him space in my office, because he didn't have any practice—he'd been on the bench all that time.

I had one colloquy with Bill when he was a judge. I represented a lovely California lady in a divorce. They had three or four children, one mentally handicapped. They reached a property agreement and custody agreement and child support agreement before she came up to establish residence and get the divorce. The agreement was generous. The husband bent over backwards to be fair and make adequate financial provisions, particularly for the disabled child, but the wife did not want the divorce. She had been persuaded by her husband, and it was obvious to her the marriage was over, he had another woman he wanted to marry. She complied, and came up to get the divorce.

I represented her when the grounds of incompatibility were new. Until that time, there were several grounds for divorce, but the one used generally was called "cruelty, mental in nature." We had a routine of questions we'd ask as to what constituted cruelty. Nobody knew what the heck incompatibility was, so in your first couple of incompatibility divorces, you didn't really know what questions to ask. This was my first incompatibility divorce, and it might have been Compton's first as judge. I prepared my questions by reading all the textbooks on incompatibility I could find as to the requisites to grant a divorce on it. Frankly, they're the questions that I ask today if I handle one of these, and most lawyers ask about the same questions.

In those days, you went in on uncontested divorce right after lunch. All of the cases sat in the courtroom until they were called. You had a courtroom full of lawyers waiting to bring on their cases, witnesses, the parties. The courtroom was full. It was a big calendar. It started at 1:30, and generally, the court might have had a trial starting at two. We're called. She's on the witness stand, and I asked these questions. We got through the property, residence, and child custody. The judge didn't say anything.

It got down to grounds. I asked the questions that established incompatibility: Is there a wide divergence existing between you and your husband as to tastes, natures, views, likes, and dislikes? Has this divergence become so great as to make it impossible for him and you to live in the true marital state? Is a reconciliation possible? I finished that, and Compton just shouted, "Those aren't grounds for divorce. What did he do to you!?"

She broke into tears. This was traumatic for her. I made a statement about the requirements for incompatibility. He snarled at me and her and granted the divorce.

After it was over, I went back to his chambers and asked his secretary if I could see the judge. She said yes, and I went in. I said, "Your honor, if you ever treat a client of mine like that again, I'm going to run against you. That client—she was a lady. She didn't deserve to be talked to the way you talked to her."

Bill was silent for a moment. He looked up and said, "Ralph, you're right. I'm sorry. It's just . . . I've got so many cases today, and I've got this trial starting. I'm sorry." We'd been friends, but I took on more respect for Bill. Other judges would have thrown me out.

One of his law partners, Madison Graves, was very colorful. Maddy was from Harvard, don't you know! [laughter] And you never forgot that. I liked Maddy. Our local bar association was informal. It was not structured, and we only met, if there was some reason to meet, at the old municipal golf course in the evening. They had a dining room and bar. Everybody would stand around and swill up booze at the bar before they ever got into the dinner and meeting. The first time I met Maddy at the bar, he said to the bartender, "Innkeepah, draw a dram for my friend, Ralph Denton." [laughter]

George Dickerson was district attorney. Of course, I knew of his family, but I had never met George. His father had been governor before my time. [Denver Dickerson was Acting Governor from 1908 to 1911, serving after the death of Governor John Sparks.] I met Harvey, who had run for state office. His older brother, Denver, was a real kick. He had this newspaper in Carson City, the *Nevada State News*, and he wrote a column titled "Salmagundi." Denver possessed a great sense of humor. Oh, God, Denver was a great Democrat! When Charlie Russell was governor, people were complaining, as they always do, that the governor traveled too much. Denver ran a story on the front page, and the headline said—like it was a news story—Russell spent Wednesday in Carson City on business. [laughter] God, he was funny!

Charlie Garner worked in the district attorney's office most of his career. When he, John Mendoza, and George Foley were partners, they were a blast. All good lawyers, active in politics; all, my dad would have said, close to the sporting element. [laughter] They would have long meetings at the bar of the Elwell Hotel. I envied them their street sense, because I didn't have much. But I had Joe McDonald. [laughter] There's a guy with street sense!

Charlie was a Las Vegas boy and a good guy, but he hated the state bar and wouldn't pay his dues. When I was on the administrative committee, we had to call Charlie in. He'd wait until it was about time to revoke his license, then pay. He resented that he had to be a member, the law *made* him be a member. That was wrong to Charlie. He always had a cigarette in his mouth; it always had long ashes; and the ashes always fell down his front. Sara used to refer to him as "Big Ash."

The Foley brothers. Their father and mother had been generous to Sara and me in the extreme when I worked in federal court. Roger, Tom, and Joe were here, and I think John. I'm not sure George didn't come later. The Foley brothers were a law firm, all good guys. I didn't know George until I came here, but I knew who he was; I remember Las Vegas High with George as their star, playing Lincoln County in Panaca with Lynn McGee as our star. Tom and I had gone to law school together, had been close friends. Joe and I studied for the bar together. We took the bar together. When we passed, he and I were admitted to federal court. His father swore in just the two of us. Joe married Betty, from a ranch at Elgin, below Caliente, whose family I had known. I met Roger in 1950 when he was running for district attorney against Oscar Bryan the summer we were out here campaigning for McCarran.[3]

Roger and I had a case against each other. It was a mining case in which I think I represented the claim jumper, and he represented the original locator. It was a well-tried case, and I heard from other sources that Roger expressed his opinion I was a fine lawyer and had done a good job. I certainly thought he had. That's the only time I remember us on opposite sides.

When I say there is no color left in the bar, you might infer that in those days, there was color. Mike Hines was one of the most colorful. Big guy from Notre Dame, always wore a big cowboy hat, rode his horse in the St. Patrick's Day parade. One time, he and Paul Price, who wrote a column for the *Sun*, entered a horse in the Kentucky Derby, One-Eyed Tom. How they got that horse, I don't know. But they got it in the Derby, and he came out of the chute backwards. [laughter] Mike was a great enthusiast for the horses.

Mike had a place he called "The Ranch" way out of town on Sahara Avenue—the middle of town now. He loved animals. He had his own zoo. You never knew what was going to be there. He would have a party for new admittees to the bar. It was informal and inexpensive, barbecues and beer. Everybody went. It would be another chance for us all to get to know each other. Nowadays, it's a formal party some place with invitations at so much a table.

I went up against Mike lots of times. As a matter of fact, I went through a time when Mike absolutely hated me. It was a terrible thing. [laughter] They were building a subdivision. Mike was attorney for the venture, and a principal. In those days, the Water District did not serve the whole valley. The lines had not been extended. If a guy got land way out in the desert from what was already developed, there was no water. They had to get a permit to dig a well, then developers would become a water company certified by the public service commission. Say there were 100 houses in the subdivision: now they had 100 customers in their water business, and they had the well.

Mike and his partner put in the water system. They no sooner got the houses built and sold than the water system was leaking. The pipes wouldn't hold water. A lawyer with an association with a Los Angeles firm filed against Mike and his partner for the purchase price of the pipe—over $150,000. About three weeks before trial, this Los Angeles firm called and asked if I would try the case in association. For some reason, the attorney who filed the suit wasn't going to handle it.

Mike's defense was clear: "I'm not going to pay for a pipe that leaks." The court gave the plaintiff a judgment, and I handled the writ of execution against the corporation. The execution was not sufficient to satisfy the judgment. I didn't do anything else, nor did the Los Angeles firm or the client.

Then I ran for Congress, and Mike was on my tail. He fought my candidacy like you cannot believe. He was pleasant when we'd see each other in court, but one time he stopped me in front of the courthouse and brought it up. He said he never could understand why I would take that case against him. I said, "Mike, you may recall, I didn't execute against you."

He was silent for a few minutes. He says, "You didn't, did you?"

I said, "No, I got my clients to walk away."

He thought for a minute. He says, "I'm sure sorry I've been such a bastard to you through the years." [laughter]

Mike was just a great guy, fun to try a case against, fun to have on the other side if you were negotiating a settlement or contract. And he was smart. Because he was such a character, some people underestimated his talents. He was a good lawyer.

I'd known of Artemus Ham, Jr.'s family for years. Art was not active in practice. His business affairs took a great deal of his time. I was involved in one estate in which he was an attorney. I saw Art go in the courtroom one time. Somebody said, "Gee, they must be giving Art an award today. He's in the courthouse." [laughter] Senior was alive at that time. I never got to know him, but you would see him—he had lunch every day in the Golden Nugget, because he was one of the owners.

I met Cal Magelby when I came here. I was familiar with Cal's father. He was the top guy in southern Nevada for the Bureau of Land Management after the Taylor Grazing Act was passed to allocate grazing licenses. The battles between Nevada cattlemen and Utah sheepmen were immense, and a lot of hearings were held in Caliente. The Utah men used to bring their sheep into Nevada, right through the middle of Caliente and to Pahranagat Valley across the Delamar flat, and north up toward Lund. That was their winter range. It was always a bone of contention between the cattlemen and the sheep men. Mr. Magelby had the thankless task of trying to bring order out of chaos. The net result was, I believe, the Utah sheep men don't come into Nevada anymore.

I remember three women attorneys: Virginia Miller, Nelle Price-Rossi, and Emilie Wanderer. I'm sad to say the bar was pretty chauvinistic. I had dealings with all three and thought they were nice. Nelle had been married to Roland Wiley, the attorney that had all that property down in North Las Vegas. He was here, had run for governor, later had this place out in Pahrump Valley, died just recently. He owned a lot of that where Main Street and Las Vegas Boulevard come together. Nellie, I think, was married to him once or twice. Emilie's son practices law here now—John Wanderer.

John McNamee was married to Pete Rittenhouse's sister. John was a delight to be around, a typical McNamee—great sense of humor, no pretense. I've never known a member of that family that was not like that. Strong Republicans in their politics, egalitarian in their views.

I had not met George Rudiak before I came here. George was a fine lawyer, but I never discerned even the hint of a sense of humor in George. [laughter] It was all business. I used to dread George on the other side of a negotiation. We would spend hours over every word to the point it would exasperate you. Keep in mind, it was the McCarthy era. You would hear whispers that he was a communist, which, of course, he never was. I think it's a credit to George that, notwithstanding those allegations, he lived them down. People respected him, lawyers respected him—he was a good man.

I know from George's business activities, he was certainly a capitalist. He was one of the owners of Valley Hospital. George represented Valley, and it was a tremendous success. George had also been the attorney for the teamster's union. He was in the legislature with my mother. She has caustic comments in her diary about some of her colleagues. [laughter] But I don't recall her having anything about George, except she thought he was bright and admired his courage. He introduced a civil rights bill, and that gained my mother's support and respect for him, because that was a courageous thing to do.

William "Wildcat" Morris was not here when I came here; Wildcat came later, even after I'd moved to Boulder City, which was in January 1959. He'd gone back to Washington to go to law school, I think, just before McCarran died. He was under Bible's patronage and went to law school, and I think was an integral part of Bible's organization. One of the funniest men I've ever known. (Oscar Bryan was the funniest man I'd ever known. Bill was a close second, with a charming, delightful wife.)

Notes

1. After a brief appointment as Clark County's district judge, Clifford A. Jones was elected lieutenant governor in 1946, defeating Republican Ernest Brooks, 26,540-22,602. He was re-elected in 1950 against Leo Schmitt, 31,356-29,571. Jones also served in one Assembly session (1941).

2. In 1954, Sheriff Glen Jones (no relation to Cliff and Herb) sued the *Las Vegas Sun* for libel. Publisher Hank Greenspun and reporter Ed Reid, with the Clark County district attorney's office, ran a sting operation, hiring a private detective to pose as a mysterious Eastern hoodlum. On tape, Jones and Wiener told him about their power, with Jones explaining that his sister, Florence Lee Jones, was married to *Las Vegas Review-Journal* managing editor John Cahlan. Cahlan's older brother, Al, was managing director of the paper and a co-owner.

3. Roger Foley was elected district attorney in 1950, did not seek reelection in 1954, was elected attorney general in 1958, and resigned in 1962 to succeed his father as a federal judge. He retired in 1982, but continued to hear cases until 1993.

16 | You Used to Try Cases

Bill Morse was in Las Vegas when I came, and I've enjoyed my friendship with Bill, although our political affiliations are different. He's a strong Republican, and I hope I'm a strong Democrat. Something he told me illustrates, I think, one big difference in the practice of the law now and what it was then: After Bill passed the bar, the first day he came to work, his dad handed him a file and said, "The trial's at ten o'clock. Go try this case."

You used to try cases. A judge would listen to the evidence, you'd make your argument on the law, and the judge would rule. Oh God, that's a terrible thing now! Now you have to have pre-trial statements and briefs before you go to court. This contributes to the cost of litigation. Back then, if the judge wanted a brief, he'd say so after he heard all the evidence if he wasn't sure. They might even tell you what they were interested in.

In that mining case against Roger Foley, the judge asked for briefs. He was interested in one point of law he wanted briefed. He said, "Mr. Denton, you have the laboring oar." He was telling me he wasn't certain what the law was on that point. What an orderly way to try to settle a dispute! Try it, put the facts on, argue the law, the facts, then let the judge decide; or let him say if he doesn't think he has enough information, ask for briefs. Now, I don't care what the case is, both sides have to file pre-trial statements, trial briefs. That costs money. The clients have to pay for all of that.

I don't think it leads to better lawyering. It leads to poorer results, because they're making up their minds on written materials the law clerks are reading. That statement is extreme, but the tendency is to have everything in writing only. Submitting matters on affidavits where the judge isn't looking a witness in the eye, doesn't have a chance to judge the credibility of a witness; where everything is in written affidavits, and the law clerks are reading the affidavits and giving the memoranda to the judges . . . . I suspect I'm way out of tune with most of my colleagues on that.

There were three judges when I came to town: Frank McNamee at department one, Bert Henderson at department two, Ryland Taylor at department three. It was such a pleasure to me, all three judges, compared to what I was used to.

I had known Frank when he was juvenile officer for the eighth judicial district court, which included Lincoln County.[1] Thank God I was never one of the people he was investigating. Frank generally dropped by and said hello to my mom and dad, and I knew him when I was a little boy, and when I came down here renewed the family's relationship.

Frank told me something sound from a judge's standpoint. I had an estate matter, and I was going in on the first and final accounting. In Elko, you put your client on the stand and went through every item. No objections had been raised, and the judge reviewed it and had no questions. Yet it would take you thirty to forty minutes to put on a first and final account and petition for distribution. I had the first one in McNamee's court after I came to Las Vegas, and I was surprised that he did it in chambers.

I did what I used to do up in Elko, and I took up a lot of McNamee's time. He didn't say a word. After it was over, he granted the petition and signed the order. We started to leave, and he said, "Oh, Mr. Denton, would you mind staying a minute? I'd like to talk to you." I went back in.

"Ralph, this petition was sworn to by your client. An attorney, a member of the bar—you—signed this petition. I have no reason to suspect that everything in it is not true. After you've been a judge for a while, you get to know which attorneys you can rely on and which ones you can't. I know you would not knowingly tell a lie in this petition, because you signed this petition. So, a judge has to rely upon his attorneys if he's going to conduct his business in an orderly fashion." I've remembered that conversation for so long, because now it seems most judges regard the attorneys as their enemies, expect to be bamboozled. [laughter]

Arguing before Frank was wonderful. Frank was very smart. He would never embarrass you in front of your client, but he would do a little thing during a trial I've never seen any other judge do. Fran Butterfield was his clerk. Let's assume I'm questioning a witness, and I'm going on and on. Frank might write a note, hand it to Fran, and say, "Give this to Denton." The note might say, "For God sakes, Ralph, haven't you been on this point long enough? Why don't you move on?" Never say anything in the courtroom that would indicate any criticism, but he'd let you know, "You're not impressing me. Will you just finish with this witness?"

I remember the first case I had. I had only been in town about a week. I'd done the research, and Joe asked me to argue it. Just a matter of pure luck, we got an advance sheet from the supreme court about three days before, which dealt with this same question. I read it. During my argument, Judge McNamee interrupted me and says, "Well, how about the case of such-and-such? That just came out."

I think Frank figured he had me. I said, "Oh, yes, your Honor, I'm glad you brought that up. That case holds . . . ." Frank was impressed. He was always prepared.

If I would have a criticism of Frank—I suppose this is reasonable, because a lot of judges do that—he would try and avoid cases that involved prominent people in the community he'd known all his life or that were politically sensitive, and bring in a judge from northern Nevada to hear it. He'd grown up here. He knew everybody in town. Chances are, he heard a lot of cases where both sides were friends of his. But if they were really tough and sensitive cases, he'd get somebody in from the north.

A. S. "Bert" Henderson was in department two.[2] Fine old gentleman, dead square honest, good judge. I enjoyed going before him. Toward the end of his career on the bench, maybe he should have retired a couple of years before he did. He taught school in Panaca at one time. I think Henderson was born in Eureka. The first time I went in, he called me to the bench and asked if I was any relation to Foghorn Denton. I said, "Foghorn Denton?" He says, "Yes, Senator Denton." He referred to my great uncle, a state senator when Clark and Lincoln were one county. Judge Henderson said, "I never heard such a political speaker in my life. We called him Old Foghorn."

We had a cordial relationship with Judge and Mrs. Henderson. He retired and bought a house on the west side of town. One evening, I thought I'd say hello. I drove *way* out in the desert to Arville. Now happens to be in the center of town. We sat on his front step a few minutes—nothing between his house and Mount Charleston. He was saying how he was enjoying it, how beautiful the desert was, and telling me he'd spent a career as a lawyer and judge. He wasn't rich, but he had income from a few investments to lead a decent life on his pension. Republican, though. He was in the legislature representing Clark County at the time they legalized gambling.

Ryland G. Taylor's reputation was that he'd been reversed a lot by the Supreme Court, and some of the lawyers were critical.[3] But he called them the way he saw them, did what he thought was right, and used to refer to the Supreme Court as the Court of Final Error. Among the three, he was the toughest in the sense of being severe with you. But he was a gentleman in every respect.

Some northern judges would come down to Las Vegas when local judges would have to step back. Merwyn Brown used to come down from Winnemucca quite a bit, and Jack Sexton started coming down a lot and became almost a fixture here.

When I was still in Elko, I had a case against the Shoshone Coca Cola bottling company in Reno. A client in Winnemucca bought a bottle of Coke, was drinking, and felt something funny. A mouse was halfway out of the bottle and had been in her throat. She became terribly ill. I sued the store where she bought the bottle and Shoshone Coca Cola. I go to Winnemucca to put on my case; Pete Echeverria comes up from Reno to defend; we settle. I'm happy; my client's happy.

I go back to Elko to await the check from the insurance company payable to my client and me. I get the check, and it's countersigned by Merwyn Brown! Judge Brown was an insurance agent all the time he was a judge, and he was an agent for the company liable on that policy. He was going to try that case without telling me. First time as a lawyer that I thought, "Do judges behave this way?" [laughter] I haven't had that thought many times. There are exceptions in my opinion, but most of the judges I know and have known are hard-working, dedicated, very attentive to that sort of thing.

We went through a string of justices of the peace—Joe Pavlikoski, Art Olsen, Jimmy Down, John Mendoza, Tom Pursel, Jim Brennan, Oscar Bryan. It was an unwritten law they could only serve one term, because they figured they got enough money from marriages that one term was enough. Hell, two years would damn near kill them. Most of them would sleep at the court a lot of times to be available for weddings. One term as JP in the Las Vegas township was enough to put you in the promised land financially. [laughter] Nobody knows how much money they made as JPs.

When I first started practicing law, district court judges did weddings, too. You could be trying a case, and all of a sudden you've got a recess while the judge marries somebody. [laughter] Happened a lot! That was the great source of income for judges in those days. There was no limit, and lawyers used to joke about it. Every time I see Pursel, I ask him, "It's been many years ago. Have you dug up the last can?" [laughter]

Just watching them on the bench, I never did have a desire to be a judge. I enjoyed practice so much. One of the wonderful things about practicing is your association with other lawyers. A judge is removed from that. You can never have the same relationship as a lawyer with a friend who becomes a judge; by necessity, it changes. You don't feel at ease, particularly if you're going to have cases in his court. In those days, you were more apt to do that. Now we've got so many judges, I suppose you could be good friends, and if you had a case in his department, go in a different department. But I've had judges complain that one of the things about being a judge they didn't care for was their isolation.

Notes

1. Frank McNamee was appointed a Clark County district court judge in 1946 and subsequently elected. In 1958, he was appointed to the Nevada Supreme Court and elected to a term. In 1965, he was severely injured and thus incapacitated; he died three years later.

2. A. S. Henderson served as district judge, 1946-60, when he resigned. He also was a Republican Clark County assemblyman, 1921-27, and state senator, 1927-35.

3. Ryland Taylor served as a district judge from his appointment in 1953 until his death in 1959.

17 | Not Political; Definitely Leaders

I suppose this is typical of most communities, but you've got two different groups of leaders: political leaders, who think they lead everything, and community leaders, who, perhaps, are completely behind the scenes. If they're involved in politics, it's only tangentially. When I came here, I was close to a political campaign to start with—Bible, then Sawyer in 1958. Most of what I would call the leaders at that time were political leaders; whereas, in years to come, I got to know other people, definitely leaders in business, social, and professional activities.

I hope what I say about Parry Thomas is not embarrassing to him, but Parry is one of the finest men I have known. Parry is more responsible for the growth of Las Vegas than almost anybody I know. When the Salt Lake group he was a part of bought out the Bank of Las Vegas, Parry came down to run that bank. For the first time, a bank in Las Vegas would loan money to a gambling house. The first high-rise built on the Strip was that small high-rise at the Sahara, surrounded now by big high-rises. That was the first one financed by a legitimate bank loan. I don't believe the Stardust would have opened when it did, except Parry was willing to loan the money to finish it.

The bank prospered and grew, and Parry continued to serve the gambling industry. He didn't ask questions as to who they were. He found them to be reliable customers. (The growth of the bank should attest to that!) I've heard Parry say a gambler's handshake is as good as a lot of businessmen's written contracts. I certainly have found that to be true.

This is how Parry and I became friends: When I moved to Las Vegas in 1955, I wound up the year busted, but I owed money on income tax. McDonald and Denton's account was at First National Bank on Third Street, so I went over, not anticipating any problem in borrowing the money. I think it was $1,500. That old geezer, the manager, turned me down on the ground I hadn't lived in Las Vegas long enough.

I was panicked and didn't know what the hell to do, so I called Harvey Sewell at the Nevada Bank of Commerce. He said, "Go see Charlie Canfield, manager of the Bank of Las Vegas, and tell him I sent you." The Bank of Las Vegas was organized by Las Vegas people. It was the first new bank charter for years in southern Nevada. They hired Canfield to come from a small bank in Idaho to set it up and run it. I went over and met that nice man, who immediately loaned me the money and started giving me legal work.

I was doing legal work for the Bank of Las Vegas when the Cosgriff group in Salt Lake City (which owned the bank) sent down sent down Parry and Jim Clifford. These two men had equal authority. It was interesting to have two heads to the bank—they actually had two desks in one office. Eventually, Clifford went back, and Parry stayed. Then they put Harvey on the board. There was talk of Nevada Bank of Commerce and Bank of Las Vegas merging.

In the meantime, I had gotten to know Parry and Peggy. They lived not far from our house in Las Vegas. Mark, my oldest son, was just a little boy, and he used to play with Parry's son, Roger. They went to the same school. We became friends, and it's a friendship I have valued, although our paths became separate, and we don't see that much of Peggy and Parry. But we still regard them as friends.

The merger did not go through. Harvey resigned from the board. I'm sure between Harvey and Parry, they put me on the board. Valley Bank opened in Reno. Through Parry, I was one of the original stockholders. Valley merged with the Bank of Las Vegas, and it became Valley Bank of Nevada. I stayed on that board until I resigned after my defeat for Congress because I was busted. Parry didn't ask me to resign, but I told him, "I just can't be on the board of directors of a bank and be busted," because I had to liquidate my stock to pay campaign debts. It didn't look good to customers to have some guy on the board who's busted. Doesn't speak too highly for the bank.

Parry played an important part in my early life in Las Vegas. He was very helpful when I ran for Congress. He didn't try to dissuade me and helped me, and through his efforts, several people contributed to my campaign. He helped me out through the years. I owe a deep debt of gratitude to Parry.

C. D. Baker was the ideal state party chairman: smart, had the respect of people not just in Clark County, but around the state—and he knew his role. Often, a candidate has some statement he'd like to make about the other side, but he doesn't want to get accused of that type of campaigning. C. D. was always available to issue a statement attacking the Republican candidate. The candidate could claim, "Well, I didn't know anything about that. God, did C. D. say that? Oh, my goodness!" He was scrupulous about not getting involved in a Democratic primary—he would not. The primary is always in September. He would always go to Hawaii in August, so he wasn't there to get mixed up in the primary or to raise money for primary candidates.

C. D. was mayor of Las Vegas. For a time before he died, I represented him, Hap Hazard [Harry E. Hazard], and Ted McCuistion in some of their business ventures. He and Hap were old buddies. Hap had been in the legislature from Clark County in the 1930s. He and C. D., through Red McLeod, acquired a lot of the public domain in Nevada when the only way you could get it was to know the surveyor general, McLeod.[1] Then you could buy it for $1.50 an acre. Hap and C. D. got quite a bit of this land, and they were partners in real estate.

Hap was an old-time Democratic-type politician. Go back to *The Last Hurrah*; you'll find a guy like Hap in it some place. I don't remember Hap going to any parties or rallies, but old Hap sure liked to sit around and make medicine. Other local leaders were in gambling, like Marion Hicks, Cliff Jones, and Joe Wells. When they sat in somebody's living room and made medicine, it was *real* medicine.

Al Cahlan had the *Las Vegas Review-Journal*. Al Cahlan and McCarran had been close, and Al and Eva Adams were close. I saw Cahlan several times at his office. When Chet Smith and I were partners, Al and Chet were close. Particularly during Sawyer's 1958 campaign, I called on Cahlan several times on political matters, and he was always cordial; but it wasn't until two days before the primary that he, Marion Hicks, and old Kell Houssels asked Grant to come for a discussion. They saw, "This kid's going to win; we'd better know him." I took Grant and sat in the car. Grant went in and talked to them. When they see they've been on the wrong horse, they come back. [laughter] And strength depresses them.

When I moved to Las Vegas, the senator was already dead, but I thought his friends would be mine. But none of the McCarran people lifted a finger to help me. Cliff's firm could have thrown me a power of attorney once in a while on a divorce case. Never did. Then they seemed terribly upset when I represented Hank Greenspun. Never could understand that. "Why shouldn't I represent Hank? You bastards never did anything to help me!"

Once the senator was gone, nothing bound the old McCarran people together. Maybe I was wearing my heart on my sleeve. This was soon after the senator's death, and I had developed a personal affection for him after I came back to Nevada. I thought we all felt that way about him, and it would give us something in common. It didn't. I should have been a big enough boy to realize it. Most people are in the racket for what they can get out of it.

Many of us have objected to a term through the years: "the McCarran machine." [laughter] I know Eva was close to Al and Mrs. Cahlan, Ernie Cragin and his wife, Lil Hicks, Marion Hicks's wife—you could conclude it was on a political basis, but Eva had known the Cahlans when she taught here. I know the Cahlans and other old-timers were proud of Eva and her accomplishments.

At the time I got here, Kell Houssels was a big owner at the Showboat. I never really knew him. He was at the Tropicana, and had a joint down-

town, I think the old Vegas Club. He was an old-time gambler, came up here
from Long Beach, where he got in the gambling business.

Ernie Cragin had the insurance agency and the El Portal Theater. Ernie
had been mayor off and on and was a close friend of McCarran's. That's why
McCarran never forgave Baker, because he beat Cragin for mayor. Paul
McDermitt worked in the Cragin and Pike insurance agency. Pike had been
his partner and long since died or left. On Ernie's death, McDermitt acquired ownership. Paul was active in the Republican party and on the tax
commission when Russell was governor. I found it interesting that McDermitt,
one of the big Republican leaders, worked for Cragin, one of the big Democratic leaders; but since I've grown up, I've seen politics didn't drive
everybody's life—it was a sideline, in aid of their business.

Ed Converse started Bonanza Airlines. Bonanza started with one DC-3.
When I was familiar with it in 1950, it flew from Las Vegas to Tonopah to
Hawthorne to Minden to Reno. It had a hard time getting certification from
the Civil Aeronautics Board. They sat on this application. McCarran brought
a lot of pressure to grant it. Now, all the board members appear before
McCarran's appropriations subcommittee. McCarran calls the hearing to
order. "Before we start," he says, words to this effect, "Isn't there an application pending before you now for Bonanza Airlines to fly from Reno to Las
Vegas and back and forth? Can you tell me, before we get started, the status
of that?"

Some of them spoke up, "Well, that has been pending a long time, and
we're processing it as rapidly as we can."

McCarran says, "What is the particular problem?"

"Well, we're . . . ."

McCarran says, "I'll tell you what. I'm going to take a little recess, and
all of this board is here. I've arranged for you to have a meeting in the room
next door, if you'd like to go consider this at this time."

He recessed the hearing on their appropriation. They all went next door,
came back, and announced to the senator that, by gosh, they'd approved
that application! Notice would go out tomorrow. [laughter] Converse built
Bonanza into a big operation. They later merged with some other airlines,
then sold the whole thing to Hughes.

When I got to Las Vegas, I got into party precinct meetings right away.
Oh God, it was a riot. They'd hide them. Let's say my precinct meeting was
going to be at my house at 6:00 at night. At 6:00, I'd lock the door and have
the meeting in my backyard where nobody could find it. (I didn't really do
that, but that's the way it used to work.)

They wanted to control these meetings. Half the time, you couldn't find
where your meeting was. You wanted to get there early and make damn sure
you were at the right place. Why? You want to be a delegate to the county
convention. Why? By God, you wanted to be a delegate to the state. Some

even had serious resolutions they wanted passed. At a precinct meeting, those trying to run the thing didn't want to get bogged down with a bunch of damn resolutions. So they would hide precinct meetings and give false addresses in the notices. [laughter]

They wanted to control it, because once you got to the state convention, the majority would cast all of the votes [the unit rule]. (I think during the Sawyer administration, we got rid of the unit rule.) So help me God, I don't understand why it was so important to control the organization. We've seen the results of it in Nevada, because nobody's interested anymore. We didn't even have precinct meetings in Boulder City. For the last several years, you had to go to Las Vegas to a central place. There used to be eight or ten people at most precincts, and we would have a big Boulder City delegation to the county convention. The importance was nomination of the presidential candidates. But that doesn't mean much anymore, does it, with the primaries? What do parties have to do?

Notes

1. Wayne "Red" McLeod, a Democrat, served as surveyor general, 1939-51.

18 | Everybody, Including Grant, Had a Good Time: The 1958 Primary

Grant and I didn't talk about his plan to run for governor in 1958—when that process was going on, he was in Elko and I was in Las Vegas—but I know he would very seriously consider how he was going to pay for a campaign. That may be one reason he held off so long in announcing, to make the campaign as short as possible and have some assurance he would have some money available. He would have consulted his father; he might have talked to Pete Petersen. He might have talked to Dutch Horton—they were close. Dutch had influence through his representation of mining companies and was knowledgeable politically.

Of course, Grant confided in, and sought advice from, his wife Bette. One of the important factors in their decision was consideration for their daughter Gail. Grant and I discussed the possible effects of a campaign and election on Gail, who was just a little girl.

I'd had what I figured was a special relationship with Gail from the time I first saw her in 1951. (I hope she reciprocates that.) I was concerned, as were Grant and Bette, about what effect being the governor's daughter would have on Gail. We had known children of people in high office and some of the problems that created. It was always paramount in Bette's mind to create as normal an atmosphere as possible for Gail to grow up in, but she did everything she could have been expected to do during the campaign. Many say she didn't enjoy it, and I don't think she *did* enjoy it, but she did it.

After Grant was elected, Bette made it a point to be at the mansion at noon every day, so when Gail came home from school, her mother was there to fix lunch. Bette did everything in her power to give Gail as normal a childhood as possible. They didn't want her to get a big head. They wanted her to grow up a normal human being. It worked.

Once when Grant was governor, they were here, and Gail was staying with a friend. Grant or Bette asked me to pick up Gail. They gave me an address in Henderson, and I got there. I was so proud: here was a house in the Victory Village area, a minority family living in public housing, and this cute little girl was Gail's best friend.

Grant and Bette did a magnificent job in the campaign. Bette knocked herself out, but there were invitations and political things she would refuse, because she didn't want to abandon Gail. When they first got to Carson City, it was tough—Gail going from the Elko grammar school, where she knew everybody, to the one in Carson City, where most of the kids were friends of Charlie Russell's kids. Bette, in my opinion, sacrificed a lot for Gail's sake. And I think it worked. Gail's a lovely girl, she and her mother are close, and she and her father were close.

Before I talked to Grant, three of his people came down from the north to talk to Chet Smith: Graham Hollister, his wife Janet, and Hazel Erskine. I didn't know them, and they didn't know me. They were in Chet's office a long time. They wanted Chet to be chairman of Grant's campaign, and Chet didn't feel his way clear to do so. The next day, they came back to see me. They said Grant would run for governor. I said, "Well, God, I hope so. I'll certainly do anything I can to help him." I was obviously second choice to handle things in Clark County. That didn't surprise me, because Chet was the political pro. I was younger than all of them. I didn't care. What the hell? Grant wants to run for governor, I'm going to do anything I can for him.

Fred Anderson from Reno filed for the Senate against George Malone. Fred was a friend of mine and Grant's, highly regarded. Joe McDonald had come back from Washington to run Fred's campaign. I don't know whether that was a sign of Bible's support—it would be to some. Fred and the McDonald family were close; Bible and Anderson were close. But Bible would not get involved in Fred's campaign. Joe was there because he was asked to run a campaign, and he loved that. I think he expected some compensation, therefore.

Grant didn't file until the closing day in June. He was playing his cards close to his vest. You had Grant, Roger Foley, Howard Cannon, all trying to make up their minds. As I understand it, on the closing day of filing, Cannon sent Jack Conlon, his chief aide, referred to as "Shady Harry," to Carson City. He had two declarations: one for governor, one for Senate. I think he was waiting to see what Foley was going to file for, because I don't think Cannon would have run against Foley. Grant files for governor, Foley for attorney general, and Cannon in the Senate race. It's my opinion there was never any doubt in Sawyer's mind what he was going to do. Keep in mind who announced for governor. Who would you rather run against: Harvey Dickerson and George Franklin, or Foley or Cannon? It looked like a better race for Sawyer. So, he filed for governor.

But isn't it unusual? Candidates for the top offices waited till the day of closing to file. You hear today, "You've waited too long." Franklin used to tell Grant all the time, "I've been campaigning for the last six months. I've

194

Everybody,
Including
Grant,
Had a
Good
Time

been all over the state. You don't have time to catch up." George was convinced, as always, that his position was correct, and Grant had gotten in too late. "I like the kid," he says. "Nobody here knows him." [laughter] The last day is as good a time as any, because most people make up their minds who they're going to vote for in the two or three weeks before the election.

Grant was so effective. Grant Sawyer was Grant Sawyer's greatest asset. His ability to speak, think on his feet, his sense of humor. Grant never came across as mean or vindictive—he came across as a rational man with a magnificent voice.

I said, "It's true, isn't it, your voice was so important? It didn't make any difference what you said."

He smiled. "That's true. I was blessed with this voice." Franklin came up with one statement, critical because Grant had been in the Little Theater in Elko. "That's why he was such a good speaker. He was a trained actor." [laughter]

Nobody was on the payroll in the primary. We had no press secretary. When we needed press releases, Grant would write some of them. Some of the press guys helped us. Hazel wrote releases, I think, even in the primary. I think Chet Smith wrote some. I wrote some.

Graham Hollister was wealthy and liberal, and it was certainly the hope that he would kick in money. Graham was of the California family that had the big ranch in Santa Barbara. The town of Hollister, California, was named after that family. His brother or uncle was a Democratic state senator in California, close friend of Pat Brown, and Graham's wife Janet was a woman of substantial means. Graham had gone to some prep school in Pasadena, where rich kids went. Janet's family had been involved in steel, I believe, with the Carnegies. They wintered in Pasadena, as rich people used to do. I think Janet and Graham met there. They moved into the Washoe Valley, bought a ranch just before World War II or possibly just after. They had lived in the Washoe Valley for a long time and were both liberal Democrats.

They met all of the people in Washoe Valley and Reno who shared their political views. David Vhay was an architect in Reno, a classmate of Graham's in Pasadena. They met Hazel Erskine, whose husband, Graham, was an architect in Reno. Graham and Hazel were graduates of Columbia University. I believe Graham's father had been on the faculty at Columbia. Hazel was bright, interested in politics. For years Hazel ran the ACLU in Nevada out of her house. She was well-regarded in . . . I don't know what you call this field—samplers of public opinion. She became attracted to Grant after talking to him, and she used this phrase: he was educable. He would listen and had the ability to learn. Hazel certainly had the ability to teach, and she did.

In Reno, Tom Cooke, an attorney, was an old-time Nevada man who became an immediate supporter of Grant. His father had been a mining lawyer in Tonopah and Goldfield, maybe even Virginia City, and in politics. Tom became chairman in Washoe, and we started having meetings at houses with people we thought were dissatisfied, willing to vote for somebody not

196

*Everybody,
Including
Grant,
Had a
Good
Time*

from Clark County. Bruce Thompson and his wife were active. Bruce might have been one of the ones Grant talked to. They became close on the board of regents. I started meeting Reno people soon after I met with the Hollisters and Hazel.

Grant's strategy and mine turned out correct. Grant would sweep Washoe and the small counties against two candidates from Clark. If the two from Clark came close to each other, we figured we needed 1,600 votes in Clark to win. We started looking for 1,600 people dissatisfied with the status quo. There's bound to be 1,600 not satisfied with whatever is going on.

We started trying to set up an organization in Clark County. Hazel was close to George Rudiak, who had been active in Democratic politics, done work for the ACLU, and met Dick Ham, who lived in Boulder City. Dick was liberal and knew people of that persuasion. Dick had the title of county chairman, if anybody had a title, or we had co-chairmen. Dick let us in to several people who became supporters of Grant and remained friends: Dr. Carl Kaufman, a physician; Sig Stein, a druggist; Dorothy Dorothy, active in the Democratic Party through the years. I was able to take him to my old friend from Lincoln County, Gladys Dula. C. D.'s secretary, Ethel Woodbury, and other women in the party became friends. Hank Greenspun became a supporter. Clesse and Alice Turner immediately started to help in any way they could.

Jack and Lu Lehman . . . Jack was working for Jack Melvin in a P.R. firm here in town and doing television commercials. Among his clients was the Lucky Strike Casino downtown. Jack also had a kiddie program on TV—Captain Lee, I think it was. ("Captain Lee . . . Captain Lee to flight line . . . ." I can hear it yet.) [laughter] He and Lu were perfect delights. They came to work and devoted their time. It was, in truth and in fact, a volunteer campaign.

Another volunteer, Lee Page, a bright young Korean war veteran, had come to Las Vegas and formed Las Vegas Insurance Adjusters. I had gotten to know Lee through personal injury cases where he was the adjuster. He was one of the first I called when we started this campaign to introduce Grant and see if he wouldn't get involved. Lee did, and he and Grant remained good friends. Lee was always willing to work his tail off. He was effective.

My friend Jimmy Garrett made a contact with one dealer on each shift in each gambling house. He did a remarkable job. Every time at night or in the daytime, if we went to a hotel to meet working people, there would be a man on each shift we would know to see, who would introduce Grant to other workers and arrange for Grant to go in the room where they were taking their breaks and talk. Jimmy would invite a lot of them for a barbecue in his backyard, where Grant could meet and talk to them. Immeasurable job, Jimmy did.

He played an integral part in the campaign. Harry Levy was a prominent businessman, a very early supporter. Jimmy Garrett had been a friend of Harry, and introduced Grant and me to Harry. I hope—I'm sure it's true—Harry and I, and Grant and Harry, became friends. Harry had a big grocery store on Charleston. His son was Al Levy.[1] Heinie Zigatema, another friend of Jimmy's, owned a dairy. Heinie became a supporter. I think he contributed money, as did Levy. It wasn't much, but it was important that they were talking. They made no secret that they were supporting Sawyer.

197

*Everybody,
Including
Grant,
Had a
Good
Time*

We had extra help. One evening, two twin boys, seven or eight, dressed up nice, cleaned up, knocked on our door. They wanted bumper stickers. Sara was talking to them, and I was just watching. She was apprehensive about giving this stuff to kids, because it costs money, and we were a little short; and what they were going to do with it? She gave them a few, and hell, they were back soon wanting more. They were serious campaigners—little Brent and little Bruce Adams. Brent now is a judge in Reno, and we lost Bruce. They were the cutest kids you ever saw. They were active Sawyer supporters. Their parents turned out to be strong supporters of Grant's.

One of the wonderful things about that kind of a campaign: people are not there for a paycheck. You see qualities in people and get to know them and treasure having known them and learning about them. People are willing to spend their time to help somebody else, if it's a candidate in whom they believe or just a candidate they like, to get involved. It's rewarding, indeed. Thank God there are people like that. I don't see it anymore. Everybody's on the payroll now. Any volunteer that comes in, they try to figure a way to shuffle them out the door. They don't want to be bothered.[2]

We lived on Oakey in Las Vegas. We had a carport at the side of the house. We had sawhorses, and we'd get sheets of plywood and saw them to build our own signs. Sara would mix paste, we'd cut out plywood, and Sara would nail it to a two-by-four. We'd load up our station wagon with as many as we could get and head out. Sara was *really* pregnant, because Jeffy was born in October. (This is late July or August.) After I got home from work, we'd go all over town and dig holes in the caliche. A couple of days later, we'd go, and somebody had torn them all down. You always expected the gamesmanship, and it was something you could laugh about. You'd be annoyed as heck, too, but you'd take some pride in the ones that stayed up.

We had some bumper stickers, and I had a 1952 Ford station wagon. We put bumper stickers on every part of the surface of that automobile. If you saw that car drive down the street, it was a conglomeration of Sawyer bumper stickers. Some said, "Sawyer for Governor." Others said, "Nevada is not for sale," in accordance with our theme that E. L. Cord was not going to buy the election for his candidate.

When Grant was in town, which was a great deal of the time, he'd stay at our house. We'd go out in the evenings, going through places, sometimes to precincts and back, have meetings with people and try and plan, "How can we get to this guy?" and figure out how best to campaign Clark County, which was a mystery to us. We weren't that well known and didn't know many people. But it was what a campaign should be. Grant came out of left field. Not many people thought he had a chance. We thought he did.

Grant never had much help writing speeches until he became governor. Then there were so many. Grant spoke extemporaneously, unless it was a formal event. We did a lot of coffees, friends having parties at their house to introduce their neighbor. Grant worked all the time, and I went to different places with him. I was running for district attorney of Esmeralda County. That was fun. I'd leave to do a little campaigning on my own. [laughter] Grant and I would talk about those things. No job was too menial for Grant.

One night, we'd gotten a little money, and we had a bunch of leaflets printed. They had the "Night of Stars" at Cashman Field.[3] You've got all the cars in this parking lot. Grant, Dick, Sara, and I went there with boxes of these pamphlets, and we were running, putting them behind the windshield wiper on every car. We had the boxes on the side of the parking lot. When we ran out of what we could carry, we'd run back and get some more. I'm running back to get some about the same time Grant's running back.

Grant looks at me. He says, "It isn't seemly for a governor to be doing this kind of work," with a smile.

I said, "It sure as hell is, if he wants to be governor," and he laughed. He was willing to do everything that needed to be done, even if it meant addressing envelopes or passing out handbills.

All that changed after the primary. Grant didn't have time after that. Now you've got the power structure coming back, and they want to take over . . . and they do, to a certain extent. But it was always a matter of great pride that that primary was run without any paid employees.

My fondest memories of that campaign are meeting people on the Westside and going to their homes. So friendly and serious about the issues, it was always a pleasure. Grant made a lot of friends among the black population. It was a long time before the Civil Rights Act of 1964. You had piecemeal federal legislation defeated. The civil rights bill had been introduced in the state legislature . . . no chance of passing. Grant was frank about the fact that there was no question he would favor a civil rights bill. I think Grant was the first major candidate who didn't try to get the Westside simply by the standard way people went for the black votes in those days: go over, give money to the preachers, and they're supposed to deliver the vote.

A lot of people helped on the Westside: Charlie West, Jim McMillan, Helen and Oscar Crozier, Dave and Mabel Hoggard. Marion Bennett was new in town—a Methodist preacher.[4] I can't remember all of the preachers. Marjorie Elliot was a real estate broker, whose son, Lonnie Sisson practices optometry. Gwen Weeks had come to Las Vegas with the opening of the Moulin Rouge, and I think was a dancer. I think Alice Keyes worked with Charlie at the newspaper, the *Voice*. He devoted a lot of time to that. It not only reported the news, but it was also a political paper. Charlie practiced medicine all day and worked half the night on political issues, trying not only to help the civil rights movement and Grant, but to improve conditions generally. All of them had strong character, but Charlie in particular. He and Grant were close.

It became a matter of great pride with Grant and me, that people accepted us as truthful men, sincerely believing. I would not have blamed them if they distrusted every white politician, Republican or Democrat (they'd only see them on election day), but they accepted Grant and knew the minute they got to know him that there wasn't an ounce of bigotry in him. We went into their homes. We laughed, joked, and talked about things. Grant was warm and friendly, didn't feel self-conscious or frightened. They reciprocated.

There was little contact between Grant's black and white supporters. I think it's pretty much the twain not meeting. Civil rights was not an issue in white neighborhoods in 1958. There had been civil rights acts introduced in the Nevada legislature that were not even brought to a vote—there was no chance. Blacks were realistic enough to know that it wasn't in the cards in the legislature. I think they saw in Grant someone who believed it was a goal that should be striven for, maybe was achievable with strong leadership over a period of time.

There wasn't much money. Any time we really got short, Janet would call her mother. Granny would come up with a little more. It was fun to run a campaign where you weren't worried about people on your payroll. Depending on volunteers, however, is a problem; you have no way to control or discipline them. You can't fire them, can you? But there never was anybody in *that* campaign that anybody ever wanted to fire. People came out of friendship or true belief. It's difficult to separate volunteers during the primary and those who came after; at that time, a lot of party people became involved. The campaign changed substantially after the primary.

Grant conveyed in his oral history [*Hang Tough!* Reno: UNOHP, 1993] how much fun he had. Everybody had a good time. Grant had a great sense of humor and could laugh at himself faster than almost anybody I ever knew, and I hope I have a good sense of humor. Sara and Dick and Betty Ham, certainly.

Betty was Major Sweeney's secretary at Pioneer Title. He was the president of Pioneer, the only title company in town, I believe, in those days. She worked a full day, lived in Boulder City. She and Dick would stay in town and work and come home late, back early in the morning.

There are not enough things I can say about Dick Ham and his devotion to Grant. He worked his tail off. Keep in mind, we were looking for people mad at the establishment. Certainly Dick was, but Dick brought into the campaign early-on George Rudiak, who was effective in giving expression to issues when issues became important.

What issues were there? I mean, everybody was taking the same position. We had to have strong control of gambling, that sort of thing. I don't recall in the primary there being that many issues. But, much to our later chagrin, in the general, the third term was an issue. Came back to haunt us. [laughter]

200

Everybody,
Including
Grant,
Had a
Good
Time

We made E. L. [Errett Lobban] Cord the issue. The establishment, the power structure was going to run Cord, a wealthy rancher in Fish Lake Valley who had moved to Nevada, like a lot of people did, to escape taxation. He wrangled his way into an appointment representing Esmeralda County in the state senate. He had all the money in the world. Bill Woodburn, that Reno power center . . . . Biltz and Mueller probably were in on this; Wingfield, the whole bunch of them. They'd all been Cord people, and for some reason Cord—I don't know why—decided he couldn't run. But he threw all of his support to these people. They selected Harvey Dickerson, who was, to use a current phrase, "anointed" to seek the Democratic nomination and get all of their support.

That looked like a good issue. The first theme and bumper stickers in our campaign was, "Nevada is not for sale." Cord was an easy opponent to run against. Not only was he rich and trying to get control of the state, but there wasn't much he could say to fight back, because he wasn't running! [laughter] I don't think we said anything detrimental or derogatory about Dickerson or Franklin. In that primary, we ran against Cord and won.

Pete Petersen had been close to McCarran. I don't know if he was on the outs with the Cord people or if he was ever close to them. He was McCarran's right-hand man. Pete was Swedish, and he was head of the bakers' union in Reno. Pete took a liking to Grant; Grant took a liking to him. Pete was smart. He spoke with a brogue. He was always masterminding. I can remember, you'd ask Pete a question, he'd say, "Let's count the wotes." Pete would sit down and start counting the wotes.

I don't think Biltz and Mueller ever became close to Grant, even after Grant was elected. They didn't figure in his calculations too much. Grant prized his independence a great deal, and that's also true of Bible. Those fellows couldn't figure a way to get them in their pockets. I think that's true of Bible; I know it was true of Grant.

It is interesting that some in Grant's campaign, even in the primary, had been for Tom Mechling. Although Grant was identified as a McCarran boy, I think Grant made it clear at Democratic conventions that he thought McCarran's attempt to control the party injured the party. He had credibility. With McCarran's death, there was no party, and we needed to build a party. The machine we're talking about was essentially Republicans—Biltz, Wingfield. But McCarran fought Wingfield and that bi-partisan thing until he became strong, and then he was their boss. They no longer controlled it. He was stronger than they were. Jack Conlon used to say, "If you're not part of the deal, knock it." [laughter] McCarran knocked it, and very effectively. Grant many times publicly stated we had to rebuild the Democratic party.

Hazel Erskine did a lot of polling and detailed reports on her projections and issues. She didn't have the facilities they have now, but she was great. Money was awful short. I kept a list on a yellow notebook of monies collected in Las Vegas. I didn't collect all of it, but even some I didn't collect, I knew about. Grant would tell me so-and-so had given him . . . . By God, after the primary, the whole damn thing only came to $21,000. One person on the payroll up north, and nobody on the payroll in Las Vegas. Everybody was a volunteer—everybody! Nobody in the established economic group, even in Las Vegas, ever came around that headquarters. Grant stayed at our house when he was in Las Vegas. The Hollisters stayed in our house. There wasn't money to pay for hotels.

201

*Everybody,
Including
Grant,
Had a
Good
Time*

One of the funniest stories was about Edgar Nores. In the primary, Grant borrowed Graham's Volkswagen Beetle, making a tour of the state, leaving the Hollister ranch in this Beetle, which had no air conditioning, to go to Fallon, Austin, Eureka, Ely, Pioche, and meet me in Caliente. In 1958, my mother and uncle were still alive. In those days, the Union Pacific was still on its regular route; you could get on in Las Vegas and get off in Caliente. I was to take the train from Las Vegas and meet Grant in Caliente. Then we were going to tour Lincoln and wind up in Las Vegas. A great trip, but you couldn't get that Volkswagen out of second gear—hot, oh!

I get on the train, and who do I meet but Nores. What a character! Edgar took to strong drink on occasion. Edgar and I go to the club car, and we have a couple of drinks. I was telling him I'm working in Sawyer's campaign. Edgar called everybody kid. He tells me, "Harvey's gonna win, kid. All the people up north are for Harvey. Cliff Jones, all the guys in Las Vegas, they're all for Harvey."

I said, "No, I don't think so, Edgar. Grant's got a really good chance."

Edgar's swilling up bourbon and water. We get into Caliente and get off the train. There on the platform to meet me is Grant. Edgar says, "Grant, it's good to see you. We're all for you. You're a cinch, kid." [laughter]

On that trip, we were going in and out of stores in Caliente. I was introducing Grant to everybody. Grant went up to two old ladies on the street and introduced himself. "I'm Grant Sawyer. I'm a Democratic candidate for governor."

One lady says to the other, "What did he say?"

Grant repeated himself.

"What did he say?"

The other lady said, "He says he wants to be somebody." [laughter]

We campaigned Lincoln County: to Eagle Valley, Pioche, down the canyon to Elgin, saw the ranchers, out to Pahranagat Valley and Floyd Lamb's ranch and saw Senator Lamb, who of course was with the establishment.[5] But he assured us he was strong for Sawyer. We finally made it to Las Vegas. Again, couldn't get that car out of second gear, and it was summer and hot, no air conditioning. We made it to our house on Oakey and got under that swamp cooler.

That was the wonderful thing about campaigns in those days. Politics is a game, and you make a mistake if you take it too seriously. You want to win, but you do not want it to control your life. It's a game that should be played

202

*Everybody,
Including
Grant,
Had a
Good
Time*

fairly; if it's played fairly, a lot of funny things happen, and you have to be able to laugh at them. An example in the general election: Doc Knollor was a strong Russell supporter. He put out a pamphlet, "What Grant Sawyer Has Done to Be Governor." It had about 20 blank pages. I thought it was funny; Grant thought it was funny.

Campaigns weren't like they are now. Grant talked to everybody we could find in Lincoln County on the street, in a store, in a bar, at their house. That's the way you campaigned Nevada. We started by getting publicity, making a contact with somebody in every county to just give us five or six names we could use. Then, we'd do a press release. That didn't cost anything. Sawyer would announce a "Sawyer for Governor" committee in Lincoln County. John Jones is chairman, so-and-so and so-and-so are members. We were hitting the papers almost every other day with a story like that for each county. You'd be surprised—you give those papers something, they print it. First thing you know, we have committees in every county. The important thing was the story in the paper. It looks like a groundswell.

It was helpful that Grant had gone to the university in Reno. In almost every town, he found a classmate—in most, a fraternity brother. There was always somebody you might not have seen for a long time, but, "Yes, I'll be glad to be chairman of Grant's committee." We did coffees, and at night a lot of walking. You couldn't walk every precinct, but Hazel would furnish information. You might pick out a precinct and only go to two houses, but word spread, "Grant Sawyer was here last night. Too bad you weren't home." Maybe we'd hit two houses in a block and then move to another area.

Also, we were trying to get to know the press. Gus Guiffre was working at Channel 13 on the grounds back of the El Rancho Vegas, a little shack. Gus had this late-night program where he ran movies. Gus didn't have much to do. He'd start the movie, then he would sit. We'd talk to Gus, and he'd help us cut TV spots, like a slide with Grant with a little message. Gus would write the message and help us make it. Didn't cost anything. Then, if we could raise some money, we could start running these little TV spots.

A few times during the campaign, Grant and I in our naiveté were shocked by some of the working press. They wanted to be on the payroll. That *really* shocked us. Grant and I did not want to become cynical, but this commercialism shocked us, particularly coming from an institution that he and I had considerable respect for.

Grant met with Al Cahlan, but I never established a relationship with Cahlan. I would stop in once in a while to deliver something or talk to him. I got to know John Cahlan (Al's brother) better, but never became a close friend, because he was so bitter toward me for representing Hank Greenspun, which I had not been doing at that time.

At the beginning, Dick and I went to talk to Hank. I arranged an appointment. Dick went with me—it was in the evening—and we had a long talk. Hank started writing his column, turned to me, and said, "Now, tell me why I should be for Grant Sawyer." I'm telling him, and he's writing his column. I don't know to what extent other people talked to Hank before me, including Grant. But nobody in the old McCarran group could have talked to Hank about Grant.

203

Everybody,
Including
Grant,
Had a
Good
Time

I remember three things to do with money as significant and of interest. A couple of nights before the primary, we wanted to get a simulcast on the three Las Vegas stations. The candidate would come on live and speak for one or two minutes. It cost $500; we didn't have $500. I had met Beldon Katleman, the owner of the El Rancho, during the Bible campaign and on other things. Grant, Sara, and I are sitting in our living room in Las Vegas trying to figure out where the hell we could get $500. I said, "Let me try Beldon Katleman."

I call the El Rancho and ask for him. Grant's listening on the extension. I told Beldon what we're trying to do. Beldon didn't let me finish the sentence. He said, "No chance. I'm a Russell man." You can imagine Beldon's attitude when Sawyer won. I think Grant had an opportunity to say, "No chance" on something that Beldon wanted.

The second was that a couple of nights before the primary, Grant, Sara, and I went to see the show at the Stardust. Word was starting to get around that Sawyer is going to win. I had a friend, Johnny Achuff, a floorman. I called, trying to get the fix in and get three comped to the dinner show at the Stardust that night, and Johnny says sure. We get a front row seat. None of us had seen the Stardust show, although it had been playing for a while. Oh, God, it's a dandy show!

The show's over, and here's one of the owners. "Ralph, why didn't you call me if you wanted to come to the hotel? I would have been glad to take care of you. Hi, Grant! Why don't you come over to my office in the Desert Inn? We'll have a little talk."

We went over, and believe it or not, one of the owners of the Desert Inn-Stardust complex wanted to make a contribution.[6] He didn't want to do it in front of me. He takes Grant out on a little patio off his office to talk privately. That's important when they're giving a candidate money and don't want anybody else to know. I am told Grant said, "Well, gee, I'm sorry sir, but the campaign's over. I don't need any money." I was proud of Grant. If he'd have taken it, I'd have known about it. He'd have had a wad in his pocket, and he would have given it to me to put in the bank.

We had gotten a contribution from Doby Doc before that. When we went to see Doc, he told us, "These barracudas here eat kids like you for breakfast and spit you out." [laughter] He wasn't optimistic about Grant's chances, but he did help. He was at the Horseshoe. I don't think Doc ever left the premises. I think Doc made every count when Benny was away to "college."

The third money thing is, I was contacted by Hy Raskin before the primary. Hy, I found out, had been Stevenson's campaign manager in 1952 and involved in 1956. Hy was a lawyer in Chicago, counsel to the national party,

204

Everybody,
Including
Grant,
Had a
Good
Time

and—this is 1958, keep in mind—he's in Las Vegas, and somebody told him he should talk to me. I learned he had already talked to Dickerson, Franklin, and the so-called "big shots" and had been told Dickerson was going to win the primary. He wanted to find out why I thought Sawyer would win. I told him.

I explained the north-south rivalry in Nevada. He understood, coming from Illinois—the rivalry between Cook County and downstate. I told him people in the north are jealous of Clark; they see it as a threat. "Grant's going to come out of Washoe and the small counties with 70 to 75 percent of the vote." I don't know where I got that figure; I probably pulled that out of the air, but it was strong. I said, "The only way Sawyer can lose is if Franklin or Dickerson completely run away with Clark County. Sawyer only needs 1,600 votes in Clark, and there are always 1,600 people any place who are mad. My job is to find those who are mad."

We became friends. Hy believed me, took me to see Ross Miller at the Riviera.[7] It was a big contribution in those days: $1,300. I remember it. Hy went to work calling people around the country to raise money for Sawyer.

Why did he do it? At the Democratic convention in 1956, Jack Kennedy had greatly impressed Hy when he ran for vice president.[8] They had become close, and Hy was one of the people at that first meeting at the Kennedy compound at Hyannis Port to start Kennedy's campaign for president in 1960. Hy already was in charge of the western states. They were out there two years ahead to lay a foundation for 1960.

Hy believed the state house was where power was politically in the state, not senators or congressmen. They were trying to be on the side of the Democratic governor, so that governor would be in the Kennedy camp. Hy made the right judgment, and they sure were here in 1960 for help! [laughter] That's significant, how far in advance those people planned. And boy, he was active in the Kennedy campaign in 1960. Teddy Kennedy had the title of western states man, but he was sort of under Hy's tutelage.

A couple of things stick out about the primary fight between Howard Cannon and Fred Anderson for the Democratic nomination for U.S. senator, and they explain why a lot of Democrats in Clark County were not involved in the Sawyer campaign. Many were longtime friends of Cannon's, working in his campaign. The second thing is, Grant and I and our friends in northern Nevada were close to Fred. We had to strive to keep the campaigns separate, although I did take Fred on a trip up to Lincoln and White Pine. I thought the world of Fred, still do. I was for Fred, and I voted for Fred.

After the primary, all the Democratic candidates were taking a tour of the state in a caravan. They were going to get to know each other and appear in every town on the same platform and campaign as a party, which was a good idea then and would be good now. The first stop was North Las Vegas. The morning they were to leave, Grant was staying with us. Foley, Cannon, and Bible were going, even though Bible wasn't a candidate. Bible came to pick up Grant. They're all sitting in my living room.

My son Mark would have been seven. He would listen to everything. Mark had been playing in the backyard, came running in, saw Cannon, and took a double take, because he had seen him on television and recognized the face. Mark stopped and says, "Are you Howard W. Cannon?"

Cannon said, "Yes," and smiled, that this kid would recognize him.

Mark says, "Did you beat Fred Anderson in the primary?"

Howard's smiling again that this little kid would recognize him and his achievement. He said, "Yes."

Mark said, "That was a shame," and he kept running on by. I thought, "Oh, my God." Sawyer, of course, was in hysterics. [laughter]

And how many years did Mark wind up working under Cannon's patronage in Washington when he was going to law school? [laughter] If Cannon remembered, he never said. Mark is very fond of Senator Cannon, and Senator Cannon, I think, is very fond of Mark.

There were little tensions perceived, but not real, between the Cannon and Sawyer campaigns. No substance to them, yet the perception approaches reality—some people in the Cannon group were bitter at the Sawyer people, thinking they supported Anderson. Fred was my friend, I took him up from Lincoln into White Pine. Joe McDonald was running his campaign. There was reason for the Cannon people to be suspicious, but, frankly, there was no effort on the Sawyer campaign to get involved in anybody else's campaign.

Having characterized the campaign as fun (it was), interesting (it was), and requiring a lot of time (it did), it brought heartaches, too. Not for me, but some for Grant. Grant was wounded when old friends didn't support him. You expect friends to help you, and it hurts when they don't. They're not bound to, but Grant was hurt in a couple of cases by close friends who didn't want to stick their neck out. Not long after the election, he and I were talking about that. Grant said, "I'll never wear my heart on my sleeve again." He had to learn not to be disappointed, because if you don't expect anything, you're not disappointed when they don't come through. Grant was fortunate to learn that early in his political career. But there were times it wasn't all fun, where it was, "Why won't he help?" It is also different from someone you go to and say, "I'm running for governor," and they say, "I'm already committed to so-and-so." That is different. It's when the guy isn't active, and you call on him. "Oh, it's liable to hurt my business. I won't sell as many cokes next week if I get involved in politics."

I never could figure out what they were scared of. If they were in the racket and intended to run, I can see a sound political judgment being made. "I can't get mixed up in anybody else's campaign." At times your friends are justified. Those times are understood. But when you have somebody whose only relation to politics is that he's a citizen . . . why do people think if they come out and support somebody, it's going to injure them in some way?

206

Everybody,
Including
Grant,
Had a
Good
Time

I used to tell Grant I thought in many cases it was motivated by jealousy. Grant had the courage and guts to do it, and they didn't. I hesitate to say this, because it sounds self-serving, but Grant and I talked about this. He expressed one thing that typified our relationship: I was never the least bit jealous of Grant. I recognized his abilities. I was as proud of his accomplishments, I think, as he was or had they been my own. I was never jealous. I think—Grant did—that was an unusual part of our relationship. I don't know if that makes any sense to you, but it did to us.

I treasured our friendship from the day it started, and I think Grant did. It was never marred by jealousy of any kind. There might have been a time when Grant doubted this—but he knew if he asked me, I would give him my honest opinion, colored only by his best interest. That would be my only motivation. Because of my association with Hank Greenspun, later a bitter enemy of Grant's, some people around Grant tried to make him believe I could no longer be trusted, but Grant didn't feel that way, and he told me so.

Election night, Grant's up north. The rest of us are awful happy. My station wagon had a sign on top that stuck up vertical, so you could read it from the sides. Some of us—not me—took to strong drink, got in that wagon, and thought we'd go park it in front of the El Rancho. We drove under that portico, and it knocked the sign off the car. [laughter]

I haven't analyzed the vote, but it came close to what Grant and I thought to begin with, and it confirmed our theory about why we thought he could win. Grant carried the north big. He got more than 1,600 votes in Clark County. He beat Franklin and came close to Dickerson. Grant lost White Pine; Dickerson, through the old family name, won, and it might have been with labor help.

Notes

1. Al Levy was a longtime Las Vegas city councilman, realtor, and businessman. Harry Levy served a term as president of what was then Las Vegas's only synagogue, Temple Beth Sholom.

2. After this was taped, Mark Denton was appointed district judge and subsequently elected. The campaign included an advertising agency with television and radio commercials—and the judge's parents, family, and friends volunteering, including Ralph and Sara Denton hammering in signs, and the interviewer for this oral history writing press releases and commercials.

3. Cashman Field was a stadium near the corner of Las Vegas Boulevard North and Washington, since renovated. Then and now, it has been a baseball stadium and multi-purpose meeting facility.

4. Oscar Crozier owned the El Morocco in West Las Vegas and was a go-between for McMillan and the NAACP in achieving the Moulin Rouge Agreement of

March 26, 1960, which desegregated Las Vegas casinos. Helen Crozier was the first African American elected to the state board of education. See James B. McMillan, Gary E. Elliott, and R. T. King, *Fighting Back: A Life in the Struggle for Civil Rights* (Reno: University of Nevada Oral History Program, 1996), 74-75, 83, 94-97. Mabel Hoggard was a longtime Southern Nevada educator; her husband David headed the Economic Opportunity Board and was a policeman and truant officer. Marion Bennett was a Democratic assemblyman from Clark County, 1973-83.

5. Raised in Alamo, Democrat Floyd Lamb served in the State Senate from Lincoln County, 1957-67, and Clark County, 1967-83. He later served a term in a federal prison after being convicted of accepting money to use his influence. His first name is for Ralph Denton's father. His brother, Ralph Lamb, served as Clark County sheriff, 1961-79.

6. Tony Cornero was building the Stardust and in financial trouble when he died while shooting craps at the Desert Inn, whose owners took over operations at the Stardust.

7. Ross Miller represented what might be euphemistically called Chicago-interests at the Riviera. His son, Bob Miller, a Democrat, was Clark County district attorney, 1979-87; lieutenant governor, 1987-89; and governor, 1989-99. In 1998, he appointed a Clark County district judge, Mark Denton.

8. In 1956, Adlai Stevenson won the Democratic presidential nomination. At the convention, John Kennedy sought the vice-presidential nod, losing to Estes Kefauver.

19 | King of All You Survey: The 1958 General

Things changed after the primary. "Supporters" were coming out of the woodwork. I was at that little headquarters on Fourth, this little house, the day after the election. I was surprised at the people who came in congratulating me and being so happy. Cliff Jones, we hadn't seen him before. [laughter] Herb, Wendell Bunker, Mahlon Brown . . . . My God, they were for him from the beginning! Berkeley Bunker became helpful. I could understand Las Vegas Democrats not wanting to get involved. Dickerson had a lot of friends among old-timers, and Franklin had his group. And I have to mention C. D. Baker, who was mayor—he was knowledgeable of the community and political forces within the community.

Now we had some resources, but the resources did away with some of the charm. Things didn't change completely, but we had what would be the normal, before-primary group, and then there was the after-primary group. We knew from the Bible campaign, McCarran's campaign, a Democratic candidate had to win it in Clark County. We knew Grant's strength in the Democratic party in the north was overwhelming. But there were certainly more Republicans in the north than in Clark County, and Russell's vote would essentially be the north. Charlie had a lot of friends up north. We figured Clark County was very important to us.

I just was running for district attorney of Esmeralda in the general (no primary contest), so I started going up to campaign after Grant's primary victory. I felt comfortable in leaving then, because we had all these folks. When they started coming in, they all wanted to be chiefs. Nobody wants to be an Indian. Grant was good at handling them and making decisions. And so, comes November, and by God, he wins. We were proud of that campaign, and it was basically a clean campaign.

The money started coming. We got an advertising agency. I think we got Tom Wilson up in Reno, who had a man here too, and started designing material and doing more television, radio, and newspaper ads. We'd had some newspaper ads, but we'd written them ourselves. Grant and I talked about this—looked to us like some of the stuff we'd written was better than what the pros gave out. We used to say the toughest part of the campaign after that is trying to get your advertising agency or P.R. people to do what you wanted them to. But they seem expert, and every time you got an idea, they would tell you it wouldn't work. You have to take their advice or none at all, I guess.

Support from the casinos started coming in. I'm not certain if it was just before or after the primary. If it was before, it was close to the election. Grant got help from some gambling people in northern Nevada before the primary—not a great deal. Bobby McDonald in Reno was helping in the primary, and Bobby had clients in that business. [laughter] Bobby was always a great help. He and Grant became good friends.

There's always dissatisfaction against whoever is governor, and it builds. Grant used to say, "It's hard to survive eight years without having them all mad at you over something." Among the gamblers, there was a fringe group mad at Bob Cahill, one of the finest public servants I knew. Bob was executive secretary of the tax commission under Governor Russell. If there was a czar, it was Bob. I used to say, "I think we'd be better off with a czar—if the czar was Bob Cahill—than all the boards in the world." Bob was honest and knew the business.

Some people not in the business, because they hadn't been able to get licenses, wanted in. They think the way you do it is to help some candidate that's got some power. Most of them wound up disappointed. [laughter] Which points out a political truism. One of the roles I was able to play was to take the heat from those people. Grant and I were so closely identified, they felt more at liberty to talk to me. After he became governor, it was a hell of a lot easier to chew me out than it was to chew him out. That's a role someone has to play. I played it without rancor. [laughter] I never enjoyed taking the heat, but it didn't annoy me. I expected that. Everybody in high office needs somebody like that. All the time, you'll hear people cussing out appointments of a governor or a senator. "I can't stand that so-and-so. Wow, the governor made lousy appointments." They're not criticizing the governor, they're criticizing people close to him.

Beldon Katleman at the El Rancho became friendly after the primary, but I never had much to do with Beldon. I represented Beldon one time in a matter that required me to go to New York City. He made the arrangements and put me up in first class at the Hampshire House on Central Park West. Small, beautiful hotel. Got me tickets to "My Fair Lady." I had to meet this lawyer in New York. If you can believe this, I'm leaving for the theater, walk out the front door of the hotel, and run right into a kid I was in the army with. Never got to see "My Fair Lady." He and I walked around the corner to a local saloon and sat there reminiscing for three hours.

Roscoe Thomas at the Golden Nugget was an old-time Las Vegan and became a friend and a supporter of Grant's early on. Grant and I, and I'm sure he alone, met most of the partners there: Roscoe, Matt Martin, Charlie King, Tex Cooper. Several dealers had been friends through Jimmy Garrett. Roscoe and I became close. He used to own the Palace Theater before he became a partner in the Nugget. I handled his late wife's estate.

Tom Hanley, who had a terrible reputation as a labor leader, was giving us a lot of trouble. He was trying to organize a dealers' union. He was trying to get every candidate to pledge support. I didn't think a dealers' union was appropriate in those days, because there's a temptation in a gambling house for a dealer to, in the vernacular, "swing." The only way a house can protect itself—at least this is their view—is to be able to fire a dealer without having to prove he's cheating. It was a sensitive issue.

We were able to schedule things so Grant was able to avoid many meetings. I would meet with them. [laughter] Of course they were disappointed, just meeting with me: they wanted to talk to that candidate. I got a kick out of it. Tom's explaining how they need the union, how unfair management is: they walk into a pit and just fire everybody. That's terrible! We get to talking more. His beef wasn't that the house was stealing money from the public, it was that they weren't cutting it up with him fairly. He wanted a share of what they stole. [laughter] He didn't mind them being a thief, he just wanted his share. I thought, "This is hard to rationalize."

If organized labor was supporting Sawyer, it was piecemeal, not a unified push. There was a feeling, too, that labor as an organization wasn't as effective then. The culinary union's Al Bramlet was supporting Cannon for the Senate. George Rudiak had been attorney for the Teamsters; I think George had them supporting Sawyer. I never did understand why Jimmy "Sailor" Ryan was never a Sawyer supporter. Ryan sort of led the opposition to Sawyer in the 1960 Democratic convention in Ely, and he'd led the opposition to McCarran's position in the state convention in 1952 and 1954. He'd opposed McCarran, and he continued that, it seemed to me, with Sawyer. Jimmy certainly was never enthusiastic about Sawyer; I never saw him enthusiastic about anybody but Jimmy Ryan, anyway.

There were two big issues in the 1958 campaign. We felt gaming control had to be tough, or Nevada ran the risk of being put out of business by the federal people. Russell's bid for a third term as governor was also an issue, but nobody would say anything bad about Russell personally. As far as I know, nobody did.

I think I knew we had it won. Hazel was sampling voter opinion all along. We didn't have the polling they have now, but we used to pass a rumor that a poll in Oklahoma showed Sawyer way ahead. We made that up: "Did you see the Oklahoma poll? Grant's way ahead." [laughter] Hazel was a professional; no question about that. If she was doing a great deal of polling, she kept it close to her vest and might tell me on the phone or in person, or I'd tell Grant. That wouldn't be published.

The night of the general election, we must have been at the headquarters. I remember trying to get Grant on the phone in Elko and could not get through. The phone was tied up most of the night. I don't think he and I spoke until the next morning. He was overwhelmed with telegrams and calls from all over—not just Nevada, but all over the country.

After the election, Dick Ham, myself and Sara, Grant and Bette, Tom Cooke and his wife, Graham Hollister and his wife—I think that was the campaign people there and friends from Elko—went to Furnace Creek Inn in Death Valley. In a month or two, he's going to make a big speech, a budget, all of that. He's got to start getting a crew around him, start the early planning, but rest and have fun too. Sara and I were going to come back to Las Vegas, Grant and Bette were going on to Elko, and everybody was going to go where they came from. But a mutual friend of the Sawyers and us, George Boucher, died. So, we went from Furnace Creek to Elko to go to George's funeral.

That trip was funny, because people from Elko had their cars, and we had our car. Grant was going to ride with me. I had this 1952 station wagon. We told everybody we would meet at the junction where that highway up Smoky Valley meets U.S. 50 going from Ely over to Reno, just east of Austin. We're sailing along. I don't know if they're behind or ahead of us. Grant and I are reviewing the campaign and discussing things friends discuss, and one of my valves got stuck. It's backfiring. "Papoomp. Papoomp." We're going in fits and starts. It takes us forever to get to that junction. So, we wait. We thought sure they were ahead of us. The other cars aren't there. Dutch Stenovitch and these other people and Bette, they're not there.

If you get to Highway 50 at the intersection, if you turn left a few yards, there's a station. But I was precise. I said we'd meet at the junction. We waited. They'd gotten to the junction; they'd gone into that station, waited for us. We didn't show up, so they got worried about us. One car went back down Smoky Valley looking for us, but they didn't see us, because there was sort of a little cut-off into the station from the road up Smoky. Another car went on into Austin to see if we'd gone to Austin, so now we've got cars all over, and I'm sitting there, wondering where they are. I said, "Just think of it, Governor, here you are, and king of all you survey."

20 | Esmeralda County: "You've Got to Take Control"

In 1958, in addition to running Grant's campaign, I decided to run for Esmeralda County district attorney. Billy Crowell, a Democrat I'd met, called. I think he was state chairman during one of the Stevenson campaigns. He was a lawyer in Tonopah. After he went out as district attorney of Nye County, he was district attorney of Esmeralda, although he lived in Tonopah and only had to go to Goldfield when they had business. He had moved to Carson City and was trying to find somebody who would run. He said, "You ought to do it. You only have to go up there once or twice a month, to county commission meetings and if they have any serious criminal cases. You'd really be doing me a favor."

I decided to run for two reasons: one, I wasn't making a great deal of money, and it paid $5,000-$6,000 a year—a good retainer. The salary looked good, to tell you the truth. Second, I thought, "I'd like to try it, see what it's like to run for office." I'd been campaigning my tail off for Grant, and I wanted to see how I could do. I didn't know anybody there. I had fun meeting people—some of the old-timers who swore the camp would come back. That's what old miners always say, "The camp will come back."

Bob Santa Cruz, a lawyer from Las Vegas, ran against me. I campaigned door-to-door when I wasn't doing things in the Sawyer campaign. I went all over that county, saw parts of Nevada I'd never seen, met wonderful people. I won by running a clean campaign. [laughter]

I talked to Grant two or three times election night before results were in. The first time he called, he wanted to know how he was doing in Clark County. (When Grant ran for district attorney in 1950, McCarran was running for reelection, called, and wanted to know how he—McCarran—had done in Owyhee, this little Indian reservation precinct. Before Grant told him, he told him how well *he'd* run for district attorney, and McCarran let him know he didn't care. He wanted to know how he had done in Owyhee. [laughter])

I remembered this. I said, "Well, I don't know how you're doing, but I'm doing well up in Goldfield." He started laughing, and I told him what was happening. It gave me a great deal of pleasure to discover I outran Grant in Esmeralda County when I ran for district attorney up there.

One time I'd been up there a couple of days, and Sara got tired of me being away. She called the sheriff and told him to find me and tell me to meet the bus. The sheriff found me and told me to meet the bus. She sent the three kids to me. Scott came off holding his toothbrush in front of him. The four of us got in the car. We went out to Coaldale, Silver Peak, through Dyer, on the California line in Fish Lake Valley, up through the mountains, through Lida, and back to Goldfield. The kids seemed to like it. They were good. We found a little dog somebody had abandoned, and we brought the dog home.

Coaldale Junction is one of those typical little bar and restaurants in the middle of the desert, a restaurant counter on one side and a bar on the other. The four of us sit at the counter to have a sandwich. I'm waiting to order so I can introduce myself to everybody. This loudmouth at the bar yells, "A hell of a politician you are. You never buy a drink." I said, "You son-of-a-bitch, you never vote the way you drink anyway," and left it at that. We had our lunch, and I put a few cards on the bar and shook hands with the other people. After I was elected and went to the first meeting of the county commissioners, when the meeting was over, they convened the county road board. It consists of the commissioners, district attorney, and assessor. Not only am I on the board, I am chairman. Guess who's head of the road department? My buddy at Coaldale. I gave him a wink and smiled, and we became friends. But he thought he was going to have a lot of trouble with the road board.

My experience as district attorney was a lot of fun. The sheriff, Ed Kitchen, I enjoyed after I really got to know him. Xenia Baird was county clerk. Xenia and her whole family—old-time Goldfield people—all believed the camp would come back. Lena Hammond was recorder and auditor. All of the office holders had double jobs. I think the county clerk was also treasurer or secretary. Ed was sheriff and, I believe, assessor.

I went to my first meeting in January 1959. They didn't have television at that time in Goldfield, and the only entertainment in town was the county commission meeting. Everybody showed up, and everything was an issue. The chief issue on the table was that Lena Hammond, the treasurer, had refused to pay Charlie Cecini's salary for three months. Charlie was the constable. That was the first great legal matter I had to confront, and the statute provided that if the commissioners approved the bills for the month, they endorsed their approval and sent it to the treasurer, who writes the checks. Lena wouldn't write a check for Cecini, although the commissioners approved it.

The law provided that if the treasurer objected to the payment of any bill on the list, she would return it to the commission with her reasons for not paying and endorse thereupon. Then, if the commission approved it by unanimous vote and sent it back, she's supposed to pay. They had done that twice, and Lena wouldn't pay it. Lena had a deep conviction that Charlie wasn't earning that money—that he was spending a lot of his time at the Santa Fe Saloon, or wasn't really out patrolling the streets of Goldfield as he should.

This had become a great community issue. The room is full of people, and the issue before the board is: what are we going to do about the county treasurer not paying Cecini's bill? There were people in the community on Charlie's side and people there on Lena's side. I'm sitting at my desk looking down at the floor, listening to this great public debate.

Everybody wondered what one guy there was doing. Somebody moves into Goldfield and doesn't have a reason for moving there—a job or something—you wonder why on earth would somebody just move to Goldfield in 1959. He was a bright guy and took a very active part in the discussions. He was up speaking on Lena's side to convince the commission. Keep in mind, Charlie had been elected by a free and democratic vote. This guy is haranguing about Charlie, and all of a sudden, I hear a "whap." Charlie had had about all he could stand. He had walked over and belted this guy, knocked him hind end over teakettle, right there in the commissioners' room. [laughter]

I thought, "Oh my God, what have I gotten myself into?" I have a battery committed in my presence. They start yelling at Ed, the sheriff, to arrest Charlie for battery. I thought, "What the hell am I gonna do?" I got Ed's eye, like I want to talk to him about what the hell we're going to do.

The man gets up from the floor, goes to the door, and opens the door to leave. He says, "I'm going home and getting my shotgun, and I'm gonna come back and kill you, you old son-of-a-bitch," to Charlie.

With that, I said, "Ed, arrest that fellow." Maybe he would have carried out his threat. Feelings were high. We took the poor guy who got hit down to that old jail in Goldfield. I wanted to print him, find out who he was and what he was doing in town. Ed didn't really know how to print him. He looked, and in the drawers, he found a fingerprint card. So, I printed the guy. When I went back to Vegas, I took it to the FBI office. He had things on his record that indicate he would not have been a desirable citizen.

We never did charge Charlie with hitting the guy. I wound up asking the fellow if he wouldn't mind moving out of town, and I would dismiss any charges we had against him. That's what happened. I shudder at the thought of trying something like that nowadays, but he signed a release releasing the county and me and the sheriff from all liability. That was my first meeting of the county commission in Esmeralda County.

It was common in those days to float people out of town. It was terrible. I ran this guy out without any due process. I gave him until five that night. He said, "OK." I'd had him in jail two weeks. He'd never been arraigned or gotten bail; he was glad to leave. That used to happen all the time. The police would put a guy in a car and drive him to the city limits. Well, Goldfield was a more peaceful society after he left. [laughter]

Charlie got his salary. I did give an opinion that Lena had to pay him. Another guy there was a lawyer from some other state and ran for attorney general even though he wasn't a member of the Nevada bar. I learned for the first time our constitution didn't require that the attorney general be a member of the Nevada bar. [laughter] I think Lena got advice from him, and he told her she should pay him. Lena was always mad at me thereafter. That issue divided the community. There was them as thought Charlie had a right to go to the Santa Fe Saloon; he didn't have to be on the streets twenty-four hours a day. And there was them as thought he had to be out policing the community.

I did a lot of stupid things. I made terrible mistakes. I had to submit a budget for the district attorney's office to Xenia Baird. They gave me the budget for the preceding year to follow. On it was a secretary. It was a high salary in that day, $6,000. I thought my job was to look out for the public interest. I didn't need a secretary. I went to Xenia and told her to delete that. Near as I could tell, it was a waste of county money. I soon learned the secretary was Martin Duffy's wife, and Duffy was state senator from Esmeralda County.[1] [laughter] In the interest of heeding the ancient admonition to protect the public's funds, I had fired the state senator's wife, earning his undying enmity. In those days, remember, each county had just one senator. Duffy was just as powerful a senator as Mahlon Brown, the senator from Clark County. That was my first mistake, and that was a dandy, but I still thought I was right, and that sort of got over.

Les Carlson, chairman of the county commissioners, worked for E. L. Cord, who had the big ranch in Fish Lake Valley. Grant later appointed Les to the public service commission. He had a county credit card. I reviewed the county bills and see these credit card charges for gas. The legislature was in session, and he was Cord's point man up at the legislature, lobbying. Esmeralda County is paying his gas bill from Fish Lake Valley to Reno and every day from Reno to Carson. If you're on official business, you're supposed to get so much a mile. I required him to turn in his credit card. He did, but I didn't make any friends with Les on that one.

Then I discovered when the legislature wasn't in session, and he wasn't up there handling Cord's business, Les was a painter. One time I came up, and he's painting the courthouse. I didn't recall the commissioners putting out the job to bid. I discovered this had been going on for a while. He'd paint enough of the courthouse to be under the statutory limit, then he'd quit for a week and start again. I put an end to that, fully cementing his enmity. [laughter]

It was fun being district attorney, but it got to the point where I came to the conclusion, I think fairly, that I could not do justice to the county without spending a lot more time there, although that's the way it had been for several years before I came, and continued for several years after I left. Every time I was in Goldfield, I was neglecting something in Las Vegas. I'd come back to Las Vegas, and I was neglecting something up there. I'd only go up for commission meetings, maybe the night or afternoon before and go through their agenda and see if there was anything. I was always on call if they had a criminal case. Bill Beko was district attorney of Nye County.[2] I appointed him deputy district attorney of Esmeralda, so if any emergencies came up, Bill would take care of it until I got there. I think about eight or nine months after I'd taken the job, I resigned.

A lot of people I knew were mad at me. I had run, they had given me their support and good faith, and now I was quitting. Most of them, however, said they understood the job was not of a type that would warrant living there. They wished something could be done so they could have a district attorney who lived there. They hadn't had one since Pete Breen.[3] Pete had been district attorney for years. [laughter] He'd run Esmeralda for years as district attorney, packed a pistol. They tried to recall him a couple of times.

The first day I got there, Pete sent word in. (He had been appointed district judge, and he happened to be in Goldfield that day for court. That district included Esmeralda, Nye, and Mineral Counties.) When I got free, he'd like to see me in his chambers. What an absolutely delightful man! He said, "Ralph, if you could get elected in Esmeralda County, you can get elected any place in the world. This is the toughest place in the *world* to get elected to something and hold onto it after you got it. So, if you got elected here, you can get elected to anything." Then he said, "But you've got to take control of this county. You have to run the county, not that bunch of dunderheads they always have on the board of county commissioners."

I said, "Well, Judge, I take it my duty is to give legal advice to the county officers and the county commissioners."

"Oh, forget that. You've got to run this county." [laughter] I disagreed. He never did accept my view. But there's a lot of truth in it. In some small counties. the district attorney better play a more important role in the government than ordinarily he would.

Breen is an old legal name in Nevada. His father was a lawyer.[4] His son Peter is a district judge in Reno. The Peter Breen I met in Goldfield was some kind of man. I got the biggest kick out of him. He told me, "The last time I was elected district attorney, I won by sixty-one votes. Six months to the day after the election, they filed a petition to recall me. We had a recall election. I won that by sixty-one votes. Not a son-of-a-bitch in the county changed their mind." [laughter] I don't know if that's true, but six months after he took office in his last term, he had a petition to recall him. God only knows why! They don't need to have a reason in Esmeralda. [laughter] Maybe they thought he was spending too much time at the Santa Fe. Who knows?

I got to know a lot of people around Goldfield. They were all characters! Kirby had the Silver Dollar Bar, and he called it the Silver Dollar Bar for good reason: he had a bunch of silver dollars imbedded in the bar. If you were going to get a drink in his bar, get it in one that came in a container. Don't get anything Kirby had to take his hands and put ice in the glass or anything like that. [laughter]

There were just an awful lot of nice people out there in rural Nevada we don't get out there enough to get a chance to know. I don't get back long enough to maintain a friendship. A lot of them have died, but we still get Christmas cards from a lot of those people and send Christmas cards to them. It was an important experience in my life—one I enjoyed.

What made it important was, at bottom, being able to deal on a personal basis with people I didn't know and hadn't known and accepted me, voted for me. We became friends. It's not the most important legal position, but it gave me some feeling of satisfaction that I could go into an area where I didn't know a soul and ask them to vote for me. It gave me a feeling of confidence I probably had not had before. At least, I knew I could campaign among strangers without being scared to death. And working with people in county government on that kind of a level in that kind of a community that was economically dead . . . . Hell, the only economic activity in Goldfield was the courthouse. You had a few tourists going through, so you had service stations and bars. No mines were operating. Not many ranches in that part of Esmeralda. Just a few old-timers who had faith the camp would come back.

For years, I would go through Lida Junction. If you're going to Goldfield, you leave Beatty and go across that big flat—Sarcobatus. About sixteen miles this side of Goldfield is a road that turns off to the left to Lida, a little old mining town, and there's a ranch. Then it continues through those mountains into the lower end of Fish Lake Valley. At Lida was a restaurant and gas pump. Margie Guyat ran that service station. I stopped there when I was campaigning. For years, if I was driving to Reno or Tonopah or Goldfield, I'd always stop at Margie's and have a hamburger.

I tried to find out as much as I could about Margie, if she had family. She's in the middle of the desert by herself. She was from Connecticut. She'd come west years before, got that property, and stayed there. I came through one time and that station had burned down. Down the road from it was the Cottontail Ranch, a house of prostitution. (Incidentally, when I was district attorney, I wouldn't let them in. They tried a couple of times to see if they could get permission to open, and I wouldn't let them.)

I wondered what had happened to Marge! I continued toward Las Vegas, and down the road a little ways was that junction you take to go to

Death Valley. There was this service station and restaurant and bar, bigger than Margie's, maybe fifteen miles closer to Vegas. Slim Riggs ran that joint. I went in, found Slim, and said, "Slim, what happened to Margie?"

He said, "Them God-damn whores burned her out."

I said, "Well, where is Margie?"

"She's sitting in the kitchen with Mrs. Riggs." I went back in to see Margie, and sure enough, she was sitting there. She used almost the same words: "Them God-damn whores burned me out, and I'm scared." She told me she had given them a lease, and they were paying her some rent. The lease was up. She wanted to raise the rent, and they burned her out, thinking she'd sell them the land.

I got back to the office, wrote those people, and told them I represented Margie. If they wished to negotiate a lease, I'd be happy to do so. I never heard from them. Then I see a story that the lady who owned the Cottontail Ranch applied to the Bureau of Land Management for a lease on government land. The county commissioners had written the BLM recommending it, saying it was for commercial purposes—Esmeralda was a poor county, and they needed any business they could encourage—without telling the BLM the nature of the business. [laughter] I sent a letter to Drew Pearson, I think with a copy to the secretary of interior, telling them that the government was about to lease land to a madam in Nevada to run a whorehouse. I said, "We have a word out in Nevada that refers to people who own whorehouses. We call them pimps. Is the United States contemplating going into the pimping business?" [laughter] That was the end of the lease from the government. Pearson wrote a little bit in his column, and the BLM backed off. Margie finally sold to the madam, and I never heard another word from Margie.

Ed Kitchen was a grand man. God, Ed must have been eighty. His daughter lived in Las Vegas and was married to one of the executives of the Bank of Nevada. She was born and raised in Goldfield. Ed served with me and the three county commissioners on the county road board. One day, we decided to inspect the road system. Generally, the road department consists of one caterpillar and the guy driving it. [laughter] You'd blade the road to somebody's mining claim. But we went clear into Silver Peak and Fish Lake Valley, and back into Tonopah. The police car had a big red light on it. Ed's driving. We wind up in Tonopah late in the afternoon. We figured it had been a long, dusty trip, and we'd better have a drink. We go in the old Bank Club and belly up and have a couple of shooters. Then we get in the car and head for Goldfield. Ed's in pretty good shape. [laughter] We pull up behind a big Las Vegas-Tonopah-Reno bus. My God, Ed turns on the red light and siren and goes by them. [laughter]

In 1960, I was chairman of the Kennedy-Johnson campaign in Nevada. About three days before the election, I got a call from Bobby Kennedy wanting to know how Esmeralda County was going to vote. I thought, "Well, who the hell cares?" [laughter] On that level? But he wanted to know. I found out in talking to him he'd checked the records, and Esmeralda County had never been wrong in a presidential election for I don't know how many years. I said, "I don't know, Mr. Kennedy, but I will find out, and I'll get back to you." I called Xenia, who said, "Oh, Kennedy's going to carry Esmeralda County." I called Bobby back and told him. Seemed to make him happy. [laughter]

Notes

1. Democrat Martin Duffy represented Esmeralda County in the State Senate, 1959-63.

2. William Beko went on to serve as district judge, 1975-91.

3. Peter Breen served as district judge for Mineral, Nye, and Esmeralda Counties from his appointment in 1957 until his death in 1967. His son is a Washoe County district judge.

4. The elder Peter Breen was a district judge from 1903 to 1922. His district, the third, included Eureka and Lander Counties.

21 | We Knew What Our Relationship Was

Sara and I went with Grant and Bette to the mansion the night before Grant was sworn in, and we spent the night. There was little furniture, but the dining room table was beautiful. Bette was worried about moving from Elko: "Do we bring our own furniture?" It turned out, to a large extent, that they did.

The next morning, we went with them to the governor's office. It came as a surprise that nobody was there to greet the new governor and his wife—when we get to the office, the door is open, but nobody's there. I thought it was bad manners. [laughter] We went in and sat down, and then people started showing up. People around Charlie Russell were bitter about the election results, but Marge showed Bette around the mansion, and Grant had a couple of discussions with Charlie. Grant wanted an office in the capitol. The legislature wasn't in session at the time, and I think they gave him the lieutenant governor's office.

We prided ourselves that nobody in the campaign wanted anything—everybody was a volunteer. But we discovered soon after the election that many people *did* want things. [laughter] Grant felt a deep sense of gratitude for people who had really stuck their necks out," . . . but what do you do if people come to you? Do you help them?" When Harry Truman went to the Senate, he said Pendergast told him, "I'll have to write letters of recommendation, but don't pay any attention unless I sign in green ink." Grant and I had a similar understanding. He knew I would be called upon, but we agreed that if it was someone really deserving and able to do the job, I would call him. I wasn't to worry about writing letters; he would know those were just routine. That worked well through the years. There were very few times that I called him on behalf of somebody, but I wrote a lot of letters. Disappointed people would get mad at me, not at him—part of my responsibility as his friend was to take the heat. How do we protect Grant? That was always my view.

222

*We
Knew
What
Our
Relationship
Was*

Going in, we didn't have any idea how many hundreds of appointments there were to boards, and it came as a surprise that so many people wanted to serve. I thought, "Jesus! Why would you want to, unless you wanted to perform a public service?" But people didn't care, they just wanted to get appointed. Hell, even before the election, people were putting pressure on for public service commission, tax commission. Then you had appointments like state engineer. Grant had no more idea than the man in the *moon* all of the boards people would kill to be on. I'd never heard there was a dairy commission, but we've got people fighting to get appointed to the dairy commission! [laughter]

All the Nevada State Athletic Commission had was boxing. George Foley is a good guy. Grant liked George and George liked Grant, so Grant appointed him; but one of our supporters didn't like George, and she was furious. (Everybody should like George. He's a jewel.) I asked George one day: "Gladys Dula—God, she's upset, George. She doesn't think you're qualified. What are your qualifications to be on the boxing commission?" George replied, "Just tell old Gladys I've been in more boxes than anybody else in Clark County." [laughter] George was a good commissioner.

There were sensitive jobs you expect to change with administrations. Warden in the state prison was one. Warden was a plum; it was a great job! They called his house the "warden's mansion" on the penitentiary grounds. Before you went in, there was this big stone house. The prisoners worked as cooks and houseboys, and the warden's wife had a salary as matron. Keep in mind, the state was smaller back then, and a lot of guys on the inside had been friends on the outside. [laughter]

Some major things had to be done, and done quickly. We talked about meeting with department heads. We agreed, in principle, that if they were doing a good job, why should they be fired just to make room for somebody else?

There had been a lot of talk during the campaign about gaming control. We knew there was going to be an awful lot of pressure. Grant knew how to handle that, but there was doubt about some of us who now had the reputation of being close to him. He was interested in creating due process in the field of gaming license revocations, and he thought the governor should not be on the board that did that. The gaming commission was the result, taking supervisory responsibility out of the tax commission and removing the governor from micro-managing that field, which I think was wise. That gained him a lot of time.

Poor old Grant. Grant was bright, had worked in the Senate, been district attorney, knew county government, knew state government as well as or better than most, but had not had any experience dealing with these agencies and making these appointments. Now he's in Carson City—all these things to do—and I'm in Las Vegas trying to practice law and make a living. As soon as I get involved in something, I have to run off to Goldfield. So I did not play much of a role between the election and when Grant took office, and I didn't play any role in his early administration. The governor had the right to hire a personal attorney, and Grant hired Charlie Springer for that.

I know from discussions we had that Grant was interested in a reorganization of state government, which he accomplished. And he was interested in trying to move civil rights legislation along, recognizing how difficult it was and trying to figure out how to deal with legislators on that issue, particularly small county legislators. Remember, before the "one man, one vote" rule, each county had one senator. You had fifteen from small counties, one from Washoe, one from Clark. He devoted a lot of his intellectual ability to trying to figure out how to advance civil rights law in that legislative environment.

By now, Bruce Barnum was in charge of the governor's office. Dick Ham was in Carson, head of the employment security department, and available. I think Hazel Erskine was appointed to the welfare board and was a valued member. Jack Lehman was appointed head of economic development. Jack had been a loyal, effective supporter. (Jack and Lu had two children at the time. I take some credit for convincing him he wasn't too old to go to law school. He went to Los Angeles, worked full time with one of the government agencies, and went to school at night. Came back to Las Vegas and had a successful career as an attorney, and now is a district court judge.) That's the old group, but you have a lot of people in state government knowledgeable in their fields that Grant could consult with. And many people volunteered advice to him.

Dorothy Dorothy got mad at Grant. Oh, God, did she get mad! That's one of the reasons I think she didn't follow his leadership at the 1960 convention. You never know why somebody will get mad. Dorothy had been an early supporter. She had been appointed to a board, but there came a vacancy in justice of the peace in Las Vegas. Dorothy wanted her husband appointed. Of course, county commissioners fill the vacancies. Grant had no power over who got appointed. Dorothy found that difficult to understand. When Dale didn't get appointed, that ended her affection for Grant. [laughter]

Grant worked hard to do things that needed to be done. Hazel hit the nail on the head when she said he was educable. Not a great deal had happened in state government since the beginning of World War II—Robbins (Bob) Cahill makes reference to this in his oral history. [*Robbins E. Cahill.* Reno: UNOHP, 1977.] Bob had served under Governors Kirman, Carville, Pittman, and Russell, and he had good things to say about them (particularly Russell), but he said Grant was, without doubt, the best governor he worked with.

224

*We
Knew
What
Our
Relationship
Was*

One night in our house in Boulder City, we had a dinner party. There was a spirited discussion. I was in disagreement with Grant. He got annoyed with me and made a pretty cutting remark. I said, "Well, Grant, if all you want around you is a bunch of yes-men, I'll be glad to join. Yes sir, whatever you say is right, if that's what you want."

He was silent for a minute. Then he looked at me and said, "No, Ralph. Don't change. I've got enough yes-men around me now." That was the only time I remember any annoyance by him or me as to the other's view. My view was always: he was the governor; I was his friend. My duty was to give him my honest view on any given issue, but once he made the decision, that was the end of it. Nobody would ever hear that I disagreed.

How to describe my role? Friend and confidante, maybe. Henchman, maybe. Many perceived me as a henchman, bagman, tool, all of those things, but Grant and I knew what our relationship was, and it didn't make any difference what other people said. My underlying relationship was that of friend. I think he trusted me, as I certainly did him; and if I ever did anything that embarrassed him, he knew it wasn't intentional. And I *did* do things that embarrassed him, no question. But generally, he asked me to do them. [laughter]

Grant told me, long after he'd gone out as governor, "All those years, there was never one thing you ever did in my name that embarrassed me." I took that as a serious compliment. McCarran would never have an office in the state, because he didn't want anybody here to speak for him. He thought they would become, in the vernacular of the day, "juice peddlers." That is what Grant made reference to, that I never "peddled juice." But you could have called me a henchman. [laughter]

My association with Grant created problems for my law practice, but it also helped. I became much better known. (Keep in mind, I'd only been here three years when he ran for governor. I had to learn. There was a lot of naiveté.)

One of the owners of a Strip hotel invited me to lunch. They wanted me as one of their lawyers. At most big hotels, their lawyers were in Los Angeles, and they used local lawyers as go-fers more than anything. This hotel had a local attorney—well-known, capable. I asked about that. He said, "There are times when he can't handle matters, and we would like to have you as our attorney. We'll give you a $500 a month retainer." I didn't smell any wolf manure. I thought that was wonderful. A $500 a month retainer was big in those days. Three days after that, the guy called and told me he wanted So-and-so appointed to the gaming control board. I said, "I can't do that, and we better rethink this. I don't think I want to be on your retainer."

A so-called legitimate business in town called and had recognized my great legal abilities, too. It was a utility. I had gotten to know one of the principals during the campaign, and we had become friends. They wanted me to become their local attorney. I knew their local attorney, and he and his father before him had been their attorney for many years. I asked about that. "We're going to keep them, but we're growing. We need more help." I thought that was wonderful. Again, I didn't smell any wolf manure. After all, these were square Johns. This wasn't a gambling house. I went running back to the office and told Cal and Chet. Boy, that was good!

I read in the paper two or three weeks after that they'd applied to the public service commission for a rate increase. I wondered who prepared this petition. I hadn't received their first check for the retainer, and I thought, "Maybe they had it in the mill before they decided to engage my services." I didn't hear any more. Then, I get a call from the big firm in Chicago that handles these things. (That firm was so old that Robert Todd Lincoln's name was still on the letterhead.) This guy tells me he would be in Las Vegas in a couple of days to meet with me and go to Carson City on the hearing on this rate increase.

I said, "What rate increase?"

He said, "We filed a petition quite some time ago to get a rate increase. The company's entitled to a rate increase. We need a rate increase."

I said, "Well, I haven't seen any petition for a rate increase."

"Oh, didn't we send you a copy of that?"

"What do you people think I am? Do you think I'm a political whore? I'm not a political whore; I'm a lawyer. I'm not going to Carson City with you, and I'm not going to sit at the counsel table. I don't know anything about the case; I haven't seen the petition."

This guy got upset. He asked if I would reconsider. He was sorry they overlooked this, and they could make it up.

I said, "No, I'm not interested in representing you."

I came home. Later that night, I got a call from the senior partner asking me to change my mind. I refused. "Well, I'm very sorry, Mr. Denton, the way this happened, but I would like you to know I admire your position, and I'm happy to have had a chance to know you."

My friend who had arranged it was upset and thought I was a nut. "Are you crazy? Grab it while you can. It won't last forever."

That happened quite a bit, so I had to learn. That hurt the practice, but people didn't believe it. I could not completely quit representing anybody that had business before the state of Nevada and be an active lawyer. So, I decided I would not represent anybody before the gaming control board or commission unless they had been clients before Grant was elected or they were dear friends, in which case, I figured I'd have to do it.

I did appear before the gaming commission several times. When I did appear, people accused me of political influence. Ed Olsen answered that by saying, "Well, if you look at the record, the gaming control commission and board have turned Ralph Denton down more than they've approved his applicants." There weren't many, but that was true. They called it the way they saw it. I am convinced to this day from the time that commission was created through Sawyer—I don't know much about it after that—it was dead on the level. If anyone had told me that corruption or political influence affected the outcome on license applications, I would not have believed it.

226

*We
Knew
What
Our
Relationship
Was*

Grant started changing the laws, creating the gaming commission. From a governmental standpoint, it had a sound basis. It removed the governor from direct participation in gaming control, because he was a member of the tax commission. The chairman of the public service commission had also been a member of the tax commission, but this new law removed department heads of state government from the commission. That was the chief change, initially.

Soon after Sawyer appointed a new gaming control chairman, that board and its enforcement officers took some unusual steps. They went into some of the big casinos on the Strip and took cards and dice off the tables to check them. You can imagine the hue and cry, and the Las Vegas politicians on the telephone to the governor complaining. They didn't seem to concern themselves as to whether the gambling joint was flat . . . whether the dice were crooked, or the cards. They complained stringently, and the governor backed the board. As far as I know, most—not all—old-time gamblers when Grant became governor, after eight years, were still friends, although he had been tough. He had done things that I don't think they liked.

The old time casino operators were nice people, by and large, to deal with. In his oral history, Cahill talks about never having trouble with the Desert Inn group. Anything he asked them to do, they did. But they were smart. The Desert Inn group had several partners. One would be the front man supporting Russell. There would be another, and he'd say, "Well, all my partners are for Russell, but I'm for you, Grant." [laughter] They always had somebody in the joint who was a contact with the other guy. Everybody knew they were helping both candidates. Might help one a little more than another, but by and large, they were helping everybody. Consequently, nobody felt really obligated to them. They weren't trying to buy control in those days, they were trying to be let alone, the chief difference between now and then, I think.

The truth of the matter is, I don't think either of us would have known a mobster if he hit us in the head with a flounder. At that time, stories were in the papers, but if you're a decent, normal human being, you accept people at face value. They didn't wear signs on their backs that said, "I'm a member of the Chicago mob." Naiveté ruled.

One good thing happened as a result of appearing before the commission and board on occasion: I met Charles LaFrance, chief investigator for the board under the Sawyer administration. He had a background of early FBI service—he was a lawyer. Charlie was raised in upstate New York state, went to law school at the University of Alabama in the late 1920s or early 1930s. Charlie went to work for the FBI in the early days, when it was a small organization. He knew the director; he was in on some of the great arrests of the day: Baby Face Nelson, Dillinger, things like that. Then he fell out with Hoover and left the FBI. There were agents he thought were badly treated by Hoover, growing out of those thrilling arrests, Bonnie and Clyde and all, with Hoover trying to claim credit, showing up and not brooking any degree of criticism or suggestion. Charlie was one of the few ex-FBI agents who didn't think Hoover was the greatest guy that ever did it behind shoe leather.

Charlie was knowledgeable in organized crime. One time, I represented this bookmaker from Louisville, a friend of Jimmy Garrett's. I could not turn down Jimmy. We were called to Carson City for an investigative hearing. I'd never met Charlie, and we were there all day with Charlie asking about his background. On the way back to Reno, this fellow said, "The grand jury of Jefferson County investigates me every year. The internal revenue service audits me every year. The FBI has all my phones bugged, at the book and at my house. And that little son-of-a-bitch knows more about me than all those agencies put together." Charlie asked him questions going back to his childhood and associates he'd had in bookmaking—Charlie knew everything. When he'd tell where he laid off bets, Charlie would know who worked at that place. Charlie stayed with the control board into the Laxalt administration, but he was opposed to things the Laxalt administration was doing insofar as corporate gambling was concerned, so he quit.

He came to Las Vegas and went to work in one of the small hotels. I think it was the Bonanza. (It was on the Strip; it was just there a little while before it was torn down.) But he didn't care for that, or they didn't care for him—one or the other—and he figured they owed him money, so he came to my office and wanted me to be his lawyer. I said, "I'll be glad to be your lawyer, but hell, you can do all the work." Charlie came into the office; he wrote the briefs; we tried the case; we lost it, appealed to the ninth circuit court, got a two to one vote. We didn't reverse the trial judge on it, but we got one circuit judge on our side. Charlie did all the work.

By now he was in the habit of coming to the office, so he kept coming, and he worked for me for several years. As fine a man as I ever knew in my life, dead square honest—would not go to an ex-FBI agents' meeting if Bob Maheu was there.[1] For some reason, he did not like Bob. If he wasn't going to be there, Charlie would go. Charlie was a little guy, one of those treasures you meet by accident and get to know them. He was remarkable.

I had a couple of run-ins with the control board, one in particular where I thought they were doing something they didn't have any right to do. Jimmy asked me to represent a guy who had been in gambling in Cuba. In those days, it was well established that if all a guy had in his background was gambling, that was not grounds to turn him down on a license. This gentleman didn't come here to get a license, just to work. He had a job downtown, and a control board agent came by and told his boss, "You ought to let this man

228

*We
Knew
What
Our
Relationship
Was*

go." If somebody from the gaming authorities come and tell a licensee to get rid of somebody, they're going to get rid of him. That had happened two or three times, and all he wanted was a job. Jimmy brought him to me.

I didn't see how they can do that. (They have more law on their side now; they didn't have this law on the subject at that time.) I called Olsen and said, "I represent so-and-so. They're rousting him. They won't let him work any place. That doesn't seem right to me. But if you will look through your files and tell me that, in your opinion, you've got enough in your files to keep this man out of Nevada, I'll back off." He said he would look.

The control board had an office on Las Vegas Boulevard South. They had a couple of auditors and investigators. Most of the action was out of Carson City. Two or three days later, I went down. Ed and Butch Leypoldt, two members of the board, were there; Ned Turner, I guess, was in Carson. They agreed to see me, and I went in. They looked at me like a bull at a bastard calf, I guess would be the way to describe it. They didn't want the man to work in Nevada.

I said, "Do you have enough in your files to justify that conclusion?"

They said, "We just don't want the man working in Nevada."

I said, "Well, piss on you then. I'll see you in court."

There was a club in town that wanted to hire the man, but was scared to. I said, "Go ahead and hire him. I don't think you'll ever have any trouble." They hired him and didn't have any trouble. There wasn't anything in his file.

About six or eight months after that, Grant was inaugurated for his second term. He gave the State of the State speech in the assembly chamber. I was sitting on the platform, and I look out, and there's Ed and Butch. Ed cups his hands around his mouth so nobody can see and moves his lips as though saying, "Piss on you. I'll see you in court." [laughter]

Ed Olsen had been the AP reporter in Reno—a first-class reporter. Grant and I had known him a little, because when Joe McDonald and I were partners, and we'd go to Reno, Alan Bible and Bob McDonald's office was in the same building where the *Nevada State Journal* and the *Gazette* were published. The A.P. had a desk there.

My recollection is that Ed got hired as public relations man for the tax commission . . . or maybe it was not until the gaming commission was formed. When Ed was P.R. man for the gaming commission, he did a good job, and Grant was so pleased with him and had such respect for him, that he appointed him to the gaming control board. At that time, I think, Bob Faiss also came to work for the state. I think he came as a news guy or secretary of the gaming commission. Bob moved into Grant's office later.

I considered it my responsibility as Grant's friend to conduct myself in such a way that it would not embarrass him. That's a little hard to do when the press and everybody else is referring to you as his bagman, and every time a political vacancy came up my name was always mentioned, all the time the poor son-of-a-bitch was governor. [laughter] I made it clear I didn't want anything. He asked me. I don't know why I didn't want any kind of appointment, except all I wanted from the time I was a boy was to practice law. I didn't want to work for some agency. I didn't want to be second fiddle to anybody. I often said I didn't go to college and law school and work hard—I hope I worked hard—to work for somebody else.

Justice Charles Merrill resigned from the Nevada Supreme Court on October 1, 1959, and Miles Pike was appointed.[2] One columnist reported Roger Foley, the attorney general, would get that job. I don't know what that writer had been smoking, because Merrill was from Washoe. An unwritten compact had grown over the years. The state was divided into three areas: Washoe, Clark, and the small counties. The Supreme Court consisted of three justices. It was agreed, and it generally worked out, that one of the justices would be from Washoe, one from Clark, one from the small counties: Merrill from Washoe, McNamee from Clark, and Milton Badt from Elko. I remember a discussion that it should go, in all probability, to somebody from Washoe, as it did.

When Attorney General Ryland Taylor died, his replacement might have been Grant's first appointment, before Pike. He talked to Foley, and Roger wished to be appointed. Roger's ambition had been to be a judge. The governor came to our office, anxious about who he would appoint attorney general before half the lawyers in Las Vegas were on his tail. He didn't want to go to the state building, where everybody was waiting to put the lug on him. He, Cal, Chet, and I—we had a small conference room—sat and tried to figure out what was best for him to do. Grant took notice of what I had heard from McCarran—I don't suppose it was original with him—that every time he appointed somebody, he made ten enemies and got one ingrate.

Grant offered the appointment to Cal. Cal would have distinguished the office, but Cal said he would have to talk to his wife Beth, and he couldn't get Beth. Grant wanted to get the appointments made, go on with his job of being governor with his first legislature. He did ask me, at that time, "Well, if Cal won't take it, will you take it?"

I said, "Oh God, Grant. Let this cup of hemlock pass my lips. But if that's what it takes, I will do it, until you can get somebody to take my place."

Then, for whatever reason, Roger changed his mind. My impression was that he had talked to his father, and his father said he owed the people the duty of serving out his term. Who now? Just Grant and I participated in that discussion.

The man Grant wanted to appoint, John Mowbray, was a bankruptcy referee, and his office was in the federal court in the old post office. I went to see if he'd accept it. He said he would, I ran back to Grant and told him,

230

*We
Knew
What
Our
Relationship
Was*

Grant appointed him, and it was done before anybody else could try to get the appointment. Mowbray served the state well as district judge and went on the supreme court for many years—fine man, fine judge.

Sawyer did give me one appointment, and Snowy Monroe in Elko joked in his column that it wasn't much of a payoff. But it was important to me: the one for the McCarran memorial statue on Capitol Hill. I succeeded Ernie Cragin, a dear friend of McCarran's, when Cragin died. I remember going to Washington for the unveiling. There was a picture taken in Statuary Hall—worst ever taken of me. I looked like a big dummy, which is probably what I am. The majority leader spoke; the minority leader spoke; Bible and Cannon, I think, spoke. It was a good reunion of old-time Nevada people, many who'd lived in Washington for years. That's why all those people went back to it.

That's the day Grant and I went over to the sergeant at arms's office, and Bible took Sawyer off. I visited Joe Duke, my old friend, and waited for Grant. After he finished with Bible and Lyndon Johnson, Grant came by Duke's office and visited for a minute, and then we left. That's when he told me Johnson had done everything in the world to get him to commit to support him in 1960 for the presidential nomination, and Grant withstood the pressure. Whether that's the time Johnson offered him secretary of interior, or if that was after a rally in Las Vegas, I'm not certain. Grant later said he promised that to every western governor who was a Democrat. [laughter]

Notes

1. Robert Maheu was an FBI agent. Later, he was right-hand man to Howard Hughes, who eventually turned against him.

2. Charles Merrill served on the Nevada Supreme Court from 1951 to 1959, when he was named to the Ninth Circuit Court of Appeals. Miles Pike, appointed to succeed him, was a former U.S. attorney. He was elected to a term of his own the following year, then resigned in June 1961.

22 | Could a Catholic Get Elected?

In preparing for the state convention at Ely in May of 1960, we had two objectives. One was to remove Bill Woodburn as national committeeman. The second was to get control of the delegation to Los Angeles for Kennedy. What happened with Bill Woodburn was that he and E. L. Cord and the big powers in Reno and their satellites—some always flock to power—had decided to pick the Democratic candidate for governor in 1958. They decided Cord would be the governor. That didn't fly. Then they decided Harvey Dickerson would be. Well, Grant Sawyer won the primary and became the candidate!

We believed that party officials should stay out of primaries to be in a position to support whoever the Democratic nominee is. Grant believed that, as governor, he had a responsibility as titular head of the party to impose party regularity. That was the reason we wished to get rid of Woodburn: Teach committeemen to keep out of primary elections. That's why we have a primary.

In the primary of 1960, both Nevada senators were committed to Lyndon Johnson. Grant had committed himself to Kennedy and put his prestige on the line a bit. (Hy Raskin believed the strength of a party in any state was with the governor, and the governor's strength would surpass that of the senators. Ninety percent of the time, he's correct, but that hasn't always been true in Nevada. Witness the power of Pat McCarran.)

Our objective at the state convention was to get control of the delegation. In those days, before they had these rules designed to promote democracy, you had a lot of people participating, going to conventions, precinct meetings. It started with our Clark County convention. We had the same thing going on in conventions all over the state, but Clark County was the big one. We had to get delegates from Clark County to the state convention. That became important. And who's going to be on the nominating committee? In those days, the nominating committee would come up with a list of the delegates that was automatic.

I was chairman of the county nominating convention. That was difficult, because we had so many delegates and didn't want to offend any Democrat who had always been a delegate. We wanted to get people friendly toward the governor, so they would take direction at the state convention. I was convinced we had a majority who would pay attention to the governor's request. Grant wasn't sure he could put that much faith in me. [laughter]

We go through the same thing at the state. Any convention starts with mob rule. You haven't had the credentials committee appointed and the delegates accepted, so a temporary chairman is elected. First thing the temporary chairman does is appoint a credentials committee. Credentials comes back with a report. It deals with challenges, if any. Then the convention is properly constituted. You know who the delegates are. There might be 300 of them or whatever the hell it is. Once that is done, the temporary chairman presides over the election of a permanent chairman. That's where the fight is, because the convention chairman appoints the committees.

We had a hell of a fight in Ely. We got Bill Briare elected temporary chairman, and he presided while we elected Dutch Horton convention chairman. They did everything they could to beat old Dutch, but they couldn't. With that, I'm appointed chairman of the nominating committee.

Grant and I had a discussion. It had been a knock-down, drag-out fight. Grant makes up a list of who he wants to be delegates. At that point, much to his credit, he did not want to humiliate Senators Bible and Cannon, Johnson's two principal supporters in Nevada. All he wanted was enough votes to have a majority for Kennedy. Bible had not taken part in the fight. He was a friend of Woodburn's, and all things being equal, had he been called upon, he would have voted for Woodburn. To what extent Cannon participated, I don't know, but his people did. Shady Harry, Jack Conlon, was leading the fight against the Sawyer forces, aided by most of the Foleys, but they were in the minority. Grant wanted to be sure Cannon and Bible got good representation on that committee, because the Kennedy people we picked were Grant's people, and we were sure of them. Ha! [laughter]

It was also our job to suggest names for the state central committee. That was generally done by county caucuses. Jimmy "Sailor" Ryan violently opposed us, fought us every step of the way, but once Jimmy recognized that they had lost, he came to me to make a proposition. We're in a period of reconciliation. He says they would have no objection to me being on the state central committee if he were put on. Each county only had two. I said, "Jimmy, I certainly have no objection to you being on the state central committee, but I don't want to be. I'll tell you what I am going to do. I'm perfectly happy to make you one of them, and I am going to recommend one of the black people from the Westside, Jim McMillan, if you'll have it. It's never been done in Nevada before, but they're entitled to it. They've stood shoulder to shoulder with us from the beginning of this convention." Ryan shrugged his shoulders. He didn't say anything.

So, I found Jim to tell him we wanted him on the state central committee from Clark County. Jim said no, "Put Prentiss Walker on." He was a preacher on the Westside who'd worked his tail off. I said, "OK." The nominating committee made recommendations that were followed by the convention. For the first time in the history of Nevada, a black man was elected to serve as a member of the state committee of a major party, Prentiss Walker. I wished it had been McMillan. [laughter] But Prentiss was a good guy.

Now it comes time to elect a national committeeman. [laughter] I took the floor and nominated Vail Pittman, to honor this former governor and fine old man. How can anybody object? Some did. It was a battle. Horton's rules of order were attacked, but we only did was what had been done in Democratic conventions for years. We had "the wotes," and we took control. Grant wasn't certain about Clark County, because a lot of the power was on the Woodburn side—the Cannon bunch. But I'd gone through that list when I was chairman of the county convention. That was the key. We had the wotes. [laughter]

I don't remember any fight over the platform being in favor of civil rights. People by then were of the attitude that platforms didn't mean anything, anyway. I do remember walking the night before the convention out of the Nevada Hotel with two of my black friends. We went across to the Bank Club to have dinner. One of the delegates from Washoe wanted to talk to me. I walked over, and he wanted to know where was I going with "those niggers." I said, "I'm going to have dinner. You want to join us?" He didn't want to.

In 1960 John F. Kennedy spoke to a Nevada joint legislative session, and a reception for state delegates to the national Democratic convention followed at the mansion. Joe Kennedy had been staying at Lake Tahoe and was there. He could not have gotten a good impression of the Nevada delegation, because most of them were drunk out of their skulls. [laughter]

Sara and I went to Reno one time for a Democratic function. Dick Ham and I met Kennedy at the airport and took him to the Holiday Hotel. Tom Cooke was to take Kennedy to mass the next morning, and Tom waited in front of the hotel with his station wagon and his wife and kids. Sara and I got on the elevator taking Kennedy down. The lobby was full of people by the elevators waiting so they'd see Kennedy, and when the elevator opened to all of these Nevada people, out stepped Jack Kennedy with Sara. [laughter] Kennedy's running late, and Tom, by God, he's not going to wait. "He'd better get here quick, or he can get to his mass on his own." But he got there in time, got in Tom's car, and took off.

When we went to Los Angeles for the convention, Nevada was way down on the totem pole when it came to hotel accommodations. We stayed in the old Alexandria. It was all right, but we didn't get the Biltmore or one of those. Kennedy's people were at the Biltmore. I guess Johnson's people were. I went to the Biltmore probably the day before the vote and ran into Bobby Baker, who I hadn't seen since I left Washington. He expressed himself harshly because I was a Kennedy man. I was equally harsh and told him it was none of his God-damn business who I was for.

When Adlai Stevenson came onto the floor, the convention went wild. Sara was on the floor with me, and Grant and I were standing on our chairs cheering. Sara disappeared. Bible did not stand up on his chair, and looked up at Grant and me, and I caught a sparkle in his eyes of what could best be described as contempt. The demonstration went on a while. The first thing I know, I look up, and Stevenson is marching in—and right on his arm is Sara. My wife got right in the crowd. She's just the most aggressive woman you ever saw in your life! [laughter]

Mrs. Roosevelt was at the convention, hostessing a reception for Stevenson. Sara and I wanted to go to that. All things being equal—all things weren't equal—I probably would have voted for Stevenson. From a practical standpoint, Stevenson could not win the convention and probably could not have been elected. But that didn't lessen my admiration for the man and his abilities. At any rate, I wanted to go, but that reception was so mobbed that we couldn't get in.

The morning after that, we held our caucus. I think Kennedy, Symington, Averell Harriman, and Stevenson came and spoke.[1] Then we took the vote. And wham! All Grant had wanted was a majority for Kennedy, and we had figured we had that by one or two votes. [laughter] But now there were defectors—people we counted on. We lost Tom Cooke, Graham Hollister, Dorothy Dorothy, Charlie Springer, George Rudiak . . . .

I was stunned, Grant was stunned. The night before the big vote on the floor, we're sitting in Grant's room—Grant, George Jolley, Dick Ham, and me. We're going over the ones who left us, and what could we do about it, if anything. Everybody had a different idea. My idea was there wasn't a hell of a lot we could do. It was around 1:00 in the morning, but it was decided that I should go to every one of these defectors, wake them, talk to them, tell them how important it was to the governor—that he would be terribly embarrassed if they reneged.

I went, and, of course, as at most political conventions, there's a fair quantity of booze flowing. I think Tom, Graham, and Charlie were in the same room. They believed in Stevenson, that it was a tragedy he hadn't been elected president, that the best thing they could do was to vote for Stevenson. I told them I respected their opinion, but I tried to get practical. "You know he's not going to get the nomination. I'm telling you, Grant committed a majority of our delegation to Kennedy." Again, they wouldn't do anything. Then I went to Dorothy. I woke her up and tried to explain to her how important this was to the governor. I didn't realize that by that time, she was mad at the governor. I reported back to the room that my mission had been a complete failure. [laughter]

The Kennedys had a sort of pre-fab house outside the convention center. On the day of the floor vote, Hy Raskin was in charge there, in contact with the guys on the floor. The Kennedy people had walkie-talkies—first time. Hy could talk to them, and you couldn't hear half the time for the static. They're talking to each other about this delegation and that delegation. It sounded like absolute chaos. I said, "Hy, this has got to be the most magnificent example of political organization I've ever seen."

Hy said, "I'm glad it looks that way from the outside, because inside, it's f___ed up." [laughter]

Then we talked about the Nevada delegation, which was important to Hy. Hy was in charge of Kennedy's campaign in the western states. I told him what the caucus vote was, but I think he'd already heard. He said, "It doesn't really make any difference. We've got it on the first ballot." It wasn't certain. At least in the public view, a couple of delegations were uncertain. Hy told me, "I feel bad about it, Ralph, because it's going to make Grant look bad." It was the first time I got an indication that the people on that side of the table were tough.

At any rate, Kennedy got the nomination, but Grant felt humiliated. He and Bette and Sara and I had left the convention. We didn't stay for the next day when they had the Kennedy speech in the Coliseum. We came home and tried to figure out what we'd done wrong. We had control of that state convention. Where did we make these mistakes?

I made it clear to him: "Well, what the hell? You picked the delegates!" I was really helpful in his time of humiliation. [laughter]

He kind of smiled and said, "Didn't you have a hand in it?"

I said, " I guess."

Soon after the convention, there was a Democratic party meeting at the Dunes. Bible called me aside and chewed me out. Apparently, Dorothy had gone to him complaining about my visit trying to get her to change her mind, and he accused me of improper pressure and threats. He chewed me out, and I gave it right back to him. I said, "Of all the people in the world, you ought to know that whatever I did, I did because I'm part of a team. You ought to understand that." I wanted it clear: I had done it willingly and didn't see anything the matter with it.

I noticed after that a coolness from Bob McDonald. We stayed friends, but drifted a bit apart over that. I never could understand the senator's attitude, because being in the game himself, he would expect his people to take his directions. I felt kind of bad about that, because I treasure Bible's friendship—good man and a fine senator. Bob got over it, and I think Bible did.

That was one example of where people will hit back at an underling and not the top guy. Every man in a high office needs somebody like me that people can express their anger to. It's OK if they get mad at Ralph Denton. Just don't hold the governor responsible. I think that's a legitimate role for somebody to play in politics, and I believe if a guy gets himself in that role, he'd better understand it, because it's going to happen all the time. People won't attack the strength. People would attack me, and the next time they saw Grant, just be lovey-dovey and everything. It's amazing how people lack the courage to attack power. It really is.

I wasn't there for what went on over the Kennedy-Johnson ticket, but from a pragmatic standpoint, I had no objection. I thought, "If the big guys think this will help in the South, maybe they're right." My recollection is, though, that a lot of delegates were upset that Johnson was a nominee, and they threatened to run somebody else. I remember thinking, "I hope there isn't a floor fight over vice president." I don't recall Sawyer expressing an opinion. I think we felt so whipped that, "What the hell do we do now?" [laughter] This may explain Kennedy's campaign in Nevada, because the old fight at Ely erupted. That became a matter, then, of some importance as to who runs the campaign.

Lyndon Johnson came to the Senate in 1949. He was a new senator at the time I was a new deputy sergeant at arms. He never came in the sergeant at arms office for a belt, which makes me think he probably went up to the secretary of the Senate, Les Biffle. Some guys came to the sergeant at arms, and some went up to Biffle's office.

I met John Kennedy only one time when I was in Washington. I was running the elevator when he was in the House. It was late in the afternoon, and I wanted to see a debate going on on the House floor, so I told the guy running the elevator across from me that I was going to shut mine down for a while. I walked into the gallery and watched.

All of a sudden, a guy grabs me by the shoulder. He says, "Are you running that elevator?"

I turned around; it was Congressman Kennedy. I said, "Yes, sir."

He said, "I want to go down."

I said, "Yes, sir," and I go down. [laughter] He was nice, but he made it clear I ought to be doing my job instead of watching. I felt like saying, "Why aren't you on the floor, Congressman? That's your job." [laughter]

Kennedy appealed to me in 1960 because he was saying the right things. (I've learned a lot more about the campaign now than I knew when it was going on.) He was talking about civil rights, but the major issue was his religion. Could a Catholic get elected president? They tried it once before with Al Smith in 1928, and Democrats by the droves voted for Herbert Hoover. I thought this country has to be above that. This country *cannot* have a religious qualification to be president. There is something the matter with us if we do. That was a big issue with me. Had I been left to my own devices, though, I probably would have been a Hubert Humphrey man. There was a man I really admired. But Kennedy was our candidate.

Why was I attracted to Jack Kennedy? Hy Raskin? Grant Sawyer? [laughter] Practical politics. People I admired were supporting Kennedy, but the pitch Bible made was, "Who would you rather see negotiating with

Khrushchev—Lyndon Johnson or Jack Kennedy?" I felt like saying, "I won-der why we're in a position where we have to negotiate all the time." That was the pitch from the Johnson people. At least Bible did talk to me about that. Probably one of the reasons he got mad at me, he was disappointed I hadn't followed his leadership. Again, that was something I thought he had to understand.

When we came back from Los Angeles, Grant felt embarrassed that he hadn't delivered the Nevada vote to Kennedy at the convention. There had been some discussion by Kennedy people about setting up Citizens for Kennedy-Johnson committees in every state, and not just relying on the state party organizations to conduct the campaigns. The philosophical ra-tionale was that citizens' committees could attract people not interested in participating in Democratic party politics—they could also attract Republi-cans or Independents who wanted to support Kennedy. Citizens for Kennedy-Johnson committees were formed all over.

Now, it became, "Who's going to run the campaign in Nevada?" The issue was, "Are Sawyer's people going to run the campaign in Nevada, or will it be that group we had the big fight with at the Ely state convention?" (Essentially, the Clark County Democratic Party—John Bonner, Foley, Bill McGarry, and the Shady Harry group. There have been many stories about rivalry between Sawyer and Cannon, but that rivalry did not extend to Saw-yer or Cannon personally. It was among the various people involved in their operations. Jack "Shady Harry" Conlon was relentless. Jack always viewed Sawyer as a potential opponent of Cannon's, assuming he would run for the Senate when he left the governor's office. Jack was an old-time political figure, had been in campaigns a long time, and he believed you ought to knock down, whenever you can, anyone who might be a potential oppo-nent.)

So, to the dismay of the Clark County people, I was chosen to coordi-nate Kennedy's campaign in Nevada. What the hell did I know about run-ning a presidential campaign? Maybe the Kennedy people, knowing how the senators felt about Johnson, realized they might have to work outside the state party structure. If they were going around that group, they would go to Sawyer, wouldn't they? There was one report that "members of the Kennedy organization" had met with me about the chairmanship. Hy Raskin might have been in town, and if so, Hy and I would have visited. Hy might have come in to talk, but I got most of my information from Carson City rather than Washington. [laughter] I've got a lot of friends in Carson.

A fight within the state party ensued when it was announced I was go-ing to be the chairman for Kennedy-Johnson in Nevada. The Clark County people started contacting the Kennedy people in Washington, asserting that the campaign should be run by the state central committee, not a separate committee. It got frenzied. Teddy Kennedy came to town, he had a meeting, and I attended. So did the opposition.

We met at a strange place: Eddie Levinson's office at the Fremont. I sat like a bag of grits and listened to these people giving all of the great reasons I should not be chairman, there shouldn't be a committee, the campaign should be run by the state central committee. I don't know why I was always in these fights! I didn't really give a damn one way or another. I didn't want to be chairman of anything, although I was strong for Kennedy.

The matter finally went before Bobby Kennedy. It was made clear to him that I was going to be chairman, or they could look to somebody else to assign responsibility to handle Nevada. Kennedy didn't blink. He said, "Ralph Denton will be the chairman."

I started looking for people I could delegate responsibilities to in each county. I thought one of my first jobs was to assure these dissident groups, "Look, I'm not trying to steal your thunder. There's plenty of work for both groups—the party organization, as well as an independent committee." Herb Jones was a good Democrat, and he and the governor were friends. He was also a friend of Bible and Cannon. Herb graciously accepted the appointment as Clark County chairman. Given that Al Cahlan and Herb Jones were among the dissidents, it's a fair assumption we did that to win them

Left to right: Ralph Denton (Nevada chair of Citizens for Kennedy), Keith Mount (chair of state Democratic Party), Gov. Grant Sawyer, Ted Kennedy, Emily Hilliard, Bruce Thompson, Mildred Krause, Charles Cowen (Reno councilman), August 30, 1960. Ted Kennedy, western states manager for his brother John's campaign, was visiting Reno with a delegation of prominent Nevada Democrats. (Don Dondero photo.)

over. [laughter] It all went back to what had happened at Ely, and I saw this as a chance to ameliorate the situation, because we were looking two years down the road to the governor's campaign. At least I was—I don't know if Grant was.

Vail Pittman was a gentleman in every sense. He thought the citizen's committee was a fine thing to give an umbrella under which people who were not active in the party organization could fit into the campaign. C. D. Baker was state finance chairman. C. D. was circumspect and nice about everything. I named Bruce Thompson to chair Washoe County. He and Sawyer were close. I think one of the things that made some people angry at me—if it was me they were really angry at—is that all of the people in that citizens committee for Kennedy-Johnson were Sawyer people. [laughter] Well, who the hell am I going to appoint? I'm going to appoint somebody I know.

Once organized, we looked for a place to hang our hat, and then for volunteers. In those days, you tried to find somebody who had a building where you could open a headquarters. I got an old furniture store on what is now Las Vegas Boulevard South. (I think then it was still Fifth Street, probably in the 300 block.) George Marshall, a Republican, had something to do with the ownership of that building. It was vacant, so they donated the building. As soon as I got a headquarters, I started looking for somebody to paint signs, so we could get a big sign up showing, "This is where you go. This is the headquarters." We got volunteers. I was pleased that my old friend from Lincoln County, Gladys Dula, who was *very* active in the Democratic party, came in and agreed to manage the office.

Then we started trying to get publicity—keep in mind, in 1960, television was not the factor it is now. We also tried to raise some money. We picked up donations and got in touch with the national committee. They started sending us materials: signs, bumper stickers, all the paraphernalia you need to make it look like you're busy and doing a job. You know one of the toughest parts about running a campaign like that where you're doing all volunteers? It's finding something for the volunteers to do, so they don't think they're just wasting their time.

I can truthfully say every campaign I've ever been involved in has been fun. The stories you hear, the things you hear people say, the things that happen . . . . It was a lot of fun, a lot of worry, a lot of sweat. One thing I remember particularly was the Kennedy speech before the ministerial association in Houston. The headquarters was full of volunteers that night. I don't remember whether we could see it on television or hear it on the radio. Everybody was so pleased and took heart from what he said. The effect it apparently had on all the commentators and on the people . . . that was a highlight in the campaign.

Laws on campaign contributions and expenditures were not like they are today, but we were told in the citizens' committee that we would have to raise all of our own money. We could expect very little financial help from

the national campaign. I don't have any list of contributors or a precise

One casino owner downtown called and wanted to make a contribution of $10,000, but he was smart like the old school: he wanted to give it to Kennedy personally. I called Hy. "What the hell do I do with this?"

Hy says, "Obviously, Jack can't go to a casino in Las Vegas and accept $10,000 in cash, personally." He said, "Tell your friend to make the check payable to Jack Kennedy, and then he'll have the check back when it's paid with the endorsement on it."

That's what I told the fellow, and, by God, he went for it like a hog goes for slop! I got the check. Then I called Hy and said, "What do you want me to do with this check?"

Hy said, "They're awful short of money up in the citizen's committee in Wyoming. Send it up to them." [laughter] I don't know how it was cashed, but that's what happened to that $10,000. I felt kind of guilty, because, obviously, the man wanted to make certain Kennedy knew he had put up this money. My guess is that Kennedy never had any idea about it.

Bart Litton owned First Western Savings and Loan in Las Vegas. I had known him because I had several suits against him. He left Las Vegas and started a big savings and loan operation in Los Angeles in 1960. He was also treasurer of the California Democratic Party. Litton had been a screenwriter, and during the witch-hunt, he testified for the House Un-American Activities Committee, admitted he had been a communist on two separate occasions, but claimed he had quit the party. They applauded him for his frankness and candor. Litton was active in politics, and he was a man who just had to be known by people.

During the campaign, Kennedy was making a whistle-stop tour of the Central Valley of California. They'd stop at every town, and he'd make a speech off the platform. Hy told me Litton wanted to make a $50,000 contribution to Kennedy's campaign. That was wonderful, except he had a condition: if he couldn't be on the train with Kennedy, he wouldn't make the contribution. Hy discussed it with Kennedy, who he always referred to as "Jack." Jack says, "The campaign really needs the money. Take it, but you'll come on the train too, and it will be your job to keep him away from me, to make sure he never gets back to the car where I am and never gets up on the platform." Hy said every time the train would stop, Litton would jump off and start running to the back of the train, where the speech was made. Hy spent the whole trip chasing after Litton and getting him back on the train.

Hy Raskin was absolutely devoted to John Kennedy. Kennedy lived in a house in Georgetown before he became president. The press was outside all the time, and the president-elect would see people, like when he was selecting his cabinet. They would go out on the front step, and he would, with his arm around whoever it was, announce he was going to nominate so-and-so for whatever the big job was. Pictures would be taken.

Hy goes to the house to see Kennedy. "He asked me what job I wanted," Hy said. "I smiled and said, 'I don't want anything, Mr. President. Just have my picture taken with you out on the front step with your arm around me.'" [laughter] He said the president laughed, said, "OK." Out they went. They stood on the front step, and Kennedy says to all these people, "I'd like you to meet my good friend, Hy Raskin." [laughter]

Hy then moved to Washington and practiced law until the president was killed. Hy immediately closed his office, never opened one again. He was absolutely devastated, moved to Palm Springs and lived out his life there. When he was living there, we used to get together quite a bit. He'd come up here, and we went down there a few times to see Hy and his wife.

Last time Kennedy was here, he spoke at the convention center. Hy was on that trip with the president. I was behind the platform, and Hy and I were discussing it. Hy hadn't seen him for quite a while. He said, "He's the same old Jack. God, he's a good guy." That was Hy's feeling toward Kennedy.

Election night was tiring, interesting . . . . I was worried I was going to have to pay off bets, and I didn't have the money to pay them. [laughter] What was it, 2:00 or 3:00 in the morning before we knew who won? Nevada has been listed as one of the states where there were irregularities. I don't recall our attorney general investigating any charges, nor do I recall anybody ever having said there were any. I think they probably lumped Nevada in because of the connection a lot of people here had with Chicago.

Kennedy's victory absolutely thrilled me. We went to the inauguration. It was a fun trip, quite an event in our lives, but not only were the Dentons short of money, so were the Sawyers. We went to Reno, met Grant and Bette, and flew to Washington in tourist class. On the same plane was Pat Brown, the governor of California, in first class. But when we landed in Baltimore, because of Bible's position as chairman of the Senate District of Columbia committee, he had a limousine and motorcycle escort meet the governor, whereas Brown had to take a cab. [laughter] We went to the hotel. Grant and Bette got a one-bedroom suite at the Shoreham. We stayed with them on roll-away beds in the living room.

We had to have formal dress and morning formal dress: striped pants and ascot tie and the hat, the whole thing. We rented those things. There was a big gala out at the armory, Sinatra and all these great entertainers. But it snowed and snowed. God, it was cold, so we couldn't make it. A lot of the Nevada people who couldn't make it came to the governor's suite. We had a pretty good Nevada party that night. There was a reception in the Senate office building. It seems to me we went to that—we went to the reception put on by Bible, Cannon, Baring, and their wives.

We all went out to Georgetown and had dinner—Major Riddle and a bunch of Nevada people. First time I ever saw my wife drink very much.

This was a small restaurant, but they had a small orchestra in the lounge. The first thing I know, after dinner, Sara's singing with the group. They were going to close the place if they could just get this lady to quit singing! [laughter] Riddle went up and told them she was opening next week at the Desert Inn in Las Vegas. He gave them some money if they would play a little longer. She was great. The problem was getting back—the snow. We left this restaurant, and last thing I saw, she and Grant were arm in arm, walking up the middle of the street in Georgetown, and Bette and I were looking for a cab to get back to the hotel. We finally got a cab and got back, and Grant and Sara beat us there. [laughter] It was just a grand, happy evening.

There was one function at the Wardman Park Hotel before the inaugural. The president-elect came, and each state had a booth. We were in the Nevada booth. He would march down the aisle and speak to everybody. He only stopped and shook hands with governors from states that voted for him. When he came to Nevada, he stopped and shook hands with Grant, Bette, me, Sara, and whoever else was in the booth. That was a very impressive function. Sara made a beautiful gown for the ball. She looked lovely.

We had good seats for the inaugural—we actually had seats across from the reviewing stand on Pennsylvania Avenue in front of the White House. I didn't think Robert Frost would ever quit reading his poem. Oh, God, it was

"Sara made a beautiful gown for the ball. She looked lovely."

cold! We wanted it to get over with. It was an impressive speech, and then the people up there went inside the Capitol, where it was warm, and had a nice lunch. We made our way back down to the parade.

I don't remember the inaugural address that well. "Ask not what your country can do for you, ask what you can do for your country." I thought that was a well-turned phrase. I remember the gist—we were stronger than wolf manure, nobody ought to screw around with us, and we were going to be stronger. I felt a little bit uncomfortable about the threats . . . . "Pay any price, bear any burden." It seemed to me we were flexing our muscles a little too much, but I read it afterward, and it was a beautifully written speech.

I was proud of Kennedy as president. I was thrilled with the way he handled the missile crisis, and I did not give him any blame for the Bay of Pigs, based on what we knew at that time—we believed that was an Eisenhower thing gone sour, and Kennedy shouldn't be blamed. I was thrilled with what I believed to be his commitment to civil rights. I was proud to be a part of that, but disappointed he wasn't more strident.

It's hard to think back without having my memories colored by things we've learned since. At that time, I thought Kennedy was magnificent. Certainly, my views have changed with what has come out since. He was a lech. I have always had the highest regard for the president, but it was a disappointment to learn, if true, of his personal weaknesses, and I wish people would leave it alone. The man's dead. He has a family. What useful purpose does it serve to bring these things up now?

I never even hated Bobby Kennedy. [laughter] I hadn't yet met Bobby when (I don't remember whether it was before or after the inaugural) he called and asked what I wanted.

I said, "Nothing."

He said, "Would you like to be United States attorney?"

I said, "No, but I certainly appreciate the offer."

I knew those people, at that stage, as efficient, bright people who looked out for their own, but I didn't want to say, "Yes, I'd like to have it," and then have him call and tell me he couldn't get it on. It wasn't his appointment to give. When he got involved in wire-tapping and trying to do injury to Nevada's basic industry (casino gambling), I'd be less than frank if I didn't say I thought *everybody* ought to be doing whatever they could to get rid of the mob. God, the mob was a terrible thing.

John Kennedy was not as popular in 1963 as in the first year of his presidency. Many thought he was going to have a tough time getting reelected, and in Nevada there was a lot of animosity toward him because of Bobby and the casino operations. There was a fear that if JFK came here, he wouldn't get a good crowd.

Grant called and asked what I thought: If they scheduled Kennedy, and if they packed the convention center, would he get booed? I said, "Grant, I believe the people of Las Vegas will come out in droves to see the president. And I don't believe the people of Las Vegas will boo the president. I don't think you should worry about that at all."

The trip was scheduled, and this was about the time Grant and the state gaming commission were revoking Frank Sinatra's gaming license. Grant rode in from the airport to the convention center with Kennedy, or back to the airport, or both. Grant told me Kennedy asked him in the car, "Is there anything you can do for Frank?"

I said, "What did you say?"

"I said no, but the president did ask if he could help Sinatra with the problem he had with the state."[2]

When Kennedy was shot, I was in Elko at the Ranch Inn, at a meeting of the state association of county commissioners. I was on the board of county commissioners, representing Clark County at this meeting, and I had taken my daughter Sally with me. Sally was ten. The Ranch Inn was a nice hotel, so I felt perfectly all right leaving her alone in the room while I was at my meeting. She had her dolls all set up on the floor, playing with them, and the television was on. She heard on the TV that President Kennedy had been shot. Sally came down, found the meeting room I was in, and told me, "Daddy, President Kennedy has been shot."

I said, "Oh my God!" I went rushing out. Other people went to find out what was going on. By then, they had a TV set going in the casino part of the Ranch Inn, and everybody was watching. I will never forget . . . the meeting just went on as usual. They went ahead. They had the luncheon. I couldn't believe it! I grabbed Sally, and Sally and I went up to our room. I started making arrangements to get home, trying to see if I could get a plane. When we left, that same group was in that room having the meeting. The president had been killed, and they're still having the goddamned meeting of the Nevada Association of County Commissioners! I thought it was the most insensitive thing I had ever seen. Get *that* on the record!

Notes

1. Stuart Symington was a senator from Missouri, 1953-76. W. Averell Harriman, governor of New York from 1955 to 1958, also served as secretary of commerce (1948-53) and in numerous diplomatic posts.

2. The state forced Frank Sinatra to surrender his license for hosting Chicago mob boss Sam Giancana, who was in Nevada's "Black Book," at the Cal-Neva Lodge.

23 | Old Ralph Put His Hand in the Fire

Grant and I were on a trip to Washington in 1962 when he appointed Maude Frazier to be his lieutenant governor after Rex Bell died in office. He had thought about appointing Vail Pittman to serve out Bell's term. Who could get mad if Pittman—distinguished ex-governor—was appointed to give him that honor in his twilight years? On the way back in the plane, however, Grant mentions Frazier. I said, "I think that would be a wonderful appointment." Obviously, she wouldn't run for re-election. This was at the beginning of the campaign, and by appointing Maude, Grant wouldn't be demonstrating any preference among the candidates for lieutenant governor. (Grant, all the time he was governor, never had a lieutenant governor of his own party, except during the short time that Maude Frazier was lieutenant governor. During most of his first term, Rex Bell was lieutenant governor; and during his second term, Paul Laxalt.)

When Sawyer looked for someone to run for lieutenant governor with him on the ticket in 1962, old Ralph put his hand in the fire again. [laughter] Grant was concerned. It appeared that the 1962 campaign was going to be tough. Rex Bell, his lieutenant governor, was going to run for governor.[1] You had this whole new concept of gaming control under Grant, and some of the people in the business were a little upset. Ray Abaticchio, the chairman of the control board, had conducted raids on hotel-casinos. He had gone in and picked up dice and cards off the tables to check and make sure they were on the square, doing pretty close surveillance to make sure the casinos weren't flat. A lot of Las Vegas gamblers were mad at Grant—mad at his gaming control board—and it appeared Rex would have great support from the gambling industry. In other words, we start with the premise that this is going to be a tough son-of-a-gun.

Hank Greenspun had kicked the traces, was no longer a Sawyer supporter, and had written that Berkeley Bunker would be a fine man to run for governor. Bunker had been a senator, then a congressman, and he was highly

246

*Old Ralph
Put His
Hand
in the
Fire*

regarded in the community, high in the LDS hierarchy. He would have been a tough candidate, but he had decided not to run for governor.

Grant recognized the strength of the LDS population in Clark County. Bill Taylor owned a steel fabrication company and was a reform mayor in North Las Vegas—God knows it needed reform—and high up in the LDS church, president of the Las Vegas North Stake. I knew Taylor; I didn't know him well, but I was an admirer. Grant asked me to talk to Taylor and see if he would be interested in running for lieutenant governor. I thought it was a bad idea to talk to him, because it would get out. We knew a lot of people wanted to run, and they would resent it if the governor was getting involved. Sometimes Grant and I disagreed, but when he made a decision, that was it. Grant thought Bill would maintain the confidence, so I went to talk to him.

The first thing I told Bill was, "this has to be in absolute confidence." Then I told him the governor had asked me to find out if he was interested, possibly, in running for lieutenant governor. He indicated he was not. I returned to my office. I was going to call Grant later in the day and tell him, but hell, there was no need . . . the news was in the afternoon *Review-Journal!* Taylor could hardly wait to tell people. Everybody else who wanted to run for lieutenant governor—namely, Phil Cummings—was awful mad at me. [laughter]

In the *Sun*, I said, "I have talked to three or four others in addition to Mayor Taylor who have indicated interest . . . and I hope no individual Democrat gets the impression that I would support him over others who might seek the office." The story said, "Denton, who is a close friend and advisor to Governor Grant Sawyer, recalled that the governor also has repeatedly stated he will not become involved in the Democratic primary for lieutenant governor or any other office except his own." What do they call it? [laughter] "Spin control." God, it makes me sound terrible. [laughter]

But we didn't leave it at that. I performed the same role insofar as Bunker was concerned. I went to his mortuary and talked to his brother. (In 1950, my Uncle Lloyd had gone to Las Vegas for a meeting of Democrats, and they had it at Berkeley Bunker's mortuary. Pat McCarran was there. Lloyd walked in, looked up, saw McCarran, and says, "Pat, what are we going to do, bury the Democratic party?") That thought entered my mind.

I'd worked under Bunker's patronage in Washington. Berkeley was a friend and a man I admired greatly. I went into great depth and detail with Wendell on why Berkeley should give serious consideration to running for lieutenant governor—that the governor would look with favor upon his candidacy. Wendell told me Berkeley was out, but he would be back, and he would call the governor that night.

I called Grant; we decided I'd better fly up there. Grant and I sat in the mansion waiting. The call came, and Berkeley told Grant how much he admired him and what a fine governor he had been. He invoked the blessings of the Lord on Grant and me and said he would run. The deed was done . . . which led to *Paul Laxalt* becoming Grant's lieutenant governor. [laughter]

247

*Old Ralph
Put His
Hand
in the
Fire*

Jack Conlon, Cannon's administrative assistant, had a part in that. Bunker had been appointed to the Senate by Governor Carville. Then he had been defeated in the primary in 1942 by Jim Scrugham. In 1944, he ran for Congress and was elected. In 1945, Scrugham died, Carville resigned, and Vail Pittman became governor and appointed Carville to the Senate. Carville had to run for re-election in 1946. Guess who filed against him? Bunker! Did McCarran have something to do with that? [laughter] McCarran had something to do with everything. I thought he saw a chance to get rid of both of them.

The old part of the Democratic Party that had been strong Carville people resented the fact that Berkeley had run against Carville in 1946. Jack Conlon had worked for Carville, and, in 1962, Jack took the lead in getting Carville people to say, "We're going to show Bunker!" In droves, old Carville Democrats voted against Bunker in the general election. I could just hear them: "Do you realize Bunker bit the hand that fed him?" Powerful, wasn't it?

The result was, Laxalt beat Bunker. Shady Harry saw Grant as a potential opponent to Cannon and wanted to lock him in with a Republican lieutenant governor; but I don't think it was in the cards that Grant would run against an incumbent Democrat. He had better sense than that. (I didn't. I ran against a Democratic incumbent in 1964.) [laughter] Conlon didn't want Grant to run against Cannon in 1964, but guess who did? Paul Laxalt. Created a monster, huh?

The Sawyer campaign was, of course, the most important race in 1962, and Grant and I and Dick Ham and some of the other people recognized it would be extremely difficult against Rex Bell. Rex was very popular. We were anticipating Rex would be well-funded, probably better than Sawyer, but there was no reason to think Grant would not be able to raise the necessary money.

We planned to do what we had done in 1958. In 1958, we had addressed our campaign against E. L. Cord. We tentatively decided that we would address our 1962 campaign against Moe Dalitz, because it was hard to say anything bad about Rex Bell—he was a nice man. Grant and Rex got along well, and Rex bent over backward not to intrude in the governor's territory and never attacked Grant in any way. (For example: The state bought Grant a new governor's car with a number 1 license plate. It was, of course, kept in Carson City. Grant sent the car he had driven before, with a number 1 license plate still on it, down to Las Vegas so Rex could use it. The first time Grant came down, Rex called to make certain the governor understood that the car, with its number 1 plate, would be available for him. They had a good personal relationship.)

We opened a headquarters on North Third, the first home of Frontier Fidelity Savings and Loan. They had built a building over on Charleston,

248

*Old Ralph
Put His
Hand
in the
Fire*

moved out, and donated that office to us. We had *lots* of volunteers coming in and working. I was chairman, but the ladies ran that headquarters—Virginia Catt, Ethel Woodbury, Gladys Dula, Marie Ripps.

We were anticipating opposition in the primary. Didn't know who, because by the time we got around to the short strokes, Berkeley was no longer a potential candidate for governor, he was our running mate. But there had been talk. Hank had been promoting Berkeley in the *Sun*, and we thought Hank would find somebody else. There was dissatisfaction in the party, tension between the Cannon and Sawyer forces—not between Cannon and Sawyer, but their people. There was dissatisfaction over the Kennedy-Johnson campaign. We were concerned that we would have to fight somebody in the primary—expected it.

Then Rex Bell died on the Fourth of July, 1962. The next day we were leaving to go to Atlanta with the Southern Nevada Industrial Foundation, which toured around the country to tell business about the benefits of coming to Nevada. I belonged to that. We were sitting at my house, and I think Bob Faiss came out to the patio and told us Rex had dropped dead. Grant decided immediately that he couldn't leave the state. I went on the tour in his place and made the speeches he would have made.

Now the ball game was up in the air—only a week or two until filing closes. Although I'm not privy to Republican counsels, I understand considerable pressure was put on Laxalt, who had announced for lieutenant governor, to run for governor. Instead, the Republicans had two candidates: Hank Greenspun and Oran Gragson. We're going to have a serious Republican primary, and surprisingly enough, Grant got only token opposition in the Democratic primary.

From a personal standpoint, the election was difficult for me. Hank Greenspun was a client by then. I took his files to his office, and I said, "Hank, I can't seek to advance your interests in the daytime and plot your downfall at night. I can no longer represent you. And you understand that I will be as active as I can be in the Sawyer campaign."

Hank was a perfect gentleman. He said, "I understand that, Ralph. I know how close you and Grant are, and I wouldn't expect you to do anything other than support Grant. It's going to get a little rough."

I said, "Well, that's what makes life interesting."

About the same time, the Sawyer people were getting things set up and having meetings with people, among them Adam Yacenda, a participant in Grant's second campaign.[2] Adam didn't trust me because of my relationship with Hank, but it never bothered Grant at all. He didn't place much stock in the criticisms of others around him. What the hell? I'm trying to make a living practicing law. These other guys are on payrolls.

Gabe Vogliotti showed up at the *Review-Journal* and wrote a column using Denver Dickerson's old title, "Salmagundi." He was paid to cut up Greenspun. And guess who's coming up with all this strong money to destroy Hank? I understand it was Moe Dalitz and others, but I was not privy to

the actual arrangements that were made for Gabe to come back to Nevada
and write a column. I had known Gabe in Washington; he had done some
ghost writing for McCarran. He was a Reno man and a good writer, and oh
my God, did he take after Greenspun! Those columns were terrible. But
that was part of the political process.

In the general election after Gragson beat Hank, many of those supporting Gragson in the primary went over to Sawyer, leaving poor Oran standing there naked. I think Moe and those other casino gambling people had
been scared to death that Hank would win. (Hank had run their pictures in
his paper with numbers on their chests.) [laughter] Oran expected them to
continue to support him in the general election, and I think Bob Brown, the
editor of the *R-J*, did.³ But they didn't think Oran had a chance to beat
Sawyer, and a gambler doesn't want to book no losers. So, they just dumped
Oran.

During that campaign, I met Don Reynolds.⁴ The *Review-Journal* was
giving Oran so much publicity! We'd have press releases, and they wouldn't
run them, but there would be four of Oran's. So, we set up a meeting with
Reynolds, who lived in a house in Twin Lakes—modest from the outside,
but you went inside, and here's a butler. It was in the summer, so we had this
meeting with the great man by the pool. With Reynolds was Bob Brown.

I was kind of ashamed to be there, to tell you the truth. Our purpose was
to complain we were not getting equal coverage. Our people had done enough
research that we could tell him how many inches of print there had been in
the *Review-Journal* dealing with Sawyer, and how many inches for Gragson.
Somebody had taken a ruler, for God's sake! I sat and looked at the ground a
lot. Reynolds turned to Bob. He was insulting and said he didn't want to see
Gragson's name in the paper again for anything. Not once. Then, with a
smirky smile, he said, "Well, unless his mother dies." Even the mayor's paper
let him down.

We had every right to go to a paper and say, "We're not getting fair
coverage." But for that man to talk to Bob the way he did was offensive. I
don't know how Bob could work for him.

The campaign went on, and Grant won overwhelmingly. We were not
surprised and did not let up. When I say "we," I mean Grant didn't let up.
During the campaign, you have the Cuban missile crisis. I remember sitting
in the headquarters worried about my wife and children, visiting in Paducah,
Kentucky, and how am I going to get them home before some missile ex-
plodes over the United States?

I didn't really have the role in the 1962 campaign that I'd had in 1958,
because in 1962, you had people on the payroll, advertising agencies, things
a professional campaign needs. We old-timers would talk, and I got a hell of
a lot more credit from the press than I deserved. I was sort of in charge of the
headquarters, but the ladies were doing all the work. Whenever Grant was
in town, we'd meet and talk and figure out if there were any problems. Little
things happen all the time in a campaign. People get their noses out of joint.

249

*Old Ralph
Put His
Hand
in the
Fire*

250

*Old Ralph
Put His
Hand
in the
Fire*

How do you get them back in? How did we repair ourselves with Democrats who had wanted to run for lieutenant governor, but who hadn't because of me sticking my nose in and getting Bunker to run?

This time, Sawyer had his team, but the team had increased in size and number over 1958, because now he had all the department heads he'd appointed in state government. Bob Cahill made the point that Grant let them all know that politics and government are the same. They were political and needed to concern themselves with what they said and did, because everything they said and did reflected upon him. They wouldn't be there if not for him. A lot of these guys seemed to think it was all above them, but Bob was right.

Election night, I go by the *Las Vegas Sun* to see Hank Greenspun. The polls are closed. I had plotted his downfall, and now I was going over to headquarters to see the results. Hank said, "Either way, Ralph, now that the campaign's over, I'd like you to take your files back." I did. Then, in 1963, when I got appointed county commissioner, I returned them to him and told him I thought it was a conflict of interest to be on the county commission and represent a newspaper. Hank accepted that too.

Notes

1. Rex Bell, a one time cowboy actor, husband of silent screen star Clara Bow, and father of a two-term Clark County district attorney, served two terms as lieutenant governor (1955-62). Owner of a ranch in Searchlight, he was long active in state and local Republican politics. In 1944, he was defeated for the House of Representatives.

2. Adam Yacenda had been reporter, editor, and managing editor for Greenspun at the *Sun*, 1950-58. In 1959, he began publishing *The North Las Vegas Valley Times*, which he sold in 1973. He was involved in numerous political campaigns and was a noted backroom operator.

3. Bob Brown, a former United Press foreign correspondent, edited the *Review-Journal* from 1961 to 1964 and was an active behind-the-scenes political operative, mostly for Republicans. He bought *The Valley Times* from Yacenda in 1973 and published it until he died in 1984.

4. Donald W. Reynolds bought out Frank Garside's interest in the *Las Vegas Review-Journal* in 1949 and then Al Cahlan's in 1960. His Donrey Media Group owned a chain of newspapers throughout the southwest, including in Las Vegas, Carson City, Ely, and Winnemucca, and radio and television stations in Las Vegas and Reno.

24 | "He's Entitled to It"

When Roger Foley seemed about to be appointed a federal judge, there were reports I would be named to replace him as Nevada's attorney general. "But," one report said, "insiders are inclined to doubt that Denton's under consideration." Their reasoning? "Denton has so successful a practice, he is unlikely to leave it to take a job he'd have to campaign to keep less than a year from now." I was flattered when they said I was making all this money. I wasn't making much . . . never have, to tell you the truth.

There was speculation about me every time something came up, and my name always brought a lot of flak. I don't know whether Grant or I was more fearful of a charge of cronyism if Grant appointed me to something. (I think I was. People didn't have the guts to strike at him, so they'd strike at me.)

When Foley got the judgeship, I discussed the vacancy situation with Grant. Probably half the lawyers in Nevada were hoping they would get appointed attorney general, and, as the senator said, when you appoint somebody, you get one ingrate and ten enemies. That proved true in this case. Grant appointed Charlie Springer, but it was only with the understanding that Charlie would not be a candidate for the position when the unfinished term expired—everybody else who wanted it would have a fair shot. So Charlie waited a few years to run for elected office, then ran against Grant for governor. And we had always thought he was on the team from the start!

Meanwhile, I was reported to be running for the House, and I announced I wasn't. In 1962, I had no intention of running. The thought had never entered my mind. However, although I didn't enjoy seeing my name in print, what the hell? It didn't hurt anything, and I'd let the press go for a while and then stop them. My reluctance to run was based upon my friendship with Walter Baring, the incumbent. He had become extreme in his views, but we'd been friends since he first went to Washington in 1949, and I'd supported him every time he'd run.

In 1962, Art Olson was re-elected to a term on the Clark County board of commissioners at-large, that is, county-wide.[1] Then, in 1963, Art got involved in a transaction in which he wanted to acquire land from the county near McCarran Airport and put in some sort of a flying museum or exhibit. To do it, he had to do business with the county. Art felt that would have been an unethical conflict of interest, so he resigned to pursue that. And it never went through. (I, along with other commissioners, voted against it.)

Grant was charged with the responsibility of appointing a replacement to fill Olson's seat on the board. He and I talked about it two or three times. I suggested Myron Leavitt and other names.[2] Never mentioned my own name. I was trying to help him make a good appointment that would bring as little political heat as possible. Grant called me. He said, "I've got to make this appointment quick. Everybody in Clark County's on my tail. The only person I could appoint that everybody would say, 'Well, he's entitled to it,' is you. If I appoint anybody else, all the others who want it are going to be mad at me. But if I appoint you, they've got to say you were entitled to it—if you wanted it, I had to give it to you." The thought had never entered my mind, but he asked me to do it, and I did it. I had no more idea than the man in the moon what I was going to get into. I'd worked with the county commission in Elko County when I was deputy district attorney, and the county commission in Esmeralda County when I was district attorney. But the county commission of Clark County is a whole different ball of wax—even in those days.

By and large, the reaction to my appointment was favorable. While I was commissioner, both newspapers treated me well, but I was sort of controversial; there were a lot of 4-1 votes, things I voted against that most other people voted for. A couple of them, I got editorial support from both papers. [laughter] One time, the Desert Inn wanted a special-use permit to have a skeet-shoot, although they weren't going to use clay pigeons. They were going to use live pigeons. [laughter] God, I wished I'd known about pigeons what I know now. I'd have approved it. [laughter] Flying rats. [laughter] I opposed that, and Dalitz and those people were furious. But I won that one! Sally Murphy scared everybody. She was active in the community, head of the humane society. She mounted a campaign, so I found an ally or two.

I enjoyed my time on the board. It was interesting work, and we accomplished several important things. We established the county recreation department and appointed its first director. We also acquired our first county manager, and I did what I could to get the appointment for Bob Cahill, one of the finest public servants I've ever known. Since I didn't know the other board members that well, I talked to Grant Robinson (the state superintendent of banks), and he persuaded his good friend, County Commissioner Bob Baskin, to back Cahill. Bob became Cahill's strongest supporter, and Cahill got the job. (Robbins Cahill later became head of the Nevada Resort Association, eventually leaving that moving back to Reno. I think he kept his hand in gaming control until he got too old to do it. He was a fine man.)

Lou LaPorta was chair of the commission at the time. Lou had been in Henderson almost from the end of World War II. He was in the insurance business and active in things in Henderson. Bill Briare, I think, came here from San Francisco, first working for Bill Peccole's insurance office in Las Vegas.[3] Then Briare opened his own business as an independent insurance agent. Jimmy "Sailor" Ryan. [laughter] Winston Churchill described Russia as a mystery wrapped in a riddle inside an enigma. Jimmy and I never became close friends, never became bitter enemies. You never knew where Jim was going to be . . . . I thought one department head was on the take, so I brought up the possibility of firing him. Jim raised hell against it in our meeting in the conference room. Then I picked up the afternoon *Review-Journal*. There was a story in the newspaper that Ryan urged that so-and-so be fired. [laughter]

Bob Baskin was a dandy. Bob had come here in the thirties, I think, from Arkansas or Oklahoma, and was a baker, then got in the restaurant business. He'd been on the city council. His restaurants were where political hangers-on would meet for breakfast and "cut up the pie," so to speak. He was in with Poppa Gar for a while. After the commission would meet, we'd go to Baskin's restaurant, and he'd have a big lunch upstairs. Everybody would swill up that food, and Bob would swill up some other things. Then we'd go back in the afternoon. All the lobbyists who had things pending for the commission would drop in, and it was a circus.

Bob led me into a jillion terrible votes on zoning matters. I thought it was going to be difficult for me to have friends asking for variances, but I found out it wasn't that tough. You called it the way you saw it and let it go. But I liked Bob, and he'd say, "Ralph, this town has been awful good to me. The only reason I ran for the county commission was to try and help out some of my old friends. Now, give me this vote. In ten years, it's not going to make any difference anyway, the way this town's growing. Whatever zoning you have now, it's all going to be done over." So, I reluctantly voted for a lot of variances I shouldn't have. I also voted against a lot of them.

I did learn something from a political standpoint—and keep this in mind as you watch present bodies: if somebody comes before the board and wants something, and you vote against him in the public interest, you've made an enemy for life. The public doesn't care; they don't even know. That's why you see so many things being granted that shouldn't be. I found that out.

I did another stupid thing on that board. When the freeway came through, Major Riddle wanted to change the name of Flamingo Road to Dunes Road. If there was ever anybody I might have owed something to, it would have been Major Riddle. He had been an early supporter of Sawyer's. We must have swilled up a jillion dollars worth of his free food through the years at the Dunes when we took comps. Everybody did. I didn't think anything about it.

The Flamingo and businessmen on that street protested the name change. I think Louis Wiener represented the Flamingo and spoke against changing the name. I could not see a public interest for changing, so I voted against it. It lost three to two. Had I changed, it would have carried. Maje never said anything, but he never forgave me. Parry Thomas, a friend of Major's and mine, told me Maje was upset about it. Parry said, "I told him, Ralph would do anything in the world for you, but that doesn't include taking something away from somebody else." But he never forgave me. Incidentally, the state highway department went along with Maje and changed the freeway exit to Flamingo-Dunes. But that just ran to the Strip. [laughter] After that, it stayed Flamingo.

My vote against the name change was a mistake—it wouldn't have hurt anybody. If you're in public office and you have a friend that needs your help, and you're not hurting anybody, give him the help. What the hell are friends for? But I just didn't see the point. I could see no reason for this. I was so naive, I didn't dream Major would be mad at me. I thought he would recognize my job was to act in the public interest to be a good county commissioner. That worried me for a long time. It ended what had been a close relationship with Riddle, and I regretted that.

A lawyer active in the practice should not be in public jobs; if I was going to be in government, it would be full-time, because I was constantly hit with conflicts of interest. A man would come to my office, make an appointment. I don't know him. He hires me to prepare a will. There's a commission meeting three days later, and here's this same man in for a permit. Obviously, a conflict. Public office is, indeed, a public trust. In a trust, you have a high fiduciary duty to the beneficiaries of that trust. In public office, the beneficiaries are the public. You owe a duty to the public. It's a shame that often the public doesn't recognize that. Once my appointed term had expired, I could not, in good conscience, run for the board of county commissioners.

I look at what's happening in our county today and what's happened in our county and city government for time immemorial, the conflicts of interest. Hell, when I was on the board, you had two insurance men on it. I never knew a finer man than Lou LaPorta, but Lou was in the insurance business, and hotels bought insurance from him. That was accepted as common. It had been happening in Las Vegas from day one, but people didn't see anything the matter with it. To me, that was the tragedy—not that the commissioner was acquiring monies from industries he regulates, but that the public didn't see anything the matter and still doesn't. So maybe I'm nuts.

I assumed everybody on the board would be good friends, and everything would be fine. They're nice folks, but I was surprised by how political most everybody was—kept their mouths shut. There was a little room, and if you got there early, you'd go back and have a cup of coffee. After Cahill became county manager, he'd be there and give us a hint of things before the board, in addition to the agenda. You would try to get some idea of what your colleagues were thinking. Jimmy Ryan wouldn't tell you the time of day. Bob Baskin would always tell you. [laughter] Everybody was looking out for themselves, which came as a surprise. But we were friendly; I don't think anybody hated anybody. It helped when Cahill became county manager, because his thinking was so sound. He would appear before the commission, and if he felt strongly about something, make a presentation. Oftentimes, the commission didn't follow him, but he just researched everything.

A gambling license application came up for a man at the Sands. His name had been in all the newspapers, which alleged that he had mob contacts, but the state gaming control board had voted two to one to approve him, the gaming commission three to two, or something like that. (Gambling licenses don't come before the county commission until they've been approved by the state.) Keith Campbell did reports to the county on gambling applications, and I looked at Campbell's report. There was nothing derogatory at all in it, but I reserved the right to make my own judgment on these matters. I went to the control board. I wanted to talk to friends I had on that board. They wouldn't tell me anything. They didn't trust the local licensing procedure, and they were afraid any information they gave the commission might get into the hands of our sheriff's office or some other people. (Ralph Lamb was sheriff.) I voted against the license, but the county commission granted it by a vote of four to one. The man was a notorious outfit guy.

It surprised me, too, that a few guys had sacred status—you couldn't touch them. Before I was on the board, I discovered that the parking lot out at the Commercial Center belonged to the county, which meant that the Commercial Center have to pay any taxes on it, and the county had to maintain it like other county roads. Once on the commission, I made a couple of motions to put parking meters on it. I didn't get any help, any support at all on that. Of course, Commercial Center was owned by Moe Dalitz, Merv Adelson, Irwin Molasky, and that group.[4] I made a stink to the point where I was contacted by my friend Parry Thomas. He told me they donated land to the county to widen Sahara Avenue. In return, the county agreed to take title to the parking lot. That happened, and there was nothing you could do about it. I didn't have any support other than from the county manager, but he didn't have a vote. [laughter]

Then there was the plan to build Winterwood. The same developers, Moe, Molasky, Adelson, Harry Lahr, were building this subdivision in the county off Nellis Boulevard, near Sahara. Golf courses were not big money makers in those days. A developer would put in a course to increase the value of his lots and attract buyers. The only problem was, after the lots were sold, he was stuck with this golf course.

I think this deal was made before I even knew about it, but it hadn't been officially done: the county was going to buy the golf course from them after it was completed for what it cost them to put it in. To me, it was ridiculous that the county would subsidize the construction of the golf course. If the county wanted a golf course, and I don't gainsay that, it should go out to bid. Clearly, we could get land from the federal government, the BLM. In-stead of this, we were just going to give back Dalitz and that group every-thing the golf course had cost them.

Before I objected, I went around trying to check my thinking. I'm not the world's best businessman, and I recognized it even then. I went to two or three real estate developers and two or three brokers. I talked to C. D. Baker. He agreed public money should not be spent in that way. I talked to George Von Tobel, an engineer and real estate broker in Baker's office. George thought it was terrible. I said, "Would you mind coming to the county com-mission meeting and testifying against it." He said he would.

The meeting came. None of the guys I asked to testify showed up. Cahill spoke eloquently opposing it, as did Elmer Anderson, the first director of our recreation department, who would be charged with administering it. There had been other objections about flood control, but that was all window dress-ing. Briare voiced a possibility it would create problems, but he was satisfied after investigating it. Therefore, he was for the deal. I don't know how they played it, Sailor and Baskin and Briare and LaPorta—the ones who voted for it. I don't think anybody led Lou around by the nose.

The vote came, and it was four to one, even though I got editorial sup-port in both newspapers. Jude Wanniski told me after I was off the board that he interviewed Dalitz, and Moe bragged that he had every city and county commissioner in his pocket except Ralph Denton, "and we don't need him." I don't know if that's true, but Jude told me that.[5]

There was another deal later. The same developers were building the Boulevard Mall. Twain used to go through to Boulder Highway, but the county changed that. Twain doesn't go all the way any more. They had a meeting in their offices in Commercial Center and made the presentation and drew the maps. I couldn't see the public interest in giving up the property. Maybe I'm a nut about it, but I made reference to my belief that public office is a public trust. I remember the phrase my father always used: When you're dealing with the public's money, you must be as clean as an angel's drawers.

My old friend Jack Sexton was judge from Eureka and Lander Counties. Jack moved to Las Vegas and was sitting as visiting judge all the time, but he was putting in for per diem every day. I didn't mind Jack getting per diem, but the state's supposed to pay the expenses of the visiting judge. The county was doing it. At a meeting, I objected to the county paying on the grounds that it was a state obligation.

About 7:30 the next morning, the phone rings at the house. It's Sexton's bailiff telling me the judge wants to see me in his chambers at nine. I'm a lawyer before his court, so at nine I'm there. He starts raising hell with me about stopping his salary. I said, "Your Honor, did you call me in your cham-bers to talk to me about a matter that I have pending in your court?"

"No, I want to talk to you about your God-damn stopping my . . . ."

I said, "Well, then, you want to talk to me about county business, right?"

He said, "Yes."

I said, "Then come upstairs to my office." [laughter]

Oh God, he bellowed like a bull. So they got an opinion from our district attorney that the county could pay the state's bill. Here I am, just trying to save the county money like you're supposed to do. [laughter] They womped up a contract, and a little resolution the county commission adopted, that the county would pay the judge's per diem and expenses.

(I tried to be as fiscally responsible as I could be on that board. That stems, I guess, from my mom and dad. I just don't understand how office holders spend so much public money on travel expenses. I never charged mileage. I was entitled to get mileage from Boulder City to Las Vegas whenever I had to go to a meeting, but I had to be in Las Vegas anyway—I went into my office every morning. Why would I charge the county for that? God, it just seems to me everybody's got their hand out—they want everything! It is public money. What makes these people think they're entitled to it?)

Soon after I went on the board, an issue came up over air pollution—smog. The commission paid some Los Angeles firm to do a study. This firm had done a first class job and prepared proposed ordinances to pass to correct it. Some of the large offenders were the plants in Henderson at that time. (Remember the Henderson Cloud?) The consulting firm made its presentation, and I thought it was just wonderful. I'm all for enacting that ordinance.

Then Julian Moore, head of Basic Management, Inc., appeared. He said the county should get Russ McDonald, legislative counsel in Carson City, to review the ordinance before we voted—our district attorney wasn't sufficient. So the county retained Russ, and Russ removed most of the teeth in the ordinances. And then you learn Russ was also attorney for Basic Management. So, they spent the money for the study, passed watered-down ordinances that didn't cause any problems, and didn't correct the smog.

As a commissioner, I chaired the board of equalization. God, that was funny. That board consists of representatives of the county commission, each city. People have a chance to protest their taxes. Constitutionally, they're supposed to be equal. You shouldn't pay any more taxes on your house than I pay on my house, assuming they're the same value. If your house is appraised at more than mine, and you think your house isn't worth more than mine, you have a right to come in and appeal it.

One of the guys on that board was Albert Franklin. He represented Boulder City. Very rich man. A guy bought a whole bunch of apartments from busted savings and loan associations that over-built. They were doing everything to sell these apartments. They had been assessed at 35 percent of what he'd paid for them, like they should be, but he was protesting the taxes.

Albert says to him, "You think that's too high?"

The guy said, "Yes."

Albert said, "I'll buy them from you right now." That took care of a lot of protest. Albert offered to buy their property. [laughter]

I thought that was interesting work. People you never saw in politics or government, just regular taxpaying citizens, would come before the board and state their case as to why they thought their taxes were too high. It was refreshing. The nicest bunch of people would state their case and accept the ruling in most cases. We granted equalization in lots of cases.

We granted a 20 percent reduction in assessed land value in the triangle between Bonanza, Charleston, Main, and Twenty-Fifth, now Eastern Avenue. I dissented. It appeared to the state that those properties were terribly under-assessed. There were some gambling joints in there. So, the state came in and did its own appraisal, which, of course, fell in conflict with the distinguished assessor, James Bilbray. I thought the state was right—they were under-assessed, as was most of the county, particularly large land-holders and large hotels. I didn't have too many victories.

At my expense, I went to Eugene, Oregon. I'd heard about their county government. We had a five-man board, all part-time. It appeared to me we needed more. They had a five-member board, two full-time, elected. They were commissioners every day. Then three public commissioners would come into the meetings. I thought that was great. I brought it back and talked to people in county government and didn't pique anybody's interest.

When I was on the board, Oran Gragson was mayor. He and I had a couple of breakfasts. I was going to talk to the county and he was going to talk to the city about getting a large parcel—40 acres or more—to build a civic center on, so we would have county government and city government, maybe state government offices at one place. I don't know how it got out, but Oran and I had hardly talked about it before there was already great opposition, which put an end to it. I was accused of wanting to move the courthouse near my office on Sahara. Oran was accused of trying to hurt downtown.

The unincorporated area wasn't as big, either. It seems ludicrous that the city of Las Vegas and the urban area adjacent to it in the county are separate governments. It's asinine for people in the county to be paying less property tax than people in the city. Somebody's going to have to bite the bullet and say, "Either the city's got to annex all the surrounding and unincorporated area, or if that's too strong, consolidate into one massive city-county government." I don't think Henderson or North Las Vegas needs to come into the super-government. They handle their municipal problems well. But the county government was never designed to govern a municipal area.

When I was on the board, your sanitation district and water district had separate boards of trustees. They were created under state law, and directors were elected. But the legislature has continued to expand the powers of the county commission to turn them, in effect, into a municipal government. They have taken over the sanitation districts. They've taken over the Las Vegas Valley Water District, the county hospital. Their powers have been made enormous, and they don't want to give up any. That seems to me to be short-sighted thinking. They're not there to serve their self-interest, they're there to serve the public interest. And a blind man with a stick can tell that they've got to consolidate, I think. I guess that's just human nature.

Relations between city and county government were good, except Bill Taylor flexed his muscles a lot out at North Las Vegas. I took on respect for Bill. He was a strong mayor. The change was dramatic with city government after Bill and those reformers came in. Clay Lynch was North Las Vegas city manager—smart, conniving. If Clay was in it, you'd figure somebody was going to get it, and Clay was going to come out on top. [laughter] I don't think there's any doubt about that. I never had that much trust in the man, but I found out later he was highly regarded by a lot of people. I might have misjudged old Clay. He sure did a job for North Las Vegas.

Finally, my appointment on the commission was running out, and I didn't feel I could run for a full term and continue to be a practicing lawyer. It would have been a conflict of interest. Murray Posin, a lawyer here, had a brother, Bernie. Bernie had been an assemblyman (1961-65). He announced he was going to run against me. I remember Sara and I laughing, because I wasn't going to run. But we got even with him, because every time we'd go out to a hotel, they would bring us a comp ticket, which they did in those days. I'd sign Bernie's name. They never looked. I figured if anybody did any checking, they would catch old Bernie free-loading all the time. [laughter]

(I abused the comp privilege. Two people I knew did not do it: Alan Bible and John Mowbray. One time Bible asked me to drive him to the airport. He had to stop at the Flamingo and get his luggage. I went in with him. We're at the desk, and they say, "Oh, this is complimentary, Senator Bible."

He said, "I pay my bills. No."

The desk clerk was really upset. "Oh, no, Senator."

Bible made a real issue out of it. I later learned the way Mowbray handled it. When he would go out to a hotel and they would comp him, he'd go ahead and accept the comp. But when he got back to his office, he'd send them a check rather than make an issue of it. But everybody else—it was such common practice. It was wrong.)

Sawyer said he was proud of the job I'd done on the county commission. He also said how grateful he was that I had never done anything that embarrassed him. Grant was a wonderful friend. Yes, a wonderful friend. He never put me in a bad position.

The county commission appointment was Grant's initiative, not mine, and I accepted it more as a duty to him. I had no desire to be a commissioner—they tie horses to county commissioners, don't they? (Actually, it's a big job today, and I guess it was a big job then.) I tried to do the best I could, but I wasn't going to be there long. I knew that. [laughter]

Notes

1. Art Olsen also represented Clark County as a Democratic assemblyman, 1965-67 and 1971-73.

2. Myron Leavitt has served as a justice of the peace, lieutenant governor (1979-83), unsuccessful candidate for governor (defeated in the 1982 Democratic primary), Clark County district court judge (1984-99), and Nevada Supreme Court justice since 1999.

3. Briare also was a Democratic assemblyman from Clark County (1961-63), mayor of Las Vegas (1975-87), and unsuccessful candidate for lieutenant governor in 1998.

4. Commercial Center is one of the Las Vegas area's older shopping centers. It is located on East Sahara Avenue, less than a mile east of the Strip. Moe Dalitz, Irwin Molasky, Merv Adelson, and others were partners in Paradise Development, which built Sunrise Hospital, several country clubs, and several malls.

5. Jude Wanniski was a *Review-Journal* reporter-columnist who went on to write for *The Wall Street Journal* and the *National Observer*, then became a close economic adviser to Ronald Reagan.

25 | Grant Was Magnificent in Defeat

Some people around Grant put a lot of pressure on him to run for a third term. In some instances, they were thinking more of their position than his. I knew he was concerned, but my responsibility as a loyal friend was to support any decision he made and do whatever I could to help. I thought he could win, and I was concerned that I'd hurt him by running for Congress and giving the Walter Baring wing of the party more reason to oppose him and vote for a Republican. (But run I did, and that's a worry I'll have the rest of my life. Grant never said, "God damn it, why did you run? If you hadn't run, I'd have . . . ." But it may be true that many Baring supporters voted for Paul Laxalt against Grant in the governor's race.) Grant's biggest concern was that *we* had made an issue of Charlie Russell running for a third term, but he made a political judgment that he could overcome that, and I felt he could too.

In the primary, the second highest vote-getter was Ted Marshall, publisher of "I Accuse News." [laughter] Marshall was a lawyer in southern Nevada who had been district attorney. His father, George Marshall, who had been a district judge, used to be a customer of mine when I was a shoe-shine boy in Caliente. In 1950, his father had taken on Pat McCarran for the Senate. George was always active in politics, and he was a Republican.

I never had any dealings with Ted Marshall, but I remember clearly that when he ran, he was on a mission—the Lord told him he should run for governor. He thought the business people, the banks, controlled Nevada, and we had to put an end to it. It was an unholy alliance—Parry, Julian Moore, Grant, and me. I had been a county commissioner. We had done big things. It's kind of funny that he was running in 1966 much as Grant did in the 1958 primary. Of course, when *you're* making the charges, there is merit to them. When somebody else is making them against you, they have no merit at all. [laughter] And we hadn't attacked the whole power structure, just E. L. Cord. [laughter]

Charlie Springer had gotten the appointment as Grant's personal counsel when Grant became governor; Grant appointed him attorney general when Roger Foley became federal judge. With Grant's help, Charlie became chairman of the state party. Grant had done everything a governor could do to help his career, and I never could understand Charlie's rationale for running against Grant. I believe there was a combination engineered largely by Charlie Bell to destroy Sawyer—and me in the process—because of his bitterness toward me for running against Baring. I have always believed that.

George Ullom got his name on the, ballot, and you can see what he got: around 2,000 votes. I think Bell had found an ideal situation for him to kill two birds with one stone. I always believed there was a quid pro quo insofar as Ullom was concerned, and I don't know what Charlie's was. Springer might have thought he could win.

Charlie is very liberal, but I don't think his decision to run had a philosophical basis. In the Democratic convention that year, Herb Jones ran against Charlie for state party chairman, and I think Charlie felt the Sawyer people hadn't gotten deeply involved, or they could have put him over. That is my memory. I could not understand how Charlie would feel that the governor, in the year he was running for reelection, would get involved in a party fight, particularly where one of the southern Nevada guys, Herb, who'd been a strong supporter of Grant's, was his opponent. If he was mad at Grant for that, he had no right to be, which meant his self-interest was the only thing important to him.

Sawyer didn't have any trouble in the primary—he got about 41,000 votes. Between them, Marshall and Springer got about 27,000. Sawyer's margin of victory is 14,000 votes, but why would so many vote against him? I was surprised that Springer ran almost as well in Clark as Marshall did—Clark being Marshall's home. I couldn't understand Springer's votes here unless there had been some real group support, and after the primary, Springer did not come back into the fold.

Going into the general election against Laxalt we felt guarded optimism, realizing it was going to be a tough fight. As the campaign wore on, our optimism continued. With me, it continued forever, because I wasn't privy to any polls. Grant and I were several hundred miles apart. I remember the last few days before the election, there was some concern. Still guarded optimism.

What came as a shock—and it shouldn't have—was how Paul cut into Grant's small county strength. The small counties had been Grant's bread and butter. Initially, we could always count heavily on those. When you saw Laxalt cutting into that vote, that was inclined to strike terror in your heart. Laxalt used to say the cows are still there, referring to the cow counties. I heard him use that phrase when he was running for the Senate against Harry Reid. Washoe was not that surprising; it was principally Republican. It seemed, all over the state, the counties that Grant carried, he carried less than he had before. Even true in Clark County.

I had a theory. Grant had been in the hot seat for eight years issuing orders with his board, controlling gaming—disciplining, revoking licenses, refusing to grant licenses. Almost every day you make one enemy. I didn't think any governor could survive eight years with that responsibility without having enough people in that business mad enough at him to beat him. Charlie Russell couldn't do it. That was what I really thought about it. The state is different now. The town's different, the attitude toward gambling is different, the people in the business are different to some extent.

You can't survive eight years of having to tell people no. There were a lot of problems with the gaming industry during Grant's administration. Grant and I agreed that the minute he became governor, attrition set in, insofar as the gambling industry was concerned. They spend a lot of money and don't expect anybody to tell them no. [laughter] Grant and his control board—Butch Leypoldt, Ed Olsen, and Ned Turner, principally—had courage to tell them no. You might recall, through the years, where Laxalt was complimentary toward his friend, Moe Dalitz. I think that group did everything they could to defeat Grant. They were mad at him,[1] but somebody should note there was never a scandal in gaming control while Grant was governor. I hope that's remembered about him.

Grant took on J. Edgar Hoover because of illegal wire-tapping on Nevada businesses. Grant was, as a man and as a lawyer, incensed that that agency of the government would violate its own laws and adopt a philosophy that the ends justify the means. Grant resented it as an intrusion upon Nevada's sovereignty. They felt at perfect liberty to come into the state, violate the laws not only of the United States but of the state, and illegally wire-tap citizens of Nevada. Grant was right; it *was* wrong. He took on Hoover, and Hoover was not used to being taken on. Hoover, for the first time in his career, interjected himself into a political campaign and wrote a letter to the *Las Vegas Sun*, in which he attacked Grant.

I was proud of Grant. He knew the public attitude toward the FBI, that this wonderful agency was beyond criticism of any kind. He knew he was taking on an awful tough opponent. I was always so proud of him that he had the guts to do it. By God, he did! He took them on! Criticizing Hoover in those days was like criticizing Mama and apple pie and the flag, even the Chevrolet, I guess. [laughter] But Grant had the courage, and he was right. He suffered the consequences in good graces. (I'm proud of Harry Reid for introducing the bill to change the name of FBI headquarters in Washington and take Hoover's name off it. Hoover was despicable, absolutely despicable.)

The day after the election, Laxalt flew back to meet with Hoover and apologize for this terrible thing the governor of Nevada had done and assure Hoover that *his* administration would cooperate with the FBI in every respect. To me, it was one of the disgraceful times in Nevada's history. A governor calls on a federal official to apologize for the former governor who wanted to prevent violations of the law. That's all Grant was objecting to, wasn't it?

Hoover had written to the *Sun*. Hank was not happy with Sawyer, either. Hank was a bitter enemy of Grant's, would do anything he could to destroy Grant. His two chief political enemies in Nevada had been Pat McCarran and Grant Sawyer, both friends of mine. I have this picture of McCarran on the wall in my office. Hank would come in, look at that picture, look at me, and smile. I think Hank had regard, if not for my legal ability, for my integrity. He never heard me say a bad word about McCarran, when I might have been inclined to curry his favor, if I was seeking his business, and he never said a word about Grant in my presence, because I think we knew we would have been in a fight.

I personally liked Paul Laxalt, but after he became lieutenant governor, I was shocked at some of the things he did to hurt Grant, and I lost considerable respect for him. It's always been my view you can be political opponents; that doesn't mean you have to be personal enemies. You've got to have some respect for each other. It takes a lot of guts for people to run for office, to put their name on the line. Unless they do things really out of line, we still ought to be friends. Paul showed a bitterness, a willingness to cross that line. I don't know why. Political ambition. Paul's not the first one, nor the last. I and some of my friends might have been guilty of the same thing through the years. I don't profess great innocence and great virtue.

One time, Grant was absent from the state; Laxalt got a grand jury convened to investigate the state government. It was serious. It shocked me; it shocked, I think, the press; it shocked a lot of people in Nevada—it was so obviously a political move. (None of that when Rex Bell was lieutenant governor. When Grant was out of the state or anything, Rex never took any steps that weren't just routine. If something out of the ordinary had to be done, he could get Grant on the phone, wherever Grant was.) Grant had to go to court over these things.[2] It left me with a sour taste in my mouth. Paul was constantly personally attacking Grant, and it was an unhappy arrangement with him being lieutenant governor and Grant having to watch his back all the time.

However, to say I like Paul very much is true. He's nice. You enjoy seeing Paul. He has a down-to-earth quality about him that's amazing to me when I look at him dressed immaculately—beautiful suits, shined cowboy boots, the kind of scarf or kerchief the Basque sheepherders wear . . . when he's dressed in western clothes. Handsome devil.

John Foley was at the meeting at Lake Tahoe. I got the impression that he wanted to run his own campaign and not be too closely tied to Sawyer. They might have made a political judgment that they were better off not getting mixed up with the governor's campaign, which might have been true, although the vote didn't indicate that—Grant ran ahead of John.[3]

The lieutenant governor's primary was a real battle. John was a formidable candidate. You also had Mike O'Callaghan and Harley Harmon.

Harley's father had been district attorney of Clark County early on. At one time, Roger T. Foley had been his deputy. Old Harley and old Roger had been active together in the Democratic party. Here you had two old-time families taking after each other for lieutenant governor. Harley's father had run for governor twice, and I think Harley wanted to carry on that tradition.[4] I assume that his next step would have been, had he been elected, to run for governor. John later ran for governor; Mike got elected.

Donal N. "Mike" O'Callaghan had come here as a schoolteacher in Henderson, been active in the party. He worked in the juvenile program here. There was a rumor O'Callaghan was a Cannon man, and I think he was in the Cannon camp in the days when the Cannon and Sawyer camps were sort of at odds—not over state or federal government, but party politics. Mike was very effective. Grant respected his ability a great deal and certainly wanted him in our tent. Grant appointed him head of the state welfare department and never regretted it—Mike did a wonderful job.

There were other candidates. Bill Galt had been on the city council in Sparks. Bill Flangas was a Democrat, and I'd be surprised if he ever voted for one. He turned out to be a *strong* Laxalt supporter. He was a mining engineer; graduate of the University of Nevada, Reno; in the test site, the engineer in charge of digging all those holes. Bill has been to Russia as one of our inspectors to see the nuclear facilities, before the Cold War ended. Bill was a bright, hard-working, nice guy, and a cousin of Peter Flangas, the attorney.[5] Victor Whittlesea, a Reno man, owned Whittlesea Cab. Vic died, and I think the Bell that runs the company now is a relative of Vic's. Vic was active politically. Charlie Bell became his lobbyist. The Taxi Authority is another chapter of Nevada political history.

In that campaign, insofar as civil rights was concerned, O'Callaghan was entitled to every vote on the Westside. I understood he didn't get those votes, that Harmon did the politically smart thing, followed the patterns of the past, concentrated his campaign with the preachers, and got a big vote. Neither Harley nor John, to my memory, had been great supporters of civil rights. Mike worked with people on the Westside a lot.[6]

In the race for congressman, I did well in West Las Vegas. I'd have won if more of the residents had gone to the polls . . . a traditional problem. I worked mostly with the leaders, but some of those preachers were active with West and McMillan. One time a group of the preachers called me to a meeting and asked me to give them money, because they were working for me. I took after them. The result was that the Sunday before the election, I appeared in about four different churches on the Westside, and I spoke. One of them got a collection hat, had a guy stand in front of the altar, and called on the people to come up and make donations to me.

In 1958, we had had a tour of the state—the candidates together, the whole party. In 1966, we didn't really have that to the same extent. Harvey Dickerson won that year's attorney general's election against Bill "Wildcat" Morris. We'd run into each other when we were campaigning. Wildcat was a funny man, a riot. The press in Reno just treated him beautifully, maybe to the point they didn't take him seriously because he was so funny. We had Keith Lee running for reelection as controller, and he was defeated. The Republicans elected a governor, a lieutenant governor, state controller.

I thought the race would be tight, but Grant could pull it off. I didn't recognize the Republican sweep it would be. I thought Foley would win, for sure. From an old-time Nevada family, known all over the state, and running against Fike, a handsome, slick Las Vegas fellow who hadn't lived in the state that long . . . .[7] The Republican running for state controller, Wilson McGowan, was an old-timer, so I figured Lee was in a bit more trouble than Foley.[8]

I was surprised by the outcome of the election, but Grant was magnificent in defeat. He didn't show real acrimony. He just started making plans for what he was going to do with the rest of his life.

My greatest political disappointment was that Grant didn't run for the Senate in 1974 when Bible notified everybody he wasn't going to run. (It may be true, as the joke went, that Bette said, "If he files, I file," But if Grant had decided to run for the Senate, Bette would have been with him.) From the time I first knew him, I believed if Grant had gone to the Senate, he would have been in leadership within a short time and a national candidate. Yet, Grant took seriously what McCarran had told him: nobody from Nevada, no matter how brilliant, effective, or forceful, could be on a national ticket because of the attitude toward Nevada in the rest of the country. I think that had changed. I believe Grant would have gone on to be a great political leader. He had all of the qualities, and then some, to become a great political leader. He was deeply committed to a general political belief in the duties of government to the people of the country. And whenever principle was involved, he'd stand up and fight.

I think when Grant came out as governor, he may have felt he had lost his skills as a lawyer; knowing full well, though, that he could get them back quickly. He said to me one time he didn't want to wind up like Governor Carville. Carville had been a governor, a senator, and after that was practicing law in Reno like everybody else, hustling divorce cases. He didn't want to become that. I think he felt he owed a duty to himself and his family to get in a sound financial position. Of course, I never knew any governor to come out busted, but he didn't leave office rich. [laughter]

I think this is kind of a compliment: as governor, Grant was paid twice a month. He lived on one paycheck and saved the other. Grant never had a lot of money, but he saved a decent nest egg to help him get started when he went out. And he took great pride in building that law firm [Lionel, Sawyer & Collins]. He was happy with what he was doing and with his financial success.

Grant came to Las Vegas. He formed the partnership with Sam Lionel. Sam's a fine lawyer. He's a money-making son-of-a-gun. Grant was proud of that firm, as well he should be. It was funny how I was representing Hank Greenspun and Sam was representing Howard Hughes, and we're going at it tooth and toenail.

Why not Sawyer and Denton? Grant and I were dear friends, no question. But there's a basic rule: If you want to bust up a good friendship, go in business together. I think Grant and I both sensed that we would have been compatible practicing law together—we had done so for a couple of years in Elko—but I would not have been happy being in a subservient position to anybody. If you're practicing with an ex-governor, you're in a subservient position.

I told Grant he was welcome to join me, but he didn't want to practice law the way I always wanted to practice, with friends and neighbors and the common man for clients. Grant made a magnificent law firm—as honorable and ethical a man as I ever knew in my life, but his clientele was different from mine. [laughter] Big money. I just never was able to establish any rapport with big operators.

Notes

1. In 1965, Ruby Kolod, a Desert Inn co-owner, was convicted of strong-arming a co-investor in an oil deal and put in the Black Book, which would have forced him to sell his casino interests. When that was set aside, he was removed from the Black Book.

2. *Sawyer* v. *District Court* held that the lieutenant governor could act in place of an absent governor only in emergencies, not, for example, to make appointments.

3. In 1966, for governor, Laxalt defeated Sawyer, 71,807-65,870. For lieutenant governor, Ed Fike defeated John Foley, 71,728-63,705. Thus, Laxalt ran seventy-nine votes ahead of Fike, while Sawyer ran 2,165 ahead of Foley.

4. In 1934, Harley A. Harmon ran second in a six-man field in the Democratic gubernatorial primary, losing by 484 votes (6,058-5,574) to Richard Kirman. In 1938, Harmon lost to E. P. Carville, 12,279-9,558.

5. Peter Flangas is a longtime Las Vegas attorney who was involved in a politically controversial estate case before Noel Manoukian, then a district court judge in Douglas, Churchill, and Lyon Counties and later a Nevada Supreme Court justice who was defeated for re-election in part due to the controversy.

6. In the primary, Foley received 14,733; Harmon, 14,524; O'Callaghan, 14,419; Galt, 12,442. Three other candidates received approximately 13,000 votes.

7. Ed Fike represented Clark County in the 1965 legislative session in the Assembly.

8. Wilson McGowan represented Pershing County in the State Senate, 1957-65. He defeated Lee, 69,507-52,351.

26 | Two-Time Loser[1]

In January 1964, I announced that I was considering running for Congress. I had become convinced that Walter Baring was not a good representative. He opposed everything I believed in, and he had become so extreme that I felt I should run against him, even though I considered him a friend.

One of the moments that crystallized my thinking came when Martin Luther King spoke at the convention center—late 1963, early 1964. They had a fund-raising dinner on a Sunday afternoon. I was a county commissioner and sat at the head table, but King did not visit with the people at the head table. He sat by himself, kept his own counsel.

I'd never heard such a speech! Then I found out that, because it cost quite a bit of money for people to attend, King would not make a speech of that kind unless a facility was also provided where people could hear him speak for free. Arrangements had been made—after his fund-raising speech, he was going to speak again in two hours to anybody who wanted to hear him. Sara and I beat it home to Boulder City to get the kids and take them back, because I wanted them to hear it. The black people of this community came in droves. He made essentially the same speech as before, but he employed metaphors and language that this audience clearly understood. Sara and I were just overwhelmed.

I think that speech gave me some impetus to run for Congress. We simply could no longer be represented by the John Bircher that Walter Baring had become. Baring opposed civil rights. He opposed almost everything designed to ameliorate conditions in this country for the average citizen. And he saw a communist behind every bush—he'd even told the city of Henderson not to put fluoride in their water because it was a communist plot to take over the municipal water supply.

Walter didn't start that way. He was a Truman Democrat, and all of a sudden, he started switching. I think he saw in the John Birch Society a source of money for his campaigns, and he became a captive of that element. They were so extreme in their views! (Pappy Smith in Reno, a Harolds

Club man, contributed to Birch causes. Pappy believed the whole communist party was just on the other side of Peavine Mountain, all armed with .30-.30s, and the first one they were going to get would be Pappy.) To me it was shocking that Nevada could be represented by a man who espoused these extreme positions.

Walter was out of step with the rest of the Nevada delegation in Washington. They could not depend upon him. I don't want to overstate the case, but Walter was just inept. Our two senators had been successful in getting the Department of Interior to accept that the proposed Great Basin National Park met the criteria of a national park, and then to get the bill passed in the Senate. In the House, Walter held it up. He stopped it because the ranchers and mining industry in the state did not want it. Not that there were any mines in the area; there were not, and there were only about 1,300

··· *Meet* ·····

RALPH

DENTON

·······································

DEMOCRAT

·······································

for
Congress

·······································

a.u.m.s [animal units per month] of grazing. But those organizations objected to anything that would exclude ranching, grazing, and mining from any public land.

I understood their principle, but they were wrong. The traffic projection showed tourists would come to southern Utah parks, across Great Basin National Park, then across Highway 50 into Yosemite. It would have increased tourism in those towns in north central Nevada that, God knows, needed an economic stimulant. I felt strongly about that. Plus, I thought it would be a feather in Nevada's hat to have a national park. Had there been mines or a great cattle industry, that would have been different. However, a friend of mine, a service station man in Boulder City, told me he couldn't support me because he used to go hunting in that area. Christ, we've got 110,000 square miles of land in the state, most of which you can hunt on!

I think Walter tried to pattern himself after McCarran. The constituent service, for example—make sure every letter is answered and represent your constituents' interest. But no thought of fighting the vested interests in Nevada ever entered Baring's mind, while McCarran had no hesitancy about fighting Wingfield and people like that in his political career.

Unlike Baring, McCarran did not deserve the title of reactionary. His blind spots got him the reputation for being an extreme right-winger, though. He was convinced the Communist Party in the United States was bigger than it was, and he was not a civil libertarian. I doubt he would have supported the civil rights act; he probably would have sided with the southern senators. He was wrong, but not a right-winger, and he had a history of supporting social legislation.

Unlike McCarran, Baring never acquired a chairmanship of a major committee with his seniority. He got a couple of sub-committees of interior. That's as far as he went. Christ, people in the House with much less seniority than he had major assignments—Judiciary, Ways and Means . . . . I think he was ineffective, that his colleagues had little respect for him.

In the elections of 1964, I was stunned by the strength of the arch-conservatives, the John Birchers. You had radio talk shows. Friends of mine were involved, had meetings, study groups. I was frightened. Most of us viewed Johnson as the great hope. Those of us who had doubts about our involvement in Vietnam saw Barry Goldwater as a threat. He talked about the use of nuclear weapons and defoliating the whole country. He was regarded as a real extremist along the line of the John Birchers, and he voted against the Civil Rights Act. (Many years later he said he was wrong, and I'd like to say my opinion of Goldwater has changed. Although we saw Johnson as more moderate insofar as Vietnam was concerned, Johnson took us in up to the hilt.)

I thought Goldwater would do better than he did, that Johnson would have lots of trouble in the South, particularly having been the architect of civil rights legislation. So, I was surprised at the size of Johnson's victory.

I knew going in my chances of winning were slim. Walter had been reelected by overwhelming margins since 1956. But optimism springs eternal in the prospector's heart. I thought maybe I could convince the people his policies were wrong. I wasn't motivated by any desire to hold high office. I don't expect anybody to believe that, but I never had that sort of fire in my belly. I did honestly believe Nevada was entitled to better.

In deciding whether to run, I talked to Sawyer. Grant was frustrated with Baring, but he was in no position to get involved in a Democratic primary. I understood that. I talked to newspaper people, among them Bryn Armstrong at the *Sun* and Bob Brown. I wasn't talking much politics to Hank, because he had become so bitterly anti-Sawyer. I talked to Lee Page, to friends around Reno: Tom Cooke and Hazel Erskine; Drs. Laird, Morrison, Gorrell, and Harvey in English. I talked to Eleanore Bushnell and Don Driggs in political science. I'm not certain I talked to anyone in the black commu-

(Ed Kelly, *Las Vegas Review-Journal*, 1964)

nity. I might have talked to Charlie West and Jim McMillan. I'm not one to hide my light behind a bush. I probably talked to every son-of-a-bitch I ran into from time to time. [laughter] Most of my friends wished I would run, but they recognized, as did I, that the possibility of victory was remote. [laughter] Nobody wants to talk a friend into doing something that's going to wind up not working out.

Sara was very supportive, on a basis I should explain: she made clear it was my decision, and whatever I wanted to do was fine with her. That's been Sara throughout our marriage. If she felt I shouldn't do it, she wouldn't have told me.

When we went to file, we stayed at the Holiday Hotel in Reno and got up to go to Carson City. We're up on a high floor. We're looking out the window over the Truckee River and across the valley. I said, "God almighty, Sara, we're going to Carson City to file for Congress, and look out this window. There's not a son-of-a-bitch we know out there." [laughter]

I didn't pay attention to the good advice I got, which was, "Don't do it unless you've got the money," because I felt the money would come. I felt so strongly about it that I thought I'd be able to raise whatever money I needed and hopefully wouldn't spend any I didn't have. It turned out I was wrong on both counts. I didn't raise all the money I needed, and I did spend money I didn't have, which I had to pay for later. [laughter]

Given the rumors about problems between Cannon and Sawyer, I knew I would be perceived as the Sawyer candidate, and I worried about the possibility of it hurting Grant. It didn't seem to bother him; he did not discourage me from running, he encouraged me. Cannon was up for reelection at the same time, and it was obvious he could not get involved in supporting me. They were both scared of Walter. But Cannon's office gave me considerable help, including Conlon. (I won't call him Shady Harry now.) [laughter] Jim Joyce in Cannon's office would send information published in Washington on Walter's record and other comments in the paper back there that we wouldn't have out here.[2]

Bob Brown took a different view. Referring to the *Review-Journal*, he said, "We could support you if you'd run against Cannon." I responded, "Well, Cannon, as far as I know, is a good senator. Why would I want to run against a man who I think's doing a good job?" I didn't smell wolf manure for a while, that Bob had his own agenda. He was thinking if I beat Cannon, or had a big Democratic fight and weakened Cannon, Paul Laxalt would have an easier time. I think subsequent events proved how close he was to Laxalt. I thought, "That's so nice of Bob, to think I have the potential to be a senator." I don't believe he really did—it's just that we had such overwhelming Democratic registration, that the best way for a Republican to win was to have a bitter fight in the Democratic party.

I made an arrangement with Spike Wilson's dad Tom Wilson's advertising agency and met some of the people in his office. In those days, agencies were compensated by getting a commission on advertising material they placed. You didn't pay big fees, you paid for production work. When I filed, Wilson's office arranged a press conference at one of the hotels in Reno. I went over to submit to questions. I told them to feel at liberty to ask any question on any subject, and I would answer as honestly and fully as I could. If they thought I was trying to dodge something, tell me. I said, "You're entitled to know everything about what I think about any subject that you think is material to the people of the state of Nevada." I was interviewed on television—first time I'd ever seen myself on television. Everybody seemed to think that was all right. I thought the reaction to my filing was good. Hank outdid himself for the headline he had in his paper. That wasn't uniform around the state, but Lincoln County was fine.

When I filed, I talked about issues. I made reference to "archaic" laws dealing with public lands; I wanted an orderly disposition. I said, "The cattle industry is really hurting. It would be hard to find another industry where you get so little back on your investment." [laughter] I'd learned on the board of county commissioners that almost every urban area in Nevada was surrounded by the public domain. These cities couldn't grow. I felt cities and counties ought to be able to acquire public domain for municipal purposes and future development—parks, things of this kind. A lot of that has happened. Henderson got a great amount of federal land they've sold and developed into Green Valley and other areas.

I believed then and believe now there is a tendency to overregulate the public domain as far as grazing rights are concerned. There were probably twice as many cattle in Lincoln County when I was a kid as today. Lincoln didn't even have a BLM office. You had the Taylor Grazing Act, true, but we didn't have an office in Caliente. We were under the Ely office. I don't know how many cattle are grazed in Lincoln today, but I'll bet you've got fifty to seventy-five federal employees around Caliente now. That doesn't mean the government should give the land to the states.

I talked about the John Birch Society and the value of moderation: "All I can do is talk about what I believe, tell them I'm a moderate and that I don't believe problems call for radical solutions. Problems we Nevadans have call for a reasonable approach by reasonable men." I anticipated Walter and his people would paint me as some kind of radical. Calling somebody a liberal in most of Nevada was not flattering, and we liberals tried to shield ourselves from that charge. [laughter] I was trying to say something that wouldn't make anybody mad, and negate the impression I was a far-out radical. To some, I was. In their view, my support of civil rights made me a radical.

There was a sense that Lyndon Johnson was too progressive for Nevada, a threat to state's rights. Walter always described himself as a Jeffersonian state's rights Democrat.[3] In the campaign I went to great lengths to assure everybody I was independent of Johnson, that I would not be a rubber stamp. Walter capitalized on how he opposed all of these matters like civil rights. That had considerable support in Nevada, as it does now. Nothing's really changed. There's an awful lot of opposition in Nevada to federal programs.

I said if elected, I was going to try to get on the Judiciary Committee. It's a major committee, and I was making a point that Walter had been there all these years and never made it to a major committee. McCarran had been chairman of the Senate Judiciary Committee, and, as a lawyer, I was interested. The Judiciary Committee handles a large percentage of legislation. We already had representation on the Senate Interior Committee. That was an important committee to Nevada, but there wouldn't be much point having a senator and the only House member on the same basic committee. Better to spread our action. Most legislation that had to do with gambling would find its way into Judiciary. If you're on that committee, you're in a position to wield a little influence with other members. At least, you can say to Congressman so-and-so from Oklahoma, "Look, partner, don't be fooling with us." [laughter]

I came out for the Great Basin National Park. Joy Hamann, our press secretary, took the call from Burrell Bybee in Ely, who pledged his support and wanted to talk to me about the park. I was for it. The people in Ely knocked themselves out to get this park. However, it brought me into conflict with some labor people in White Pine; by God, they wanted to hunt, too. They didn't care about economic welfare. I had friends in the labor movement there, and we'd talk about this. I said, "Look, you work in the mining industry. You know what happens when the mines shut down. Don't you want to raise your family in a community that has some stability so your kids don't have to leave here when they grow up, don't have to follow the booms and busts like you've had to follow them all your life?" I met a lot of wonderful people in White Pine who were strong, but most cattlemen and real estate brokers were opposed. They didn't want restrictions on the public domain at all.

Baring had voted no on the Civil Rights Act of 1964, and I knew it was an issue. Every time I'd be with more than two people, the question would come up. To a large extent, my campaign was based on coffees—all day, every day. You could see it. Things would be going well, then I'd make a speech. Never had a written speech. Spoke extemporaneously all the time. Sometimes I was good, sometimes lousy. I made a mistake—a guy should have a canned speech. I'd open it up for questions. Everything would be fine until civil rights would come up. I would try to explain why I supported the legislation, why I thought it was important. You could see their eyes go down. To me, it was so logical. I thought I could convince people. A black person who tried to travel couldn't eat in a restaurant in Nevada. I just thought the moral imperative was so great that I could persuade them.

I didn't think I was critical of Walter when I declared, but he attacked me—called me "a liar, a juvenile, and low caliber." [laughter] How do you respond to that? I accepted it as part of the game and said to myself I wasn't going to do that. He said, "You're conservative here and liberal there." I responded I was liberal on some things and conservative on others, which was true. I considered myself liberal on human rights, democracy, but a fiscal conservative. My record on the county commission would demonstrate that. I was always raising questions about spending.

Walter accused me of fronting for a Las Vegas publisher. "He is a mouthpiece for his boss," Baring said. "His boss is a newspaper publisher." He was referring to Hank.

I replied, "The only two bosses I have are my conscience and my wife, Sara. I'm pretty sure she does not own a newspaper, but I'll ask her." God, I got flip. If my two bosses were my conscience and Sara, Sara was the most efficient, important one. [laughter]

Walter had the story that my dad belonged to the Ku Klux Klan. I'm sure that was true. My position was, "If Walter wants to run against my dad, let him run against my dad." [laughter] Dad used to joke about how funny it was.

There were attacks from rural counties. Two come to mind. I was in Yerington, and in those days, at night, you'd go through the saloons and buy everybody a drink. I went in this bar, and this bartender was telling me Walter had been in a few days before. He told the people there he knew my parents in Caliente. They were fine people. He had known me in Washington. I was a fine boy. He just doesn't know why I turned communist. [laughter] I thought, "How the hell do you answer that?" I thought that was funny.

One was not funny. During the campaign, they had the American Legion convention in Tonopah. I had been commander of the post in Elko. I got a phone call from Wally Blohm, an old-timer in Elko, a World War I veteran active in the Legion. It meant a great deal to Wally. Nobody from Elko could go. Would I represent the Elko post? I went and Sara went with me. The next day, I'm back in Las Vegas, and people are calling a radio talk show saying that while I was at the convention, I spent a lot of time in Bobby's Buckeye bar, which was a whorehouse.

I simply answered truthfully: Sara was with me; the charge wasn't true. That ended it, but I can see Charlie Bell's hand in that. For many years, Charlie was Baring's right-hand man. He was in charge of his office in Las Vegas. He drove a car with "Congressman Walter Baring's Staff Car" on the sides. Charlie was the old-time school of politics, and there would be a legitimate question as to whether he operated as Walter's alter ego or Walter operated as his alter ego. [laughter]

To Charlie, anything was fair in love, war, and politics. The first time I was on the campus in Reno, three students came to see me at the student union and played a prominent role in my campaign: Keith Lee, Mike Sloan, and Dave Cooper. Dave fell by the wayside because he wanted to get paid, and I didn't have any money. But Mike and Keith helped like the devil. Mike was traveling around the state putting up signs. Some guys were tearing down the signs and muscling him about putting up more. One night in Reno someone threw a rock through our headquarters window. But that's part of the game.[4]

During the campaign, I brought up the idea that Baring might vote for Barry Goldwater in the November election. I'm sure he did, but he disagreed. He said he was a Democrat, a state's rights constitutional Democrat. I said I never thought the word Democrat demanded an adjective. [laughter] Nevada was very much an L.B.J. state. I recall the charge that I would be nothing but a rubber stamp. Nevada prided itself in its independence—our senators and congressmen. All I could do to answer that is to just assure everybody that I would vote my conscience . . . that or Sara's directions. [laughter]

I had another opponent: Ed Fountain. Big Daddy. [laughter] Remember the movie, "Cat on a Hot Tin Roof"? Burl Ives played Big Daddy. Ed was a lot like Big Daddy.

Big Daddy was a likable guy, on the city council in Las Vegas for a long time. He was out of the south. I think he owned a soft-drink distributorship. Later he owned Ed Fountain Toyota. There was a lot of dissatisfaction in the party with Walter, and I certainly wasn't the only one in the state considering running for his seat—Big Daddy saw a chance. [laughter] The campaign starts, and Big Daddy decides he wants out. There was a rumbling he was trying to get money from Democrats, and Sawyer blocked it. I don't think that's true. My guess is Ed couldn't get any money, because nobody thought he had a chance, and he blamed Sawyer. But he spent money he didn't have, and he needed help.

I thought, "If that's what he wants, I'll see if I can raise the money, then I'll go see Ed. If he's going to withdraw, I'll reimburse him." But it didn't work that way. Word came that at 11:00 one night, I was to drive to the Showboat Hotel and park out in the middle of the lot where nobody would observe us. A car would pull in alongside me. I was to give the money to the person in the other car, and Ed would withdraw.

Sara and I thought it was hysterical. Sara went with me. We drove down and parked in the Showboat lot in the dead of night. Up comes the other car. In the other car is Big Daddy. Big Daddy comes over to the driver's side of our car, and I say, "Hey, Ed. How are you?" and hand him the money.

Big Daddy said, "I'll withdraw," and he left.

I thought, "Jeez, are we playing 'cops and robbers'?" [laughter]

When I opened my headquarters on Sahara, there was a tremendous crowd. Some who came surprised me. It appeared I had a shot.

I was surprised by people who helped and disappointed by friends who didn't. I will never forget Carl Cohen of the Sands. The Sands contributed to Baring, and they would be contributing more to Baring than to me, but Parry Thomas told me to go see Carl. He had a little office next to the counting room. (He had a big one upstairs.) We go in, I introduce myself, and he gave me $1,000. Then we started to talk. He was one of the few in that business who asked me about issues. He was familiar with civil rights. The hotels were concerned about the effect it would have on big spenders from the South, what it would do to their business. He asked me my feelings about civil rights. I told him, and I think he agreed. He says, "Thousand dollars isn't enough for you, Ralph." He left and came back, and he gave me $3,000 more.

That impressed me. He made the contribution based upon our conversation. You hope somebody's voting for you because it's you, and they're not just voting against the other guy. Many who were supporting me didn't even know me—they were just against Baring. Money people, particularly in the gambling industry, didn't ask any questions about issues or anything else. Carl came up with more than they anticipated they'd have to give me to get me off their backs, and he did it based on our discussion of the issues. I had another experience along that line. Milton Prell at the Sahara went into great detail talking to me about national issues. Most people didn't.

I was told to go to the Desert Inn to see Moe Dalitz. I come into this reception room. Half the candidates on the ballot are there. It appeared to me, here we are as supplicants at the table of this great man, and he set this time aside to get the politicians out of his hair and give them their payoffs. I sat for about ten minutes, thought, "I can't do this," and left. So, of course, I never received any money from the Desert Inn.

Harvey Gross owned Harvey's gambling house at Lake Tahoe. I called on him, and he said he would send me a check. A week later, I got a check drawn on a corporation account for $100. I sent it back and pointed out in my letter it was against the law for a corporation to contribute to a federal election. I said, "And when I view the amount, it would appear you need the money worse than I do." I never received anything further from him, although we became friends later. One would suspect he was a Baring supporter. [laughter]

Baring got more money from the casinos than I did. I didn't get much. You didn't have to file in those days. There's no way you can know, but all you had to do was look at the money he was spending. It may have been simply that he was the incumbent, I was the challenger, and he had the better chance—he'd been congressman for a long time. I assume he built close relationships with these people. He was close to Major Riddle of the Dunes. The Sahara used to have a suite he used. Charlie Bell was well connected with these people in the gambling industry, but I didn't know that many.

The hardest thing for me was to ask for money. Somebody else would have to arrange for me to see somebody, and even then . . . . Prell, Cohen, and Dalitz, how differently the three men handled it! Imagine yourself begging, running for a high office that should be respected, treated like a two-bit ward politician come to see the boss to get your payoff. That's extreme, but that's the way I felt. Parry put the lug on a few people. Hank did; other friends did. But I was impossible as a fund-raiser. Of course, I wound up busted, so that's proof of the pudding, isn't it?

Hank supported me. I was his attorney, but I don't think Hank and I had any ideological differences, when you come down to it. Hank did everything he could to help. The political columns were favorable. Bryn, his political writer, was helpful. Whatever Hank could do, he did—without question. I think he thought I was absolutely crazy when I told him I was going to run for Congress. If so, he was right. [laughter] If he tried to talk me out of it, I might have listened. I wish somebody had. [laughter]

A lot of people helped with fundraising. I don't recall all of them. It came in cash, went out in cash. It went into the bank to pay bills. I was really surprised by some in Reno who contributed. I tried to call on as many lawyers as I could. An older lawyer, Dave Sinai, who had been in Reno for years, who I didn't know, gave me a nice contribution. Clark Guild, Charlie

Russell's brother-in-law, a Republican, gave me a contribution. Dr. Fred Anderson helped as much as he could. None of the McCarran people signified good wishes or contributed. That hurt a little, but it didn't surprise me. I'd learned the same thing in Sawyer's campaign.

As for who else who didn't help that surprised me, there were so many. [laughter] I was disappointed in the attitude of a lot of friends in Elko. The rivalry between north and south was so strongly felt, friends would say, "We can't support you, Ralph. Why don't you run against Cannon?" You can tell when you're talking to somebody, and they're looking at their shoes. They just would not vote for anybody from Las Vegas and give up that seat from the north. Why should they? He'd do anything they wanted. They opposed the park, any attempt to increase regulation of grazing, mining, on the public domain. Walter, my God, he was with them, and he was born in Esmeralda and had grown up with everybody there.

If you're a friend, you help your friends. I've always tried to be that way, a matter of conscience. I found it hard to accept that so-called friends would not support me and give as an excuse that I came from Las Vegas. That's painful, when you think a friendship didn't mean as much to the other person as it did to you, where you think some guy's your closest friend, and they look at you like a bull at a bastard calf. That happens to all of us. I'm waxing too emotional, because I learned, about the time Grant did, not to wear your heart on your sleeve. If you don't expect anything, you're not going to be disappointed. It made me more appreciative of people, some of whom I hadn't known before, who knocked themselves out for me. I sometimes suspected it was because they were against Baring more than for me, but it turned out many of them were for me. [laughter]

George Foley and I had been friends, and he came immediately to help. My friend Lee Page devoted full time to my campaign from the day it started until the day it was over. I got to the point I hated to see Lee; every morning at seven, no matter where Sara and I were, there would be the knock on the door, and it would be Lee to start the day. That went on from seven in the morning until eleven at night. Lee and Bill Kellett were partners in insurance adjusting, and they, Lindsay, and I owned a building on Sahara, across and down from the old Plush Horse bar. We had a big mortgage on it. That became the headquarters. It was ideally suited. Later, Art Lurie, the father of the former mayor of Las Vegas, owned a bar, Art's Place, on that lot.

Sara was into everything from the beginning, worked constantly. Joy Hamann had been a reporter for the *Review-Journal*, and she came to work as my press person. She was the only one on the payroll. She worked her tail off. One of the most remarkable women I've ever known, she was a constant surprise—the things that would come out of Joy's mouth! She was smart, a good writer, and didn't go over that well in the small counties. [laughter]

One of the things we started early in the campaign was coffees at people's houses, where friends of ours would arrange to invite their neighbors in, and we would appear. There were hundreds of people like that, because we did it

Denton Headquarters. Ralph with Art Revert, "who owned most of Beatty," and was an old Carville man and a client.

---

all over the state, not just in Las Vegas. That's how I met a lot of wonderful people in Washoe County, particularly.

I went to Minden to a chamber of commerce luncheon we had been invited to. I made a speech. After it was over, this lady told me how strong she was for me and how she had supported me in the past. Of course, I'd never been on the ballot in the past. She thought she was talking to Walter. Then the editor of the newspaper made clear he wouldn't support me because I was from Las Vegas. I asked him the last time he'd been in Las Vegas. He said he'd never been there, and he wasn't going to go.

I opened other headquarters. In Henderson, Rae Smalley ran it. Rae was a Caliente girl, a school nurse, active in politics then and now. Her husband Jim was a school teacher who later served in the legislature [1971-74]. We had a headquarters in Boulder City. In North Las Vegas, we had Andy and Ruth Berg. Ruth, from time to time, wrote for the *Las Vegas Sun*. Andy was a strikingly handsome man. You would put Andy and Ruth into the liberal column.

We formed a couple of organizations. Sara and Eunice Kellett, I guess, put together "Dolls for Denton." They'd campaign all over. They'd go up to the test site, and as people were coming out or going in, give them donuts and coffee, and campaign. Some of those young women became life-long friends, and we were friends with most of them before. "Young Nevadans for

Denton" was Keith Lee and Mike Sloan. They worked in the entire campaign, never got a nickel, Keith principally in Reno and Mike here.

The mining companies, of course, opposed me, because Great Basin National Park meant they couldn't prospect there. I talked to the head guy out of Kennecott at McGill. He was cordial. I didn't change my views, nor did I commit that I would, and he didn't change his. I think they wanted to support me. Maybe, had I given a little accommodation to their views . . . . I think Dutch Horton, their attorney, one of the McCarran boys, supported me.

But that's one thing you do: get your headquarters open and the first thing you do, get signs printed, get this stuff distributed, and start with a schedule. Hazel Erskine in Reno took it upon herself to handle my county scheduling—when I would be in Clark and different counties. She made it a point to know what was going on in each county and what I should attend. She would send forms, and Sara would take the day-to-day scheduling. Hazel was polling constantly. She was good. She was the one who had told me when I began that only 9 percent of the people in the state recognized my name.

Don Ragon was a first-class musician we'd met in Elko when he had a four-piece band in one of the hotels. He could play anything, plus he was smart. His wife was a vocalist, and they worked all over. They were playing at the Stockmen's Hotel when we moved there, and Sara met his wife Alice. Sara was pregnant with Mark, and she'd go to the park in the daytime. Alice

was a vocalist in the band that appeared in the hotels at night, and she'd go to the park in the daytime.

The Ragons would leave Elko after an engagement, then maybe they would come back the next year for an another. After we moved to Las Vegas, we hadn't seen them for years. One time we were downtown, looked up on the Golden Nugget marquee, and there they were! We renewed our acquaintance. They later moved to Las Vegas and made it their home base.

Don Ragon got some musicians together, and he

wrote this piece to go on the radio with kids singing: For effective representation, vote Denton, vote Denton, vote Denton; for Nevada and for the
whole nation, vote Denton, vote Denton, vote Denton." We ran that son-
of-a-bitch on the radio all over Nevada to the point everybody knew the
name Denton and hated it. But people still come up to me, "Vote Denton,
vote Denton, vote Denton." [laughter] They remembered my name. I found
that effective. That was a fight in the campaign. It was driving my handlers
crazy, and they wanted to take it off the air. I'd say, "No, leave it on."

I found billboards effective too. Particularly in Reno, I had two or three
well-placed billboards that had my picture. They're hearing that song on the
radio and seeing my face on the billboards. People say billboards are not
effective; I thought they were.

Television was really in its infancy. Don Bowers was the editor of *Nevada* magazine, a Fallon boy. He wasn't under McCarran's patronage, but I
met him in Washington and we became friends. He worked for the state
department—the U.S. Information Agency in Russia—and was on the staff
of (or maybe even editor of) that magazine that they put out in Russia called
America. Don had come back and worked on the newspaper in Fallon. Russell
gave him a job as head of *Nevada* magazine, and Grant kept him on. Don
helped immeasurably, finding pictures, always writing things for me, sending
me ideas.

Jude Wanniski said we made the most effective use of television they
had seen in a Nevada campaign. We went to Los Angeles, and Don hired an
announcer to ask questions. I was sitting on a desk, and the announcer was
in front of me. The camera would go in on him. He'd ask a question, then it
would come to me. I did not know what the questions were going to be—
Don prepared the questions. He knew the issues, and we gambled that I was
familiar enough with them that I could handle them without a script, because most people come over better extemporaneously than reading a speech.
Certainly, I do.

In one day, we cut every commercial used during the campaign. We
were there all day long, and I think we wound up with fifteen or sixteen
tapes. Didn't have to do many of them over, and they were long enough that
you could get a message across. They weren't sound-bites. Gun control, the
John Birch society . . . . They thought it was so professional. Professional,
hell. We did it off the top of our heads.

My neighbors did a lot. Cliff and Gene Segerblom and some others put
on a picnic in the park, well attended by Boulder City people. Sara and I
didn't spend much time in Boulder City. We figured if we didn't have Boulder, all the campaigning in the world wouldn't do it, and I worried about
whether I'd carry Boulder. I did. Sally and one of her friends set up a card
table in front of Central Market, "Dimes for Denton," and stayed all day
getting contributions. [laughter] It was a family operation.

Campaign breakfast on the lawn of the Dentons' home in Boulder City.

Leonard Atkison donated a storefront on Nevada Highway in which we had a headquarters. We kept literature and material there. People staffed that and handed out brochures and things of that kind. [laughter] The Godbey family worked like the devil. Bob Georgeson is now a Republican, but he helped. There was a good Democratic organization in Boulder City in those days. Even some people whose natural tendency would be to support Walter helped.

A hell of a lot more went on in Boulder City than in Caliente. In Caliente, they had a picnic and barbecue. Not many came. I spoke. Didn't get any money, but I carried Lincoln County. I think Uncle Lloyd was shuddering all the time about my positions on the national park and civil rights. I'm sure whatever vote I got in Lincoln County was a tribute to him and to my mother and my father.

George Foley helped in hundreds of ways. He worked his tail off. George was a strong supporter, and not only on a friendship basis. Philosophically, he and I were in tune.

During the campaign, there was a little brawl. George, his law partner John Mendoza, and Chuck McKenna were in a bar. Mendoza had run against Baring in 1962. Chuck was the bomb-thrower type—he had worked for Baring for years, and he and Bell were buddies, but Chuck had his own agenda. Although he would do almost anything, he was dedicated to the labor movement.

Chuck took to strong drink that evening. He and Mendoza exchanged words, then they started exchanging blows. I don't think Chuck weighed 135 pounds soaking wet. They wound up on the floor. George lost his glasses in the fracas, and Chuck stomped on them. That infuriated John, and, allegedly, John whacked Chuck around. At least, I think that's what happened. [laughter] I wasn't there, of course.

Things happen in saloons late at night. [laughter] I think nowadays there's so much money in campaigns that all the people working in them have three-piece suits, they're all on the payroll, and nobody feels that strongly about anything.

My campaign had a sense of crusade about it for some. They were believers. Had they been serving their own self-interest, they wouldn't have gotten involved in my campaign. It was an impossible chore. They had nothing to gain. Even if I got the job, there wasn't anything I could do for them. A congressman has little patronage. He has little staff compared to senators, and he doesn't have a bunch of jobs to give out. Fortunately, none of the people in my campaign wanted anything, because I had nothing to give anybody if I won.

One of the things I found most pleasant was the people I got to know on the Westside and the work they did on my behalf. I still count many of them as dear friends. It was a pleasure to go to meetings, rallies, people's homes to talk. I first got to know these people during the Sawyer campaign, and there were others. Jim McMillan was supporting me while running in the Senate primary against Cannon (that was a bit of a problem), and Charlie West, all of those guys, did everything they could to help me.

The town was segregated then, so when you say the Westside, you're talking about the black community. I carried the Westside by a tremendous margin, but turnout was so low. Had turnout been higher, I think I could have won that thing.

Some Las Vegas old-timers felt I was making a mistake with my close association with leaders in West Las Vegas. A lot of people used the argument that the Civil Rights Act interfered with states' rights. I thought the argument was specious. They were trying to preserve the states' right to do wrong. And it was *wrong*. They would like to have repudiated the thirteenth, fourteenth, and fifteenth amendments.

They were always saying, "What, do you want your daughter to marry a nigger?" You got a lot of that.

I would say, "I want my daughter to marry whoever she wants to marry, whoever she is in love with."

"Do you want to live next door to one of them?" That's the sort of stuff you got all the time.

I'd say, "Jesus, I've faced some awful assholes in my life, and they were white." Those arguments were insulting to me, to the intellect of any person who thinks at all or believes in what our government documents tell us to believe and what we're taught in whatever church we belong to. That's the way I thought about it, and that's kind of the way I'd answer those questions when I was put to it.

The guy who later became president of the Mormon church, who'd been Eisenhower's Secretary of Agriculture, Ezra Taft Benson . . . his son was active in the John Birch Society. By and large, the church hierarchy opposed civil rights. At that time, almost every ward had a club where they would discuss public issues. They didn't do it at the church, but they violently opposed civil rights legislation.

Charlie West was an owner of a paper on the Westside, the *Voice*. He wrote many favorable stories about me. A pre-election flyer distributed in predominantly Mormon neighborhoods in Las Vegas had a picture of Charlie and me, captioned, "The colored people are calling for the defeat of your congressman, Walter Baring, because he has the courage to stand up and vote against the unconstitutional civil rights bill. He warned that if the bill were passed, there would be riots and unrest in this country. Congressman Baring stood for us, now let's stand up for him. Vote for Congressman Baring for Congress on September 1."

They had the story in the *R-J*: "The *Vegas Voice*, a weekly newspaper published in the west Las Vegas Negro community, has begun a campaign to remove Walter Baring from the political scene. 'Every eligible Negro in Nevada is compelled by self-respect to vote against Walter Baring in the Democratic primary next September. Baring was only one of two northern Democratic congressmen to vote against the civil rights bill now being debated in the Senate.' West complained that Baring had referred to civil rights as 'special rights' . . . . He has labeled our leader as agitators and has emphasized his steady shift to the extreme right by voting against the civil rights bill."

It didn't surprise me. Nothing Bell would do would surprise me. Walter had called me a communist, a juvenile, and what else? A liar. He never indicated what I lied about. Bell put this together, and he waited until it was too late to reply, and then he delivered it in select neighborhoods just before the vote. I smiled when Walter called the Civil Rights Act unconstitutional—of course, the Supreme Court didn't agree with him.

It was cheesy for Baring to try and capitalize on the racial tension in the country at the time. He's opposed to it, fine! He has a right to oppose it. I wish I'd had time to respond. I would have gone on television and stated that Charlie West was my friend, his paper had endorsed me, and I was pleased that they had.

I ended up with the endorsement of both Las Vegas newspapers. I thought it could make the difference in a close race. The town was smaller then, and people knew each other better. I had the endorsement of both papers, and I carried Clark County, but it didn't reach into the north. I did carry Ormsby—the owners of the *R-J* had a paper in Carson City too. I carried Lincoln because of my family, and I came close in White Pine because of the park. I was so pleased with the *R-J* endorsement that I got my old bota bag (the bag that sheep herders carry in the hills with their wine in it), went to the newsroom, and passed around the bag for everybody to have a sip of wine and thank them for what they'd done for me. You could see these guys, never seen a bota bag before, holding it up trying to get the wine into their mouth. [laughter]

I hadn't known I would be defeated. People were telling me I was going to win, and I thought it would be awful close. I didn't know. Look, I'm thirty-eight, running against a guy with seven terms under his belt. I'd been around politics, but this was the first time my name had really been in the fire. I didn't know what to think. It was just, "God, I hope I win!"

Election night, we're at Joy's house. The first returns were in from Clark County. I was way ahead. I talked to Grant a couple of times on the phone. When Baring started to catch up, and you could see the trend from the north—you could see my lead diminishing—I started to write a telegram congratulating Walter. I wanted to do it before I drank too much. [laughter] I showed it to Joy, and she told me not to send it yet. Later that night I sent Walter the telegram congratulating him on his victory.

Trying to get reestablished, trying to figure out how to pay my debts—that was difficult. I owed a lot of money, and I had to earn the money and pay taxes, and with what's left over, pay my debts and support my family. I had a few assets—not a lot—which I could sell, which I did. But I still owed a lot. I'll tell you, being young is a wonderful thing. Didn't worry me a hell of a lot. I knew I would get them paid. What the hell? I'd been broke all my life anyway. Sara and I were happy. The kids were happy. That was the important thing. We could joke about some of the privations, the deep gratitude I felt for the Bank of Las Vegas or Valley Bank covering some of my hot checks, not bouncing them. [laughter]

So it's over; I'm busted. I got Sara and the kids. I had two credit cards left. I thought, "The hell with it. I'm going to take the kids on a little vacation. I'm going to take them to the beach." We took off in our car and checked into the Coronado Hotel. I didn't have any money. We'd go into San Diego to go to dinner, and we'd have to find a place that took Carte Blanche or Diners' Club. We had a good few days vacation, and then we came back home to bite the bullet.

One thing that happens to a lawyer—when you get involved in politics, you lose your reputation. Everybody thinks you're not really a lawyer, you're a politician. As loyal as your clients are, if their work isn't getting done, they're going to go some place. I started to rebuild my practice. That's not to take anything away from my partner, Earl Monsey, who did a magnificent job in holding the office together while I ran. But a lot of my clients felt neglected, and I was busted. I was just flat-ass busted. I had to figure out how to pay campaign debts and how to make a living.

Senator Cannon and Paul Laxalt ran against each other for Cannon's Senate seat in 1964. That race was controversial—Cannon was attacked because of his association with Bobby Baker. It was alleged that Baker and Cannon were close friends, which was true. Hell, Bobby was a good friend of everybody. [laughter]

Cannon beat Laxalt by forty-eight votes; then the recount made it eighty-four. Bob Brown, the editor, resigned over the *Review-Journal's* support for Cannon, and he went to work for Laxalt. All I knew about the *Review-Journal's* involvement is that they were strong supporters of Lyndon Johnson and Don Reynolds was seeking an appointment as ambassador to Australia. I remember going to the airport to meet Johnson when he came in, and Reynolds was in the line—the only time in all the years I lived here I ever knew him to be a public person.

The day after the election, I took off with a group of Nevada business-men and professional and government people for a trip to Europe. We were going to all of these European capitals to have big dinners and luncheons, which we did, and extol the virtues of Nevada. We met with tourist agen-cies. It was billed as a "sell Nevada tour," but I think it really wound up as the "buy Europe tour." I never saw so many guys with so much money float-ing around, but I got busted the first night in London. I had sold my soul to pay my debts—a client had sponsored me to be on this trip with the big shots. [laughter]

It was a wonderful trip. You had a group from Reno, a group from Las Vegas, and a few from small counties. Initially, northern Nevada guys would be in one group, southern Nevada guys in the other. By the time we'd been on the trip for one week, it was a completely integrated group with people who liked each other and were having a good time.

First, we went to London. We stayed at the Savoy. There was a lun-cheon where they had the principal travel agencies in London and some government tourism people. A pitch was made about Nevada. The first night, I went to a nightclub with Parry, Sam Boyd, and Jackie Gaughan.[5] I thought, "Jeez, I have the responsibility to hold up my end," but after I bought one round, all my money was gone. After that, Don Bowers and I went around together.

Parry and those guys were generous. Many of us were of moderate means, and there would be nice dinners. Parry and Jackie and Sam picked up a lot of tabs without making you feel like you were mooching. We were out one night in Paris, and we all wore cowboy hats. We looked ridiculous. We're at a nightclub. God, quite a few drinks! A rancher from Carson wanted the check. He took one look at it, and his face turned red. Parry very tactfully retrieved the check and paid for that.

I arranged in Berlin to have a girl from a German orphanage come live with us for a year. The group put up money to pay her transportation. While she was here, the ones from Reno and other places came down, and there

Back row, left to right: Grant Sawyer and Sara, Ralph, and Mark Denton. *Front row, left to right:* Scott Denton, Petra Kniestedt, Sally Denton.

was a big dinner for Petra. Petra stayed with us for a year. We correspond and see Petra almost on an annual basis—she and her husband and children. Sara and I went to Berlin a few years ago when Petra got married.

Petra went to Boulder City High School. They put her in the same grade with Sally, and she learned to speak English. When she got back to Germany, she was behind. She was put into that John F. Kennedy American School. I think—because she could speak English—they expected more out of her. She got over that, graduated from college, and is a social worker in Germany. She was adopted by a family after she went back from here, but she still calls Sara "Mom" and me "Dad." For me, then, the "Sell Nevada" trip had a different meaning.

Don Bowers had done a lot to arrange this trip, was familiar with most of the cities. After my first night in London, when it dawned on me I could not be a moocher the whole trip, Don and I would go out. I saw my first opera in Berlin, and it was magnificent. I've been an opera aficionado ever since. What really made me proud, the lead female—soprano—was an American black that had never sung in an opera in the United States up to that time: Leontyne Price. But she was singing in an opera in Europe, in one of the major opera houses in the world.

Before that trip, I had lined up a client who made it possible for me to borrow enough money to pay my debts, but I still had to pay him back. That was First Western Financial Corporation, with the principals in New York,

Bob Fielding by name. Sara and I had a great time lining that up. Mel Moss was their local man. Mel indicated that Mr. Fielding wanted me to come to New York to talk to him about becoming affiliated. I didn't much want to go, but I finally said, "Well, if Sara can go too, then I'll go." That's fine. They pay our expenses, and we go to New York. Grant was to be in New York at the same time, staying at the Roosevelt Hotel for some meeting.

Sara and I had made reservations at the Roosevelt, a nice enough hotel, but when we landed, Mr. Fielding met us at Kennedy Airport in a limousine. It was early in the morning, and he got up early. He's taking us into the city, and he says, "I hope you don't mind, but I've taken the liberty of changing your reservations and put you with us at the Waldorf Towers." Christ, we had a suite, and there's poor old Sawyer down at the Roosevelt. [laughter]

We check into the suite. Fielding and his wife maintained a suite at the Waldorf and invited us for cocktails that evening at 5:30. We hadn't been in contact with Sawyer yet. At 5:30, we went to Fielding's suite, had nice cocktails, and he took us to a lovely Broadway show, then to Sardi's for a late supper, and we went home. The same thing was repeated the next day. And I didn't know why he wanted to see me. But we were really living it up.

Sara said to me, "What does he want?"

I said, "I don't know."

She said, "Well, whatever it is, give it to him." [laughter]

The next day, he had asked me to meet him at his office. He wanted me to become general counsel in Nevada, but I wouldn't have to actually perform those duties, because he just wanted my advice on setting up advisory boards of directors for the savings and loan. By then, they owned a bank, a life insurance company, and a title company. They wanted to branch out all over the state and set up advisory boards of directors in whatever community they were going to be in. His bank would loan me enough money to pay whatever campaign debts I owed. I would have to secure the loan with whatever assets I had, and half of the retainer would go to pay off the loan. It was, in the vernacular of the day, an offer I couldn't refuse.

The only problem was it didn't last that long. I resigned. The reason isn't important. They declared the balance due and payable by 5:00 that day. As usual, who did I go to for help? Parry Thomas. He said, "How much do you owe them?" I told him. He had his secretary bring in a note and a cashier's check. I took it, paid them off, got my security back, came back, and gave it to Parry. It was a good loan. I paid off the loan. It wasn't a big deal to him, considering the dealings he was having every day. To me, it was an awful big deal, and I'll never forget him for that. Parry was a life-saver.

Early in 1965, stories started appearing in the press predicting I would run again. I was interviewed in Reno, and I was equivocal. Then I started thinking . . . . Although I had mostly paid my debts from the 1964 campaign, I had sacrificed a lot. I still owed the bank money, and it was tough to make that payment every month. There were groups that vehemently opposed Baring, and if I would run, they promised me help. "You came so close last time. We'll see that you get the money." I saw it as a way to get even financially.

When I make a mistake of judgment, it's a lulu. It was a terrible mistake for me to run again in 1966. I didn't deserve to be elected; my reasons for running were all wrong. In 1964, my reasons were right. In 1966, I ran out of desperation. I never had the same attitude. I would equivocate—not to a large degree, but I worried about what people would think about what I said; whereas, in 1964, that didn't bother me that much.

I've always felt guilty about that campaign. I wonder if my running at the same time injured Grant and contributed to his defeat in the general election. I was so closely identified with him. That damn Grant! I talked to him; if he didn't want me to run, he didn't say. Knowing Grant, he didn't want to discourage anybody, particularly me, from seeking office. I wish he'd have said, "Ralph, for God's sake! Are you crazy?" Sometimes I thought he owed me that. [laughter] I wished he'd tell me, "You're nuts!" But nobody did. And I lost, bigger than the first time. Walter didn't beat me to death, but he beat me by a few hundred more votes.

I had come closer to beating Walter in 1964 than anybody who had run against him before. At that point, he was the largest vote-getter in the state. Nobody likes Baring but the voters. Hell, I start out with only a nine percent name recognition in the whole damn state, and I come within one percent. After 1964, everybody thought Ralph Denton was stronger than wolf manure, but I proved to them in 1966 that I wasn't stronger than wolf manure.

Opening ceremonies, campaign headquarters, 1966. Sara made Batman capes for the kids.

[laughter] I *was* wolf manure. I was described in one column as shrewd politically. I proved beyond reasonable doubt in 1966 that I wasn't shrewd, or I wouldn't have run.

There was also George Ullom. I think Bell put him in the primary to drag off some of my votes—supposedly, he was a strong Sawyer man. Ullom was an old-time political operator, had a mind like a steel trap. He became registrar of voters in Clark County. He was city manager for the city of Las Vegas. He was head of the resort hotel association.

I always thought I had the ability to persuade reasonable

people, so I challenged Walter to a debate and offered to "let the congressman bring along his political puppet, George Ullom, for moral support." I got a little nasty, didn't I? [laughter] But Walter did not debate me. I tried to make as much of that as I could, knowing he wouldn't accept. If he had accepted, we might have gone, "Whoops!" [laughter]

I think Walter had the worst attendance record of any member of Congress. I capitalized on that as best I could. It turned out not to be effective, because he answered it with announcing he was paired. I don't know where Walter was. Wherever it was, the birds were singing, and Walter was having a nice time. [laughter]

In 1964, I had a press conference in Reno—very successful. I told it the way it was, the way I felt on everything. I repeated the same thing in 1966, and it was terrible. I waffled. Vietnam was a big issue, and I struggled trying to decide what our position should be. I wanted to believe in my government, so I took the view that, presumptively, the government was correct— I shouldn't criticize my government, particularly in something like this, unless I have convincing evidence that the government is wrong. About that time evidence started appearing that made me question my position. I couldn't put it all together.

If you're running for a high public office, for Christ sake, how do you tell the people, "I don't know." They expect you to *know*, and that's one of the tragedies of our political system. We *don't* know. So, what do we do? We try to figure out, what does the public think? We won't lead them, we'll follow them and make them think we're leading them. You discover it more and more. Our political leaders aren't leaders, they're followers. That's what I'm doing in 1966. I'm trying to weasel instead of honestly saying, "I don't know."

Breaks my heart—that war in Vietnam. I don't think that country's worth one American soldier. I don't see it as a threat to our security. All of the things I was willing to give expression to later, I didn't know at that time, and I didn't know how to tell the people. I thought public opinion was overwhelmingly in support of the war. So, to my everlasting shame, I did not at that time come out opposed to my president, my Congress, my government. I later did, but that is a shame to me. I was perfectly willing to do it when I wasn't running for office. I marched in demonstrations and stood on courthouse steps and read the names of deceased people. Why didn't I have the guts to do it when I was running in 1966? In 1964, I would have.

Part of my campaign was to have coffees. In Reno, one of the Parraguirre wives had a meeting. There were about ten or fifteen women there, all mothers. That was their question—Vietnam. I remember trying to express to them, "I don't know. What do you think?" There's no question what they thought. They wanted us the hell out of Vietnam. They were thinking of their sons.

Yet, when I did become opposed to the war, it had serious effects on personal relationships. My neighbor's son in Vietnam, a young marine, was killed. His father thought I was a traitor. I don't know how long it's going to take this country to get over the tragedies of Vietnam. I don't think we're over it yet, and I don't understand why people haven't admitted their mistake. Barry Goldwater did, but I haven't heard the rest saying, "I never should have voted for all those appropriations. I never should have swallowed the Tonkin Gulf Resolution. I'm sorry, American people." It took Robert McNamara how long? At least he's done it.[6]

I was always proud of Grant. It never was an issue in his campaign, but after he went out as governor, Grant was first in line to express his opposition to the war. Of course, that's what led me, after 1966, to being chairman of the Eugene McCarthy campaign for president here.

I avoided issues. Take gun control: Our neighbor next door, Mr. Christian, went deer hunting every year. I went with him two or three times. Never killed a deer, but I loved to go out in the hills. In the Nevada I grew up in, you're not much of a man if you don't like to go out in the hills and kill deer and any other type of animal that moves. I grew up in that atmosphere, but I can truthfully say I've never killed a deer in my life. Tom Gallagher in Elko says it's because I couldn't hit them.

In 1964, I had appeared on a radio station in Ely, and they had asked about gun control. I had said, "I favor reasonable regulation of the use of handguns." (Now, I'm even stronger. I'd like to see them take guns off the streets.) Mark's birthday is September 2, a couple of days before the primary. I was buying him a hunting rifle. That morning, I went to the sporting goods store about the 1100 block of Fremont. On the counter—and all over the state; I hadn't seen them—was this card explaining why you shouldn't vote for Ralph Denton because he wants gun control, signed by a sportsmen's association, a fictitious creation, in White Pine . . . accusing me of saying these things about gun control. That panicked the people working in my campaign.

Had to come out with something denying that. We cut a tape that ran the night before the election, with Sara and me and the whole family. I was ashamed of myself after I did that, because I was always for gun control legislation.

Walter was worried. He was scared to go on television. He just ran slides with pictures of "Walter Baring, Jeffersonian state's rights Democrat." How do you run against a guy like Walter Baring? Big old lovable Waffle-foot. That was his nickname, Waffle-foot. [laughter] "Oh, they're all against me. All the newspapers are against me." That's what he was telling everybody all the time. [laughter]

In 1966, Ted Marshall ran for governor against Grant. Ted had a campaign flyer called "I Accuse News," a technique used in campaigns through the years. You'd put a thing in newspaper tabloid format and you'd have these stories. Ted accused me of being a part of some unholy machine in Nevada that included all these corrupt politicians: former district attorney

George Foley, Julian Moore, Parry Thomas, the banks strangling the state. And he ran a picture of George's wife in a scanty costume when Irene had been a dancer at one of the hotels. Attack! That was all pretty much Bell's thinking, I suppose. I always believed it's really trying to discredit me more than Grant, actually.

Diamond Tooth Miller, with his *Nevada Democrat*—he should figure in any political history of Nevada during the '50s, '60s, and '70s. He put out this sheet before election in which he predicted the outcomes. They usually would have stories about you. Everybody knew the way to get a good story in was to give him money. If you didn't, he was going to knock you. So, the *Nevada Democrat*, from time to time, supported Republicans. Diamond Tooth was always a strong Baring guy, because Bell had been laying it on him for years.

There was a change in the *Review-Journal* from 1964 to 1966. I considered the working press at the *Review-Journal* good friends. Sara and I had gotten to know Fred Smith and his wife—he wasn't a newsman; he was Don Reynolds's man in the whole empire. Another guy was business manager, Bill Wright. We were friends. So, I was shocked a few days before the election when the *R-J* endorsed Baring. I didn't anticipate that. Politics is politics, but you get your feelings hurt when you find some friend is supporting your opponent.

A long time after that election, I ran into Fred Smith at the bar of the Las Vegas Country Club. (I am not, nor have I ever been, a frequent imbiber at the country club. That society is a little rich for my pocketbook or taste, but from time to time, I have been a guest.) Fred told me why they'd endorsed Baring: Wilbur Mills, who was chairman of the House Ways and Means Committee and later had his problems with the press and women, had called Reynolds and told him his friend Baring was in trouble.[7] The paper had to do everything it could to reelect him.

I said, "Fred, I understand that kind of political activity. I wish you'd told me a long time ago, because my feelings had been hurt. I appreciate your telling me that." The endorsement, I think, was a potent factor, considering the election was still close.

In 1966, labor came in to help. They sent a man from COPE, the Committee on Political Education, Lamar Gilbranson. In his column, Drew Pearson quoted George Meany—president of the AFL-CIO—saying they were really sorry they lost one in Nevada in 1964 that they really wanted to win. I guess they decided they could win in Nevada this time. Gilbranson actually came and lived here, set up telephone banks, forced some reluctant local labor leaders, at least on the surface, to support me. Many of them had deep personal ties to Bell.

Al Bramlet was sincere in his support, but he hurt me too. I was in Ely when I read a headline that Al had called a meeting of all culinary workers to work for Denton, and if they didn't attend, they would be fined. You can imagine the effect that had on people. "Jesus, Ralph Denton's a tool of labor!" I wanted their help, but I wished they would keep their mouths shut a little bit. [laughter]

Several people have since told me they voted for me in 1964, but didn't in 1966 because of my ties to labor. Of course, the Taft-Hartley Act was an issue. Labor was smart enough not to try and force me into making a commitment on that. They knew how injurious that would be in Nevada. I thought they felt they had a better chance with me on it than they would with Walter. [laughter] They were out in force for me, though they didn't come with the money I'd expected. But they considered all the money they spent supporting Gilbranson and his activities like money to me, except it didn't help me pay the other bills for the campaign.

I was back as Hank's attorney, and Hank supported me as much as he could—he never had much regard for Walter or the Birch society, and I have no doubt he would have supported anyone who opposed Baring in the primary. But because of my association with Hank, neither in 1964 nor 1966 did I hear from the old McCarran people—never heard from Eva Adams in either election. That hurt my feelings a little. Oh, a couple of lawyers who worked under his patronage, but I'm talking about the hierarchy. Hank was their enemy.

Your friends are your friends. Everybody brings baggage. If you've got a friend, you accept that friend. Grant and I always understood all of his friends were not necessarily going to be friends of mine, and all of my friends would not necessarily be friends of his. I couldn't hate all of his enemies, just because they were his enemies, and he shouldn't hate all my enemies. Hank was a mixed bag, both from the standpoint of politics and the practice of law. But I always was grateful for his support, and it was a hell of a lot better having him on your side than against you. He was effective, and he was sincere. He was my friend.

In the primary, I lost only by about 700 more votes in 1966 than in 1964. It didn't surprise me. We didn't have money for polls, but a candidate gets a sense of how people are treating him—their demeanor. I had the feeling before that election I was going to lose. There were two reasons for that, mainly. In 1964, an active group in White Pine was supporting the Great Basin National Park. After 1964, that was the end of the park; it didn't rear its head. By God, our two senators knew they weren't going to fight that battle again. And Grant was running. Consequently, the Carson City Democrats were more involved in that campaign and did not want to get involved in anybody else's, which made a great deal of sense from their standpoint.

The day after the primary in 1966, the day after I lost, I flew to Reno on the same plane with John Foley, who'd just been nominated for lieutenant governor, to meet Grant at Lake Tahoe and start planning the general election. So, what the hell? I wasn't surprised and heartbroken at having lost. The world hasn't ended. Let's keep going. I was glad I had tried. I didn't want to reach the age I am now and look back on my life and say, "God, if I'd have had any guts, I could have . . . ." So, take a shot. Maybe I picked the wrong time, but that was it.

My heart hadn't been in that 1966 campaign, yet I remember so many good things about it. They must have thought I was crazy, but my true good friends were there for me then: Lee, Bryn, Jimmy Garrett, George Foley, Lindsay, other people. The only one we didn't have going for us that we had before was Joy Hamann, and I don't remember why.

We got to know Nancy and John Gomes in Reno. If we'd have had Nancy and John in 1964—like in 1966—I bet we'd have carried Washoe and won. I wound up in worse debt because I didn't have the help I'd had in 1964. We had another race going on, and it was extremely difficult to get money. Some of the promises I had been given didn't come through. Of course, anybody who had been around as long as I had should have known better. You can't run on promises.

After I lost, we were going some place in the car with the kids. I think I said we owed something like $60,000-$75,000. An awful lot of money. Sara and I were talking about it, and the kids were taking it in. We were really worried about our financial condition. Scott piped up and said, "It was worth it just to get to know the Gomeses." He was dead right. To know John and Nancy Gomes was worth every penny it cost me.

We met them, I think, through Bryn and Leola Armstrong. They lived in Reno. Nancy was Leola's sister and a real activist, a true believer that Baring was a lousy congressman. Nancy was raised in Lovelock. John had graduated from the University of Nevada school of mines as a metallurgist and worked for the U.S. Bureau of Mines in Reno. He and his father had had mining properties. They had children about the same ages as my children.

Nancy agreed to manage the campaign in Reno and did a magnificent job. More importantly, we became close friends, and our kids became close. Nancy went on to have a distinguished career in politics. She was elected to the school board and the legislature [1977-79], and she was a great force for good things. Her relationship with Paul Laxalt after Paul became governor was interesting. She had a great deal of respect for Paul, and, of course, their backgrounds were similar—they both grew up in rural Nevada. Nancy always said Paul would listen. If you could persuade him, he would change. Didn't change her political views, though. She was very liberal. Through her, I met a lot of people I hadn't met in 1964.

Through Nancy, I met Maya Miller, another outstanding woman. She helped me very much. Maya lives in the Washoe Valley, on a beautiful ranch, Washoe Pines. Her then-husband was an ichthyologist. They had this Foresta Institute and ran a summer camp for kids. They had Indian tepees all around the main house, and the kids lived in those. They got instruction in science plus field trips out in the mountains, and each kid was assigned a horse.

Maya would go back to New York City to real ghettos, get kids from there, and bring them out at her expense—scholarships—to this camp in the summertime. My kids all went, thanks to Maya. Each kid had a horse they could ride, but they had to keep the horse and curry it and all that. Sally told me one black boy had never seen a horse. When it came time for him to go to New York, he cried to say goodbye to his horse. Some of them never had seen stars, you know.

Maya spent a fortune doing good things, going to Nicaragua and funding and helping build housing for the poor. Just after the Gulf War, she went to Kurdistan, and at her own expense bought food, rented trucks. There is no good cause that Maya doesn't help. That includes friends. She's helped put friends in businesses here, in Washington, D.C., and other places.

She ran for the Senate, and Harry Reid defeated her in the primary in 1974.[8] I supported Maya, of course, but I made a mistake. Maya hired a PR man from out of state to run her campaign. I met him at the Union Plaza early on, and we talked about Maya's chances—the question was whether Maya could win, not whether I would support Maya. It was always clear in my mind I would do anything I could to support Maya, but I told this man I didn't think she could win. That was my honest opinion.

I've always felt you owe your friends, particularly if they're in politics and they seek your opinion, the truth as you see it, not to just say what they want to hear. My opinion was interpreted by a lot of Maya's friends as not supporting her; but not only did I believe in Maya, she was entitled to my support, whether I believed in her or not. She's a magnificent woman. A lot of her friends believed I did not support Maya during that election. I hope Maya doesn't think that. But if she did think that, she would never say it.

I could almost say the same thing about Nancy Gomes. Nancy and Maya were soul mates, both smart as could be. Considering where Nancy came from, you wouldn't expect a brilliant liberal. Brilliant, somebody from Lovelock, maybe . . . but liberal, unusual. Yet even those who were not liberal had great respect for her. And John Gomes—just a wonderful man. Scott was dead right when he said it was worth it just to get to know the Gomeses. There are rewards in politics. Sometimes you can't put them in the cash register.

Good people did some nice things to help me. When the phone company charged my headquarters phone bill to my home, I couldn't pay it. Frank Rogers was head of the phone company—his son was my law partner—they were taking out my home phone. I said to Frank, "I've got two phones in my name. Why don't you take out the office phone?" [laughter] I told him, "Look, you'll get paid, but you'll be the last one. I owe a lot of people money who really need their money. I'll get all of these creditors paid, and you'll get paid last. The phone company can afford it better than these other people."

It was nice not to have a phone. I think we went over a year without a telephone in the house. Without my knowledge, after a year or so, my bill was paid off. I found out Maya had paid my phone bill. Lindsay Jacobson picked up another bill for $2,000-3,000, and he paid it. He'd been my treasurer. He knew they were getting ready to sue me on this particular bill, and didn't even tell me about it. I didn't find out for a long time. Scoop Garside, who owned Bonanza Printers, just wrote off the bill.

Funny things happened too. Leonard Atkison, a businessman here, told Sara, "You ought to see Sally in her office." Sally was about thirteen. Sara said, "What do you mean?" After school, Sally would go to a pay phone downtown across from Leonard's store, and her girlfriends would call her. He said she'd be there all afternoon. He called it Sally's office. [laughter]

Guess who was one of my campaign workers? Chuck McKenna, who used to throw rocks through my campaign headquarters window and have his boys rough up my boys who were putting up signs. He had come to great disagreement with Walter, and, by God, he was now a true believer! We go to Ely, staying at the Nevada Hotel, which had gambling. I paid for the room. Then, when the campaign's over, and I get a letter from a lawyer's office in Ely threatening to sue me on behalf of the hotel for a bill owed by McKenna. Certainly, I was responsible for the hotel bill, but, unknown to me, McKenna had gone to the cage and gotten a marker, for God's sake! Then he spent it over at the Big Four, one of the prominent houses of ill repute in Ely.

The Hotel Nevada sues me for, I think, $100. I wasn't going to pay that. I go into small claims court and defend myself. I wasn't liable; I didn't contract to pay his gambling debts. I paid the hotel bill, his room, his food, but I was not going to pay this marker that Chuck had spent in the whorehouse. Herman Fisher was justice of the peace. Herman gives them a judgment for half, orders me to pay $50.

There's more: The Press Club at the Riverside Hotel in Reno was pretty active. We'd try and hit there every evening around 6:00 and talk to the reporters. We had become friendly with the bartender. He calls me one day. He said, "I hate to call you about this, but your man Chuck McKenna was in, I got him a couple of girls, and he gave them a bum check."

I said, "I never heard of a hustler that would take a check."

He said, "I told him it was OK because he worked for you, and I knew you were good for $200."

I said, "Why am I responsible for that?"

He said, "The girls never would have done it if I hadn't told them it was OK." So I paid him. I must have been the only politician in the world that paid somebody else's whorehouse bill. [laughter]

1. Ralph Denton modestly suggested *Memoir of a Two-Time Loser* as the title for his oral history. Neither his family nor his friends, the interviewer among them, agreed. But we considered this title appropriate for this section, although the "two-time loser" didn't lose by much. In 1964, in the Democratic congressional primary, Walter Baring received 30,402; Ralph Denton, 28,649; and Joseph Kadans, 886; Baring's margin of victory was 1,753. In 1966, it was Baring, 35,109; Denton, 32, 654; and George Ullom, 1,994. In neither election did the third candidate draw enough votes to affect the outcome.

2. Jim Joyce was a newspaperman, Cannon aide, and advertising agency executive who became one of the most influential and successful lobbyists and political consultants in Nevada history.

3. In 1962, Walter Baring renounced John Kennedy's New Frontier and declared himself a Jeffersonian Constitutional Democrat, an advocate of states rights.

4. Keith Lee's father served two terms as state controller, during Sawyer's governorship, and was defeated for re-election with Sawyer in 1966. Mike Sloan served as a deputy attorney general, Democratic state senator (1979-83), and executive at Circus Circus and the Nevada Resort Association. Dave Cooper was later a Las Vegas advertising agency executive and political consultant.

5. Sam Boyd was a onetime dealer in southern California casinos who came to Las Vegas in the early 1940s. He worked at the Sahara and went on to be president of the Mint and built the Union Plaza and the California. His son Bill took over the company and, with his father and since the elder Boyd's death, has expanded it locally to include Sam's Town, the Stardust, and the Fremont, and properties in other jurisdictions. Jackie Gaughan came to Las Vegas in the 1940s and has owned numerous downtown casinos. Today he owns the Plaza, the El Cortez, and several others. His son Michael Gaughan built the Coast Resorts, including the Suncoast, Barbary Coast, Gold Coast, and Orleans.

6. Robert McNamara, secretary of defense from 1961 to 1968, and later president of the World Bank, eventually renounced his role in escalating the Vietnam War.

7. Democrat Wilbur Mills, longtime House Ways and Means chairman, represented Arkansas, 1939-77. He became embroiled in a scandal involving excessive drinking and a stripper.

8. In the 1974 Democratic Senate primary, Harry Reid defeated Maya Miller, 44,768-25,738, with the unrelated Dan Miller receiving 5,869. Reid lost in the general election to Paul Laxalt, 79,605-78,981.

27 | Law is a Profession, Not a Trade

Communications between an attorney and a client are confidential, and you have to make certain that everybody in your office—secretaries and clerks—understands that the client's business is confidential. Only the client can waive the privilege. It's a high obligation of an attorney to maintain the confidences of his client, and this continues even after the client dies. My problem in this oral history is to determine what information is privileged and what came to me outside of the attorney-client relationship.

Cal Cory left the firm of Cory, Denton, and Smith in 1959 or 1960. Then, we continued as Denton and Smith after Chet Smith left and went to Washington, because he wasn't certain if he was going to stay or come back. (And I was hoping Chet's name on the practice would draw in some Bible juice. It didn't.) [laughter] I don't know when the practice became just 'Ralph Denton'. I liked practicing on my own, but I missed discussing matters, the interplay with a colleague, particularly someone who fell within the same privilege, where I could discuss a case frankly and get suggestions.

I wasn't built to surrender my independence and freedom of action to the degree that I think is necessary if you're going to be in group practice. Hell, I went to college and law school so I wouldn't have to work for somebody else. I never did look for a job after I got out of law school. I thought you could open a door and start practicing law. You could, and you still can. But nowadays, it seems everybody's looking for a job with a great big firm.

I did have George Ogilvie in the office with me for a time. Dear friends of ours in Elko, George and Eva Ogilvie—George is their son. When we went to Elko, George was in Northwestern University law school. He graduated, won top awards—best writer—and went to work with this big firm in Kansas City. He was doing "blue sky" law—securities work. He didn't care for that. He missed Nevada, and wanted to come back. I couldn't afford to hire anybody, could hardly pay my bills, to tell you the truth, but we made a deal: George came out, and I would give him work to do. I didn't pay him a

300

*Law
Is a
Profession,
Not a
Trade*

Back row, left to right: Miriam Fox, unknown, Ralph Denton, Alan Bible, Joe T. McDonnell, Elizabeth Heckman, unknown, unknown. *Front row, left to right:* Grant Sawyer, Eva Adams, Cal Cory, unknown, unknown, Chet Smith, Jay Sourwine.

salary—it was on a fee basis. He was a first-class guy, a bright man, and he had the old Nevada background I understood.

It was hard for us to get started, barely making a living. The matters I referred to George weren't the best cases I had. [laughter] George understood. He was with me a couple of years. He went into public law, was city attorney of Las Vegas, attorney for the water district, county manager. George has had a distinguished career. One of the essential things in my office was a good sense of humor, and he had a great sense of humor.

I formed a new partnership just before Grant's second campaign, which was 1962. I'm going to have certain responsibilities. How am I going to make my living practicing law and devote time to Grant's campaign? Obvious, isn't it, I need help? I didn't know where to get it. I didn't have much business, so I didn't have much to offer. Grant had met Earl Monsey, a deputy attorney general. Grant had come into contact with Earl and was impressed, as well he should be. Not only did he like him, he respected his legal ability. Earl came down from Carson City to meet me, spent the night with us in Boulder City. We had dinner, and immediately, Earl's my partner, fifty-fifty.

Earl had the distinction of being Jewish, so he was considerably outnumbered growing up in Salt Lake. [laughter] He went to Stanford and graduated, applied to Stanford for law school, and was accepted for admission in the fall term. Earl's father, being more realistic than Earl, was interested in the cost of going to law school at Stanford. "What's the matter with the University of Utah law school?"

"Well, nothing," Earl says.

"Why do you want to go to Stanford then? It's so much cheaper if you go to law school here."

Earl said it was the prestige. His father thought for a minute and says, "The hell with you, Earl. You're going to Utah." [laughter] He went to Utah.

After Earl got out, he worked in Salt Lake and saw in a bar journal or something a vacancy in the Nevada attorney general's office. Roger Foley hired him as a deputy. That's how Earl and I became partners, and we were together ten years. Never a harsh word between us.

The quality of Earl's work is outstanding, and it was a pleasure to work with him. We certainly had some interesting cases. Once we were representing some people in France. They owned land in Las Vegas, and they had been sued over it here. There was a witness in France whose deposition we wanted to take. The witness came to give his deposition, and after we settled the case, the French lawyer told us it wasn't the witness at all, it was an actor. They'd hired an actor to show up. [laughter]

At one time, Earl represented the guy that had the big elephant in the floor show at the Dunes Hotel. Same guy had an elephant in the floor show at the Sparks Nugget. The elephant would come out and stand on his hind legs and do all sorts of things. The elephant had a baby, and one day the client brings that baby elephant to the office, and the baby elephant's running up and down the halls. Earl said he had the biggest client in Clark County—an elephant. [laughter]

It was fun at the office with Earl. When Earl and I were partners, and Charlie LaFrance came to work for us, a couple of nights a week after we'd close the office, we'd sit around and play bridge. I'm not so good; Earl's a great bridge player, and Charlie was a great bridge player. That's three of us, and we get Millard Sloan, a real estate agent in the building next to us.

We worked on cases separately, depending on who the client came to see. At times a client came to see me, and I was too busy—another reason you need help in an office—to devote time to it right then. I'd ask Earl if he could handle the matter. He'd come in, I'd introduce him to the client, we'd talk, and Earl would take over, or vice-versa. To avoid conflicts of interest, we started a system where a copy of everything either of us did would go onto a clipboard. Then we'd circulate the clipboard, so I would see everything that had gone out—letters, pleadings; contracts. We'd initial them, and when the clipboard got full, we'd file it away. We talked about cases a lot. That's the thing I've always missed when I was by myself.

Ours was a general law practice, and neither of us had a particular talent we concentrated on. Actually, Earl had a talent for things that bored me. [laughter.] Negotiating leases for Herb Kaufman, when he was manager of Wonder World and arguing with tenants . . . that bored me. Earl became an expert on shopping center law, and Herb was in the office a lot with Earl. One day, they call the office—the Wonder World store's on fire on Maryland Parkway. Earl had to get over there. Earl goes running out, jumps in his

301

Law
Is a
Profession,
Not a
Trade

302

*Law
Is a
Profession,
Not a
Trade*

car, and races over, pulling up in front of the store. Smoke is coming out through the roof, and Herb's standing on the sidewalk in front with the battalion fire chief. Earl rolls down his window as he's going by, and he says, "Herb, I thought the fire was tomorrow." [laughter] That's vintage Earl Monsey.

I was senior to Earl, but I didn't think of it in those terms. Earl was a partner. We split everything fifty-fifty. That's the ideal. I never could see how lawyers could practice in an office together with one of them being treated unequally, except that in a big firm someone has to be the boss. Earl and I had the same education, were doing the same work, and we were afflicted with the same fault, in that money was never the reason we were practicing law. We loved to practice law, and we had to make enough money to pay our bills and to live on. But the thought of keeping time records and billing people by the hour: oh my God, no. We always under-billed. Earl was just as bad as I was. Then we'd be busted, and we'd start scurrying around trying to make payroll.

We thought, well, the big boys were gathering into law firms. We thought we needed to build a law firm, so we had different people come in; and they'd be disappointed, I'm sure, that they didn't come in and immediately start making a lot of money. [laughter] But those ten years with Earl were among the happiest ten years of my life in the practice of law.

If Charlie LaFrance had been a member of the bar, he'd have straightened the whole damn thing out. [laughter] Charlie graduated from Alabama when that law school had not been approved by the American Bar Association. Nevada's rules provide that to take the bar, you have to graduate from a school approved by the ABA. One guy graduated from Oxford and couldn't take the bar because he hadn't graduated from a law school approved by the ABA. So, there was a procedure where you could petition the court and get special permission to take the bar.

I filed a petition with the state supreme court to give him permission to take the bar. The court granted permission. Charlie took the examination, but he had probably been out of law school thirty-five years by then. When the results came out, he was listed as having passed, but the next day he got a letter telling him he'd failed. That was heart-breaking, and he never took it again. He continued to just work for me until he retired and moved to Florida in the late seventies.

Charlie was immaculate. His shirts were ironed with the crease down the sleeve. A mind like a steel trap. Say I had a case—Charlie might have drawn the complaint or the answer. Charlie would go through that file and our discussions with the client, and he'd prepare written questions for me. When I went to the deposition, I would be thoroughly prepared. It's a great service. On estate matters, he would take care of the details. When the client came in with a box full of receipts, trying to prepare an accounting out of it, Charlie would do it. Everything he did was first-class.

Charlie was so contemptuous of the control board during the Laxalt administration that he was always trying to file some suit against it to compel them to do something. One time the board recommended a man for denial, and it was to go before the commission. Charlie had known the man. Charlie decided we would ask the commission to issue subpoenas to every agent who participated in the investigation to testify, so we could question them as to what they had in their record and why the recommendation had been to turn him down. In other words, let's look in your file, babe. [laughter] It hare-lipped them. That wound up in court. It looked like they were going to have to issue the subpoenas. Then, for reasons sufficient to me and Charlie, we withdrew. [laughter]

303

*Law
Is a
Profession,
Not a
Trade*

Charlie was gunning for the board, and I think we had them. They do these investigations, then write a report. They never tell you what charge you have to defend yourself from, unless they ask you specifically about a certain thing. Then you just got a hint. Charlie figured, well, make them tell. [laughter]

We figured we needed more help when I ran for office. Don Wynn came in. He had worked for the control board. Don didn't care for private practice, and he wound up going back to work for the board. He was a friend and kind of protégé of Charlie's at the board, and he had been an FBI agent. He went back to the board during the Laxalt administration and, I think, was the attorney who drew most of the proposed regulations on corporate gaming. He left there and went to the University of Nevada and taught.

Between 1964 and 1966, Jim Rogers came into the office. I knew Jim's father, Frank. Jim impressed me, still does, as a bright man, a fine lawyer. He brought to the firm some business ability, something we'd never had before. [laughter] I think Jim had an idea how you're supposed to run a law office, and I sure as hell didn't run it the way it was supposed to run. He became business manager of the firm.

When I got soft in the head and ran for Congress again, Jim Brennan came in—Denton, Monsey, Rogers, and Brennan. It was an equal partnership. (Some are more equal than others, it turns out.) [laughter] After so long—I don't remember how long that lasted—Rogers and Brennan left.

I would be less than frank if I did not say there were problems between Jim Rogers and me. He had legitimate grievances against the way I conducted myself, and I had grievances. The years have passed. Whatever they were, I hope have been forgotten. Jim has been a great success in not only the law, but business. It doesn't do any good to carry a grudge, and I look on Jim now as a friend. Good sense of humor, fun to be around. I defy anybody around Jim Rogers to say he doesn't enjoy his company. (Rogers since has set up the Ralph and Sara Denton Scholarship at the William S. Boyd School of Law at UNLV with donations from himself and others).

Jim Brennan grew up in Las Vegas. His mother worked for the phone company. He'd been in practice with Bill Boyd and Myron Leavitt. Then

304

*Law
Is a
Profession,
Not a
Trade*

Jim was elected justice of the peace. He was coming out of that when he came into our firm, so we assumed he was rich. [laughter] I never had personal difficulty with Jim. When he and Rogers left, they formed a law firm. Then Brennan ran for county commissioner, and they split up.

Rogers built a big firm, and Earl joined that for awhile. Earl had gotten tired of not making any money with me. [laughter] Jim knew how to handle that part of it. Later, Brennan ran for judge and was elected to a couple of terms.[1] I appeared before him and thought he was a fine judge. All the lawyers in town knew we had been partners. Brennan would remind the other side that he and I had been partners, and he'd recuse himself if they wanted him to. I don't think it would have made any difference one way or another—Jim was going to call it the way he sees it.

I hired Margaret Willoughby, a Boulder City girl, when she was in law school to work summers as a clerk. When she got out, we hired her. She's a wonderful lawyer. We represented a big company, I think in Minnesota, and brought a suit for them against some local person who owed them a lot of money. They had complicated defenses. Margaret handled that case and did a good job of it. After it was over, the company hired her as counsel, and she moved there. The last I knew, she had become general counsel and secretary, and the firm had moved to Phoenix. I still come across some of her work and think, "Gosh, Margaret did a great job." I hated to see Margaret go.

I also hired the first black legal secretary in town. I think this is when I was alone—this had to have been sometime in 1959. I needed a secretary—I had one, but I was alone, and my secretary needed help. Two black ladies came to see me. One was Mickie McMillan. I interviewed them . . . or they interviewed me. It was a few minutes before noon, and I said, jeez, I was sorry; I'd love to hire them, but I didn't have a vacancy. They were polite, and they left.

I sat and thought, "What kind of a horse's ass am I? I've been doing everything I could for as long as I remember to advance the cause of civil rights. I don't believe in discrimination, and yet the first time I'm personally put to the test, I take a cop-out." I ran out the door and caught them. Mickie became my secretary, and she was a good one. The truth is, she was probably testing me, and when I said yes, she didn't know what the hell to do. [laughter]

When she found out I had hired a black woman, my secretary didn't say anything. I later asked her what she thought. She said, "Well, I would have quit, except I couldn't afford to give up the job." Then she went on to say, "I'm sure glad I didn't, because Mickie's wonderful." I got a call from the legal secretaries' association telling me she'd better not apply for membership—she wouldn't be admitted. I simply said I didn't know she'd applied.

Among the first people we had met when we came to Las Vegas, of course, were the McNamees. Joe McDonald was representing Loy Martinet—married to Ann McNamee—and Julian Moore, married to Ann's sister Fran, in an air conditioning and heating business. Loy went into the insurance business. He had been a client, and we had become friends. Now he was opening his own office.

305

*Law
Is a
Profession,
Not a
Trade*

At the same time I wanted to have my own building. I hated signing that rent check every month. [laughter] I didn't have any money, but I got to know Millard Sloan. Sloan owned land on the north side of Sahara—it was still San Francisco Street instead of Sahara. Bertha's was under construction on the corner, and across from that was the jewelry store, Christensen's. He was boot-leg subdividing it, selling off lots. Can't do that anymore. [laughter]

I needed a partner, and Loy would be good. We could build a building. His office could occupy part of it; my offices occupy part of it; and our payments would go to pay off a mortgage. Then we'd own a building, and the payments wouldn't be any more than the rent, maybe less. We'd be paying the rent to ourselves. The problem is, where do we get the down payment? Millard agreed to sell us the lot for $50,000, and he would take a note—just a personal note—without a mortgage. Then we would apply to Frontier Savings for a loan. Millard's brother-in-law was on the board of directors of Frontier.

It's a beautiful building. It was a nice office, and we had plenty of room . . . nice place to play bridge. Sara did most of the design—ideal for a law office. We made a mistake: we put a second floor on it, because we got greedy. We thought we'd make money by renting it out. That drove me crazy. We couldn't keep the son-of-a-bitch rented because we neglected it.

When we moved in in May 1964, Lee Page pulled a trick on us. A sign goes up across the street on a vacant lot, "Coming: Future home of Mike's Motorcycle Repair Shop." God, how could the city give permission to a motorcycle repair shop to be built where it's zoned for offices? I called city hall, talked to the clerk.

"Oh yes, the city gave them the zoning."

I called Phil Mirabelli, the city commissioner: "How on earth could you do that?"

He said, "Sorry, Ralph. Nobody was here to object."

It was a scam. Lee had given a note to the telephone person in the zoning department saying that if Denton calls, tell him this. He keyed Mirabelli into it. We ended up with a dental office across from us.

When we got the mortgage paid off, Loy and I sold the building. Loy was retiring, and he sold his agency. I bought a building next door that the same architect had built, kind of a duplicate, except smaller so I would not be tempted to build a firm again. [laughter] And I wouldn't be paying rent. I think Mark was back before I sold the Denmar building. I added a library and conference room, and that got too crowded. I sold that and bought the house on Seventh Street where we are now, and that's too crowded. But

306

*Law
Is a
Profession,
Not a
Trade*

Bill Kellett (left) and Lee Page.

with great pride and pleasure, I tell folks, "I haven't paid rent to anybody since pounds on table 1964!"

Guys are paying as high as $2 a square foot per month for rent in offices now. Like the old gambler says, "They got to beat everybody they play with." They can't book no losers, or they're not going to be able to pay their rent. Can you imagine? You've got a 2,000-square-foot office, and how much rent? I think that's part of why lawyers are seen as out only for money. God almighty! What are you going to charge if you're a general practitioner? The big firms pay for enormous square footage. I have the luxury of practicing law. If I don't want to charge, I don't charge. If I just want to charge a little, I just charge a little, or I make it up on the guy that can afford it. I don't see how big firms can do it. Plus, they pay themselves good salaries and figure that's part of the overhead. [laughter]

I can't think of a better way I could have spent my life than in the private practice of law—really! I've been completely happy in my occupation. I've been fortunate. I've heard it expressed that the private, general practice of law in a small setting is the last great job in America. Think about it. You can make a decent living. You have the chance, like the prospector, of hitting a big one. Your only bosses are your clients, but if they leave, more will come in. It gives you a freedom other people don't have—a freedom to participate in politics, to run for office, because you know the worst that can happen is you lose, and you'll have to go back to practicing law.

In addition, you meet the most interesting people from all walks of life. I think of the black woman I represented years ago in a divorce. She had three children. Her husband was brutal. He made a good income. The court ordered him to pay child support and her attorney's fee, which he didn't do, and you didn't have the remedies you do now. Every time I would try to collect it, cite him for contempt, he'd go to the apartment on the Westside where she lived and make her life miserable.

Finally, she said, "Let's not try anymore. I'd rather be rid of him completely. I'll manage to take care of the kids." She paid me $5 a month. She *insisted* I give her a bill. I gave her a bill for the minimum fee for an uncontested divorce. She paid that off over a period of years. That was a *sacrifice* to her, and I felt guilty taking it; but on the other hand, it would injure her self-respect if I didn't. One of the finest women I've known—devoted to taking care of her children, to paying her way. General practice law makes an egalitarian out of you, I think.

Insofar as gambling is concerned, I've represented owners, dealers, people in menial chores. Many of my friends today, our relationship started out as attorney-client. When I ran for office, you'd be surprised how many of these people, who'd been my clients, helped me. You look across the desk and see a human being, not dollar signs. I never could have been happy in a big firm where I had to account to partners or superiors, justify what I was charging. To me, the essence has been the absolute freedom and independence.

The days of the small firm and the general practitioner, as we become a big city, are rapidly ending. Most are going into big firms. The changes are, essentially, in advertising. Most personal injury work goes to those who advertise on television, and big work goes to the big firms. Even so, my dad used to say, "Even a hog will root up a pearl once in a while." Once in a while, a good P.I. case or a large matter of some other kind—an estate matter or business transaction—comes in, and we're delighted to have it, and I think handle it well.

Those things we don't feel we're up to snuff on, we'll refer out. If a client of ours is a creditor in a bankruptcy case, we feel perfectly competent to handle those. If an old client wanted to go into bankruptcy, we might consider doing the original petition. We do not file petitions for people to go into bankruptcy: we just don't like that kind of practice. People ought to pay their debts. That doesn't mean I don't believe there's a place for bankruptcy law, but I think there's an awful lot of abuse.

A lot of cases you don't like to take, but if they're clients, you take them. I don't like to get involved in child custody and support. The lawyers in Las Vegas were all general practitioners until maybe fifteen years ago. Now we have this separate family court with a bunch of rules and procedures. It's just become a bureaucratic maze I prefer not to walk through unless I have to. I'm afraid I go to family court and I've got kind of a chip on my shoulder. I expect it to be unpleasant and distasteful before I ever get there, which isn't the proper attitude to have. [laughter]

307

*Law
Is a
Profession,
Not a
Trade*

308

*Law
Is a
Profession,
Not a
Trade*

I want to be certain our client gets the best possible result that can be obtained. If it's a will, I want to be certain it's thorough and complete, and that I know enough about the client's affairs to point out problems that can conceivably come up. In other words, I want to do a good job for people. If that involves me consulting with somebody else, I'm very happy to do it.

The practice of law isn't as much fun now as it was before, in general or for me. When my son Mark came to practice with me, I was delighted, because I never tried to interfere in his decisions as to his career. He was through college before he told me he wanted to be a lawyer, and I was thrilled to death that he did. He never mentioned coming in with me until he'd finished law school, and I was thrilled at that. I was worried for fear it might not be the right career choice for him, because it was changing. But I told him one of the great things about practicing law was your association with your colleagues, other lawyers, and the friendships and respect you develop for other lawyers, and how I found it rewarding to get to know other practitioners of the art, so to speak. There was a great collegiality.

You were taught in law school—or at least I was, and I think everybody heard the same language—that you should strive mightily as adversaries but sup as friends, that the case belonged to the clients, not to the lawyers. Sometimes, there's a little stress, and it would take a week or two, maybe a month after a case was over before you got so you weren't mad at the other guy or vice versa. [laughter] To a certain extent, we've lost that collegiality. It seems to me there's a mean-spiritedness with lots of lawyers.

I had a case recently and dreaded calling the other lawyer. I didn't know him. You're scared now, about whose word you can take and whose you can't. (Didn't used to be. You knew after a while which lawyers were trustworthy. Very few were not, so you could take a man's word.) I thought, "I'll call him and see how he views the case." I was completely charmed—as nice as he could be and interested in resolving the matter with as little expense as possible to our clients. Isn't that part of the role of lawyers—to resolve disputes and prevent the necessity of them going to court, if possible? You can't always do that, but you should try. This young lawyer impressed me greatly. We had the case settled in about forty-five minutes on the phone. *That*, now, is the exception rather than the rule. Years ago, it would have been the rule rather than the exception.

I think the public, in one respect, is wrong: lawyers are given too much credit for the outcome of the average case. A decision should be based upon the *facts*. I don't mean to minimize the efforts of a good lawyer, or the effect of legal argument to the judge or jury. Whether the lawyer is a great speaker should not have much to do with it, and ordinarily does not. But I remember we won one case, and my client said I was better than Perry Mason. Clients expect certain things out of you as a result of the television shows they've seen. If a lawyer gets all of his facts into evidence, he's done his job. Argument is more effective with a jury than a judge.

A lawyer's duty is to present the law in as well-written a fashion as possible. When I started practicing, you had a complaint and an answer, deposition or discovery was done, and you went to trial. You'd make your oral argument, cite cases, and the judge would make notes and generally rule from the bench. But the new rules and procedures don't seem to take costs into consideration. It costs the client more money to pay the attorney. We used to strive to simplify cost; we don't do that anymore. [laughter]

I haven't done criminal cases for a long time except where it's a client. Consequently, everything isn't right at my fingertips—that is, knowledge. There are no great mysteries in criminal law, but you have to keep up. I've had judges who didn't have any criminal practice tell me it didn't take long to pick up on the nuances. When I was practicing criminal law back in the 1950s and 1960s, it wasn't remunerative because most of your clients were crooks. If you got them off, they'd skip. If you didn't, most of them were busted. Now it's different. Drug dealers got money coming out of their whatever, and defense lawyers representing them get big retainers.

I defended a guy for heisting a clothing store and got him off. After the verdict, I had to go to Reno. When I came back, he was at the airport to meet me, and he had a suit of clothes to give me as a gift. No labels in them, so I thought, "Maybe old H. did knock over that store." [laughter] But I accepted the suit. That was the payment.

The bar keeps talking about public relations campaigns to make the image of lawyers more favorable. They're wasting their time. This attitude has been present since the profession started, because you're always in controversy. The best way for lawyers to stop it is to conduct themselves as lawyers should.

Half the people are going to be mad at lawyers. Maybe more, because my clients, who may think I'm a fine lawyer, think the rest of them are a bunch of . . . you know. But I'll tell you, when you need one, most people I know want the help of a lawyer. Most of them are grateful when you do a good piece of work for them, whether it be a will, a trust, contract. One of the things that has pleased me through the years, and I think this is probably true of every lawyer: I treasure some of the little notes I've gotten from clients, thanking me for the manner in which I handled their business.

I hate to admit it: at times you take an automatic dislike to somebody. Thank God that doesn't happen much. But that has happened to me, when a client comes in, and I just say, "Jeez, I'm too busy at the present time to handle this matter." A client should have the same attitude. Question them; talk to them. Find out if you think you can establish the rapport, because the attorney-client relationship depends at least upon mutual trust.

I think it's terrible that lawyers advertise. I resent it because I think it cheapens the profession. We're a profession, we're not a trade. I know there's another side of that argument. The best way to select a lawyer is like the best way to select a doctor: find out their qualifications, which you can do, and

309

*Law
Is a
Profession,
Not a
Trade*

310

*Law
Is a
Profession,
Not a
Trade*

their reputation. Ask people. There's a legal referral service. You can call the bar association. Hopefully, you find someone who knows somebody. Then, be certain that when you start the relationship, if you have any questions in your mind, discuss the lawyer's qualifications.

The legal profession is less cohesive today because there are so many of us, and we're spread around. It used to be you could see half the lawyers in town at 10:00 most mornings, having coffee at the Hickorywood Barbecue on Fremont, talking to each other. That used to be true on Saturday mornings, too, because the court's calendars were called. Every lawyer in town would meet. In each department, the judge would tell you when your case was set. Then everybody would walk over to Fremont and have coffee and go back to the office, and at noon go to lunch and then go home. We kept the offices open Saturday mornings for a long time—the courts too, until the judges wanted to shut down.

We have had a lot of great lawyers in Las Vegas, present company excepted. [laughter] Without question, Harry Claiborne is one of the finest trial lawyers I've ever seen. Quick. Able to think on his feet. A delivery like an evangelical preacher. [laughter] A great persuasive orator is Harry. And what made him such was not only his delivery, but he had a great deal of street sense and understood people's emotions, knew how to get people stirred up. Harry was a *great* trial lawyer. I was *not* a great trial lawyer, but, I think, a good one.

George Dickerson was a good trial lawyer, because he was always well-prepared and had the fire in his belly to fight for his client. You're not trying to make friends. You would call George a good speaker, but I was always most impressed with George's thoroughness and fire—he and Claiborne are completely different. Actually, I can't think of any lawyer in town I ever tried a case against that I didn't think was a worthy opponent. Might have been a couple of exceptions, but by and large, we had a good bar here.

I would say the federal bench has also been outstanding—good men who worked hard and felt the responsibility of their office . . . sometimes a little irascible, but that illness goes with the territory. [laughter] A federal judge said no man should have as much power over other men as he had. Constantly, he had to make certain he was not abusing that power. Not every judge I have known has felt that way, but most have.

I only had one appearance before Claiborne as a federal judge, and consequently have not had enough experience with him to judge his performance on the bench. First case I tried in federal court was before Roger Foley. I tried cases before Roger D. Foley, his son, Bruce Thompson, Ed Reed. My experience would lead me to conclude that they were fine judges, every one of them, a credit to the bench and bar. I don't have any federal judges any place else to compare them with, but we've had outstanding federal judges in my time here. We have outstanding federal judges on the bench right now.

Our state supreme court has been in great controversy the last few years. I don't know enough about that to judge, but I have no hesitancy in saying that until that controversy developed, I always had the utmost faith in our supreme court. That controversial period, I think, has shaken confidence in that court, as have the campaigns for election to that court.

Johnnie Rawlinson became Nevada's first black federal judge, then on the Ninth Circuit. I think it's wonderful that we have a society now where a person of color can aspire to be United States District judge, where a woman can aspire to be a United States District judge. I think that's wonderful, a vindication and a pleasure to people who worked in the civil rights movement.

There's no question in my mind that judges, at least on our state court level, should be elected. There's too great a tendency to take jobs away from the electorate and make them appointive. Vacancies should be filled by appointment by the governor until the next election. Every governor I've known took the appointment of judges as a serious matter and generally knew the people they were appointing, or knew well the people recommending their appointment. By and large, I think the system worked well.

A few years ago, in an attempt to remove it from politics, the legislature created a judicial selection committee. Now, instead of the governor just appointing the judge, this committee takes an application from anybody who wants it. They read the application, conduct an interview, and select three people out of the pool to be furnished to the governor, and the governor must appoint from that three. You're limiting the governor's original power to appoint district judges by saying, "Yes, you can appoint judges, but you only got three people to choose from."

Some governors like to get rid of as much responsibility as they can, but a good governor should be jealous of his prerogatives. In a sense, by creating this committee, you're depriving the people's representative. It diminishes the governor's power. And believe it or not—I hate to say this—all government is politics, and politics should not be a bad word. It should be as Adlai Stevenson defined it: "Politics is a struggle over policy." That is a righteous struggle. The governor should have the right to name people in whom he has confidence.

We're talking about a judge or any official—the only thing that keeps their feet near the ground is that they have to come back for reelection. I don't know why the judicial department is more sacred than the legislative and executive, that the people shouldn't have a right to determine who their judges are and the right to throw them out. Historically, once a judge is a judge in Nevada, few have been defeated for reelection. If a judge is doing a good job and the bar is satisfied, they're reelected. In the last few years, we've had some terrible campaigns and seen judges defeated.

If you don't have a basic faith in the collective wisdom of the people and want to keep chipping away at the rights of the people, you are chipping at

311

Law
Is a
Profession,
Not a
Trade

312

*Law
Is a
Profession,
Not a
Trade*

your belief in democracy and the ability of the people to govern themselves. My God, if we don't trust the people, how can we trust anything, governmentally? I do think somebody has to figure out a better way to finance not only judicial campaigns, but all campaigns. I don't think judges have a right to make the rules different for them than for anybody else.

I was never interested in being a judge. I tried once, but it was not out of interest in being a judge. Mark had been practicing with me for a while. (They were the happiest years of my life, practicing with my son.) I was worried, seeing how the town was changing, the big firms and that sort of thing, that chaining himself to a small general practice office was interfering with his career. This vacancy on the bench came up, so I thought, "I'll put my name in the hat. If I get it, then Mark will be free to decide whether he wants to continue that kind of practice or whether he wants to go with a big firm or whether he wants to go into public employment." I went before the judicial selection committee, and they didn't select me, which was all right. I didn't really want to be a judge. I've always wanted to be one of the players.

Notes

1. James Brennan served as a Clark County district court judge from 1975 until resigning in 1989. Since then, he has heard cases as a senior judge.

28 | Hank Was a Hell of a Lot Smarter Than I Am

I don't know when I first started doing legal work for Hank Greenspun. I think it was after Sawyer was elected governor, but I would like to think Hank's motives were that he needed work done, my reputation was such that he thought I could do a good job . . . and he must have gotten mad at whoever was representing him. [laughter] Hank didn't need me to have connections. I represented him sometimes, and sometimes I didn't, because there would be a political conflict of interest, and I suppose a governmental conflict when I was on the board of county commissioners.

Hank told me one of the reasons he stayed with me. Sally was away, in college or some place, and she called me. You shouldn't be interrupted when you're talking to a client, but I would always take calls from my kids. I apologized to Hank, and I took the call. Later, he said, "One of the reasons I've stayed with you is the way you feel toward your family."

How to describe Hank? Adjectives to describe one of the most interesting, complex individuals I've ever known are hard to come by. To try and capture his character and him with words, when I have as limited a vocabulary as I have, is difficult. Let me try a few: guts—I guess courage is synonymous with guts; passionate in his views, generous, sometimes downright cheap. Brilliant, ambitious, tolerant, the zeal of a missionary on causes he believed in, vindictive, forgiving, pragmatic, warm, sometimes cold. Loving. Loyal. I think he might disagree with any adjective that cast disfavor upon him. [laughter] I meant to say vain. [laughter]

Without question, Hank could be the most difficult man in the world to represent. I said he was brilliant; I should have said smart, too, great street sense. We had filed a lawsuit. Hank was having a fight with Milton Schwartz. Schwartz had a big tank of propane gas in the middle of town. Hank was mad at Milton; Milton was mad at Hank.[1] What are we going to do about the tank? I did a little research and determined it was really dangerous. If it exploded, Christ, it could wipe out that whole end of town!

314

*Hank Was
a Hell
of a Lot
Smarter
Than
I Am*

This is a real old statute: if the county commissioners find there's a public nuisance, they're supposed to instruct the district attorney to abate that nuisance. Under the statute, if the commissioners have knowledge of the existence of a public nuisance, and don't instruct the district attorney to abate the nuisance, they forfeit their offices. If the district attorney, after being instructed by the county commissioners, doesn't do it, *he* suffers forfeiture of office.

I prepared a letter. We made a complaint to the commission that this was a public nuisance, and we demanded that they abate the nuisance. They entered an order, the order went down to the district attorney, and it got into court. Howard Babcock was the judge, and it was tried as to whether that was a public nuisance and should be abated.[2]

My son Mark and Brian Greenspun were representing Hank. Of course, Hank is at the trial. When you're trying a case for Hank, if you're sitting next to him, he's telling you what you're supposed to ask the witness. Hank was a lawyer, and he'd been trying to get Mark or Brian to ask a certain

question. He finally wrote a note and handed it to Mark and Brian. We saved it. He says, "If you don't ask this question, you're both fired." [laughter] The case went on, was won, and Schwartz had to move his tank, thereby saving that part of the community from a disaster.

Very seldom does your client go up with you to the Supreme Court and argue. [laughter] When we argued the Greenspun-Hughes case, Hank sat at the table with me. I'm on my feet arguing, and he's constantly pulling on my coat telling me what to say. He did not accept your judgment as a substitute for his. [laughter] Sometimes that's a help, sometimes a hindrance. In Hank's case, it was generally a help. I make no secret that Hank was a hell of a lot smarter than I am.

Ralph in the Clark County Courthouse, mid-1970s, Hank Greenspun behind him.

I learned a lot from Hank. He sought power; that doesn't make him bad. He was criticized from time to time for the causes for which he used such power, but he had the courage of his convictions. He wasn't afraid of anybody—not the most powerful man in Nevada, the most powerful agency of the government, the most powerful man in the Senate, the most powerful man in the world.

Hank was generous, yet there were always complaints that his wage scale at the *Sun* was low. Yet I know of examples of his generosity to people that you wouldn't believe—former employees—and the manner and method in which he helped . . . there were many people in the community he lavished help on that nobody ever knew about. Had he wanted it known, he could have made it known.

Before I represented him, my daughter had to have eye surgery in San Francisco that involved her being in the hospital for six weeks. She was little, but the boys were little too, so Sara and I got a babysitter, and we took Sally to that children's hospital there. We found a room in a small hotel, the Franciscan. After the surgery, Sara stayed, and I came back to take care of the kids and practice law.

On weekends, I'd fly with the boys to be with their mother and Sally. Damned expensive, flying back and forth. In those days, the Dunes and Hacienda were flying airplanes from San Francisco, and I was sometimes able to hitch a ride. (Hell, they had pianos on the planes. The boys thought that was great.) From time to time, I had to buy tickets, and I bought them through Willis and Cole Travel Agency.

One time, I hadn't gotten a bill, and I called Mike Cole at the travel agency to ask him about it. He said, "Oh, Hank Greenspun called and asked me to send your bill to him." I hardly knew Hank at that time, but he knew the situation. I was a new lawyer having a hell of a time getting going, and he was sensitive to this child who had to have this eye operation. That's an act of kindness and generosity you wouldn't ordinarily expect. So, I used to be offended when I'd hear people talking about Hank not paying his help good wages. I don't know if that's true, but he was awfully nice to me.

Hank was funny, he had a great sense of humor. I can't really put my finger on any specific time, but I know I'd be in hysterics, sometimes, when we were talking. I don't mean funny in the sense of crude or dirty jokes—he could see humor in situations.

I mentioned loyalty. People Hank knew back in New York and law school—friends out of the past—Hank helped. One time he was going to loan a friend money. I knew the friend was not reliable, but Hank was going to loan him money upon security of a master lease on a shopping center in San Diego. I was to draw the note and the assignment of the lease. Knowing the guy, I thought I'd better check into it. The man did not have a shopping center; he had made up a lease to show to Hank.

I called Hank, and he came over. I said, "Hank, there isn't any shopping center." He laughed. A guy tried to con him, and Hank laughed. He thought

316

*Hank Was
a Hell
of a Lot
Smarter
Than
I Am*

that was funny. He said, "Go ahead and loan it to him anyway." So, I did. I did a note, no assignment of lease. We had to sue the guy in Hawaii to get the money back. But Hank was a good sport. He appreciated a good con man. [laughter]

One adjective I didn't use was conniving. [laughter] Hank could connive with the best of them. One time, Temple Beth Sholom was short of money. The elders were meeting to get contributions. (Lloyd Katz told me this story, so if it isn't true, you have to blame Lloyd. Lloyd having predeceased us, you'll have to blame Edythe, his wife.[3]) They were putting the lug on these people for donations, and Hank made a big pledge. Lloyd was presiding and said, "For God's sakes, Hank, you haven't paid your last year's pledge."

Hank says, "What's the matter? Isn't my marker good in this joint anymore?" [laughter]

Another time, two *very important* savings and loan people loaned money to Hank to rebuild the *Sun* after the fire.[4] Hank was delinquent in the payments. They asked me to set up a lunch meeting with Hank at the Sands. They're about half-scared. [laughter] They don't want to get in a beef with Hank. They pad pretty easily, but go to great lengths to explain the terrible position they're in with this delinquent loan. Hank listened sympathetically to their woes. When it was over, he said, "I understand the trouble you're in, fellows. I'll do anything in the world I can to help you. But I can't pay you." [laughter] I don't know what else he thought he could do to help.

He was a hard-working man, busy all the time. He really did love the paper. God, he was an outstanding writer. I've often thought if he did nothing but write on great issues, it would have been a *wonderful* collection. A lot of his writings, though, particularly toward the end of his life, dealt with some of his own business matters, and it injured his credibility a little.

Hank was a victim of cheating in a gin game at the Friar's Club in Los Angeles. Maury Friedman went to jail for it, and Hank was the first guy to write the judge and ask to give Maury probation. Hank figured he was three times seven: if he couldn't protect himself, that was his worry. [laughter] After Maury went to the big house, Hank wrote to get him paroled early. That's Hank. You'd have thought he'd been madder than the devil.

I did not represent Hank in connection with Howard Hughes until, if memory serves me, 1969, when he sold the Paradise Valley Country Club to Hughes and entered into contracts to sell Hughes unimproved acreage in what we now call Green Valley. Out of those transactions came the lawsuit. I'd known Hank well, but we spent a lot of time together in connection with this case, and I got to know him better. Smart son-of-a-bitch. [laughter] Hell of a lot smarter than I am.

There came time for a closing. We met at the Hughes Tool Company offices in Commercial Center. When we got there, Dick Gray, their attorney, handed me the contracts and a promissory note for $4,000,000, which they expected Hank and Barbara to sign to the Hughes Tool Company. I was

surprised—contracts weren't required, because it was a cash transaction—
and I learned Hughes Tool Company was prepared to close the sale on the
country club and pay the price for that. Hank had borrowed $4,000,000
from Hughes, and this new note was to replace the old note. The payment
schedule was different, and it would be secured differently—by stock in the
Las Vegas Sun. But they weren't prepared to close the transaction on the rest
of the acreage, so they had a little contract in which they agreed to buy it.

317

*Hank Was
a Hell
of a Lot
Smarter
Than
I Am*

At that point, I said, "I can't have my clients sign a new note for $4
million unless you return me the old note. I don't want two notes out there."
That note was in Houston, and it would take them some time to get that
note here. I asked them, "Then at least change this note and make a reference in this note—that is, the second note—that it replaces and is in payment of that other note." That was done. The sale on the golf course closed,
and we signed the contracts for the sale of the rest of the land.

Time went on, and the contract for the sale of the land never did clear,
nor did I ever get back the first note. The next thing I know, Sam Lionel,
representing Hughes Tool, recorded a deed of trust, which Hank had given
them when he borrowed the $4 million, and wrote a letter to Hank demand-
ing payment in full of the first note on it, or we're going to foreclose. I wasn't
aware that deed of trust was in existence. I filed a lawsuit against them to
cancel the first note and enjoin foreclosure. We got a temporary restraining
order, then a motion for preliminary injunction was argued before Judge
Joseph O. McDaniel from Elko, and he granted it.[5] We were involved in
that suit for almost seven years. Ultimately, we were successful. The first
note was canceled; the deed of trust was canceled; and Hughes Tool Company was ordered to pay Hank. Hughes paid punitive compensatory damages of $1 million.

To get to that point, we went to trial twice in Elko. Judge McDaniel was
from Elko, and it was either him come down to Las Vegas or us go up there.
We thought it would be more peaceful, with less harassment from coverage,
if we tried it in Elko. We could go all day long every day. And we went to the
supreme court three times. Once, we took it to the supreme court to try and
overturn an evidentiary ruling made by McDaniel, then went back to trial.
After we went to trial, John Squire Drendel in Reno became associated with
me. The second part of the trial in Elko, I wasn't on my own. Squire was
there and deserves a lot of credit for the outcome.

Then, Hughes appealed to the supreme court. The court upheld the
judgment canceling the first note and deed of trust that secured it, but reversed on punitive damages. Then we had all sorts of little battles: disquali-
fying judges, motions to disqualify judges in the supreme court, rehearings.
Ultimately, the supreme court called the case back. The judges who had
been on the court disqualified themselves, and the governor appointed four
district judges. Charlie Springer was a new judge who hadn't been on the
court when the case was first heard. The matter was briefed again, and that
court reversed the first supreme court and upheld the punitive damage award.

318

*Hank Was
a Hell
of a Lot
Smarter
Than
I Am*

It was interesting. It went on for a long time. It was a lot of work, a lot of stress. It was an experience, representing Hank with the help of Julie Yabloc, not a member of the Nevada bar, hadn't practiced law for years and years, but was a friend of Hank's and kibitzed. Getting to know Julie was almost worth the work involved in the case. Julie had grown up in New York City in the 1920s. I think he and Hank met in law school at St. John's. Julie went to Boys High School in Brooklyn—in those days, I am told, where bright kids went. Julie was bright and a good football player. He was quarterback, and he got a football scholarship to Colgate University in upstate New York. He said it was the first time in his life he realized everybody in the world wasn't Jewish. [laughter] He was an All-American quarterback, then played for the New York Yanks—the old professional team. Julie said the mob owned them. They'd come in the dressing room after the game and pay you in cash. [laughter] Julie knew every Gilbert-Sullivan operetta by heart. I'm in his house in California, he's in front of his record player conducting, leading the band and singing every word. [laughter] He was a law partner with Mickey Marcus, another boy from that area who graduated from West Point, had been in the OSS during World War II. When Israel gained its independence, Mickey was a general in the Israeli army. Nobody's sure how he was killed. A movie was made about him.[6]

I wouldn't say the case was complicated. There were serious legal questions, but complicated, no. All the people involved were complicated. So many nuances, and trying to get to the bottom of the facts: What actually did happen? Why did not the second sale go through—things of that kind? Why, out of the clear blue sky, did they record a deed of trust they'd had for two or three years, and demand payment in full?

We got all involved in the law of discovery. Did I have a right to take Hughes's deposition? He's a party to the action—his company. The court found he was a managing agent of the company, and, ordinarily, I would have had the right to take the deposition of the managing agent of the company I was suing. I served notices to take his deposition in my office, and Hughes never showed up. Shocking, and the judge decided he didn't have to. [laughter] We were fighting constantly over matters of that kind.

I don't know how Hank ended up with me handling the case, although I was doing most of Hank's work prior to that, after the 1966 election. I just was not involved in these business arrangements Hank and Hughes Tool Company had. Of course, I read the paper and knew what Hank was saying about them. I had met Bob Maheu while they were buying the Desert Inn and the Sands.

I didn't know Howard Hughes from a bale of hay, but I knew who he was, and I remembered his testimony before that Senate committee trying to catch one of his employees for influence peddling during the Eightieth Congress. It might have been one of his last public appearances. I went to listen to it. God, did he take care of Homer Ferguson! [laughter] Hughes just destroyed that committee.

Hughes really told Ferguson off. They hadn't been able to serve this employee a subpoena to appear before the committee. Finally, Ferguson says to Hughes, "Will you have him here to testify before this committee?"

Hughes was silent for a minute, and then he says, "No, Senator, I don't think I will. He's been before you so many times. You've hounded him. He's given you papers, he's talked to you. No, I don't think I will have him here." He just really did a job on that committee.

Hank's impression of Hughes obviously changed over time, but mine really didn't, not having had any to begin with. It was my opinion he's got to be half nuts, anyway, just from what I'd read. I had no contact with him. I had a little social contact from time to time with Bob Maheu, his right hand man. I had a high opinion of Dick Gray, their attorney, but didn't have that much contact with him. I was not really in that loop when the loans were being made and that stuff.

Sam Lionel, who represented Hughes, was Sawyer's partner. Grant never mentioned the case to me, nor did I ever mention it to him. We did get a little annoyed one time when we went up to the Supreme Court. We'd filed a motion to disqualify Judge Noel Manoukian.[7] The attorneys for both sides were called to meet with the court to discuss that motion. Of course, Sam came up. And Grant came, sat there, and didn't open his mouth. It seemed obvious the Hughes Tool Company had insisted that he be there. Grant had appointed a couple of those justices. I think my client might have had a thing or two to say about it, but he didn't.

The grounds for the disqualification were that word came to us that one of the lawyers from the Lionel Sawyer firm had an *ex parte* communication with one of the justices concerning a case that firm had pending in the supreme court. If such was the case, we thought that judge should disqualify himself. The darndest thing happened: Brian and I went to Reno to talk to the person who told us about this to make sure our information was correct. We prepared a motion, and Brian went to Carson City to file it in the court clerk's office. I went to the airport to catch an earlier plane back to Las Vegas. I'm sitting on the plane waiting for it to take off, and Brian gets on. He said, "When I filed it, they handed me the ruling denying our motion for rehearing." Clearly, we're a week late. I pondered that all the way back to Las Vegas, then I got an *ex parte* order from the court to recall the *remittitur*, in other words, to hold that order in abeyance until this was heard. That's when the supreme court called us up to discuss the procedure.

In the meantime, one of the justices got a snoot full of whiskey and made comments to the press about Hank. [laughter] Hell, we filed a motion to disqualify him. Now we've got two judges we want disqualified. The opinion that reversed the trial court on punitive damages was three to two. It just happened the two we wanted to disqualify were in the majority. [laughter] We got involved in procedural things, raised the question whether our affidavit was sufficient to support a disqualification. The first question was, who gets to vote? Can these two judges? We won that fight.

320

*Hank Was
a Hell
of a Lot
Smarter
Than
I Am*

We had sought to disqualify Justices Manoukian and Gordon Thompson, and when we won, Sam files a motion to disqualify one of the other judges.[8] Now, nobody knows what the hell to do, and we all go home. [laughter] A year or two later, the court called the case back. Thompson and Cameron Batjer had left, Springer came on, everybody disqualified themselves, the governor appointed four district court judges to hear it, and they reversed it.[9]

Were the judges afraid of Hank? That might have been true with a couple. Some members of the courts were prejudiced against Greenspun. It went on so long, and we fought awful tough battles. I really believe the credibility of our story was accepted by the court reluctantly to begin with. But after Hughes died, all these things came out. We had been saying these things during motions for depositions and everything. Initially, when we first went up to Elko on this case, I had the feeling the attitude was that we were a bunch of Las Vegas sharpies trying to take advantage of that nice man who had given all the money to the Elko Community College, the medical school, and all those wonderful things. That was the attitude of a lot of people here.

From what I knew, that was not the case. Hank owed no duty to Hughes. He was three times seven. That was my view. Frankly, I was always hurt when I couldn't persuade people in the community. I tried to explain to my friends that Hank had a legitimate beef, and had been injured severely by it.

The Hughes saga. [laughter] It took a lot of work and energy over that seven years. It always appeared to me if there had been anybody the least bit rational in the Hughes camp, the matter would have been resolved. But Chester Davis and those guys were so bitter. When they took over, Davis said they were going to bury Hank—*bury* him. Their threats were serious, and they should have known when they took on Hank, they weren't taking on a patsy. They started that thing, and then to threaten, "We're going to bury you." I was always convinced of the justice of my cause. [laughter]

I wound up our association with a warm, kind feeling for Hank, Barbara, and their children. In my judgment, wonderful people. His devotion to his family was wonderful to see. He adored Barbara and the kids. I dealt with Barbara from time to time on her own. Barbara's smart as a whip. She'd make a few business judgments through the years, and Hank would be madder than hell. It turned out the best judgments they made. [laughter] I like Brian. His interest went more to the business world, but a good, smart lawyer.

Mike O'Callaghan went to work for Hank when he went out as governor in 1979. When Mike came to the paper, frankly, it surprised me. Here are two very bright, headstrong men, both very ego-driven—I don't mean that as bad—able to get along. You'd expect that two strong men would ultimately clash. And I'm not being critical of either one of them when I say what I've just said. But I thought, "This is going to be interesting to see how long this will last." [laughter] And it lasted, much to their credit, both of them.

I described Hank as "tolerant." I do not recall us having disagreements over a matter such as civil rights, Vietnam. We had political disagreements, which we voiced, but he didn't think everybody that disagreed with him was a bad person. He was tolerant of other people's views, unless they reached the point of what he thought was idiocy. [laughter] As badly as he hated McCarran, he understood my loyalty to him. Hank gave loyalty to his friends, almost to a point where I think some would be critical of him.

321

*Hank Was
a Hell
of a Lot
Smarter
Than
I Am*

Hank's wife, Barbara, was an influence on him, and so was Ed Morgan, a lawyer in Washington, D.C. Hank was deeply devoted and grateful and loyal to him. I think Morgan had been in the FBI and worked for the Senate committee on political corruption. Hank had written a column about McCarthy, and the Republicans indicted Hank and accused him of violating the federal statute, in that it would incite somebody to kill McCarthy. That's a serious charge. Ed comes out from Washington to defend Hank. Hank was acquitted. In those days, Hank was doing well, but he was sometimes struggling to meeting payroll, stuff like that. Ed gave him a huge bill— $10,000—and on the bottom, marked, "Paid In Full." Ed felt so strongly about that kind of a charge being brought. I don't think Hank ever forgot that.

Notes

1. Milton Schwartz owned not only a taxi company, but also a cable television business, and competed with Greenspun's cable company. He eventually sued Greenspun for libel and lost. Brian Greenspun, Hank's son, eventually sold the cable television company to Cox Communications in 1998 for $1.3 billion.

2. Howard Babcock served as a Clark County district court judge from 1967 until his death in 1986.

3. Lloyd Katz managed several local movie theaters. He and his wife Edythe were active in politics and the Jewish community. Lloyd Katz died in 1986, and Edythe Katz remarried and remained one of Ralph Denton's clients.

4. In November 1963, a fire destroyed the *Sun's* building. Greenspun kept the paper alive by publishing it in Southern California and having it delivered to Las Vegas. While the *Sun* built a new building—it has moved twice since—it never regained the momentum it enjoyed in news coverage and circulation before the blaze, which Greenspun long believed to have been arson.

5. Joseph O. McDaniel was an Elko County district attorney who served as district judge, 1971-91.

6. *Cast a Giant Shadow*, released in 1966, starred Kirk Douglas as Marcus with, among others, Frank Sinatra and Angie Dickinson.

322

*Hank Was
a Hell
of a Lot
Smarter
Than
I Am*

7. Noel Manoukian was appointed judge in 1974 for the newly created Ninth Judicial District for Douglas, Lyon, and Churchill Counties. He was then elected to a term, but resigned in 1977 when he was appointed to the Nevada Supreme Court to succeed the retiring David Zenoff. Manoukian was elected to a term in 1978, but defeated for reelection in 1984 by Cliff Young after a drawn-out controversy involving Manoukian challenging attorneys' fees for an estate case.

8. Gordon Thompson, a brother of U.S. District Judge Bruce Thompson, was appointed to the Nevada Supreme Court in 1961 and subsequently elected to three terms, retiring from the court in 1980.

9. Cameron Batjer was appointed to the Nevada Supreme Court in 1967 when its membership expanded from three to five justices. He served until 1981, resigning to become the head of the U.S. Parole and Probation Commission in Washington, D.C. Charles Springer was elected to the court in 1980 and served three terms.

29 | And Who Could Forget These Guys?

Bob Stupak qualifies among my other all-time most fascinating clients. [laughter] I got to know Bob well. I see him now, and he says, "God almighty, Ralph! When I first met you, you were the age I am now." I met him when he came to Las Vegas from Australia in the early 1970s. Grant referred him. *Man*, did Bob love this town—and still does. He'd made a little money, wanted to get into something, and was looking for "juice." (The term should be understood. Someone who has juice is thought to have influence in all of the right circles. I don't think juice is as important as it used to be, but Bob was looking for it.) Of course, he sought out Grant. Grant became his attorney, according to Bob, and Bob says, "The first time I wanted him to do something for me, he had a conflict of interest, and he couldn't do it. So he referred me to you."

He was an interesting kid, smart, frenetic. As a promoter, compared to Bob, P. T. Barnum was a shrinking violet. He's smart as a whip, and if you don't believe me, just ask him. [laughter] I liked Bob. In those days, Charlie LaFrance was in my office, and he and Bob were kindred souls. Charlie recognized in Bob a unique, talented person who needed direction. Bob recognized in Charlie a bright man from whom he could learn and who he enjoyed being around. Charlie would chew him out. Bob can get pretty loud in expressing his views. Charlie could tell him, "Shut up and sit down! You don't know what you're talking about!" and lay into him. Didn't bother Stupak, and they would go on the town together.

First, Bob had the Cinnabar on Ogden downtown, and I represented him in the licensing. Then his great museum on Las Vegas Boulevard South burned down. That became a big case. Bob didn't help himself when he went to the fire. They've got everybody out, and he's standing on the sidewalk, some guy from the fire department next to him, and the firemen are in there. All of a sudden, flames go shooting up from the roof. Bob said, "My God, the fire department's in there pouring gas on it!" The fireman, of course, heard that.

324

*And
Who
Could
Forget
These
Guys?*

The report never indicated arson, but said "suspicious circumstances." The insurance company declined to pay, alleging arson. We had to file a lawsuit in federal court. As happens in a lot of these cases, the day before the trial's to start, it was settled and they made payment. But there was a lot of bad publicity. Somebody makes an accusation, and half the people believe it. I never saw any evidence of arson.

When I filed suit against the insurance company, I took the insurance company's expert's deposition. One of the nice things about being a lawyer, you learn about different fields. I had to do a lot of research on arson investigation. There wasn't much. I did find one textbook and made myself knowledgeable. I took note that the arson investigation unit of the Las Vegas Fire Department had done few of the things the textbook says you're supposed to do. The last question I asked the expert, "Do you really consider yourself to be an expert in arson investigation?"

He said, "No, my field's marine." [laughter] Boats.

(After that, I had a criminal case where I defended a guy for arson. By cross-examining the state's witnesses on the methods used in investigating, and demonstrating that they didn't do any of these things, I was able to get the case knocked out. The same guy went out and did it again, though, and he came back for me to defend him a second time, and I declined.) [laughter]

When that museum burned down, God, the secret service was on Bob's tail. The walls were papered with money, mostly ones and fives, but once in a while there would be a twenty. But he had a sign, "See what a $10,000 bill looks like . . . ," implying a $10,000 bill was in there. It wasn't. There was a copy of one on the wall. But when the word 'arson' reared its head, in came the federal people, because it's a federal crime to burn money. Most of the money and the walls were saved, but they thought there was a $10,000 bill. We had a hell of a time proving to them, no, there wasn't a $10,000 bill in there. The sign just said, "See what a $10,000 bill looks like." [laughter]

From there, Bob went into that Dine Out Las Vegas Club. This is the type of work he was doing in Australia. You get these restaurants in this book, then sell the book for $25 a pop. Maybe they've got $100 or more of free meals in there—a good profit margin. This is typical Bob. [laughter] When he built Vegas World, he had a restaurant and a big plaque that it had been awarded a five-star ranking as an outstanding restaurant by Dine Out Las Vegas. [laughter] He had a picture in his restaurant of a guy with a white beard. Looked like Colonel Sanders: "This fellow recommends the chicken." [laughter] God, he was funny! He borrowed a lot of the money to build Vegas World from Valley Bank. He rented a Rolls Royce, and he'd drive that Rolls down and park it in front of the bank when he went in. He talked them into loaning him a lot of money—it was a good loan.

For a long time I didn't represent Bob. When he started Vegas World, he decided he needed juice to get his license, so he sought out a lawyer who had a close tie with the current administration. Then he'd call once in a while about doing something; I was too busy. After his accident, we did some work for Bob. Not much.

I always had a fondness for Bob, but it was like some other guys: I'd rather be their friends than their lawyers. Bob is a complex man. I'm sure he'll bound back. I had no connection to Bob's entry into politics, running for mayor, but it didn't surprise me he would do that. Didn't surprise me that he almost won, either.

325

*And
Who
Could
Forget
These
Guys?*

I have to be careful that I don't violate privilege in the way I tell about this: I was appointed in federal court to defend Terry Conger. That was a very difficult case. I wound up trying it up in Reno. That's a case someone should write a book about in the nature of Truman Capote's *In Cold Blood*. Terry had a history of small crimes. When he was a boy, he came down from Overton and stole a car—just a prank. Somebody left the keys in it, and he drove all over town all day. He didn't know what the heck to do with it, so he parked it on the police department lot. [laughter] He went by the next day. It was still there, so he took it again, and he had it three or four weeks. He was leaving it there every night, thinking they'd catch it. They didn't, so he finally parked it in a no-parking zone on Fremont Street, and it stayed there about three or four days before it was picked up by the police and towed away.

Terry was charged with robbing a bank in Overton. He put people in the vault and killed them—people he knew. He had grown up in that area. He was tried in district court for murder, and there was a plea. He got two or three life sentences to run consecutively. The feds charged him under the federal statute that robbing a bank insured by the FDIC was a federal crime. That statute provided if anybody was killed, they could be given the death penalty if the jury found them guilty. The feds decided they didn't trust Nevada to keep Terry in jail the rest of his life, so they prosecuted him.

Judge Roger D. Foley appointed me to defend Terry. I got to know him, and I found him to be one of the most shockingly interesting people I ever met. I tried through pre-trial motions to get the case dismissed, and I was fortunate in one respect. Federal kidnapping law, as far as the death penalty was concerned, was that kidnapping became a federal crime after the victim had been gone seven days or something, and the accused could be given the death penalty if a jury found him guilty. That statute was attacked constitutionally on this basis: someone charged under it could be given the death penalty only if a jury found them guilty. If they pled, the judge couldn't sentence them to death. The argument against it was, I think with some merit, that the statute coerced a lot of people to plead guilty to avoid the death penalty. While I was representing Terry, the Supreme Court held that portion of the Lindbergh statute unconstitutional, which applied to our case. So, I no longer had to worry about the capital aspects of it.

I sought dismissal of the indictment on two grounds. One, I attacked the constitutionality of the death penalty, and I said Terry had been denied a

326

*And
Who
Could
Forget
These
Guys?*

speedy trial, because they waited almost two years before they brought the federal case. The constitutionality of capital punishment was upheld by the U.S. Supreme Court the last time, five-to-four. My argument was against capital punishment, but I added, "If your honor feels bound by the doctrine of *stare decisis*, maybe it's time for the Supreme Court to take another look at capital punishment. And this would be an ideal case. My client doesn't have the money, nor do I, to finance an appeal to the Supreme Court, but if you were to rule in my client's favor on this matter, the government would appeal, and I would respond on behalf of my client."

Judge Foley thought for a few minutes, smiled, and said, "No, Mr. Denton, I'm bound by the previous ruling of the United States Supreme Court in that respect," so he denied my motion. He also denied my motion on speedy trial. I hadn't expected much there. [laughter]

When Terry was kept in the Clark County jail, he escaped and was gone for a long time. He was in solitary, and they watched him—he'd escaped before—like a hawk. Every thirty minutes, they came by. He knew when they were coming, so he's trying to cut a hole in the roof of his cell. Before they came, he would cover up where he'd been cutting. He said, "I'd tell them, 'You better look up there. I'm cutting my way out. I'm going to be out of here tomorrow night.'" They just laughed.

Finally, Terry got the hole cut. There was one floor above where his cell was, and about a three-foot crawl space between the ceiling and the floor above him. He looked around. Sure enough, the contractor had left some rope up there where they'd tied the joists before they nailed them in. Now he had a rope. He crawls to the exterior wall, which was cinder block, and knocks out however many blocks it took that he could fit through, and he let himself down on the rope. He said people were across the street watching him, and they didn't know what the hell he was doing. But he let himself down on the rope. The stories when he escaped said he must have had inside help—that this was a big planned thing.

When the sheriff's office called and told me my client was back in jail, I went to see him. In those days, you pushed a buzzer outside of the jail, the squawk box would come on, and you'd identify yourself. I pushed the buzzer, and soon the turnkey said, "Yes?"

I said, "My name's Ralph Denton. I'd like to see my client, Terry Conger, if he's in." They didn't take too kindly to that remark. [laughter]

Terry said he knew once they discovered the cell was empty, they'd stand around for thirty or forty minutes looking at the hole before they did anything. He said, "So I knew I had thirty minutes to get away from there."

I said, "Well, how did you get away?"

He says, "Oh, I walked down the street to the Fremont Hotel and caught a cab down to Tom Hanley's house." His getaway car was a cab. [laughter]

We went to trial, so I had to get the facts. I read transcripts of the preliminary hearings in state court. By then they'd transferred him to the state penitentiary—after he escaped, they decided the Clark County jail wasn't

secure enough. I went to Carson to see him. They had him in solitary con-
finement in a cave with an iron door on it. (The old state penitentiary's an
old stone quarry where they took out the stone to build the capital and all
sorts of things around Carson City in the early days.) The guy opens this
door. There's Terry, a table and chair and a light hanging from the ceiling.
The turnkey says, "When do you want me to come and let you out?"

"You're going to lock me up in there with him with no one observing?"

"Oh, yes. That's the way we do it."

"Well, I'm not going to see my client under these conditions. I'm going
to federal court from here, and I'm going to file a motion saying my client's
been deprived of his right to counsel. No attorney should have to see a client accused of that crime under those circumstances."

I went and called Governor Paul Laxalt from a pay phone. Paul couldn't
believe it. He said, "I'll call the warden." They put Terry in a cell with bars
and a guard watching us.

I tried the case in Reno. Bruce Thompson was the judge, and it was a fair
trial. Terry was convicted. He was sentenced to fifty years to commence
after he served his terms in the state penitentiary.

What amazed me, when I went into court, was that people from Overton,
family of the victims, were hissing me. Nobody seemed to realize I was doing
a job important to our society—people accused of crime have attorneys who
will make certain they're afforded all of the rights the Constitution gives to
citizens. I didn't realize the full extent to which people on the other side of
a case can hate lawyers.

It's a shame that Milton Prell's a forgotten figure. I met him in the late
1950s, became his attorney in the late 1960s. I had the utmost respect for
the man. He was a gentleman. My experience in dealing with owner types in
the gambling business had been, if they wanted to see you, they'd call and
tell you to come to the hotel. Not Mr. Prell. I was maybe twenty years younger
than he, but he would call and make an appointment to come in and talk to
me, and he treated me as a professional, not his lackey. I appreciated that
very much. A couple of times, because of exigencies, he would apologize and
say, "Would it inconvenience you to stop by the hotel on your way home
tonight? I really have to talk to you." But always he did that in an apologetic
sense.

After I got to know him, I learned a little about his background. I'm not
certain what his business was before gambling, but he came here after the
war, I think, from Butte, Montana, a wide-open town in those days, and
established the Club Bingo where the Sahara is. It was not a hotel. Then he
built the Sahara, and it was like most of the hotels on the Strip at that time:
really a motel with a casino on the front of it. The Sahara Hotel was very
successful, a good operation. I didn't represent Mr. Prell in those days, and
didn't know him. I actually met him through Hank.

327

*And
Who
Could
Forget
These
Guys?*

328

*And
Who
Could
Forget
These
Guys?*

He had a great showroom policy. He had the lounge. He brought back some great acts that became prominent for the second time in their career. Louis Prima was a good example. Louis was reborn as a celebrity and national star in the lounge at the Sahara, he and Keely Smith with Sam Butera and the Witnesses. And the lounge acts—Don Rickles was not well known until he started working the lounge at the Sahara. In addition, they had the major showroom where you had dinner shows and headline acts.

Prell sold the Sahara to Del Webb. So, in the vernacular of the trade, Prell was out of action. He bought what was then the Tally-Ho Hotel, later the Aladdin, which was ahead of its time, because there was no gambling. After he purchased it, he constructed an addition on the front: a big casino, which wasn't out of character, because most Strip hotels had originally been motels with a casino. This is when I started representing him.

Mr. Prell took good care of the people who worked for him. He gave every one of his former key people at the Sahara an opportunity to come into this. They had to buy their points, but if they didn't have the money, he would co-sign their note. In effect, he loaned them the money. Prell would guarantee the loan. There must have been fifteen or sixteen key employees allowed to buy a few points. And it was an immediate success.

A couple of stories indicated Al Parvin was one of the original stockholders. That is not true. The hotel was successful for a year or two, and Mr. Prell had a stroke. After he came back from the hospital, he sold the property to Parvin-Dohrmann. They formed Recrion Corporation. I think Recrion had mob problems from the minute they started. [laughter] Parvin had been active in Las Vegas for many years. They were out of Chicago and in the business of selling interior furnishings like tables and chairs to hotels. One of the original stockholders with Prell was Al Garbian. The new people asked Al to stay, and he declined. Then it got mixed up in all sorts of things. It became a nightmare, at least for the regulatory agencies.

Prell was generous to his employees, not just key people. He had people with him for years at the Sahara, and he knew most of them and was concerned about them. Besides Al Garbian, Jim Rivera at the Sahara became an owner at the Aladdin and was in charge of baccarat. A purchasing agent at the Sahara for years came to the Aladdin. Sam Boyd was president of the Mint, did not come into the Aladdin, but he was with Prell at the Sahara. At one time, the group had a bingo house on Fremont Street between the Nugget and the California Club on the other end of the street. Al ran that. They were all devoted to Prell. Al said to me, "We were the only major operation in town that did not have connections. We knew them all, but we had no connections."

I met Al through Prell, at the time the Aladdin was built. I handled the licensing for everybody, among other things, and set up a procedure. You had that many people, you had to do all of the applications, their personal history statements, their capital questionnaires. They were in and out of my office quite a bit. After the place was licensed and opened, I got to know Al.

I think he was on the board and was director of marketing. I would see him at the hotel and on business. Later, when he had a personal legal problem, he came to me and became a client and a dear friend.

As a young man, Al had been involved in California at Venice and on the beach, and he had worked on gambling boats. He was in gambling in southern California until Earl Warren shut them down when Warren was attorney general.[1] They came to Las Vegas. Sam Boyd was in southern California. Bill Harrah went north. Al went to Reno with Harrah, then in the army during World War II. After he got out, he came back to California to visit friends and family and was on his way to Reno to go back with Harrah. He stopped in Las Vegas and went into the Club Bingo—he had friends there—and they were glad to see him. They needed a man who knew bingo. They talked Al into staying a little while. He stayed the rest of his life. [laughter] He stayed through the Sahara, the Aladdin, then with his dear friend Boyd into the California, Sam's Town, and the other organizations the Boyd group owns at the present time, until he retired.

There was one period when Al owned a place, I think before Sam built the California. Sam had gone into the Union Plaza with some other people, left, and put his own deal together and built the California and after that, Sam's Town. Al bought a little casino on Fremont Street. I represented him when he purchased that, and he later sold. He ran that by himself; he didn't have any partners. Then he went in with Sam in the California.

Al was very loyal to Prell and his memory. He often talked about how many men, successful here now, started with Prell and don't seem to remember that. Al felt very strongly about how gamblers were regarded in the late '30s and '40s and even into the '50s. His phrase was "second-class citizens." Al was very proud when he was admitted to a service club in Las Vegas. I think it was the Optimists Club. He became governor of that district. He was very active in charitable things in town: on the YMCA, different boards. He was proud that he was accepted in some areas in the community as *not* a "second-class citizen." That's a step in the right direction, because what he says is true. For many years, people in gambling were not considered worthy.

I was involved with other casino operations when I first came down from Elko. With Joe McDonald, of course. But I've represented a lot of working people in gambling. I hate to use this phrase, it's so hackneyed, but some of my closest friends started out as clients, and they worked in the business—Jimmy Garrett is the best example.

When I represented the Aladdin, there was an incident involving a New York publisher, Lyle Stuart.[2] Prell agreed to sell him three or four points in the Aladdin. I think Prell didn't want to lose him as a customer. [laughter] When we filed an application for a license, lo and behold, Stuart had published some racy books. Not pornography, but reproductions of great art, which could be erotic. There was nothing in his background, no reason he shouldn't get a license, but I'm a son-of-a-bitch—the board turned him down

330

*And
Who
Could
Forget
These
Guys?*

because he published what they termed "pornographic" books. Therefore, he wasn't fit to have a license in Nevada.

I came back from the meeting in Carson City, where the control board denied the application. Keith Campbell, Doc Pearson, and Frank Johnson, making a judgment as to what is art and what is pornography, were on Laxalt's board. I used to go on the Strip to have lunch. I went to the Desert Inn, and here are the three of them having lunch. I walked by their table on the way to mine, stopped, and asked, "Have you guys burned any books this week?"

I could not conceive of that being a reason to turn a man down for a license, particularly a minority license, when you've got strip joints operating all over town. [laughter] You had a right to appeal it to the gaming commission. I wanted to, but Stuart didn't want to do it.

Louis Prima was another client. He'd been a big star before World War II. Big band and all that. His career kind of waned until Prell brought him to the lounge at the Sahara. Prell told me when he asked me to represent him, "Be sure you get paid. Louie doesn't like to pay any bills." He said, "For example, he ordered a whole bunch of new uniforms in California for Sam Butera and the Witnesses and had them shipped to the hotel collect. Of course, he wasn't there when they came, and the hotel paid for them. Never been able to get Louie to reimburse the hotel. And he knows that when we negotiate his contract, we're going to want to be friendly towards him, so we're not going to push him." [laughter]

That was my introduction to Louie. He came to the office, and he was a perfect delight. He would imitate other entertainers. He would have everybody in the office in stitches. Louie came up for Grant's inaugural in 1963. They used to have the ball in the gymnasium in Carson, and here's Louie and the Witnesses, marching around in the middle of the crowd, Louie with his trumpet and singing "When the Saints Come Marching In." It was really nice. As I remember, he did that for nothing.

Then, there came a time . . . . Louie was building a golf course. Fairway to the Stars, I think was the name, out on Warm Springs Road. God, this was the most important thing in the world to him! Liens start getting filed against him by some contractors and material men. He hadn't paid them. This was about the time I ran for Congress. I turned these liens over to a lawyer in the office, because I was off on the campaign. They would file these liens; Louie wouldn't pay; and the people would file suits to foreclose the liens.

The young lawyer in my office would talk to Louie and file an answer, so there was a whole bunch of them with these answers filed. I told him, "You've got to settle these cases, because they're going to come to trial, and you're going to lose them." That's what happened. Judgments are entered against Louie. I get this letter from Louie, "What did I ever do to you? We've been such good friends, and you turned me over to this incompetent in your office. And these judgments!"

I read the letter and I thought, "God . . . ." I wrote him a note in which I said, "Dear Louis, Some nut's been sending me letters and signing your name to them. I thought you ought to know." Louie didn't think that was too funny, and that ended my legal relationship with him. I never really saw him after that. He had a lot of trouble there at Fairway to the Stars, and it was ultimately, I think, lost.

331

*And
Who
Could
Forget
These
Guys?*

When Earl Monsey and I were partners, I got a call from somebody in Los Angeles that some *very important* celebrity, well-known not only in this country but all over the world, wanted to get married in Las Vegas. They didn't want publicity. Could I help? My first question was, "Well, who are they?" Wouldn't tell me. [laughter] "You'll be surprised when they get there, but see if you can do this."

Earl talked to the county clerk about bringing this couple in so they wouldn't be seen. That was worked out. We decided the wedding would be at our office, and we needed a judge. Earl talked to Joe Pavlikowski.[3] Joe had a lot of experience marrying. He was justice of the peace, a great marrying job. Earl couldn't tell him who it was, and Joe Pav, he'd married enough folks—he didn't need another. I talked to Carl Christensen, a new judge then.[4] I explained the situation, and he agreed to do it. It was set. These people were coming in from Los Angeles at a certain time. Earl was to meet them at the plane, take them to the clerk's office, and get the license. Then they were going to come to the office. By then it was going to be probably 6:30 in the evening, and we'd have a wedding. Of course, we needed two witnesses, but we were careful—we didn't want anybody to know about it.

Earl and I could be witnesses, except I had other important business. We had a store at Mount Charleston. The sign said, "Mountain Mercantile: Mark, Sally, and Scott Denton, Props." We had taken a lease on a cabin in the Rainbow Canyon subdivision. We put in floors like an old-fashioned grocery. We built shelves and a counter, and we had a deep-freeze. Scott was running the store. Mark had a job as a flagman on a highway construction job, and he got off at 3:00 in the afternoon. Then he would come in to the wholesale houses and load the stuff that had to be hauled up to our store. Generally, at that time of year—it was summer—it was ice cream. For some reason, Mark could not do it that day, so I had to do go. When this big wedding is going to go on, I have to get in Mark's pick-up and haul the stuff up to Mount Charleston. Earl and my daughter Sally would be the witnesses.

Everything went according to plan. These people explained to everybody how important it was to keep this confidential. "Do not disclose this to the press or anybody." The couple was Christina Onassis and a young man whose name, I recall, was Volker. Oh, the wedding was wonderful, and Sally thought that Christina was charming. Sally was in college at the time, old enough to be a witness to a wedding.

I hardly got to the office, and the phone starts ringing. God, there are calls from all over the world, the *London Times* and newspapers all over the

United States, trying to get confirmation. Of course, I denied it. "I didn't see any wedding. No comment. Can't discuss it."

Then they read me a quote from Judge Christensen describing the wedding and saying how nice the people were. [laughter] Sally was incensed, as only a young person can be when she confronts what she believes to be misconduct by a grown-up. She wrote the nastiest letter to Christensen, pointing out he promised this would be confidential, and here it is in the paper. It was beautiful, but nasty.

A few days later, I'm in Christensen's court. After the motion was over, he called me to the bench and showed me this letter. [laughter] I thought, "Oh my God! What's going . . . ?"

I won that motion; he never held it against me. Frequently, he'd ask how my daughter is. By the time he gave that statement, the news was out anyway, and reporters were driving him crazy. In his statement, he had said something about how nice the couple were and how much class they had. Sally said, "It's too bad you don't have some class yourself." [laughter] The righteousness of youth.

Notes

1. Earl Warren was elected attorney general of California in 1938 and moved against gambling boat and casino operators, many of whom came to Nevada, including Bill Harrah. Warren went on to be governor of California (1943-53) and chief justice of the U.S. Supreme Court (1953-69).

2. Lyle Stuart published *Las Vegas Review-Journal* columnist John L. Smith's biography *Running Scared: The Life and Treacherous Times of Las Vegas Casino King Steve Wynn*. Wynn sued Smith and Stuart for libel. The case against Smith eventually was dismissed. A Clark County district court ruled in Wynn's favor, and the Nevada Supreme Court overruled on a technicality.

3. Joseph Pavlikowski served as a district judge, 1971-99.

4. Carl J. Christensen served as a district judge, 1971-93. He is part of a long-time Southern Nevada family that owns a jewelry store; his father, M. J., was an assemblyman and his brother Paul was both a city councilman and a county commissioner.

30 | Helping Liberal Candidates

Grant commented that my two campaigns for Congress took a lot out of me. They took an *awful* lot out of me. They busted me. I was not as happy in life for a while, trying to restore some semblance of family security, get a telephone, and things like that. [laughter] But it did not affect my interest in politics. Grant said he told somebody whom he was trying to get involved, "Look at Ralph Denton. He's back in Chicago on the McCarthy campaign, at his own expense."

By 1968, I had reached the view our policy in Vietnam was wrong. I might have come late to it, but I did come to that conclusion. Believing that, I welcomed Eugene McCarthy entering the New Hampshire primary. Nobody thought he had a prayer, but I saw it as a way to increase debate. You may remember sit-ins, teach-ins, where the government's Vietnam policy was being challenged.

I was disappointed that Bobby Kennedy had not been too vocal in his opposition. The only people in the government or the Senate I remember as *really* vocal were Frank Church of Idaho and J. William Fulbright of Arkansas, maybe Teddy Kennedy to a lesser degree, Wayne Morse of Oregon, Ernest Gruening of Alaska.[1] But the two that really had substance were Church and Fulbright. Morse was a fine senator, but a loose cannon—one year he's a Republican, the next year a Democrat. Another man who influenced me was General James Gavin, who had written, I think, a book opposing the war.

My change of thinking about Vietnam probably made me anti-Lyndon Johnson. If so, I had mixed emotions. I thought maybe he was a misguided soul, maybe he had not followed John Kennedy's advice, and he trusted the military. I thought if we had a public debate, maybe *he* would see the light. As I recall, in the New Hampshire primary, McCarthy got 40 percent of the vote against a sitting president. Now everybody realized that possibly, the opposition is more deeply rooted than they thought. Until that time, everybody who opposed the war was "just a bunch of pinkos." Now it was clear there were thoughtful people in America challenging our policy in southeast Asia.

After the New Hampshire primary, Bobby Kennedy comes into the picture. Maybe my judgment was wrong, but at that time I thought, "That gutless wonder! He didn't have the guts to come in here and challenge Johnson on the ballot. Now he ought to be trying to support McCarthy, instead of dividing the opposition." A lot of the people I talked to and I knew who were anti-Vietnam War switched then from McCarthy to Kennedy.

I became chairman of the Nevada committee to elect McCarthy, but I'm not quite sure how that happened. By then, Grant Sawyer had joined the anti-Vietnam forces, intellectually and publicly, and my guess is that somebody in the McCarthy organization contacted Grant and Grant suggested me. I don't recall Grant ever asking me to do it, but where else would they have gotten my name?

I'm chairman, with no money to do anything. I arranged to get bumper stickers, cards, and pamphlets. We got them. Then, a bunch of college kids descended upon me and came out to really do the work. One of them was Don Reynolds's son, who came here, and he was busted, as most of them were. He had long hair and no place to stay, so he and his girlfriend stayed with us a few nights. Jeff Zucker was in college or law school—young intellectual opposing the war. I get kind of a kick out of this. He was critical of lawyers who engaged in the pursuit of money in the practice of the law, because he was going to devote his life to helping the poor. But he's a local lawyer now, and he specializes in real estate law! [laughter]

There's a meeting back in Chicago—state chairmen and people active in the committee on the national level and everything. I went to that. McCarthy wasn't there, but they had a phone hook-up. We were in this big room. He spoke from Washington, talked about the campaign, the war—winning wasn't important; what was important was that we end this terrible war. The people there were passionate believers that this war was a tragedy that *had* to end. One of the people I met there was Barbara Tuchman, the historian.[2] Had a long visit with her about it. I don't think anyone had any illusions about McCarthy's ability to be president—his approach was so unconventional. Maybe an intellectual, a poet, would make a good President, although I held no illusions about it.

One of the people there, believe it or not, was Tom Mechling. I met him in the bar of the hotel. I was sitting having a drink after the meeting with somebody else I'd met in there. A guy's sitting next to me, and I happen to look around. By God, it was Mechling! I hadn't seen him since his run for governor in 1954.[3] We chatted a little. He recognized me, and I recognized him. We were friendly. What the hell?

That was one of the most satisfying experiences of everything I've done in politics, because in that meeting were people from the highest strata as well as the lowest—true believers doing everything they could to correct a terrible wrong. That impressed me. Then we get back to Nevada and have the campaign.

The Washoe County chairman was Don Driggs, professor of political science at the University of Nevada. The procedure had already been instituted where the selection of delegates was changed. Don was the Nevada delegate to the 1968 convention in Chicago. I think it was great for a professor of political science to see first-hand what happened and the political interplay. Johnson's activities in connection with that convention, it seemed to me, reflect no real credit on him. The way he treated Hubert Humphrey possibly prevented Humphrey from being elected.[4]

So, we lost. Kennedy defeated McCarthy in the California primary and was assassinated. It was a foregone conclusion that McCarthy was not going to get the nomination. But McCarthy had accomplished his purpose. The focus of everybody's attention now was Vietnam. Bobby Kennedy carried that opposition brilliantly, I thought, until he was killed. Poor Humphrey was saddled with an unpopular policy that Johnson would ultimately wiggle out of, in effect.

I have no recollection of the sort of thing you do in the average campaign: a bunch of people sitting and plotting strategy. Instead, we were like horse manure—we had these kids spread all over. You couldn't call it a well-run campaign statewide. I don't remember anybody in any county other than Washoe that organized, and they did that on their own—people at the university.

Hubert Humphrey was a delightful man. He came to the Senate in 1949. I was there. He had sponsored civil rights legislation on the floor of the Democratic convention in Philadelphia, which resulted in the southerners walking out. Many of those who walked out were senators. I think Humphrey was initially regarded as a brash young man who talked when he should have been listening, but I admired him, and from time to time would bump into him and say, "Hello, Senator, how are you?" He'd always speak and say, "How are you?" nice and cordial.

I met Humphrey again in 1968. Sara and I were up at Mount Charleston. Grant got in touch with me to tell me he wanted me to come down that evening to the Desert Inn to meet Humphrey. Hell, I was dressed in Levi's and a red woolen shirt, and I came down from the mountains and went right to this room. Humphrey was a good-spirited man and a man you couldn't help but like. Unfortunately, there were people who voted for Nixon instead of Humphrey that year because they felt Humphrey should have challenged Johnson on Vietnam. They couldn't understand that a vice president owes loyalty to the president.

I felt angry and sad about the 1968 convention. I could not believe the Chicago police would react so violently to what was basically a peaceful protest and demonstration. Any misconduct by the demonstrators could have been handled more moderately. The Chicago police seemed to get a thrill out of whacking these kids in the head with their billy clubs and hiking them off to jail. I don't mean to say misconduct should not have been dealt with, but the mayor's attitude seemed so adamant, so *violent*, such an abuse of power, from the things I saw on television. I was disappointed. "What on earth is happening to us . . . to our political process?" I don't understand why reasonable people can't debate, peacefully, questions of policy, why violence has to be part of every debate where people feel strongly.

Nixon had a "secret plan" to end this war, and that went on for five years after he became President. I thought Nixon was a terrible man. I didn't have to know any more than the campaign he ran against Helen Gahagan Douglas or his service on the House Un-American activities committee—the trampling on the truth, on people's basic rights.[5] I had no use for him. I was proud of Gerald Ford, though, and I think this country owes him a great debt of gratitude. He took over after Nixon left office in disgrace, and things gradually got back to normal—Watergate and the other crimes of the Nixon White House crew were forgotten about, and government went on. There was no violence, and Ford held things together. I don't blame him for giving the son-of-a-bitch a pardon. I didn't particularly care if Nixon went to jail, but being forced to resign the office of president in disgrace ought to be punishment enough.

I was active in the campaign of 1976. Grant invited me to lunch at the Las Vegas Country Club. The purpose was to talk about the 1976 presidential campaign. I arrived in that rarified atmosphere to find Bob Rose with Grant.[6] Grant wanted to assist in securing a chairman for the Jerry Brown campaign in Nevada. (He'd arranged, I think, for Jon Collins to be chairman of the Carter campaign. Grant had friendship for Jerry Brown's father, Pat, but he was not personally supporting Brown.)

Bob Rose didn't want to be chairman of the Brown campaign. If I tried to say why, I'd probably be wrong. Other than he was smarter than I was. [laughter] I said, "Sure, I'll be chairman."

I admired Brown. He was governor of California, although he appeared to be out of the normal mode of what you think of as a governor. And I was distrustful of Jimmy Carter. I was dead wrong about Carter, and I later became a great admirer, but I was fearful of a southern Bible-beating Baptist becoming president. So, I welcomed the opportunity to be chairman for Brown in Nevada. That's going strong. [laughter] "Welcomed" isn't quite right. I was willing.

That year, there was a presidential primary. It wouldn't be like the McCarthy campaign, where there wasn't a heck of a lot you could do; this was going to be a real campaign. Doris Evans was a longtime resident, real estate broker, and friend of mine and Sara's (she and her husband at one time lived in Boulder City), and her granddaughter was Brown's chief assistant in California. We got off to a great start, because almost immediately, Doris had a humongous cocktail party at her large house in Las Vegas. Oh, the place was mobbed. Brown came. We didn't get a separate headquarters, but his campaign sent young people from California to Las Vegas, and I moved them into my office and ran the campaign.

We ran quite an aggressive campaign. Jim Santini was our congressman, and apparently a Brown supporter. He had the title as chairman. Whether my title was co-chairman or executive director or coordinator, I don't remember and don't care. I never saw Santini during the campaign.

There was a big function at the Las Vegas Convention Center soon after we started putting the campaign together. Before that meeting, I met Brown and two of his aides who came to attend. I introduced them to Hank. I listened to what those great men said to each other, then rode with Brown and these two guys from Hank's place to the convention center—it wasn't very far. They're talking. I listen, and my God, they sounded like they had a candidate for sheriff. He was running for president, and the conversation I heard was on a level that I didn't think was presidential . . . but I put those thoughts behind me.

Bette Sawyer was for Brown. She made a nice talk at the convention center, and Brown made a fine speech. He spoke of things I thought a candidate for president should be speaking of. My disappointment had been a failure to recognize that presidents are human, suffer from the same weaknesses as the rest of us. I don't think Speaker Tip O'Neill's quote, "All politics is local," had been made by then, or if it had, it hadn't made an impact upon me. It's true, I don't care what you're running for. If you're running for president, you sort of campaign like one of the people in whatever area you're in.

A few days before election, we arranged for an airplane, and the candidate flew to Las Vegas, Elko, Reno. I'm not sure of all the other towns, because I had to leave the day of that tour to go to Washington, D.C., where Mark was graduating from law school. I was in Washington the day of the election. Sara and I voted absentee. By God, we won!

These young people from California were bright. I'd gotten to know and was fond of the workers housed in my office during that campaign, maybe a month. Then they departed . . . . My office was a mess, they didn't clean up, no note saying goodbye, I wasn't told to go to hell or drop dead or anything, let alone receive any thank-you note from anybody. Four years later, when Brown was going to try again, they asked me to be chairman in Nevada, and I declined.

Later in 1976, I was co-chairman with Mary Gojack of the Democratic state convention in Las Vegas.[7] I presided a great deal of the time. The new rules were being implemented that national convention delegates would be selected, so many for one candidate, so many for another, based upon their votes in the presidential preference primary. Brown carried Nevada, so he was entitled to the largest number. The way it was handled under the rules, everybody who registered at the convention as favoring Brown would meet in caucus to elect Brown delegates. Believe it or not, that was handled well, and there were no big beefs.

I was in the caucus, and I was elected to be a delegate. Always took a little personal pride and pleasure that I got as many votes as Santini, our congressman. I don't know that Santini was thrilled, but it led to a serious problem. (I was not mad at Santini at that time. We'd been a supporter of his for Congress.)

Santini was the highest-ranking Democrat in the delegation; governors and senators were a separate category. I had committed myself to support Santini for chairman. The delegation is getting ready to have a caucus to elect a chairman and make plans for going to the convention. The meeting was held in the governor's office in the Bradley building. A few days before, I find out Maya Miller wished to be chairman. I knew if I owed a deep debt to anybody, for everything she had done for me, it was Maya. I had to tell her I'd committed myself to Santini, and I couldn't break my word. I called people in Reno and around the state. Everybody was "counting the wotes." It looked like it was going to be a tough battle. Did Maya have a chance? It looked like Santini was going to win by two or three. I called Jim and asked him to release me from my commitment and explained why. He refused to do it.

We had that caucus, and they had a secret ballot. I voted for Jim. I knew then no matter what happened, I could be accused of anything. I made sure a guy sitting next to me saw my ballot. I carried out my commitment to Jim, and Maya won. I was delighted. Jim believed and will believe to this day I voted against him, and all I can say is I wish I had. I carried out my word to him. I know it hurt Maya, although we have never discussed it.

I gave my proxy to the convention to an alternate, and I didn't go. I saw no point. The primaries were in, and it was obvious Carter was going to get the nomination. But that's been a sad political fallout for me ever since. There is nobody in the world I admire or respect more than Maya Miller. It really pained me, but I've always believed if a man's word is no good, as my father used to say, nothing about him's any good. One of Santini's aides back there got drunk in a meeting and was accusing me and Sawyer of double-crossing Jim on that convention chairman thing because Maya was elected chairman. It looked awful good to me when I saw her on television.

I had no involvement in the general election. I went to rallies, hollered, and voted for Carter. I thought he was a good president. He might have been a micro-manager when he should have limited himself to policy, but he's a president we can all be proud of, and we will be more and more proud of him as time goes by. He was courageous, and he wasn't given the credit he was entitled to for that accord with Egypt and Israel. Reining in the CIA was a positive accomplishment. He was destroyed by inflation, when you think about it, and the Iran captives. All in all, it was obvious he was going to get defeated. But I thought it was a shame.

In 1980 the Democratic primary was between Carter and Ted Kennedy. I was and am an admirer of Kennedy, but he was terribly wrong. He'd better wait until he could run against somebody other than an incumbent Democrat. There was a Kennedy reception and meeting in Reno. I went for the purpose of seeing him, and did. I didn't, thereafter, take an active part in his campaign at all.

Hy Raskin was in Palm Springs, and I talked to Hy. Hy was anxious to get involved and help Teddy. Hy was ready, as the gambler says, "to get back in action." [laughter] Hy and I talked about both thinking he was wrong, but if he was going to do it, we'd be there; but he never heard from Teddy or anybody else. If I'm completely honest—and I want to be—had Hy been involved, had he asked me, I'd have been hard pressed to turn Hy down. Jimmy Bilbray sprung up in Nevada as chairman of a committee for Kennedy to talk Kennedy into running, as I recall it.

I never saw Ronald Reagan in person, never went to a rally. Saw him on television, saw what I considered a charming, likable man, personally. I could not agree with his policies: trickle-down economics. It never trickles down, never has. That wasn't new with Reagan. I thought his policies were detrimental to the best interests of the country in the long run. But he probably has been, next to Franklin D. Roosevelt, the most popular president in my time. He had the courage of his convictions. He told people when he was running what he was going to do and did it.

I haven't really been active in presidential campaigns since. Why? Nobody has asked me. [laughter] I tried to get as active as I could in the Clinton campaign. For the first time, Sara and I contributed money to a national campaign. It was the things he said he believed in and what he wanted to do. To a large extent, he did most of them. He wanted to make the government look more like the people of this country. He wanted to modify the welfare system, maybe improve it. That job hasn't been completed, but he tried. He wanted to do something about health care and got shot down. God *knows*, we have to do something about health care in this country. If I had a criticism of President Clinton, insofar as the official duties of his office are concerned, maybe he was too pragmatic. Maybe he should have been willing to make some fights, even though he lost them. That would be my main criticism, if I were to criticize him.

The party has been taken over by one-issue people. We have new rules that govern the selection of convention delegates. Under those quota rules, so many delegates have to be this, so many delegates have to be that, but there's no rule that delegates have to be interested in the party. The changes have been injurious to the Democratic party—the method of selecting delegates to national and state conventions, selecting national committeemen.

You've got how many national committeewomen? You used to have one national committeeman and one national committeewoman. Now, Christ, everybody's a member of the national committee. It's like hind-ends. Everybody's got one. [laughter]

Notes

1. Church represented Idaho, 1957-81. He was a Democrat, as was Fulbright, the longtime Foreign Relations Committee chairman who represented Arkansas, 1945-75. Ted Kennedy has represented Massachusetts since 1962. Democrat Ernest Gruening was governor of Alaska territory (1939-53) and U.S. senator from the state (1959-69).

2. Barbara Tuchman was a Pulitzer Prize-winning historian whose books included *The Guns of August*, about the coming of World War I, and *The First Salute*, about the American Revolution.

3. Tom Mechling ran in the 1954 Democratic gubernatorial primary, finishing with 9,270 votes, behind Vail Pittman (14,427) and Archie Grant (9,660). All three could have been considered anti-McCarran candidates.

4. Hubert Humphrey, the former senator from Minnesota (1949-65), had been elected vice-president with Lyndon Johnson in 1964. Johnson is believed to have denied Humphrey Democratic party money and support to hinder his chances of succeeding him, because Humphrey had begun to declare his independence of Johnson's Vietnam policy.

5. In 1950, Nixon defeated fellow Rep. Helen Gahagan Douglas for the Senate from California in the "Pink Lady" campaign, accusing her of sympathizing with communism.

6. Then lieutenant governor (1971-75), Bob Rose was defeated for governor in 1978. He later served as a Clark County district judge (1985-88) and, since 1989, as a Nevada supreme court justice.

7. Mary Gojack was a longtime liberal and women's rights advocate in Nevada. In 1980, Paul Laxalt defeated her to win reelection to the U.S. Senate. She served in the Assembly (1973-75) and State Senate (1975-79).

31 | This Was a *Lulu* of a Mistake

In 1974, Mike O'Callaghan was the winner in the race for governor in Nevada. The people running against him—five of them—got about 7,000 votes, and he got 69,000. Another name almost ended up on the ballot: mine. Thank God it didn't! [laughter]

There had been a perceived difference between the Sawyer and O'Callaghan forces in the Democratic party, but I admired Mike and the job he did as governor, and I think Grant did too. I did everything I could to support O'Callaghan, and I would have done anything Mike asked me to do. He had my vote, and whoever I could persuade to vote for him, I did. But I almost wound up running against him in the primary.

At the time, the lieutenant governor's race presented a problem. My neighbor and friend, Bob Broadbent, a Republican, was running against Harry Reid. I stated publicly that I was going to support Bob. I never hide when I'm doing stupid things. I just do them. [laughter] I had publicly supported Republicans before. I was wrong about Harry, but it had nothing to do with O'Callaghan.

I'm going to sound petty. Perhaps I was petty. I got annoyed at Reid. Somebody sent me a clipping out of Reno. Harry had been up to the university, talking to professors. There was some sort of a meeting. He was quoted as saying, to convince them he was liberal, he was just as liberal as Ralph Denton, and Denton was the most liberal candidate in Nevada. I thought, "Oh, thanks Harry." [laughter] That offended me, because I'd be surprised if Harry supported me when I ran for Congress. I wouldn't have expected him to: when he was in Washington going to law school, he worked under Baring's patronage. I assumed he owed Walter the loyalty of supporting him. I would not have expected Harry to support me.

At that time in Nevada and today, in the eyes of many, calling somebody a liberal means evil. Liberal's a *bad word*! I've never understood why. Most of us who were tarred with that didn't deny it. I never tried to hide the things I believed in. But that is a buzz word. Telling them he was just as

342

This
Was a
Lulu
of a
Mistake

liberal as I was, and I'm the most liberal man in Nevada—words to that effect—in a select audience where I assume he hoped it would never go anyplace else—I was annoyed by that.

In 1974, the gubernatorial election wasn't that clear-cut. That would have been Bible's time to run for reelection to the Senate, but he announced his retirement. As fair and decent a man as Bible was, he gave everybody fair notice so that everybody interested in it would have an opportunity to "look at their hole cards," as they say, and decide what to do. Right away, speculation started. Grant announced almost immediately he would not run.

Everybody in whom I had confidence believed Mike O'Callaghan was going to run for the Senate and Harry Reid for governor. Harry started preparing for a campaign, but he didn't announce he was going to run for governor. It was believed the delay in announcing what each one of them was going to do was to freeze other people out of making a decision till after they knew what everybody was going to do, and then it might be too late. [laughter]

If my second campaign for Congress was a mistake, I was about to make a *lulu* of a mistake. When I make a mistake, man, it's a mistake! But it was my firm belief, based upon information I received from what I considered, in the vernacular, reliable sources, that, no matter what anybody said, Mike was going to run for the Senate. A lot of people talked to me who liked Harry, but thought he was too mild, not belligerent enough that he could handle the job as governor. He's proven them wrong, but that was generally the feeling.

I was assured that Mike was going to run for the Senate, and I was approached to run for governor against Reid. I may be stupid, and I may have made a big mistake, but I wasn't dumb enough to think I should run against O'Callaghan. First, Mike was an excellent governor. Secondly, I couldn't have beaten him. I knew that.

I'm thinking about it. It doesn't take me long. I'd run. This is one place where I really was stupid. I didn't listen to my own opinion. I was advised that I should file immediately before Mike or Harry announced what they were going to do—nobody's going to give me a nickel until they know I'm committed. But my better judgment was to wait until O'Callaghan made his announcement. I voiced this to some of the geniuses by whom I was surrounded. "Oh, no, he's going to run for the Senate. You've got to file now. You've got to make a big splash about it." So, that's what I did.

In those days, you could file any time from January on up to the middle of June or July—I forget which. It wasn't open for a couple of weeks like it is now. God, would you believe this? Charlie Bell comes to me. He wants to work in this campaign. He says ever since I ran against Baring, he believed I should have won, and I was a good man. We welcomed Charlie aboard. I'd rather have him in the tent than outside.

343

*This
Was a
Lulu
of a
Mistake*

Ralph and Sara, accompanied by supporters and the press, leaving to file for governor, February 27, 1974.

We chartered a plane and flew up to Carson City. It was quite a group that went, too. My friends George Foley, Jimmy Garrett, and Lindsay Jacobson went. Joy Hamann was on board again—good old Joy—and a lot of newspaper people. After I filed for governor, I went across the street, had a press conference at the Ormsby House, made a speech, and submitted to questions. Everybody was there—the ones who flew up with us and Reno and Carson City people. I don't think I had any platform except continuation of the policies that had started with Russell and grown during the Sawyer administration; I think, gotten out of control a bit during the Laxalt administration, and resumed and continued during the O'Callaghan administration.

I didn't find anything in the O'Callaghan administration I would not have been proud to have continued to work for. I say this because I'm not as smart as Mike. [laughter] I might have gone for some people-oriented things, but I had no fault to find with O'Callaghan. He was a great governor. But he wasn't running. I knew for *certain* that he wasn't running.

A funny thing happened. John Laxalt, one of Paul's brothers, was standing in the back of the room. After the press conference, I was visiting with people. I finally got to Johnny. He says, "Paul's in the dining room. Like you to come in." He owned the Ormsby House. I sat down, and we were having a nice visit. He says, "I'd be careful going home on that airplane. O'Callaghan will have the national guard shoot you down." [laughter]

344

*This
Was a
Lulu
of a
Mistake*

Whoever told me I better file if I was going to get any money was correct. The minute I filed, money started coming in. Polls started showing me either very close or beating Harry, and I'd only been in it a week or two. A gambler who was not given a license offered me a $75,000 contribution, and I thought that was nice until he said, "If you'll see that I get a gambling license if you're elected." Of course, I had to tell him I couldn't do that. I said, "All I could do is tell you that I would do my best to see that you got a fair and complete and impartial hearing if you come before one of the agencies in the state of Nevada. But if I am governor, I certainly can't guarantee or promise or interfere in the licensing procedure. All I can do is appoint good people to handle those jobs." So I didn't get the $75,000. That was a new experience. When I was involved in Grant's campaigns, I don't remember anybody who made a contribution having any condition attached to it.

Then the announcement came that Mike was going to run for reelection. In all fairness, Mike had told me before I filed he was going to file for reelection, but I didn't believe him. The minute he announced, I immediately stated I would withdraw, which I did. But it took me two or three days to get the letter done. I had things at the office. Mike called once, said, "When are you going to file that withdrawal?"

I said, "Don't worry. I'm going to file it, pretty quick." And I did.

Before I withdrew, I had to hold up a day or two, because a couple of people in Reno said they represented a large group there and wanted to talk to me. I told them I was going to withdraw. They said, "Please give us an opportunity to talk to you before you do." Charlie Springer and Chow McGarry urged me to run against O'Callaghan. They named people in Reno, and they were speaking for them. I said, "No, no. No." I think they had their own axe to grind. We invited them to dinner at the house. They tried to persuade me, and I wouldn't do it. "Tell those people back in Reno I'm sorry, but I think Mike's been a good governor." They didn't like that, but that was the end of that.

How much did it cost not to run? Whatever income I lost at the office while I was screwing around running for governor. I collected quite a bit of money. When I withdrew, I felt an obligation to people who had contributed, so I got the checkbooks, got everything in order, and made a list. At the top of the page, I put the amount I'd received. Then, I listed every expenditure. When you got to the bottom, I had spent all the money I received and had a little deficit. I still thought I was bound to return their contributions, because they had given the money to me based upon my representation that I was running for governor, and they should let me know if they wanted it returned. Only one of all the contributors wanted his money returned, but that wasn't bad, because the guy was a client and owed me $5,000 on attorney's fees, and that's what he contributed. He said he didn't want his money back, just charge it up to his bill at the office. So, there was some deficit, but not a great deficit. I really had my fingers crossed for a long time. I did tell them I would be certain they were paid back, but it might take time. But not a one of them asked for it back, except the one.

Harry then filed for the Senate, further complicating my life, because Maya Miller filed against him. At that point, when I withdrew from the governor's race, several people, particularly in the black community, asked me to file for the Senate. I did give some consideration to that, but Maya was running, so there was no way. Yet, according to the polling at that time, Laxalt wasn't that strong. He'd come out as governor with a lot of baggage: Hughes, Delbert Coleman, the hotel in Carson City, the debate with Jack Anderson.[1] And he just barely beat Harry.[2]

I am still friendly with O'Callaghan and Reid, and I hope they are friendly toward me. I assume Mike was, if not furious with me, annoyed. Considering how close he and Harry are, I wasn't a threat to him, but I was a threat to Harry. He wouldn't be the successful politician he is if he didn't have feelings about things. I assume Harry was furious with me. And my belief is that when he was in the House, Harry was as fine and effective a congressman as we've had in my lifetime. He's a fine senator. I was wrong in my judgment of him, completely wrong. He's tough, and a man has to be tough in that job if he's going to accomplish anything. I'm a great admirer of Harry's. I told you, when I make a mistake, it's a lulu.

I've got to compliment Mike, because after Harry was defeated for the Senate, ran for mayor in 1975 and was defeated, Mike didn't give up on him. Mike knew what Harry was, and he appointed him chairman of the gaming commission [1977-81]. The people who believed he was young and weak, I think, soon after he got on that gaming commission, came to the conclusion he was neither too young nor weak. He's a strong man. I don't know what his feelings are toward me, but those are mine toward him.[3]

I have never been inclined to run for anything else. I've been asked a few times. I always thought they were pulling my leg or blowing smoke. I'd say, "What's open?" just jokingly. No, there has not been a groundswell of public opinion trying to talk me into running for anything. [laughter]

The next governor's race in which I took a great interest was when Richard Bryan ran in 1982.[4] His father Oscar was the most entertaining, humorous, funny man I ever knew. When I got to know Dick, I discovered Dick had a great sense of humor, too. That's a quality I admire in people, the ability to laugh at the world and themselves. I've always been fond of Dick, without being on intimate terms with him. Maybe it's because of his father and his mother, Lil. I got to know her, because she was a deputy county clerk for a long time—a lovely woman. I'm so proud of Dick—a local boy, a Nevada boy.

He was a good governor. He stood for things. There's nothing worse than unsolicited advice, and I've given him some . . . and I'm sure he's regarded it as such and hasn't seen fit to follow it. [laughter] If ever a man went

346

*This
Was a
Lulu
of a
Mistake*

to the Senate from Nevada eminently qualified by background and experience, it was Dick. Keep in mind: one, he was raised here; two, he's familiar with the entire state, not just a regional part. He graduated from the university in Reno, was student body president, went to a fine law school, came back to southern Nevada to his home. He served in the legislature; he was attorney general; he was governor—all before going to the Senate.

The combination of Reid and Bryan as senators ranks very favorably with teams like Pittman and McCarran, Bible and Cannon. I believe Reid recognizes his power, and he will know how to use his power. And when someone is wielding great power, they're going to be stepping on somebody's toes. Harry is tough enough to do that, and Dick was a fine senator.

After I ran against Baring, Dick Ham ran against him. I did everything I could for Dick. We had a big party on the front lawn at our house that was well-attended. Otto Ravenholt fired and fell back. But Jim Bilbray did it.[5] I was surprised that Jimmy ran so well against him in the small counties. Charlie Bell was running that campaign for Jimmy. Bell had been Baring's man. Charlie and Walter had fallen out. Through the years, Charlie had become well known as the Baring man, and had established relationships with all of these people. I always gave Charlie credit for turning around the small counties. David Towell beat him in the general election. The message hadn't got through to Republicans in the north. [laughter] Towell was defeated at the next election. He served one term.[6]

The next Democrat in Congress was Jim Santini. My feelings about him are not too hot. One, my memory is not exact, but each senator and congressman was allotted a certain amount of money to run their offices—stationery and this stuff. The Senate had a stationery store and gift shop, as did the House. When I read that Santini drew his out in cash, I thought, "What the hell is the matter with the man? Most young congressmen who go there, if they're busted, go to the bank and borrow money." [laughter]

We had scandals—remember?—in the House: in the post office, the sergeant-at-arms office, the stationery store. I used to be critical, knowing senators' offices. Somebody would go to the stationery store and buy a briefcase as a gift for some friend for Christmas. [laughter] That's petty chiseling. That was disappointing.

At the Carter inaugural, at a party for the delegation, Santini and his administrative assistant were vociferously attacking Grant for not supporting Jim for delegation chairman. That teed me off. What also teed me off is that by now Sara's working in Cannon's office. During Santini's first term, Cannon loaned Sara to him, so she went off the government payroll. That was OK. She sort of took charge of Santini's campaign headquarters to get it going. He also loaned one of his staff in Washington to Santini. When the campaign's over, Santini, without talking to Cannon, offered that young man a job in his office at a higher salary than Cannon had been paying. The young man took it. He offered Sara a job, and Sara, of course, wouldn't even consider it. Cannon had loaned her to him, and when the campaign was over, she was going back. I thought that was petty, insensitive, cheap conduct on Santini's behalf.

Cannon had given Santini all that help, helped him every way he could, when he first ran; Grant did; everybody worked their tail off. So, what does he do? He runs against Cannon in 1982. I said when I made a mistake, it was a lulu; when he made that mistake, it was a *double* lulu. But it didn't end his self-centered ambition. He couldn't beat Cannon in the primary, so the next time around, he changed to Republican and ran. Had he, as a gentleman would, gone to Cannon before he ran against him to find out if the senator was going to run for reelection, and the senator said yes, he should have stayed where he was until the next time. In all probability, he'd have been a cinch.

Jim Santini, like many others, decided, "Oh, the Democrats are through. I'm going to jump. I'm going to become a Republican, because everybody's a Republican nowadays. And besides, I want to be senator." It reminded me of when I was a little kid in Lincoln County during the Depression after the election of 1932: you hardly ever saw a Republican running for anything. All the Republicans switched to Democrats, and those who were too intellectually honest to do that ran as Independents. Santini was a disappointment to me, and I know he was to Sara, because Sara worked in his campaign, and, during the course of the campaign, had developed some admiration for him.

Notes

1. The controversies surrounding Laxalt included his close relationship with Howard Hughes's organization, the method of financing his building of the Ormsby House and its alleged connections to organized crime interests, and a debate with Jack Anderson in which the muckraking columnist attacked all of those activities. *The Sacramento Bee* subsequently published articles dealing with Laxalt's past, and he filed a libel suit against the paper; it ended with both sides claiming victory.

2. Paul Laxalt received 79,543 votes to Harry Reid's 78,932, a difference of 611. A recount increased Reid's deficit to 629.

3. Reid went on to win election to the House of Representatives from District 1—the Clark County district—in 1982. He was reelected in 1984 and elected to the Senate to succeed Laxalt in 1986. In 2001, he became Senate majority whip, ranking second in the Democratic party in the institution.

4. Richard Bryan was the first Clark County public defender, and went on to serve as an assemblyman (1969-73), state senator (1973-78), attorney general (1979-83), governor (1983-89), and U.S. senator (1989-2001). When he retired, he became an adjunct professor of political science for the University and Community College of Nevada System and a senior partner in Lionel Sawyer and Collins.

348

*This
Was a
Lulu
of a
Mistake*

5. The primary results were as follows:
1968: Baring, 40,938; Ham, 19,306
1970: Baring, 41,925; Ravenholt, 19,086
1972: Bilbray, 36,525; Baring, 31,896.

6. In the 1972 general election, Republican attorney David Towell defeated Jim Bilbray, 94,113-86,349. In 1974, Jim Santini, a former Clark County justice of the peace and district court judge, defeated Towell, 93,665-61,182.

32 | The Alpha to the Omega of My Life

Sara worked in both of Grant's campaigns and in Bible's campaigns as a volunteer. In the last Bible campaign, in 1968, she handled his personal schedule. She was very good at that, because she knew people all around the state. That was expected to be a tough campaign due to Ed Fike running against him, and it didn't turn out to be that tough.[1] When that campaign was over, Bible had an excess of contributions. He divided that up with people who had worked in his campaign for nothing. They got a check; income tax was withheld. For the first time in a political campaign, Sara got a check—wasn't a hell of a lot—and that's typical of Bible: he did the fair thing. He didn't profit from any surplus in campaign money. I don't see anybody doing that anymore. Now, I don't see any volunteers. Everybody gets paid.

In 1970, Mark and Sally were students at the University of Nevada, Reno. Sally lived in Nye Hall. Bill Raggio was district attorney. In the winter, it's co-o-o-old in Reno. They would have fire drills at 2:00 in the morning. The kids would have to get out of bed, get clothes on, come downstairs, go out onto the parking lot. Then the police would go in and search their rooms, looking for pot. That infuriated Sara; me too! But Sara was going to do something about it.

Raggio was Senator Cannon's opponent in the fall election, and Sara volunteered to work in Cannon's headquarters. As in most campaigns, Sara isn't there long until they've got her in a responsible position. She was handling Cannon's scheduling. She developed genuine fondness for Cannon and an appreciation for the way he treated her. He treated Sara—and this pleased me no end—as an absolute lady, not some peasant. That impressed me. I've been around people who treat their underlings with less than the respect they are entitled to. I got better acquainted with the senator and the people in his organization—I hadn't known them well until that time.

Now the election's over, Cannon has won, and Sara comes home.[2] Jim Joyce was in charge of Cannon's Las Vegas office, and he asked Sara if she

350

The
Alpha
to the
Omega
of My
Life

could come into the office two or three afternoons a week and help wind up the paperwork with the campaign and get everything organized. She did.

Then Jim asked her if she would work in the office. That upset me. No wife of mine had to work. I regarded it as a threat to my manhood. *I'm the one who supports this family. You're not supposed to work.*

A day or two later, I was trying a case. It was the afternoon recess. The courthouse was not crowded, as it isn't today in the afternoon. [laughter] I'm sitting in the hall having a cigarette, and George Foley comes by. He says, "Oh, I hear Sara is going to work for Senator Cannon."

I said, "By God, you heard wrong. She's not." George sensed how I felt, although I didn't express myself. "Ralph, you're making a mistake," he said. "Sara's been busy all her life, raising her children, in community things and school in connection with the children. The children are gone or shortly will be." Scott was in high school; he'd be going next year. "She's bored. She feels unneeded. She's in Boulder City. You're in Las Vegas. She doesn't know what the hell you're doing," he says, "and you're making a mistake."

I thought for a minute and said, "By God, George, you're right." I had to look into myself. I was *dead* wrong. I was about to deny her the opportunity, if she wanted, to get out of the house and do something. I came home that night and said, "Honey, if you want to take that job with Senator Cannon, I certainly have no objection."

She smiled and said, "I'd like to do that." And she did. It turned out to be wonderful. We had much more time together. We'd drive to Las Vegas together and back; we'd have lunch. She had things to tell me about what was going on in her office. And I cannot say enough of Senator Cannon and his wife, Dorothy, how nice they were and how pleasant he was to work with. I've always been grateful. It gave her a chance to be around young people other than her own children, to meet a lot of people, to do interesting things.

Jim left, and Sara wound up in charge of the office. I don't know whether that was planned. Chet Sobsey was administrative assistant in Washington. The only thing that tees me off—I don't blame the senator and Sara doesn't blame anybody—her salary never got to the point as head of the office that Jim, a man, received when he ran the office. Cannon didn't discover that until a little while before his last campaign, and he raised her salary. Chet was in charge of that, but Chet never believed a woman should . . . . [laughter]

Jack Conlon had died. Jack was administrative assistant. In the days of petty warfare between Cannon and Sawyer, Jack had the stomach for it. But after Jack died, Cannon didn't get involved. When Jack died, Chet, who had been his pressman, became administrative assistant. Chet used to be the political writer on the *Review-Journal*, the "Boiling Pot" column.

The office here was small, just Sara and two others, Nancy Lee and Lee Alverson. They had a retinue of young friends. In the Washington office was Janine Assuras, a McGill girl Sara became close to. Frank Krebs worked in Cannon's office there. He and Cannon had been shot down behind the lines during World War II and escaped together. Sara and he became good friends. Sara got to know and like other people in the office. Aubrey Sarvis was staff director or counsel at the Commerce Committee, and Sara became fond of Aubrey. A lot of them would come out during campaigns. Through them, she got to know local boys who had gone back under Cannon's patronage. Sara got to know Frankie Sue Del Papa.[3] It was a wonderful experience for Sara.

Cannon brought a lot of people back under his patronage. Roger Hunt is one of the federal judges; I knew his father from Overton. Lee Walker is an attorney. Shelley Berkley.[4] Jim Jimmerson is a Las Vegas attorney. I think Brian Greenspun was under his patronage when Brian was going to Georgetown. Helen Foley worked in the Senate. Mary Lou Foley worked in the office the last year or so Cannon was in. Patty Becker, who went on to fame and fortune in the gaming industry, and Nancy, her sister. Sam and Mary Ellen McMullen. Judge John McGroarty.[5] Eddie Feutsch was in charge of the Reno office, an old-time Nevada guy. He and Sara became good friends. I wasn't part of the operation, but got to meet these people through Sara.

It's hard to say how Cannon's operation compared with McCarran's. McCarran and Eva took a paternal interest in the Nevada kids, to the point you had to tell him your grades after each semester. They would check on where you were living. They would have get-togethers. One reason many who supped at Cannon's table didn't feel any obligation to help when he was running for reelection is because they never had that relationship in Washington. I always blamed Chet for not pulling these people in to feel like they were part of the organization.

When I was with McCarran, I would talk to kids who worked for other senators, and I might complain because I had to do this or that, and some of them would say, "God, we never have to do anything like that." But McCarran made you feel like you were part of something. I don't think Cannon's office staff integrated patronage people into that feeling of belonging. That was a mistake. Part of it is that Nevada was bigger by the time Cannon was in office. God knows it's bigger now. But when a senator's office helped you in those days, you thought it was because you were a friend of the senator. Nowadays, they just refer to it as constituent work.

During Cannon's last campaign in 1982, a grand jury in Chicago was investigating the Teamsters and trying to find out if there was anything to allegations that Cannon accepted something for his vote to deregulate the trucking industry. Allen Dorfman came to Cannon's office in Las Vegas.[6] Sara was subpoenaed to testify before the grand jury. She had no testimony of substance to give, and she wasn't there when Dorfman came to the office. We were in Mexico. When we came back, Sara was upset he'd come to the office, and she wanted to know who in the office had made an appointment for him to see the senator.

352

The
Alpha
to the
Omega
of My
Life

Sara and I went together when she had to go to Chicago to testify. She came back and was laughing about some of the questions: describe the office, and how many doors there were. The office was on the fourth floor of the federal building in Las Vegas, and they asked if he could go out a window. They hadn't done too much in the way of preparing for her. [laughter]

I believe the whole thing had started over local zoning. Cannon had a condominium in the Las Vegas Country Club. A lot of his friends were his neighbors, among them Vern Willis and General Zack Taylor.[7] There were two or three vacant lots across from where he lived, and somebody applied to build a multi-apartment building. The neighbors didn't want that. Cannon went before the county planning commission as one of the property owners to protest; they weren't successful. A bunch of them got together and thought maybe they ought to buy the lots, but they didn't know who owned them. When they checked, they found the Teamsters pension fund owned them. Cannon got ahold of them to see if they wanted to sell. They never bought it, but there were allegations that Cannon received favors over the deregulation bill. That had a substantial effect upon that election. In retrospect, had Sara been in the office, she never would have let the man in, because she knew who he was.

Then you had that really tough Democratic primary where Cannon's colleague in Congress, Jim Santini, ran against him, split the party. There was personal rancor that Santini would run against Cannon. The loss of seniority was terrible for Nevada. I can give you simple examples of what seniority meant. One, the FAA, or whoever it is, wanted to close the weather station in Elko. They thought that area would be properly served by the weather station in the Reno area, but people in Elko didn't want it closed. They regarded it as a very important service. They kept it open for several years because of Cannon. Right after his defeat, they did close it.

Another example was, until Cannon's defeat, United Airlines ran a regular schedule through Elko, Ely, and Reno. They finally were able to drop that flight after Cannon was defeated. I don't think for one minute, had Cannon remained in the Senate, the Department of Energy would have gotten as far as it's gotten in the nuclear waste dump thing. He would have had that squelched and killed. It would have died aborning, I believe.

Seniority is important, the way the Senate works. Cannon had the seniority and ability to *use* power for the benefit of Nevada. Look what Reno's going through with the railroad coming through the middle of town. The Southern Pacific and Union Pacific have merged and got more trains coming through Reno now than they used to. They had the same problem in Elko. It wasn't as great, but Christ, Cannon got the tracks moved at federal expense. They don't come through the middle of town anymore. [laughter] That shows what seniority can do if you have power and know what to do with it. So, it was a loss. Nevada suffered for that. The senator who took Cannon's seat, Chic Hecht, was kind of a laughingstock, which is too bad, because he's a nice man.[8]

Sara's pension would be a hell of a lot better if she hadn't lost that job. [laughter] What I really missed about it is that we'd drive to work together in the mornings, have lunch together, then drive home together. I enjoyed that, and so did she. It's kind of lonesome for me now, since I work in Las Vegas and she's in Boulder City. I miss her. But she comes in quite a bit.

353

The
Alpha
to the
Omega
of My
Life

After Cannon was defeated, Sara became involved in owning the Green Valley Athletic Club shop, kind of a lark, probably not the wisest decision we ever made. She had never been in any business of that kind, but we didn't think when we acquired it that she'd have to be too deeply involved. God, within a short time, she was running that store and going to Los Angeles to market, knew where to go and what to buy. I didn't realize how she hated it until we sold it. She's never been one to complain about things. God, she was glad to get rid of that. [laughter]

I cannot think of enough superlatives to describe Sara. She's without question the most efficient person I've ever known. She never sits down. She's always doing something, and it's always something of value. She's not wasting her time. She's making a quilt or painting a picture or painting the house. Her greatest ability, in my opinion, though, is that she is the greatest wife a man could have, and I think I can say the greatest mother.

Sara has a great sense of humor, and she's smart, energetic, and interested in everything. She's interested in art, and she tries to get our grandchildren interested, and she encourages them. Politics—God damn, she's a good Democrat! [laughter] I'm not sure which of us is the most devoted to the principles of the Democratic Party. But she's the alpha to the omega of my life. My greatest accomplishment was to meet, court, and marry Sara. Everything else pales to insignificance. I can't conceive of my life without her.

Mark was our first child. He was born in Elko, and I think he was four when we moved to Las Vegas. Then came Sally, born two years later, also in Elko. She was two when we moved. Scott was born in Henderson after we moved here. They're all two years apart, and they're good kids.

I did not know Mark wanted to be a lawyer until his senior year in college, because I never tried to influence the kids or direct them in any way. I'd known lawyers who weren't really happy because they were lawyers, but their dad was a lawyer and pressured them into becoming lawyers. I did not know where their talents and interests laid in that respect. I was pleased, though, when Mark told me he wanted to be a lawyer. He said, "Dad, I've always wanted to be a lawyer and to work with you."

I can truthfully say—coming from a father, this sounds like braggadocio—Mark is as fine a man as I've known. He doesn't get this from his father. I have never heard Mark say a bad word to or about anybody. He's the kindest, gentlest man I've known, but he's strong of character. He stands for what he stands for. He's a fine lawyer, a credit to the bench, the bar, and his generation. But he hides his light, to a degree, behind a bush. He's not out glad-handing everybody. He's doing his work and taking care of his family— he has four children—and having a nice time doing both.

Mark clerked for me a bit when he was going through law school. Not much, because he went to law school in Washington, D.C. After he graduated, he went on active duty in the army, then came back and came in with me. It's a wonderful thing to have that kind of association with your son. You love your son, but to be working together on an equal basis, where your son learns all of your warts and still loves you.... I worried about that, once he found out what a horse's ass I really am. [laughter] It's been a wonderful experience. Sometimes I've seen kids come in and be dominated by their father, in different businesses and things. I was worried about that, but my shadow wasn't so great, and I never tried to dominate him.

Mark wasn't much of a student until college. He was a great student in high school in things he liked, but if he didn't like them, he liked to think about what was going on in the world by looking out the window. [laughter] He came into his own academically at the university. He graduated with distinction, was a top student in political science and French. He was awarded honors in both fields and was Phi Kappa Phi. He had no problems in law school, did well, writes well. I'm very proud of Mark, of course.

355

The
Alpha
to the
Omega
of My
Life

My next one is Sally. I love her dearly. Wherever Sally is, the birds are singing, the flowers are growing, and it's exciting. Sally is a believer, energetic, talented. She has three sons, and they adore her, she adores them, and she's a wonderful mother; but at the same time, she's creative, a good writer, and she's always writing something.

Sally was always the most independent of our children. She started the university after just three years of high school. I never had any more idea than the man in the moon how Sally was doing in college. The boys had their grades sent home from the university, but not Sally. She did something so her grades didn't get sent home. When she graduated from the University of Colorado, I went to the ceremony, but I wasn't even sure she was going to graduate. There she was, she had on the cap and gown, but I had never gotten any grades from there. I had never known what she was taking. She didn't discuss that. She'd take what she damn well pleased! [laughter]

Sally has always been a great believer in causes. She's bright, loving, emotional, enthusiastic—all of the qualities I like in an individual. I'm proud of Sally and her accomplishments. She had success as an investigative reporter, working for newspapers,

A 1970s Denton family Christmas.

356

*The
Alpha
to the
Omega
of My
Life*

a television station in Kentucky, and Jack Anderson and his column in Washington. She was one of his associates. She'd worked for a paper in New Mexico, and I think she won an award for the best investigative reporter, although she was on a weekly.

Morry Zenoff was a friend of ours.[9] He lived in Boulder City. He ran the Boulder paper and the Henderson paper. He offered Sally a job when she got out of college, and she went for it like a hog goes for the slop. She started writing news stories, and soon she was doing practically everything. A schoolteacher here, a lovely lady, was a member of a minority and suffered discrimination. Sally wrote a big story, called it what it was, and gave everybody in the community hell. Then she had a column, and she wrote a great column on issues.

She believed *strongly* in the ERA. That was coming before the legislature. One of Morry's sacred cows was Jack Jeffrey, a member of the assembly from Henderson.[10] Morry went to Mexico, as he did every winter—his wife Eva was from Puerto Vallarta; they had a home there. Morry left Sally in charge of the Boulder City paper. (The Henderson people were above her; they had final authority.) Sally determined Jeffrey was speaking out of both sides of his mouth, taking contributions from pro-ERAers and anti-ERAers. He announced something along this line: he hadn't decided how he was going to vote, but was taking a poll of his district and would base his vote on that. He, in her opinion, was without conviction of any kind, and she ran a big story in the Boulder paper. The gist was that Jeffrey is two-faced or a double-crosser, words to that effect, was without conviction and had told the ERA people he was for it, and the ones against it that he was against it.

The story ran. They didn't stop it in Henderson, but they told Morry, and he fired Sally. Her comment was, "It's not too bad losing a job that pays below the minimum wage, anyway." [laughter] Morry never could understand how we stayed friends. He thought we'd be madder than hell. I said, "You own the paper. You can hire and fire who you please. None of my business. Sometimes you're pretty stupid about it, but what the hell?"

Sally was out of work and in kind of a quandary as to what she was going to do. She had heard good things about Santa Fe, and she decided she was going to go get a job on the paper. She's got a Datsun station wagon and her golden retriever, Kilgore Trout, named after a Kurt Vonnegut character. I talked to her. "Sally, what are you going to do there?"

She said, "I'll find a job . . . ."

I said, "It's going to be hard to get a job with a newspaper."

She said, "I can get a job as a waitress or something. I'll find a job."

Sally and Kilgore Trout got in that car and took off for New Mexico. Sure enough, she got a job at a good weekly at Española, the *Rio Grande Sun*. She started investigative reporting, and she took after the superintendent of the highway patrol for covering up stuff. She and the paper got sued for libel. Sally won the lawsuit, and she won the award as the best investigative reporter in New Mexico.

Sally went to work for Jack Anderson. She wrote some beautiful columns for him. You could always tell which of the associates had done the research or written the story. When you see, "My associate, Sally Denton," you knew Sally had written the story. She wrote some beautiful stories from Moscow. We went with a writers' group to Russia, and we were there when they invaded Afghanistan. Sally, peddling Anderson's name around, got some interviews with high people in the Communist Party and in government.

Then Sally married another writer, and he got a job with the big newspaper in Lexington, Kentucky, part of the Knight-Ridder chain. They had a policy of not having husband and wife teams, so she found a job as a TV reporter. The first thing you know, she had things about the underworld and Governor John Y. Brown and his wife Phyllis George. [laughter] She became a big name, and everybody was accusing her of sleeping with her sources, but the TV station was scared to fire her. They took her off the air, but kept her on the payroll. That culminated in Sally writing a book about it, *The Bluegrass Conspiracy*, that did very well and still sells in Kentucky.

That marriage ended in divorce, and she came back home and wound up going back to Santa Fe, although she left Kilgore Trout with us. After a while, I wouldn't let her take him again. [laughter] Sally's very talented. As I say, she's cause-driven, has a very deep moral sense of government and how people in public office should conduct themselves, and a deep shock when she discovers that's not always true.[11]

Scott's a lot like Sally, in the sense that he knows what he wants to do, he's going to do it, and it doesn't make a hell of a lot of difference what his old man says, never did. I didn't know until late that he wanted to become a doctor. Always a great student in school, popular. I think he was class president every year in high school and student body president his senior year. He doesn't like to be hassled with paperwork and crap like that. He didn't apply to any university except the University of Nevada in Reno. He didn't want to fill out forms. He didn't want to take SAT tests. He wanted to go up to the university in Reno, and to medical school, and that's what he did. His grades were always good, though I'll never forget this: He was in grammar school, and he brought his report card home. Of course, he had superior grades in everything, even then. But the teacher had written all over the report card and all over any place that she could write, "Talks, talks, talks, talks, talks, talks, talks, talks, talks." [laughter]

Again, this sounds like a father bragging, but I get this from doctors, from his patients, that he is an outstanding pediatrician. That's exactly what he wanted to be when he started, and exactly what he is. His patients, people we know, will come up to us and, "Your son takes care of our grandkids. They just love him." Now he's on the faculty of the University of Nevada School of Medicine here in Las Vegas. He will be seeing patients, of course, and with the students and residents, because the school now has a pediatric resi-

358

*The
Alpha
to the
Omega
of My
Life*

dency. Scott's working with them. Scott has three delightful children. Mark has four and Sally three. I'm really proud of my kids.

Scott ended up back in Elko for a while. In a medical school, in your fourth year, you apply for residencies. It used to be they all did a one-year internship. If they wanted to go on and specialize, then they would decide. Now in their senior year, because they have to get the applications in to where they want to do their residency, they make applications to medical schools all over the country. They're interviewed at that school, and medical schools all over the United States, the same day, open "The Match"— which schools accepted which ones into their programs. One of the good things about our medical school, our kids generally match.

Scott applied at the University of Minnesota, Georgetown in Washington, Children's Hospital in Oakland, one other I don't recall, and the University of Arizona in Tucson. Now he has to travel to all those places. He interviews them, decides where he wants to go. They decide among all the kids applying, if they want to take them, and "The Match" comes out. Every place he went selected him. His first choice was Arizona, so he went to Arizona. Now, why did he, in his wisdom, decide on the University of Arizona? The climate. When he went to Minnesota, there was snow hind-end deep to a tall Indian, and he figured he'd had enough snow in Reno for four years. [laughter] Scott will tell you, "Yes, the climate, sure. But it's a wonderful program," and it is. But there was no doubt in Scott's mind. He wasn't going in that snow if he could avoid it.

When he finished, he went to Elko to practice with the Elko clinic. I don't know if the winters have anything to do with it, but Scott stayed just three years, then came down and opened a practice in Henderson at St. Rose. Our friends in Elko told us the same thing I hear from people here. I don't know anything about the practice of medicine, but people tell me he's a fine pediatrician. If he wasn't, I'd still think he was—he's my son.

I'm proud of the kids—a lawyer, a doctor, and a writer. All of them went to college, and two of them pursued graduate degrees. Sally could have, but went right into writing. And they're all very bright.

Notes

1. Bible defeated Fike, 83,622-69,068. The race was expected to be closer due in part to Bible's long-standing close relationship with Lyndon Johnson.

2. Cannon defeated Raggio, 85,187-60,838. Raggio had lost to Ed Fike in the 1968 Senate primary. In 1972, he won election to the State Senate from Washoe County, and still was a member—and Republican leader—as of the 2001 session.

3. Frankie Sue Del Papa has been a university regent since 1980, when she unseated Louis Lombardi, who had held the office for 30 years. In 1986, she became Nevada's first woman secretary of state and, in 1990, the state's first woman attorney

general. She was elected to two subsequent terms and announced in 2001 that she would not seek reelection in 2002.

359

*The
Alpha
to the
Omega
of My
Life*

4. Shelley Berkley has been an assemblywoman (1983-85), a member of the Board of Regents (1991-98), and congresswoman from the first District (1999 to present).

5. Helen Foley, daughter of Joe Foley, was an assemblywoman (1981-83), state senator, (1983-87), and unsuccessful candidate in the Democratic primary for House of Representatives in 1986. She then became a lobbyist and political consultant and is now a partner in Faiss Foley Merica. Mary Lou Foley, daughter of Roger Foley, has worked for and run several non-profit organizations. Patty Becker has been a member of the Gaming Control Board and an attorney, recently a corporate counsel for Harrah's. Nancy Becker was appointed to succeed James Brennan as a Clark County district court judge in 1989, was elected in her own right, and in 1998 was elected to the Nevada Supreme Court. Sam and Mary Ellen McMullen have been active in political and educational issues. Judge John McGroarty has been a Clark County district court judge since 1983.

6. Allen Dorfman ran the Teamsters Central States Pension Fund, helping direct loans to various casinos. He was gunned down in 1983; his murder remains unsolved, suggesting a mob hit.

7. Vern Willis was a longtime Las Vegas businessman and stockbroker. General R. G. "Zack" Taylor was commander of Nellis Air Force Base and then a Las Vegas businessman.

8. Chic Hecht, a longtime Las Vegas businessman, defeated Cannon in the 1982 general election, 120,377-114,720. Defeated for reelection in 1988 by Richard Bryan, Hecht became ambassador to the Bahamas, 1989-93.

9. Morry Zenoff founded the *Henderson Home News* and *Boulder City News*, as well as the first Jewish weekly newspaper in Las Vegas. He also was an original owner of Channel 13.

10. Jack Jeffrey was a Democratic assemblyman from Henderson, 1975-91, and later a longtime lobbyist.

11. Since these interviews were conducted, Sally Denton and her husband, Roger Morris, a historian and journalist, have published *The Money and the Power: The Making of Las Vegas and Its Hold on America, 1947-2000*.

33 | Jeffy

We lost our fourth child, Jeff—Jeffrey Lewis Denton—when he was eighteen months old. I remember it so clearly. It was May 11, 1960, at twilight. We had just finished dinner. Mark would have been nine, Sally seven, and Scott five. The weather was beautiful. We didn't have a swimming pool then, and there was a brick wall around the back yard. The kids used to play in the back yard. Mark and Sally and Scott had gone outside to play with a turtle and a puppy that Art Revert had given them. Jeffy had gone down the hall to the doorway, we thought to go outside to play with the other kids.

Sara and I heard a terrible scream. We went running. Sara got there first. Jeffy had gone into the bathroom in Sally's bedroom. It's quite a distance from the dining room—the other side of the house. We didn't hear the water. He had turned on the hot water and fallen in. Sara, always the one who knows what to do, grabbed him out, wrapped him in a towel, and took off for the hospital up the hill—with me following. Mark, Sally, and Scott were standing on the front step, puzzled looks on their faces. Mom had gone tearing out with Jeff, with me behind her, and we just left them here.

The hospital staff called our doctor, Tom White, and he came running from the city council meeting. When Tom finished, we were able to see Jeffy. His body was completely wrapped in bandages, and his face looked natural. You couldn't see any burns. I thought, "Gee, everything's fine."

Tom took me aside and said, "This is very bad. We need to transport him to Southern Nevada Memorial Hospital [now University Medical Center], where he can get care." He mentioned electrolyte balances and that sort of stuff. I had no idea what he was talking about, because Jeffy looked fine, the part we saw. He arranged for an ambulance to take Jeff. I don't remember whether he called Dr. Merkin, our pediatrician in Las Vegas, but Dr. Merkin and Dr. Cap were at the hospital when we got there. Neither Sara nor I realized how serious it was. We thought, "He got burned, but he'll get better."

You never know how wonderful people are until you need them. For the following week, we stayed in Las Vegas with Jimmy and Dorothy Garrett—they didn't live far from the hospital—some nights and Lindsay and Martha Jacobson some nights. The next day, Grant and Bette came to the hospital. That wasn't easy for them. Jeffy needed special nurses. Ann McNamee Martinet had been a nurse. The minute she heard about it, she volunteered. I'd grown up with Rae Smalley, also an ex-nurse. The minute she heard, she volunteered. Those two were with Jeffy around the clock, would not take a penny.

We would stay at the hospital all day long, most of the night. Then we'd get up early in the morning, go back to the hospital. I spent some time in the hospital library reading what I could on burn cases. The doctors were talking about the fact that if Jeffy survived, he would need many years of treatment and skin grafts. They were expensive, and I should contact the Crippled Children's Society. Frank McNamee had something to do with the society, so I contacted Frank, and he said, "If that comes to pass, don't you worry about it." Through that, I met Kitty Rodman, who was active in the society. At that time, we had hope that Jeffy would survive.

They had to do the debridement, a surgical procedure where they surgically remove the dead, burned tissue. Dr. Merkin and Dr. Cap were there constantly, and they'd arranged for a surgeon. But Dr. Fred Anderson, my friend in Reno, had heard about the accident. Fred shows up, and into surgery he goes. Pretty soon, the surgeon we'd hired left. Fred was a fine surgeon, without question. He flew down at his own expense, did the debridement, flew back at his expense, and would not take a penny.

On the eighteenth, we were awakened with a call about 1:00 or 2:00 in the morning, telling us that we should come to the hospital. We immediately went to the hospital and were told that Jeffy had died. The next day, we took Mark and Sally and Scott to the mortuary. There was Jeff. He looked exactly like Scott, and I'd never seen that in him. About a week after, we buried Jeffy in Caliente.

Some time later, Dr. Merkin called and wanted me to stop by. I did after work, and he went through his whole file. From the minute Jeffy arrived at that hospital, he went through everything they had done and why. That took a while. After he finished, I asked him for his bill. He said, "There's no bill, Ralph. Nobody could afford a catastrophic accident like that." I just couldn't believe it.

That was May 18, 1960. All these years . . . you live. Life goes on, your life is normal, and your life is happy. But you never, never forget. The evening after Jeff died, Sara and I were sitting in the backyard, looking across the valley at the mountains, and there was a little star that we had never particularly noticed before. To this day, on May 18, we go out and see if that little star's there. You don't see it all the time.

We live with it, and very seldom do we get emotional about it anymore. But there were effects I didn't anticipate. I didn't fully appreciate the loss that Jeffy's brothers and sister had suffered. We didn't pay much attention to them while this was going on, or when the family gathered for the funeral and we all went to Caliente. We didn't consider that maybe they needed special love and attention from their mother and father, or maybe counseling. Years later, Mark remarked to me that he'd lost a brother and nobody ever considered that much. That wasn't the way he said it, but that was the meaning. Sally and Scott have made similar comments.

Sara and I both have felt guilt. Why, for God's sake, did we let him get into a situation where he could go in and turn the water on in the bathroom? But he'd gone outside to play with the other kids from the time he could walk. Why was the water temperature so high? I suppose in every tragic accident, somebody has to feel responsible. God knows, I don't think I should feel a deep sense of guilt, and I know Sara should not feel any.

At Fantasy Park, the Service League, now called the Junior League, helped build a monument to children where the Sawyer state building is now. Sara was a member of that, and they participated with the city in the development of that park financially. They raised a lot of money for it, and they dedicated it to children of members who had died. Jeffy was one of those. I think there were only two or three. I don't know what's happened to that plaque, since they built a building where the park is. I'd like to know where it is.[1]

When I was a boy, Memorial Day was quite a day in Caliente—it was back then in most places in the country. We'd go to the cemetery and "decorate the graves," these two little headstones in our family plot. They were my sisters.

My mother wrote a poem one time in which she referred to "those babies over there." Mother and Dad must have just been devastated by the deaths of their only two daughters when they were little girls. Until our son died, I had never fully realized what Mom and Dad had gone through, and how it had stayed in their minds through all the years.

Notes

1. The building where Fantasy Park was located is the Grant Sawyer State Office Building.

34 | Clean, Green Boulder City

Clean, green Boulder City, where gambling is illegal, growth is frowned on unless it's approved, and the sun shines every day. And every day the sun doesn't shine, you get a free beer down at the local saloon. [laughter]

I moved to Las Vegas in 1955. Mark was four. When it was time for first grade, the schools were overcrowded, and they would have double sessions. Wherever the kids wanted to go, Sara was spending her days in the heat driving them. I was hoping we could find a place where Mark walks to school from his house at a regular time . . . and we have the other two kids. So what are we going to do?

I found this house that had been vacant for two or three years. It was screwed up with mortgages, mechanic's liens, and foreclosures. Dick and Betty Ham told me about it; they lived in Boulder City. I tried to figure out how to buy it, but I didn't have any money. I got a title report. There were two trust deeds against the house. One was around $10,000-$11,000. The second was around $14,000, and owned by a Reno lady, Hancock. I called Harvey Sewell and asked if he knew Ms. Hancock.

"Oh, yes. She's a customer of the bank."

I explained she had this deed of trust and offered to buy it at face value. He called back and said, "God, she'd be glad to!"

I said, "Oh, that's wonderful. Mr. Sewell, would you loan me the money?" [laughter]

He said yes. I bought the second trust deed and then foreclosed it, sub-ject to the first. I went to Charlie Horsey, who owned Nevada Savings, and asked if he would give me a loan with enough money to pay off the first and the loan from Mr. Sewell, so he would have the first trust deed. He said they would. Then, we had the foreclosure sale. I kept worrying somebody would bid, because I didn't have any cash. Nobody did.

The house was filthy. There was a table in the dining room, and a turkey carcass on it. Apparently, the people here before opened the door to the downstairs and threw their garbage down. They knew they were losing the house and didn't care. Sara, bless her heart, didn't complain, but when I brought her here the first time, I thought she'd cry. Sara was pregnant, and we waited. Jeffy was born in November, so we stayed in our house in Las Vegas through Christmas and moved here after the first of the year.

Right away, it was wonderful. Mark and Sally could walk across the park and be in school. Mark was in second grade and Sally in kindergarten. If they wanted to go to the movie, they could just walk downtown. Just like a small town, and it was a lot smaller then than it is now. Right away they were meeting kids, and we were meeting teachers and parents. To me, it was a blessing, because when we lived in Las Vegas, it took me about ten minutes to get home from my office. A law office is a busy, nerve-wracking place on occasion. I'd still be on edge, and maybe snap at the kids or just be in ill temper. After we moved here, I had thirty minutes from the time I left the office to get home. By the time I got home, it was just wonderful. A different world completely separated my professional life from my home life.

Most everybody worked for the government, the Bureau of Reclamation, or the National Park Service or the Los Angeles Water and Power Company. They were on a schedule. Sally couldn't understand why we couldn't have dinner every night regularly like her friends did. Morewood Dowd lived down the street—you could set your clock by the time he went to work or went home. All of their friends had dinner at 5:30. It might be as late as 9:00 before I got home, and we always waited till I got home to have dinner. Sally thought why couldn't I, for God sakes, be regular and punctual? [laughter]

It was so peaceful, and everybody was so nice. We started making friends immediately. Soon Sara knew half the people in town. A little thing like this: Sara and I went out of town after the kids were older. They were in high school or junior high. If they needed something—or money—they knew to go to Central Market. The owner would give them what they needed, just put it on our bill. Bob Georgeson at the men's store would do the same thing if they needed equipment for the athletic program at school and we didn't happen to be here. They never abused that. Before we got dial telephones, if I had to get up to catch the plane to Reno, I'd call the phone company here and ask them to call me in the morning. Things that in small town life you can do.

The educational system was first-class. The high school was like an academy. The teachers lived here. Their kids went to school here. I think Boulder City High School had a higher percentage of kids going on to college and completing college than any high school in the state. Senator McCarran told me one time, too, that he'd never appointed a Boulder City student to one of the academies who flunked the test.

The kids just thrived here. I visited each child's room at least once a year in each grade. I'd be sitting in the back. I did that all through elementary school. I got to know their teachers socially. That was great. You'd meet a teacher at a Christmas party. They might tell you something about one of your children. There was a lot of parent involvement. In high school, at the beginning of each semester, one night was set aside when the teachers would be in the rooms and you would talk to them. By then, we knew them all. It was really hands-on.

It's been wonderful, and we try to maintain it. The people in the community try not to stop growth, but control growth. We've grown. I think there were 4,000-5,000 people when we moved here, and now there are about 15,000. We don't have any gambling, and cannot without a vote of the people.

When we moved here, Boulder City was still a federal reservation. We had just a lease on the lot. We paid ground rent to the government. When we were allowed to become an incorporated city, everybody who had a lease was given the option of purchasing that ground from the government at appraised value, but the money went to the new city of Boulder City. So, the city started in a sound financial position. Plus, it owned the water distribution system—the federal government conveyed that—and power system. Boulder City owns its utilities, and we probably have the lowest water and electric rate of any city in the county, if not the state. They also conveyed to the new city thirty-three square miles of land. The city can control its growth.

It's a constant struggle. Around 1974 or 1975, the city was selling a lot of land, so 74 percent of the people voted for the growth control ordinance, which limits the number of hotel and motel rooms and sub-divisions that can be built in any year. The first year was 120 units, the average of the past five years. That's how that figure came up. Then they could have a 5 or 10 percent increase each year after that. Initially, it didn't have much of an effect, because about that time, they had interest rates so high, nobody could borrow money to build a house. But the city council generally finds some way to get around the ordinance as best they can. Most of them have never thought that was a good idea. They like to sell this land. They see more revenue, more money to spend. I think new people who move here feel just as strongly about it as the old timers. That's why they moved here.

Under the Boulder City bill, there could never be liquor, gambling, or prostitution without a vote of the people. Hell, we had two elections before they even let liquor in. Even I voted against it the first time. I thought, Geez, we don't need a bunch of saloons in Boulder City. There's plenty of whiskey at Railroad Pass. The second time, I voted for it. [laughter] But we haven't had a growth of bars. I thought when it was on the ballot that if we legalized liquor, we'd have a bunch of cheap, skid row type bars around town. We haven't gotten that. It's just a lovely place to live.

Boulder City had a group of people involved in the community. Leonard and Corinne Atkison owned two stores. One was a women's dress shop, and the Navahopi sold Indian stuff. Leonard was a 31er. Bob Georgeson's father came here early; Bob had a clothing store. Doctors Faye and Vic Ahlstrom,

Cliff and Gene Segerblom. Jake Dieleman owned Jake's Crane and Rigging in Las Vegas, but lived here and was in the assembly (1959). The Bureau of Reclamation was big—a regional office for the ten western states, I think.

I'd known Elbert and Mary Edwards since I was a boy. He was from Panaca. He and my mother were good friends. He was in education, my mother's field, so I remember him being at our house when I was little. I'd known Mary when I was a boy, because I think Mary actually lived in Caliente when they were young. Mary's still here—lovely woman.[1]

Bob Broadbent was an Ely boy. I don't know when he moved to Boulder City, but he was here when we came. He ran a drug store. His wife's mother was Clarence Wadsworth's daughter, a Lincoln County woman I had known as a child. Her father, Jack Schwartz, was related to Mrs. Senter in Caliente. George Senter owned the garage in Caliente; Jack worked there. I had known them. I knew Bob's mother-in-law and Bob's wife when we moved here and met his father in Ely before we moved here. Bob was active in the committee that lobbied to separate Boulder City from the federal government, was on the first city council, and became mayor. He served on the board of county commissioners. He became commissioner of reclamation, and director of McCarran Airport. That takes Bob's political career from about 1960 up until 1998 in a rough summary. [laughter] The worst you can say about Bob is he's Republican.

Tom and Erma Godbey were 31ers, and active in everything in the community. The kids—just as smart as a whip. I never knew a Godbey that wasn't smart. Alice and Laura and some of the kids married, moved away, and come back. And they did not suffer from the same disability of Broadbent: they were all Democrats. Tom was in the legislature for several terms. He was there when my mother was [1955-59, 1961-65], so my mother and Tom were friends. When we moved here, we became friends immediately.

Histories written about Boulder City always quote Erma. She had a great memory and could describe in vivid detail what it was like living in tents and shacks on that muddy river, 115 degrees, and having babies, children, before Boulder City was created. She and Tom came here from Colorado, went to mine in Arizona, then came up here to the dam. Tom was very liberal, a strong labor supporter. I used to call him "the old Wobbly." Whether he was an IWW guy, I don't know, but he'd smile—didn't bother Tom. Hard-working, and he worked at the test site. They were people you could always count on.

Michael Ravitch is an orthopedic surgeon. His offices are at St. Rose Dominican Hospital. He and his wife Donalene are neighbors. We went back to Washington together. I tried to play tour guide, but it's a different ball game now. Now it's more roped off. I had hoped I would be able to just take them through the Capitol, like we did in the old days. You couldn't do it. Senator Reid was kind enough to have one of his staff escort us.

Cliff Segerblom was in-residence artist and photographer. Gene taught government, so we met them in connection with school activities and became dear friends. Our kids commissioned Cliff to do a painting of the house, and he gave it to us as a gift. We had prints made up to give the kids.

My Uncle Lloyd owned the Rex Theater in Caliente, and I worked in it most of my early life, passing out handbills, and wound up as projection assistant manager. That theater meant a lot to me. It had been closed since my uncle died, and Cliff went up and did an oil painting of it. I wanted it, but I couldn't afford it. Cliff was having a show, and Sara was helping. I came home one day from the office, and here's that painting in the living room standing up against the couch. I commented to Sara, "Oh, God, I wish that was mine."

She said, "It is."

"How on earth . . . ?"

She said, "Mike Ravitch bought it, and it is yours. He gave it to you." That's one of the paintings they show every time there's a Segerblom show all over Nevada. On the marquee was the title of the movie that was playing the night my Uncle Lloyd died, "When the Legends Die." The theater never opened again. It had been closed five or six years or more when Cliff painted it, and that was still on the marquee.

Cliff and Gene were politically active, both good Democrats. Cliff served as justice of the peace and municipal judge, and he did a fine job. When I was on the board of county commissioners, I appointed him JP. Both graduated from the University of Nevada. Gene was raised in Winnemucca and Reno—old Nevada family. Cliff played football at the university in the 1930s. It's unusual for an art major to be a football player, but Cliff was successful in both. They lived the most ideal life. He did great photography. He painted and took pictures of the Colorado River, Lake Mead, the Grand Canyon, this whole area, and Gene wrote stories about them. They had them published in *National Geographic* and travel magazines—Arizona, Nevada, all over. Gene went on to serve on our city council and in the legislature (1993-2001). We try to help as we can during her campaigns. She's a grand woman.

We met so many wonderful people right away. One of the first was Gordon Miles. I saw him at a rally Dick Ham put on in Boulder City when Grant was running. Here's this guy with a crew cut, pink hair. I thought, "My God, that was the Boulder City football coach." I remember him when Lincoln County High School—I was on the team—played Boulder City. He hadn't changed a bit. Gordon was manager of McCarran Airport, worked for the county. His wife Dorothy was a McGill girl, old-time Nevada family.

Ken Andre was the football coach, and his wife Joanne was a teacher. They used to have football parties when the high school played. After the game, there would be a barbecue in somebody's backyard. They were always fun, particularly if Boulder City had won. I remember completely humiliating my daughter when Lincoln County came down to play Boulder City. She and Mark were students at Boulder City at the time. They were sitting on the Boulder City side yelling for Boulder City, and I'm on the other side yelling for Lincoln County. She would hardly speak to me. Boulder won. [laughter]

The school teachers were all so good. I should mention Andy Mitchell and his wife Mabel. Andy was a principal of the elementary school and on the city council, and Mabel was at the high school. She and Madelene Garrett were excellent English teachers. John Morrison, a professor of English at the university in Reno, told me one time he'd like to meet Mabel, because they'd never had a Boulder City graduate that had any trouble in an English placement exam at the university.

Dr. Tom White and his wife Juanita . . .[2] Al and Doris Wartman . . . Of course, I met Al in town. He was an attorney in Las Vegas and a Republican. We were the only two attorneys here. Both of us commuted, so everybody was bound and determined that Al and I get in a fight. Boulder City had just incorporated, and George Franklin spread the rumor I was moving to Boulder City so Dick Ham would take over as mayor, I'd take over as city attorney, and we'd take over the town; Dick moved to Carson, and I never had any desire to be city attorney. But Al and I had an agreement that we would not talk politics. He was as strong a Republican as I was a Democrat, so there would be plenty of reasons to fight. Having reached that agreement, we abided with it until Al died and never had a beef. We would sometimes ride to Las Vegas together. I was pleased that in the last years of Al's life, he had me represent a couple of his old clients. He also hired Mark a few times to do some work for him. He had great confidence in and affection for Mark. I appreciated that and wore that as a badge of honor.[3]

Bob and Linda Faiss are perfect delights, and they fit right in to Boulder City. They're active in the community. I think they're as happy to be here as Sara and I were when we came here, as happy as clams. They're wonderful people. [laughter] He has a program on our local television station here in which he interviews people. Linda is active in the hotel and museum associations.[4]

One nice thing about a small town, you can participate in things a lot easier than in a big city. There was an active theater group. They used to have a building, an old barracks or rec hall, a remnant of Camp Sibert, the military camp during the war. Inside, it had a stage and everything.

Dick and Betty Ham were active in the theater. They were going to do "Harvey." I had never been in a play, but they asked me to try out for it. I did, and I got to play Elwood P. Dowd. After we did it three or four nights here, we did it in Las Vegas. I loved it.

Memorizing the lines wasn't that tough, but I had no more idea than the man in the moon what to do with my hands or my feet, or whether I was to walk some place or have some mannerism. Lo and behold, we got a director from Henderson who was good and taught me the movements. I learned I could follow his instructions. My Lord, I enjoyed it! [laughter] When I got good reviews in the Boulder City paper, I thought I'd quit while I was ahead. [laughter] Sara worked like heck on the scenery.

Sara has been trying to save that beautiful old hotel that was in danger of being destroyed. Everybody put their shoulder to the wheel, and a group consisting of the museum organization, art league, Chamber of Commerce, and the city did wind up acquiring the hotel. They moved in. There are commercial shops and the museum. A certain number of rooms will be run like a bed and breakfast. They have wedding receptions and things like that. It was colonial-style, and it had a great history. All the great people of the world flocked to see Boulder Dam and stayed at that hotel: presidents and movie stars, the aristocracy of Europe. [laughter] That's going well.[5]

I learned something interesting. The museum has been trying to get grants. This reminds you of the rivalry between the north and south. I went to see if we could get a grant from the Cord Foundation and learned, to my dismay, the documents that created the foundation contained a provision: no grants to anything in Clark County! [laughter] That surprised me, because the Fleischmann Foundation gave great sums of money to the Clark County organization that built the library in Boulder City. It surprised me that a foundation would prohibit gifts to a certain part of the state.

I served as city attorney two or three times. Typically, city attorney jobs are short-lived like city and county manager jobs. It's not an elective position. It's appointed by the council, so when they would fire a city attorney or he'd quit, I would take it until they found a replacement.

I did what a city attorney does: I gave legal advice to the council. I prosecuted the heinous crimes committed against the peace and dignity of Boulder City. [laughter] The building department was always inspecting this contractor's work. The contractor thought the building inspector was too tough on him, and the inspector thought the contractor was cutting corners. He red-tagged a job one time. The contractor decked him. [laughter] I had to prosecute one of the town's leading citizens for belting one of the city's employees. We were able to resolve the dispute to everybody's satisfaction. The job being done was Cliff and Gene Segerblom's house. It came out well, but boy, it was sure watched like a hawk.

I wasn't interested in keeping the job, because I was making my living practicing law, and it took time from my practice. One of the reasons I moved to Boulder City—or one of the benefits I didn't realize when I moved—was the ability to separate my personal life from my professional life. I regard Boulder City like a neighborhood. It's where I live. I don't make my living here, and I didn't want to be involved in disputes in the neighborhood. Consequently, I didn't want to be city attorney.

I don't want casinos built in my neighborhood. It's not that I'm against gambling—I don't think they should be built in neighborhoods in Las Vegas either. That may seem unfair to businessmen who want to the community to grow so their business will be better, but I'm persuaded that local businesses will suffer with growth.

We haven't been active in many city council races. I've tried to keep my nose out of it, but I got involved when the bureau of reclamation wanted to deed the park to the city. It was expensive to maintain, and it was the government's responsibility to maintain that park and make sure it stayed a park. We were distrustful: if the city got to own it, they might subdivide it. [laughter] We appeared at the city council and opposed them accepting that park from the government. The government backed off. Now the city does own it. Several years later, they quietly did it. It's no longer a federal park. So far, it has worked out. But the federal government has been cutting down on maintenance of the park. They really want to put in desert landscaping and take the park out. We have appeared at city council meetings opposing that.

Those two parks are historically significant. When I was stationed at Kingman, Arizona, during the war, they'd bring us to Las Vegas in buses for rest and recreation. A whole lot of recreation and rest you got in those days! The bus would come around this corner. Here were these two beautiful, green parks. These kids from the east who had been on that desert around Kingman hadn't seen grass. The troops would get out and roll around in the parks. Every soldier stationed at Kingman during World War II remembers these parks in Boulder City. So, we fight to keep them and keep the government paying for them, rather than the taxpayers of Boulder City.

Boulder City now has its second traffic light. Terrible. It's not the traffic light I fear so much; they've built a road across the desert to connect with the highway, which indicates that land, which is now desert, will be developed. Incidentally, the people voted against building the road. The city council did it anyway. Some of them were voted out over that.

It's hard for me to say how much Boulder City has changed since we moved here. To me, the growth has been so fantastic, and we don't know the people. I don't think the old town group has changed much, but it's smaller in relation to the total population. Many have retired here from all over the country. Some of them get active in the community, and you're just delighted to meet them. They moved here because they like the smallness of it.

Some newcomers are builders, have become investors, built things. They're solid members of the community, have been here several years, and they're all for building all sorts of things. God, we're talking about four new golf courses! [laughter] I remember the fight when the first nine holes were built. A lot of people said we don't have enough water. Now we've got eighteen holes, we're going to build fourteen more, and everybody says that's fine. We've got enough water now. There seems to have been a great increase in water. [laughter] Some of them say, "Well, if they use up the water for golf courses, then they can't build any more homes. Might work." [laughter]

We're doing everything we can to encourage "old town." Now we've got a new Albertson's that's come in right across the street from Von's. That means we only have one local market. Can that local market survive? It's a great little market. They will deliver groceries. You can call them if you're sick or can't get to the store; they'll have it delivered. I don't think Von's and Albertson's are known for that sort of service. When we moved here, there were three grocery stores in town, and the town was smaller.

Boulder City is seen as Republican and aged. It's probably true. It was always Democratic, but you see million-dollar houses around this town now. They are all rich, and, consequently, Republicans. But I'm constantly surprised at how many young people seem to be Republican. A lot of young people want to move into Boulder City and can't afford to. In my view, if Boulder City needs anything, it would be a sub-division of low to medium price houses, so young people can afford to buy them. We're going to wind up like one giant Sun City with a bunch of pensioners or retired people who wouldn't spend a nickel to support government or education. A lot moved here because the taxes are low. And a lot moved here and built these big homes, and are still living in California. These are second homes for a lot of these people.

There has been some effort in Boulder City to break away from the school district. I don't have kids in school, but I am still interested in our school system. The teachers don't live here anymore. When the bell rings, they tell me it's hard to see who gets out first, the teacher or students. You don't have that parental contact you used to have. I brought it up one time with a school official. He said, "That's one of the reasons teachers don't want to live there. They don't want to be subject now to all that parental contact." I thought, "Jeez, that's a terrible thing to say." Then he made the point: "They can't find places to live." I remember when our kids were going to school, only one teacher in high school didn't live here.

Boulder City is a great place to live, but I don't think it's as good as it used to be. I miss things like the old-fashioned service stations, where you'd go get your gas, and the guy would check your oil and your water, check the air in your tires. But that doesn't happen anymore anywhere, so I can't complain. It's a lovely place to live. It really is.

Notes

1. Elbert Edwards was a longtime Las Vegas and Boulder City teacher and historian who wrote *200 Years in Nevada*.

2. Dr. Juanita Greer White was a university regent, 1963-73. A UNLV science building is named for her.

3. Al Wartman was a Clark County district judge, appointed in 1967 and serving until 1969. For several years, he was a law partner in what then was called Lionel Sawyer Wartman and Collins.

4. Bob Faiss was a *Las Vegas Sun* reporter and city editor who went to work for the Gaming Control Board, then was an aide to Governor Grant Sawyer, an aide to President Lyndon Johnson, and, since 1973, has been an attorney at Lionel Sawyer and Collins. He is now a senior partner and succeeded Sawyer as chair of the Administrative and Gaming Law department.

5. The Boulder Dam Hotel now has hotel rooms, and was the site of the interviewer's wedding. However, Mr. Denton made those references before that event.

Appendix
Why I Switched to Malone

This is a facsimile copy of a letter from Ralph Denton to Tom Mechling:

October 16, 1952

Mr. Thomas Mechling
Candidate for the U.S. Senate
Post Office
Las Vegas, Nevada

Dear Tom:

As you will recall, when you were last in Elko I personally assured you that you had my support as well as my vote. At that time I was sincere in so assuring you. However, subsequent events have led me to change my mind, and I feel that in all honesty I should explain to you the reasons for such a change. I do not want to be regarded by anyone as anything but intellectually honest, and therefore wish you to know and understand exactly where I stand insofar as my one vote is concerned.

Prior to the primary election I actively supported Alan Bible for the Democratic nomination to the United States Senate.

This support was founded upon the belief that Mr. Bible was, due to his past experience and training, the most capable man the democratic party in Nevada could offer the voters of Nevada as its candidate for the U.S. Senate.

There were a few things in your primary campaign which upset me; by way of example, you will recall the ad you ran in the Las Vegas papers which showed a picture of a law office door in Reno which purported to convey the impression that Alan Bible and Senator McCarran are presently partners in the practice of law. It seemed to me, at the time, that honesty would have dictated that you reveal that the picture in question was taken at least 10 years prior to the date of your ad. Also, as a veteran, I resented the Veterans letter which originated in Ely.

However, I chalked all these things up to politics, and a realization that there was little else in Mr. Bible's character or background that could be attacked by you except these two things, and I frankly did not condemn you for so doing. Therefore, after the primary, I concluded that inasmuch as you were the Democratic nominee, and inasmuch as I thought you to possess qualities that would make you a credit to the State of Nevada in the U.S. Senate, and inasmuch as I sincerely felt, and still do, that the philosophy of government adhered to by a majority of the Democratic members of both houses of the Congress is the best and right philosophy, and inasmuch as I felt, and still do, that it is vital to the welfare of this great country of ours that the Democratic majorities in both houses of the Congress be maintained, I therefore determined that I would give you my wholehearted support in the General Election. As mentioned in the first paragraph above, subsequent events have led me to believe that my initial determination following the primary election was fallacious. I hasten to explain to you the reason.

First, I was greatly disappointed in your performance at the recent Democratic rally in Elko. Before you stood a unified audience, supported by a small group that had worked hard to put that rally over, a group that was sincerely interested in electing the ENTIRE Democratic ticket. I need not remind you that I was among that small group. Also in the audience were three fine Democratic members of the Congress. You chose as your theme the purported high incident of corruption in the 82nd Democratic Congress. This conduct on your part leads me to believe that you have no interest in the rest of the Democratic ticket, but are interested only in yourself, and your own political future.

Second, you have attempted to make the people of the State of Nevada believe that you were a newspaper reporter in Washington with the principal duty assigned being the coverage of the U.S. Senate and House of Representatives from the galleries of those Houses of Congress. I am unable to discover your name listed in the Congressional Directory as one of those individuals accredited to the press gallery of either House. I know, of my own personal knowledge, that you were a newspaper man in Washington for the Kiplinger Letter. Why don't you say that instead of trying to create a fallacious and false impression? This point, it seems to me, is trivial, but coupled with the other factors becomes important to me because it indicates a desire on your part to be willing and desirous of standing on half truths.

Third. Statements made by you in your radio addresses, and I refer particularly to the one printed in toto in the Elko Daily Free Press under date of October 15, 1952, make it perfectly clear that you do not want the support of people like me who have in the last few weeks since the primary election worked very hard in the interest of the campaign of the ENTIRE Democratic ticket.

Fourth. You have chosen to make an unwarranted attack upon the character and integrity of Senator McCarran. I point out to you that your opponent in this election is George Malone, and not Senator McCarran. Personal attacks upon Senator McCarran, following the primary election, set badly in your teeth, especially after Margaret stated in a post primary interview with Jean McElrath, of the Wells Progress, that you were able to have this chance because of the fact that your combined incomes in Washington were great enough to permit you to save for this campaign. I need not remind you that your wife's income was derived from Senator McCarran's Sub-Committee on Immigration and Naturalization. During the primary I attributed your attacks upon Senator McCarran to politics; their continuation after the primary I attribute to bad taste and ingratitude.

Fifth. You have failed to inform the voters of Nevada where you stand on any of the intra-state questions vital to the interests of the State of Nevada.

Sixth, you have attempted to make the testimonial dinner given in honor of Senator McCarran in Reno on the 20th of September seem a conspiracy against you, and further a conspiracy shrouded in secrecy and conceived in despotism. Nothing could be further from the truth. I deeply resent this inference, and feel that it must be prompted by a malignant heart and a malicious brain. I personally arranged the dinner for Senator McCarran, and the arrangements were completed prior to the primary election. It was designed to give those of us who have supped at the Senator's table a chance to express our gratitude to him. Many of us in attendance owe our existence as attorneys in

this great state to Senator McCarran, for
without his assistance it would have been
impossible for many of us to secure a legal
education. This expression of gratitude did
not necessarily mean we felt that we owed
him unending political allegiance. For we
all feel, and I am sure the Senator joins us
in this feeling, that reasonable men can
differ on questions of politics. This dinner had absolutely no political significance, and any statement on your part to the
contrary is an outright mistruth. I can
truthfully say that Senator McCarran has
never, and did not on the night of September
20th, and has not since, asked me to do anything of a political nature.

Seventh. I resent greatly the implication
contained in your ads and speeches to the
effect that I, like many other young Democrats in the state of Nevada, are nothing
but pawns on a chess board to be moved into
position by the player. I resent the implication that I am less than an independent
man. If you feel that we are all part of
the McCarran machine —indeed, if you feel
that there is a McCarran machine—please permit me to advise you that I deem it an honor
to be considered a member of such a machine
and shall be proud to my dying day that I
was one of those whom Senator McCarran chose
to assist in obtaining a legal education,
and shall likewise be proud of my relationship with him and shall ever treasure it as
one of my choicest memories, and shall forever be grateful to him.

The seven reasons above stated, I consider
to be a sufficient base upon which to dis-
avow you as my candidate for the U.S. Senate.

The reason I am writing you to this effect
is that I believe questions concerning politics should be treated with candor and fairness. I dislike the person who assures a
candidate that he is for him and then knifes

him in the back. I cherish honesty in others, and feel, therefore, that I should be
honest with you.

Very truly yours,

Ralph L. Denton
Asst. D.A., Elko, Nevada

Index

Capital Theater (Salt Lake City, Utah), 126
Capitol Theater (Washington D.C.), 92
Caraway, Hattie, 46, 47n.
Caraway, Thaddeus, 47n.
Carlin Canyon, 119
Carlson, C.A. "Dutch," 68
Carlson, Lester, 216
Carter, Jimmy, 336, 338-339
Carville, Edward P. "Ted," 11, 87, 115n. 131-132, 134n. 223, 247, 266, 267n.
Cashill, Thomas, 113
Cashill, William, 113, 115n.
Cashman, James "Big Jim," 80, 84n.
Cashman Field (Las Vegas, Nevada), 84n. 198, 206n.
Cast a Giant Shadow, 321n.
Castle, Doug, 133
Catholics, 93
Catt, Virginia, 248
Caudill, Robert "Doby Doc," 103, 130, 203
Cecini, Charles, 214-216
Chamberlain, Neville, 50
Chavez, Dennis, 40, 47n. 81
Chavez, Lorenzo, 40, 42
Chavez, Martin, 40
Christensen, Carl, 331-332
Church, Frank, 333, 340n.
Churchill, Winston, 253
Cinnabar Hotel (Las Vegas, Nevada), 323
Claiborne, Harry, 172, 174, 310
Clark County (Nevada), 25-27, 109, 123, 127n. 183, 188-189, 194, 196-197, 204, 209, 231, 237, 251-252, 286, 290, 301, 371
Clark County Wholesale, 25
Clark, Ed, 25-27
Clark Forwarding Company, 25
Clay, Thomas, 23
Clifford, Jim, 188
Clinton, William J., 339
Clover Valley (Nevada), 124
Club Bingo (Las Vegas, Nevada), 327, 329
Coaldale, Nevada, 214
Cohen, Burton, 154, 159n.
Cohen, Carl, 277-278
Cohen, Joe, 8
Cole, George, 38n.
Collins, Jon, 40, 77, 85, 100, 336
Commercial Center (Las Vegas, Nevada), 255-256, 260n.
Commercial Hotel (Elko, Nevada), 120-121, 132, 140
Compton, Bill, 174-175

Conger, Terry, 325-327
Congressional Country Club (Washington D.C.), 42, 47n.
Congressional Record, 82
Conlon, Jack, 194, 200, 232, 237, 247, 273, 350
Connally, Tom, 70, 83
Converse, Ed, 190
Conway, Dana, 33
Conway Ranch, 32-33, 61
Cooke, Tom, 195, 212, 233-234, 271
Cooper, Dave, 276, 298n.
Cord, Errett Lobban, 197, 200, 216, 231, 247, 261
Cornero, Tony, 207n.
Cory, Cal, 40, 42, 103, 164, 167-169, 174, 229, 299-300
Cottontail Ranch (Nevada), 218-219
Cove Tavern (Lincoln County, Nevada), 21, 23
Cragin, Ernie, 104, 189-190, 230
Crosby, Bing, 124
Crowell, William, 213
Crozier, Helen, 198, 207n.
Crozier, Oscar, 198, 206n.
Crumley, Newt, 127, 131-133, 140
Culverwell, Alice, 28
Culverwell, Charles, 24, 28, 30
Culverwell family, 27-28
Culverwell Ranch (Caliente, Nevada), 2
Culverwell, William, 28
Cummings, Phil, 246

D

Dalitz, Morris B. "Moe," 247-249, 252, 255-256, 260n. 263, 278
Daly, Zeke, 104
Daugherty, Robert, 41
Davidson, Lou, 149
Davis, Chester, 320
Del Papa, Frankie Sue, 351, 358n.
Delich, Helen, 68
Delich, Sam, 68
Delphinian Society (Caliente, Nevada), 6
Delta Theta Phi, 93
Demman, Doc, 40
Demman, Mary, 40
Democrats, 6, 10-12, 38, 66, 69, 181, 188-190, 195-196, 199-200, 204, 209, 269, 271, 273-274, 276-277, 283-285, 347, 354, 368-369
Denton, Betty Jeanne, 15-16
Denton, Floyd "Babe," 1-5, 8-10, 12-13, 15-17, 19-20, 22-27, 29-31, 33-34, 36, 38-43, 50-52, 56, 182, 275, 363

Escobar, Francis, 109-110
Esmeralda County (Nevada), 198, 200, 209, 279
Eureka Palisades Railroad, 75
Evans, Charles R., 36, 38n.
Evans, Doris, 336-337
Evans, Gene, 130, 133n.

F

Fairway to the Stars Golf Course (Las Vegas, Nevada), 330-331
Faiss, Linda, 370
Faiss, Robert, 228, 370, 374n.
Federal Bureau of Investigation, U.S., 226-227, 263, 321
Ferguson, Homer, 318-319
Feutsch, Eddie, 351
Fielding, Bob, 289
Fike, Ed, 266, 267n. 268n. 349, 358n.
First Presbyterian Church (Hempstead, New York), 1
First Western Financial Corporation, 288-289
First Western Savings and Loan (Las Vegas, Nevada), 240
Fisher, Herman, 297
Flamingo Hotel (Las Vegas, Nevada), 253
Flangas, Bill, 265
Flangas, Peter, 265, 267n.
Fleischmann Foundation, 371
Fogliani, Jack, 13, 14n.
Foley, George, 176, 222, 279, 283-284, 293, 343, 350
Foley, Helen, 351, 359n.
Foley, John, 265-266, 267n. 294
Foley, Joseph, 108
Foley, Lucy, 89, 93
Foley, Roger D., 106, 114n. 229, 310, 325-326
Foley, Roger T., 10-11, 14n. 98, 114n. 123-124, 176-177, 179n. 181, 194, 204, 251, 262, 265, 301, 310
Foley, Tom, 89, 93
Ford, Dayton, 88
Ford, Gerald, 336
Ford, Tennessee Ernie, 126
Foresta Institute (Washoe Valley, Nevada), 295
Fort Bragg, North Carolina, 55, 57
Fort Sill (Blocker, Oklahoma), 56
Forty-Second Infantry Division, 53-54
Fountain, Ed, 276-277
Fox, Miriam, 300
Franklin, Albert, 257-258
Franklin, George, 108, 172-173, 194-195, 204, 206, 209, 370

Frazier, Maude, 245
Friar's Club (Los Angeles, California), 316
Friedman, Maury, 156-158, 316
Frost, Robert, 242
Fulbright, J. William, 333, 340n.

G

Gallagher, Doc, 135-137
Gallagher, Dorothy, 122, 125-126, 127n. 137, 143
Gallagher, Morris, 125
Gallagher, Tom, 122, 125-126, 137, 143, 292
Galt, Bill, 265
Gaming Control Board, Nevada, 114n.
Garbian, Al, 328-329
Gardner, Ava, 147
Garner, Charlie, 176
Garrett, Dorothy, 362
Garrett, James, 153-155, 196-197, 211, 227-228, 295, 329, 343, 362
Garrett, Madelene, 370
Garside, Frank, 250n.
Garside, Scoop, 297
Gaughan, Jackie, 287, 298n.
Gaughan, Michael, 298n.
Gavin, James, 333
Gedeny family, 125
Geisler, Jerry, 147
Gentry, Laura, 173
George, Phyllis, 357
Georgeson, Bob, 283, 366-367
George Washington Law School, 71, 93
Gerry, Peter G., 43, 47n.
Getchell, Noble, 110
Giancana, Sam, 244n.
Gilbranson, Lamar, 293-294
Glaser, Norm, 124, 127n.
Godbey, Erma, 368
Godbey, Tom, 368
Gojack, Mary, 337, 340n.
Goldfield, Nevada, 37, 38n. 214-215, 218
Goldwater, Barry, 83n. 271, 276, 292
Goldwater, David, 145, 147
Gomes, John, 295-296
Gomes, Nancy, 295-296
Gordon, Loma, 40
Goyeneche, Xavier, 137-138
Gragson, Oran, 248-249, 258
Graham, Bill, 37
Grand Ole Opry, 66, 70n.
Grant, Archie C., 26, 34n. 79
Grant, Zora, 26-27
Graves, Madison, 176

Lurie, Art, 279
Lynch, Clay, 259

M

McAfee, Guy, 25
McCall, Quannah, 25
McCarran, Patrick A., 2, 36, 38, 41-
    42, 46, 53, 63, 66-69, 71-88, 91,
    97-104, 106-112, 114, 115n. 130-
    132, 135, 141, 147, 161, 166,
    168, 172-173, 177, 179, 189-190,
    200, 203, 209, 211, 213, 230,
    246-247, 249, 261, 264, 266, 270-
    271, 274, 279, 282, 294, 321,
    346, 351, 366
McCarran, Sam, 103
McCarthy, Eugene, 292, 333-336
McCarthy, Joseph, 81, 84n. 111-112,
    321
McCrea, Joel, 124
McCuistion, Florine, 131-132
McCuistion, M.E. "Ted," 40, 131-132,
    133n. 141-142, 189
McDaniel, Joseph O., 317, 321n.
McDermitt, Paul, 190
McDonald, Bob, 161, 210
McDonald, Joe, 37, 78, 83, 85-87,
    143, 145, 147-149, 155-156, 158,
    161-163, 165-166, 176, 182, 187,
    194, 205, 304, 329
McDonald, Mary Gene, 147, 156, 166
McDonald, Robert, 228, 235
McDonald, Ross, 257
McDonnell, Joe T., 85-86, 300
McEachin, Malcolm, 127n.
McElroy, J.F., 132, 134n.
McFarland, Ernest, 72, 79, 83n.
McFarland, Verla, 137, 139
McGarry, Chow, 344
McGarry, William, 237
McGowan, Wilson, 266, 268n.
McGroarty, John, 351, 359n.
McKay, Jim, 37
McKellar, Kenneth, 46, 47n.
McKenna, Chuck, 283-284, 297
McKnight, William, 115n.
McLaughlin, Tom, 99
McLeod, Wayne "Red," 189, 191n.
McMillan, James B., 153, 159n. 198,
    206n. 207n. 232-233, 265, 272,
    284
McMillan, Mickie, 304
McMullen, Mary Ellen, 351, 359n.
McMullen, Sam, 351, 359n.
McNamara, Joe, 125, 135
McNamara, Robert, 292, 298n.
McNamee, Ann, 305, 362

McNamee, Frank, 27, 113-114, 115n.
    172
McNamee, Frank Jr., 27, 182-183,
    184n. 362
McNamee, Graham, 18
McNamee, John, 178
McNamee, Leo, 19, 27, 147
McNamee, Luke, 27
Madrietta, Celso, 139
Magelby, Cal, 178
Maher, Florine, 40-41
Maheu, Robert, 227, 230n. 318-319
Malley, Ed, 38n.
Malone, George, 58, 66-67, 69-70, 86,
    101-102, 121, 194
Malone, Ruth, 69
Mann, Pat, 137, 142
Mannario, JoJo, 150, 158
Mannario, Sammy, 158
Manoukian, Noel, 267n. 319-320,
    322n.
Mapes Hotel (Reno, Nevada), 106
Marcus, Mickey, 318, 321n.
Marshall, Edward G. "Ted," 261-262,
    292
Marshall, George, 10-11, 14n. 25,
    239, 261
Martin, Anne, 6, 13n.
Martinet, Loy, 304-305
Masonic Lodge (Caliente, Nevada),
    5-6
Mathews, Wendell, 20
Maybank, Burnet, 90, 94n.
Meadow Valley (Nevada), 16, 21, 28
Mechling, Thomas B., 101-102, 106,
    129, 200, 334, 340n.
Melvin, Jack, 196
Mendoza, John, 108, 124, 127n. 176,
    184, 283-284
Merkin, Dr., 361-362
Merrill, Charles, 229, 230n.
Mesquite Club (Las Vegas, Nevada),
    26, 34n.
Michel's Restaurant (Washington,
    D.C.), 45
Midas, Nevada, 118
Miles, Dorothy, 369
Miles, Gordon, 369
Miller, Bob, 207
Miller, Dean "Diamond Tooth," 293
Miller, Maya, 295-297, 298n. 338,
    345
Miller, Ross, 204, 207n.
Miller, Virginia, 178
Mills, Wilbur, 293, 298n.
Minden Inn (Minden, Nevada), 25
Minden, Nevada, 280
Mint Club (Las Vegas, Nevada), 328

Mirabelli, Phil, 305
Mitchell, Andy, 370
Mitchell, Mabel, 370
Molasky, Irwin, 255, 260n.
Monroe, Warren "Snowy," 125, 131, 133, 230
Monsey, Earl, 20, 286, 300-304, 331
Moore, Julian, 257, 261, 293
Moran, 126
Morgan, Ed, 321
Mormons, 3, 11, 28, 93, 246, 285
Morris, William "Wildcat," 179, 265-266
Morrison, John, 370
Morrison-Knudson Construction, 87
Morse, Bill, 182
Morse, Wayne, 74, 83n. 333
Moss, Mel, 289
Moulin Rouge (Las Vegas, Nevada), 198, 207n.
Mountain City, Nevada, 119
Mowbray, John, 123, 127n. 229-230, 259
Mueller, John, 113, 136
Murphy, Sally, 252

N

National Gallery of Art (Washington, D.C.), 45, 92
National Observer, 260n.
National Security Agency, U.S., 64
National Symphony (Washington, D.C.), 92
Neely, Matthew, 90, 95n.
Nevada Association of County Commissioners, 244
Nevada Bank of Commerce, 102
Nevada Club (Caliente, Nevada), 39
Nevada Democrat, 293
Nevada Federation of Women's Clubs, 7, 14n. 27
Nevada magazine, 282
Nevada Resort Association, 252
Nevada State Athletic Commission, 222
Nevada State Journal, 87
Nevada State Prison (Carson City, Nevada), 327
Nevada Supreme Court, 89, 267n.
New York City, New York, 210, 289, 296
Ninth Circuit Court, 26-27, 311
Nixon, Richard M., 44, 68, 335-336, 340n.
Nores, Edgar, 130, 201
Norris, George, 109, 115n.
North Las Vegas, Nevada, 258-259

North Las Vegas Valley Times, 250n.
Norton, Hugh, 40, 45-46, 61, 68, 88, 94
Novakovich, Nada, 164-165
Nye, Gerald P., 43, 47n.

O

O'Callaghan, Donal N. "Mike," 264-265, 267n. 320, 341-345
Odd Fellows Lodge (Caliente, Nevada), 5-6
Oddie, Tasker, 36, 38n.
Ogilvie, Eva, 124-125, 127n. 143, 299
Ogilvie, George, 124-125, 127n. 143, 299-300
Old Prince Mine (Lincoln County, Nevada), 4, 25, 27, 30
Oldham, Johnny, 133, 134n.
Olsen, Art, 184, 251-252, 260n. 263
Olsen, Edward, 225, 228
Olson, Hans, 23
Olson, Hans Jr., 23
Olson, Otto, 23
Onassis, Christina, 331
O'Neill, Tip, 337
O'Reilly, Bill, 158
Orr, William E. "Billy," 10, 14n. 26-27
Owyhee Indian Reservation, 119-120

P

Page, Lee, 196, 271, 279, 305-306
Pahranagat Valley (Nevada), 7, 10, 29
Palace Club (Reno, Nevada), 105-106
Palm Saloon (Elko, Nevada), 37, 124, 133
Panaca, Nevada, 7, 10-11, 13, 16, 20, 23, 25, 28, 183, 368
Parvin, Al, 328
Pavlikowski, Joseph, 184, 331, 332n.
Pearl, Minnie, 66, 70n.
Pearson, Doc, 330
Pearson, Drew, 219
Peccole, Bill, 253
Pechart, William, 105-106
Pence, Betty, 87
Pence, Marge, 85, 87
Pentagon (Washington, D.C.), 42
Peraldo, Louie, 17
Persons, Roy, 107-108
Persons, Wilton B., 63
Petersen, Peter C., 193, 200
Phipps, Verne, 153-155
Pike, Miles, 229
Pioche, Nevada, 7, 13, 18, 20, 22-24, 27, 35
Pioche Record, 42, 47n.

Wilson, Thomas Cave, 209, 273
Wilson, Thomas R.C. "Spike," 273
Wines, Barbara, 122
Wines, Lorinda, 124
Wines, Taylor, 102, 114n. 121-122,
    136, 142-143
Wingfield, George, 37, 110, 200, 271
Winnemucca, Nevada, 118, 124-125,
    130
Witter, Dean, 124
Women's Democratic Club of the
    District of Columbia, 66
Woodburn, William, 200, 231-232
Woodbury, Ethel, 196, 248
Woodruff Manifesto, 3
Wright, Bill, 293
Wright, George, 125-126, 127n.
Wunderlichs, 122
Wynn, Don, 303

Y

Yabloc, Julie, 318
Yacerda, Adam, 248, 250n.
Yerington, Nevada, 276
Yoachim, Archie, 23
Young, Cliff, 161, 165, 169n. 322n.

Z

Zenoff, David, 147, 159n. 322n.
Zenoff, Eva, 356
Zenoff, Mary, 356, 359n.
Zigatema, Heinie, 197
Zucker, Jeff, 334

A LIBERAL CONSCIENCE

Text designed by Mary A. Larson

*Composed by the University of Nevada Oral History Program
in Goudy using Adobe PageMaker 6.5*

Printed and bound by Edwards Brothers.